Accounting
Theory

Accounting Theory

ahmed belkaoui
university of illinois
at chicago circle

HBJ

HARCOURT BRACE JOVANOVICH, INC.

New York   San Diego   Chicago   San Francisco   Atlanta
London   Sydney   Toronto

Printed in the United States of America
Library of Congress Catalog Card Number: 80-82704
ISBN: 0-15-500470-0

Material from the Uniform CPA Examination Questions and Unofficial Answers, copyright by the American Institute of Certified Public Accountants, Inc., is adapted with permission.

*To Janice, in fond recognition
of her understanding and continuous support.*

Preface

A single generally accepted accounting theory does not exist at this time. Several attempts have been made to formulate such a theory. Starting with different assumptions and using different methodologies, the various attempts have resulted in different frameworks for financial reporting standards.

To construct an accounting theory requires one to justify or to refute existing accounting practices. Under the traditional approach, construction and verification of a theory were considered virtually synonymous. In the past ten years, however, a new approach has emerged, under which a distinct verification process is required. The underlying objective of both approaches is the same: to develop a conceptual framework for what accountants do or are expected to be doing. A coherent system of objectives and assumptions is necessary for the promulgation of consistent standards that define the nature, function, and scope of financial statements and the techniques for producing them. In other words, the standard-setting process, or generally accepted accounting principles, must be guided by a generally accepted accounting theory.

Constructing and verifying an accounting theory, therefore, consists of defining and selecting the objectives of accounting and financial statements and delineating the elements of financial statements, the attributes of these elements, and the appropriate unit of measure to be used.

Given the diversity of assumptions within the accounting environment, writers, researchers, and practitioners have tackled the task of theory construction in various ways. The result has been a state of continual crisis or revolution within accounting in which (1) various accounting paradigms, or models, have competed for primacy, (2) vested interests have argued for the domination of their particular paradigms and resulting theory, and (3) a gradual politicization of the standard-setting process has taken place.

Accounting Theory presents the principal approaches and proposed solutions to the problem of formulating an accounting theory. The emphasis is on the current issues in defining the elements of an accounting theory, namely, the objectives of financial statements, the fundamentals of accounting, the asset valuation and income determination concepts, and the future scope of accounting. In an attempt to provide a clear picture of all the issues, this book presents the elements of an accounting theory as conceived in the literature and the consequent competing conceptual frameworks. The reader is in a position to take sides on the issues confronting the discipline and to evaluate the points of view expressed in the literature. Where positions are taken and solutions proposed, however, the author is the first to admit that they can be but tentative in such a dynamic field as accounting.

The references at the end of each chapter are a guide to a more profound examination of each of the issues. A student of accounting theory is urged to examine these articles to appreciate the challenges facing the profession and the tremendous unfinished work that will need his or her active participation.

The questions at the end of each chapter are designed to lead the student to consult the literature for answers. Although theoretical questions may be answered on the basis of value judgments (which should be encouraged), evidence in the literature should be required.

Accounting Theory is intended for junior, senior, and graduate courses in financial accounting, financial accounting theory, seminars in asset valuation and income determination, and contemporary issues in accounting. It should be useful to students who wish to study for professional accounting examinations and to those who wish to keep up to date with current accounting research and education.

Accounting Theory consists of nine chapters. Chapter 1 describes the traditional approaches to accounting theory construction. Chapter 2 presents the new approaches, which require verification as an additional step in the formulation of an accounting theory. Chapter 3 discusses the first step in the development of a conceptual framework, namely, setting the objectives of financial statements. Chapter 4 identifies and explains the theoretical structure of accounting. Chapter 5 commences the examination of the asset valuation—income determination issue by focusing on current-value accounting. Chapter 6 presents general price-level accounting as an alternative. Chapter 7 presents a synthesis of the asset valuation and income determination models. A clear differentiation is made between the attributes to be measured and the unit of measure chosen. A glimpse into the future of accounting is provided in Chapter 8. Finally, Chapter 9 presents a philosophy of science view of accounting as a multiple paradigm science.

I wish to express appreciation to the offices of the American Institute of Certified Public Accountants (AICPA), the Canadian Institute of Chartered Accountants (CICA), and the Society of Management Accountants of Canada (SMA) for their kind permission to reprint and adapt some theory questions from their respective professional examinations. I wish to thank Abt Associates for permission to reproduce their Annual Report, 1973.

I am indebted to numerous people for their help and reviews of the manuscript. Steve Dowling, Karen Bierstedt, and Robert Watrous, from the staff at Harcourt Brace Jovanovich, have been both helpful and enthusiastic throughout the lengthy process of producing a finished book. A special vote of thanks goes to them. Literally scores of changes were made in the final product as a result of comments and suggestions received from those who provided insightful reviews of the manuscript at various stages. My thanks go to Alfred Kahl, University of Ottawa; Peter Holzer, University of Illinois, Champaign; Nicholas Dopuch, University of Chicago; John B. Barrack, University of Georgia; and Bill Parrott, University of South Florida, Tampa.

I wish to thank Jane Hilmers, Constance Hunt, Thomas Ryan, and the typists of the University of Chicago faculty secretarial service—

Vicky Longawa, Cynthia Nelson, and Evelyn Shropshire—as well as Louise Moreau, Irene Turmel, and the typists of the University of Ottawa faculty secretarial service for their ever cheerful and intelligent assistance.

Ahmed Belkaoui

Contents

Accounting Theory

chapter one

The Traditional Approaches to the Formulation of an Accounting Theory

The Nature of an Accounting Theory

Methodologies for the Formulation
of an Accounting Theory

Approaches to the Formulation
of an Accounting Theory

Nontheoretical Approaches
Deductive Approach
Inductive Approach
Ethical Approach
Sociological Approach
Economic Approach

The Eclectic Approach
to the Formulation
of an Accounting Theory

Entities Concerned with Accounting Principles
Development of Accounting Principles

Conclusions

References

Questions

The Committee on Terminology of the American Institute of Certified Public Accountants originally defined accounting as follows:

> Accounting is the art of recording, classifying, and summarizing in a significant manner and in terms of money, transactions and events which are, in part at least, of a financial character, and interpreting the results thereof.[1]

More recently, accounting was defined with reference to the concept of information as follows:

> Accounting is a service activity. Its function is to provide quantitative information, primarily financial in nature, about economic entities that is intended to be useful in making economic decisions, in making reasoned choices among alternative courses of action.[2]

The above definitions refer to accounting as either an art or a service activity and imply that accounting encompasses a body of techniques deemed useful for certain fields. *The Handbook of Accounting* identifies the following fields for which accounting is useful: (1) *financial reporting*, (2) *tax determination and planning*, (3) *independent audits*, (4) *data processing and information systems*, (5) *cost and management accounting*, (6) *internal auditing*, (7) *auditing*, (8) *fiduciary accounting*, (9) *national income accounting*, and (10) *management consulting*.[3]

Although accounting is a set of techniques useful for specified fields, it is practiced within an implicit theoretical framework. This framework is composed of principles and practices that have won acceptance by the profession because of their alleged usefulness and their logic. Known as "generally accepted accounting principles," they are a guide to the accounting profession in the choice of accounting techniques and the preparation of financial statements in a way considered to be good accounting practice. In response to changing environment, values, and informational needs, generally accepted accounting principles are subject to constant reexamination and critical analysis. This is reflected in *APB Statement No. 4*, which describes the principles as follows:

> Present generally accepted accounting principles are the result of an evolutionary process that can be expected to continue in the future. Changes may occur at any level of generally accepted accounting principles. . . . Generally accepted accounting principles change in response to changes in the economic and social conditions, to new knowledge and technology, and to demands of users for more serviceable financial information. The dynamic nature of financial accounting—its ability to change in response to changed conditions—enables it to maintain and increase the usefulness of the information it provides.[4]

---

[1]*Accounting Terminology Bulletin No. 1*, "Review and Résumé" (New York: American Institute of Certified Public Accountants, 1953), par. 9.

[2]*Accounting Principles Board Statements No. 4*, "Basic Concepts and Accounting Principles Underlying Financial Statements of Business Enterprises" (New York: AICPA, 1970), par. 40.

[3]*The Handbook of Accounting*, 5th edition. (New York: The Ronald Press, 1970).

[4]*APB Statement No. 4*, pars. 208 and 209.

Changes in the principles occur mainly as a result of the various attempts to provide solutions to emerging accounting problems and to formulate a theoretical framework for the discipline. Thus, a definite link exists between accounting theory and accounting practice in the sense that the process of accounting theory construction attempts either to justify or to refute existing practice. Accounting theory construction stems from the need to provide a rationale for what accounts do or expect to be doing.

The process of accounting theory construction should be completed by theory verification or theory validation. Fritz Machlup defines this process as follows:

> Verification in research and analysis may refer to many things, including the correctness of mathematical and logical arguments, the applicability of formulas and equations, the trustworthiness of reports, the authenticity of documents, the genuineness of artifacts or relics, the adequacy of reproductions, translations and paraphrases, the accuracy of historical and statistical accounts, the corroboration of reported events, the completeness in the enumeration of circumstances in a concrete situation, the reproducibility of experiments, the explanatory or predictive value of generalizations.[5]

This statement implies that theory should be subjected to a logical or empirical testing to verify its accuracy. If the theory is mathematically based, the verification should be predicated upon logical consistency. If the theory is based on physical or social phenomena, the verification should be predicated upon the relationship between the deduced events and observations in the real world.[6]

Accounting theory, therefore, should be the result of both a process of theory construction and a process of theory verification. A given accounting theory should explain and predict accounting phenomena, and when such phenomena occur, they verify the theory. If a given theory fails to produce the expected results, it is replaced by a "better" theory.[7] This well-accepted idea in the philosophy of science also applies to and is accepted in accounting, as shown by the following statement by the Committee on Accounting Theory and Verification:

> Scientific theories provide certain "expectations" or "predictions" about phenomena and when these expectations occur, they are said to "confirm" the theory. When unexpected results occur, they are considered to be anomalies which eventually require a modification of the theory or the construction of a new theory. The purpose of the new theory or the modified theory is to make the unexpected expected, to convert the anomalous occurrence into an expected and explained occurrence.[8]

---

[5]Fritz Machlup, "The Problem of Verification in Economics," *The Southern Economic Journal* (July 1955), p. 1.

[6]"Report of the Committee on Accounting Theory Construction and Verification," *The Accounting Review*, supplement to vol. 46 (1971), p. 54.

[7]Thomas S. Kuhn, "Anomaly and the Emergence of Scientific Discoveries," *The Structure of Scientific Revolution* (Chicago: University of Chicago Press, 1962), pp. 52–65.

[8]"Report of the Committee on Accounting Theory Construction and Verification," p. 53.

To date, this line of thinking has not been strictly followed in accounting. Instead, two approaches have been used: in the traditional approach to accounting theory construction, accounting practice and verification are considered synonymous; second, in the new approaches to accounting theory construction, attempts are made to logically or empirically verify the theory. In this chapter, we shall elaborate on the nature and contribution of the traditional approaches to accounting theory construction. Chapter 2 covers the same issues for the new approaches to accounting theory construction. Before introducing the traditional approaches, however, we shall elaborate on the nature of an accounting theory and the methodologies adopted for the formulation of an accounting theory. The traditional approaches we shall examine are (1) the nontheoretical, pragmatic, and authoritarian approach; (2) the deductive approach; (3) the inductive approach; (4) the ethical approach; (5) the sociological approach; (6) the economic approach; and (7) the eclectic approach.

The Nature of an Accounting Theory

The primary objective of accounting theory is to provide a basis for the prediction and explanation of accounting behavior and events. We assume, as an article of faith, that an accounting theory is possible. **Theory** is defined as "a set of interrelated constructs (concepts), definitions and propositions that present a systematic view of phenomena by specifying relations among variables; with the purpose of explaining and predicting the phenomena."[9]

It must be recognized at the outset that at the present time, no comprehensive theory of accounting exists. Instead, different theories have been and continue to be proposed in the literature. Many of these theories arise from the use of different approaches to the construction of an accounting theory or from the attempt to develop theories of a **middle range** rather than a single comprehensive theory.[10] Accounting theories of a middle range result from the differences in the way researchers perceive both the "users" of accounting data and the "environments" in which the users and preparers of accounting data are supposed to behave. These divergences led the American Accounting Association's Committee on Concepts and Standards for External Financial Reports to conclude that:

1. No single governing theory of financial accounting is rich enough to encompass the full range of user-environment specifications effectively, hence,
2. there exists in the financial accounting literature not a *theory* of

---

[9]F. N. Kerlinger, *Foundations of Behavioral Research* New York: Holt, Rinehart and Winston, 1964) p. 11.

[10]Theories of the middle range have been introduced and defined by Merton as: "Theories that lie between the minor but necessary working hypotheses that evolve in abundance during day-to-day research and the all-inclusive systematic efforts to develop a unified theory. . . ." In Robert K. Merton, *On Theoretical Sociology: Five Essays, Old and New* (New York: Macmillan, 1967), p. 39.

financial accounting, but a *collection of theories* which can be arrayed over the differences in user-environment specifications.[11]

Despite the presence of accounting theories of a middle range, few authors of these theories have attempted to prove that an accounting theory is possible. Two exceptions deserve our attention.

E. S. Hendriksen used a definition of "theory" that may apply to accounting. According to *Webster's Third New International Dictionary*, **theory** represents "the coherent set of hypothetical, conceptual, and pragmatic principles forming the general frame of reference for a field of inquiry." Hendriksen, therefore, defines **accounting theory** as "a set of broad-principles that (1) provides a general frame of reference by which accounting practice can be evaluated and (2) guides the development of new practices and procedures."[12] This definition allows us to perceive accounting theory as a basis of explanation and prediction. The main objective of accounting theory under this definition is to provide a coherent set of logically derived principles that serve as a frame of reference for evaluating and developing accounting practices.

D. L. McDonald argued that a theory must have three elements: encoding of phenomena to symbolic representation, manipulation or combination according to rules, and translation back to real world phenomena.[13] Each of these theory components is found in accounting. First, accounting employs symbolic representations or symbols. "Debit," "credit," and a whole terminology are proper and unique to accounting. Second, accounting employs translation rules. The encoding, or symbolic representations of economic events and transactions, is a process of translation into and out of symbols. Third, accounting employs rules of manipulation. Techniques for the determination of profit may be considered as rules for the manipulation of accounting symbols.

Methodologies for the Formulation of an Accounting Theory

We have now established that an accounting theory is possible if: (1) it constitutes a frame of reference, as suggested by Hendriksen; and (2) it includes three elements: encoding of phenomena to symbolic representation, manipulation or combination according to rules, and translation back to real phenomena, as suggested by McDonald.

As in any other discipline, a methodology is required for the formulation of an accounting theory. The divergences of opinions, approaches, and values between accounting practice and accounting research have led to the use of two methodologies, one **descriptive** and the other **normative**.

In the professional world of accounting, it has been a widely held belief that accounting is an art that cannot be formalized. The methodology traditionally

---

[11]Committee on Concepts and Standards for External Financial Reports, *Statement on Accounting Theory and Theory Acceptance* (Sarasota, Florida: American Accounting Association, 1977), pp. 1–2.

[12]E. S. Hendriksen, *Accounting Theory*, 3rd ed. (Homewood, Ill.: R. D. Irwin, 1977), p. 1.

[13]D. L. McDonald, *Comparative Accounting Theory* (Reading, Mass.: Addison-Wesley Publishing Co., 1972), pp. 5–8.

used for the formulation of an accounting theory has been essentially descriptive. In other words, according to this view, accounting theory is an attempt to justify *what is* by codifying accounting practices. Such a theory is labeled **descriptive accounting**, or a **descriptive theory of accounting**.[14]

The descriptive accounting approach has been criticized by proponents of a normative methodology. Normative accounting theory attempts to justify what *ought to be*, rather than what is. Such a theory is labeled **normative accounting**, or a **normative theory of accounting**.[15]

At the risk of over simplifying, we may assume that, given the complex nature of accounting phenomena and issues, both methodologies may be needed for the formulation of an accounting theory. The descriptive methodology will attempt to justify some of the accounting practices deemed useful, and the normative methodology will attempt to justify some of the accounting practices that ought to be adopted. Among the descriptive theories of accounting are Grady's "Inventory of Generally Accepted Accounting Principles for Business Enterprises," *Accounting Principles Board Statement No. 4*, and the works of Skinner and Ijiri.[16] Ijiri's book differs from the other three attempts to formulate a theory in that not only is it descriptive, but it is an analytic examination of what accounting is through a pronged inquiry: (1) a mathematical inquiry examining the logical structure, (2) an economic inquiry examining what is measured, and (3) a behavioral inquiry examining how accounting is practiced and used. A distinction is made between two different orientations: One called **operational accounting**, is aimed at providing useful information for management and investor decisions, especially decisions concerning resource allocation; the other, called **equity accounting**, is aimed at reconciling the equities of shareholders and other interested parties inside or outside an organization in order to achieve an equitable distribution of the proceeds or benefits from operations.

Among the normative theories of accounting are the studies by Moonitz, Sprouse and Moonitz, the American Accounting Association's *A Statement of Basic Accounting Theory*, the theory of Edwards and Bell, and the Study by Chambers.[17] A good review of the descriptive and normative methodologies and the resulting theories is provided by McDonald and the AAA's *Statement on Accounting Theory and Theory Acceptance*.[18]

---

[14]*Ibid.*, p. 8.

[15]*Ibid.*

[16]See Paul Grady, *Accounting Research Study No. 7*, "Inventory of Generally Accepted Accounting Principles for Business Enterprises," (New York: AICPA, 1965); R. M. Skinner, *Accounting Principles: A Canadian Study* (Toronto, Canada: The Canadian Institute of Certified Public Accountants, 1973); and Yuji Ijiri, *The Foundations of Accounting Measurement: A Mathematical, Economic and Behavioral Inquiry* (Englewood Cliffs, N.J.: Prentice-Hall, 1967).

[17]M. Moonitz, *The Basic Postulates of Accounting* (New York: AICPA, 1961); R. T. Sprouse and M. Moonitz, *Accounting Research Study No. 3*, "A Tentative Set of Broad Accounting Principles for Business Enterprises," (New York: AICPA, 1962); *A Statement of Basic Accounting Theory* (Evanston, Ill.: AAA, 1966); E. O. Edwards and P. W. Bell, *The Theory and Measurement of Business Income* (Berkeley: University of California Press, 1961); R. J. Chambers, *Accounting, Evaluation and Economic Behavior* (Englewood Cliffs, N.J.: Prentice-Hall, 1966).

[18]D. L. McDonald, *Comparative Accounting Theory*; Committee on Concepts and Standards for External Financial Reports, *Statement on Accounting Theory and Theory Acceptance*.

Approaches to the Formulation of an Accounting Theory

Although there is no single comprehensive theory of accounting, various accounting theories of a middle range exist, resulting from the use of different approaches. As we mentioned, for the sake of clarity we shall limit our discussion in this chapter to the traditional approaches to the formulation of an accounting theory. These traditional approaches have reached a higher level of acceptance and exposure than the new approaches, which we shall present in Chapter 2. The traditional approaches are the following:

1. Nontheoretical, practical, or pragmatic (informal)
2. Theoretical
    a. Deductive
    b. Inductive
    c. Ethical
    d. Sociological
    e. Economic
    f. Eclectic

We shall examine each of these approaches below.

Nontheoretical Approaches

The nontheoretic approaches are a pragmatic (or practical) approach and an authoritarian approach.

The **pragmatic approach** consists of the construction of a theory characterized by its conformity to real world practices and that is useful in terms of suggesting practical solutions. According to this approach, accounting techniques and principles should be chosen because of their usefulness to users of accounting information and their relevance to decision making processes. Usefulness, or utility, means "that property which fits something to serve or to facilitate its intended purpose."[19]

The **authoritarian approach** to the formulation of an accounting theory, which is used mostly by professional organizations, consists of issuing pronouncements for the regulation of accounting practices.

Because the authoritarian approach also attempts to provide practical solutions, it is easily identified with the pragmatic approach. Both approaches assume that accounting theory and the resulting accounting techniques must be predicated on the ultimate uses of financial reports if accounting is to have a useful function. *In other words, a theory without practical consequences is a bad theory.*[20]

The use of utility as a criterion for the choice of accounting principles links accounting theory construction to accounting practices, which may explain the lack of enthusiasm generated by the pragmatic approach. In fact, the pragmatic and authoritarian approaches have been largely unsuccessful in reaching satisfy-

---

[19]James M. Fremgem, "Utility and Accounting Principles," *The Accounting Review* (July 1967), pp. 457–67.

[20]Hendriksen, *Accounting Theory*, p. 23.

ing conclusions in their attempts to construct an accounting theory. For instance, Skinner claims that:

> In essence the pragmatic approach to development of accounting principles has been followed by accounting authority in the past, and attempts to reduce conflicting practices have until recently been extremely cautious and tentative. It is apparent on the basis of experience that this approach will never, by itself, come close to solving the problem of conflicts in accepted accounting principles.[21]

Utility has been cited as a main objective of accounting by various writers in the literature, including Fremgem and Prince.[22] Mueller also argued for accounting principles to be developed through a pragmatic approach.[23] The practical attempts should not be discarded simply because they are basically nontheoretical. Practical approaches are necessary to any theory with an operational utility. In fact, pragmatic considerations permeate the field of accounting through the generally accepted standard of relevance.[24]

We may also think of the pragmatic approach as including a theory of accounts. This approach, which rests on a rationalization of double-entry bookkeeping, was contained in Fra Luca Paciolo's *Summa De Aritmetica Geometria Proportioni et Proportionalita*, published in Venice in 1494. Although the *Summa* was a review of the literature of the then-current mathematical technology, it included 36 short chapters on bookkeeping, called *De Computis et Scripturis* (*Of Reckonings and Writings*).[25]

The theory of accounts approach rationalizes the choice of accounting techniques on the basis of the maintenance of the accounting equations, namely the balance sheet equation and the accounting profit equation.

The balance sheet equation is usually stated as:

$$\text{Assets} = \text{Liabilities} + \text{Owner's Equity}$$

The accounting profit equation is usually stated as:

$$\text{Accounting Profit} = \text{Revenues} - \text{Costs}$$

These two equations in the theory of accounts approach led to the development of two positions within the standard-setting bodies, namely a balance-sheet–oriented position and a profit-oriented position. In any case, the theory of accounts approach, like the pragmatic and the authoritarian approaches, suffers from the absence of theoretical foundations.

Deductive Approach

The **deductive approach** to the construction of any theory begins with basic propositions and proceeds to derive logical conclusions about the subject under consideration. Applied to accounting, the deductive approach begins with basic

---

[21]R. M. Skinner, *Accounting Principles*, p. 302.

[22]Fremgem, "Utility and Accounting Principles"; T. R. Prince, *Extension of the Boundaries of Accounting Theory* (Cincinatti: South-Western, 1973).

[23]Gerhard Mueller, *International Accounting* (New York: Macmillan Co., 1967), pp. 27–30.

[24]*A Statement of Basic Accounting Theory*, p. 9.

[25]J. B. Geijsbeek, *Ancient Double Entry Bookkeeping: Luca Paciolo's Treatise* (Denver: University of Colorado, 1914).

accounting propositions or premises and proceeds to derive by logical means accounting principles that serve as guides and bases for the development of accounting techniques. This approach moves from the general (basic propositions about the accounting environment) to the particular (accounting principles first, and accounting techniques second). If we assume at this point that the basic propositions about the accounting environment consist of both objectives and postulates, the steps used to derive the deductive approach will include the following:

1. Specifying the objectives of financial statements;
2. Selecting the "postulates" of accounting;
3. Deriving the "principles" of accounting;
4. Developing the "techniques" of accounting.

In a deductively derived accounting theory, therefore, the techniques are related to the principles, postulates, and objectives *in such a way that if they are true, the techniques must also be true.* The theoretical structure of accounting defined by the sequence of objectives, postulates, principles, techniques rests on a proper formulation of the objectives of accounting. A proper testing of the resulting theory is also necessary. According to Popper, the testing of deductive theories could be carried out along four lines:

> First, there is the logical comparison of the conclusions among themselves, by which the internal consistency of the system is tested. Secondly, there is the investigation of the logical form of the theory with the object of determining whether it has the character of an empirical or scientific theory, or whether it is, for example, tautological. Thirdly, there is the comparison with other theories, chiefly with the aim of determining whether the theory would constitute a scientific advance should it survive our various tests, and finally, there is the testing of the theory by way of empirical applications of the conclusions which can be derived from it.[26]

The last step is necessary to determine how the theory stands up to the demand of practice. If its predictions are acceptable, then the theory is *verified* or *corroborated* for the time being. If the predictions are not acceptable, then the theory is said to be *falsified.*

Although not necessarily adopting the same steps that we have defined for the deductive process, some accounting writers, who have dealt primarily with the conceptual underpinning of accounting, may be categorized as deductive theorists. Such writers as Paton, Canning, Sweeny, MacNeal, Alexandre, Edwards and Bell, Moonitz, and Sprouse and Moonitz,[27] are deductive theorists. In addition to their search for some conceptual rigor and their adoption of a deductive approach, these writers unanimously agree that users should use current price in-

---

[26]K. Popper, *The Logic of Scientific Discovery* (London: Hutchinson, 1959), p. 33.

[27]W. A. Paton, *Accounting Theory* (New York: The Ronald Press, 1922); J. B. Canning, *Tax Economics of Accountancy* (New York: The Ronald Press, 1923); H. W. Sweeny, *Stabilized Accounting* (New York: Hayer & Brothers, 1936); K. MacNeal, *Truth in Accounting* (Philadelphia: University of Pennsylvania Press, 1939); S. S. Alexandre, "Income Measurement in a Dynamic Economy," *Five Monographs on Business Income* (New York: AICPA, 1950); E. O. Edwards and P. W. Bell, *The Theory and Measurement of Business Income;* M. Moonitz, *The Basic Postulates of Accounting;* R. T. Sprouse and M. Moonitz, *A Tentative Set of Broad Accounting Principles for Business Enterprises.*

formation in their resource allocation decisions. In fact, the search for rigor in the formalization of the structure of accounting theory led some deductive theorists to resort to mathematical, analytic representations and testing. Known as the **axiomatic method,** it is found in the writings of Mattessich and Chambers.[28]

Inductive Approach

The **inductive approach** to the construction of a theory begins with observations and measurements and moves toward generalized conclusions. Applied to accounting, the inductive approach begins with observations of financial information of business enterprises and proceeds to draw, on the basis of recurring relationships, generalizations and principles of accounting. Inductive arguments are said to lead from the particular (accounting information depicting recurring relationships) to the general (postulates and principles of accounting). The inductive approach to a theory involves four stages:

1. Observations, and recording of all observations;
2. Analysis and classification of these observations to detect recurring relationships, "likes" and "similarities";
3. Inductive derivation of generalizations and principles of accounting from those observations that depict recurring relationships;
4. Testing of the generalizations.

We may see that, unlike the case with deduction, the truth or falsity of the propositions does not depend on other propositions but must be empirically verified. Induction, the truth of the propositions depends on the observation of sufficient instances of recurring relationships.

Similarly, we may state that accounting propositions resulting from inductive inference imply special accounting techniques only with more or less high probability, whereas the accounting propositions resulting from deductive inference lead to specific accounting techniques with certainty.

Some accounting writers have relied on observations of accounting practice to suggest a theoretical framework for accounting. Inductive theorists include Hatfield, Gilman, Littleton, Patton and Littleton, and Ijiri.[29] The underlying objective of most of these authors is rationalizing accounting practice to draw theoretical and abstract conclusions. The best defense of the inductive approach is provided by Ijiri's attempts to generalize the goals implicit in current accounting practice and defend the use of historical cost. He states:

> This type of inductive reasoning to derive goals implicit in the behavior of an existing system is not intended to be proestablishment to promote the maintenance of the status quo. The purpose of such exercise is to highlight where changes are most needed and where they are feasible. Changes suggested as a result of such a study have a much better chance

---

[28]R. Mattessich, *Accounting and Analytical Methods* (Homewood, Ill.: R. D. Irwin, 1964); R. J. Chambers, *Accounting, Evaluation and Economic Behavior.*

[29]H. R. Hatfield, *Accounting* (New York: D. Appleton & Company, 1927); S. Gilman, *Accounting Concepts of Profit* (New York: The Ronald Press, 1939); A. C. Littleton, *Structure of Accounting Theory,* Monograph No. 5 (Evanston, Ill.: AAA, 1953); W. A. Paton, and A. C. Littleton, *An Introduction to Corporate Accounting Standards,* Monograph No. 3 (Evanston, Ill.: AAA, 1940); Y., Ijiri, "Theory of Accounting Measurement," *Studies in Accounting Research* #10 (Evanston, Ill.: AAA, 1975).

of being actually implemented. Goal assumptions in normative models or goals advocated in policy discussions are often stated purely on the basis of one's conviction and preference, rather than on the basis of inductive study of the existing system. This may perhaps be the most crucial reason why so many normative models or policy proposals are not implemented in the real world.[30]

It is interesting to note that while the deductive approach starts with general propositions, the formulation of the propositions is often done by inductive reasoning, conditioned by the author's knowledge of and experience with accounting practice. In other words, the general propositions are formulated through an inductive process, while the principles and techniques are derived by a deductive process. Yu suggests that inductive logic may presuppose deductive logic.[31] It is not surprising, therefore, that some of the inductive writers sometimes interpose deductive reasoning, and deductive writers sometimes interpose inductive reasoning. It is also interesting to note that when Littleton, an inductive theorist, and Paton, a deductive theorist, collaborate, the results are of a hybrid nature, indicating a compromise between the two approaches.

Ethical Approach

The basic core of the **ethical approach** consists of the concepts of fairness, justice, equity, and truth. Such concepts are used by D. R. Scott as the main criteria for the formulation of an accounting theory.[32] He equates "justice" with *equitable* treatment of all interested parties, "truth" with *true and accurate* accounting statements without misrepresentation, and "fairness" with *fair, unbiased, and impartial* presentation. Accountants since Scott have considered the three concepts to be equivalent. Yu, in contrast, perceived only justice and fairness as ethical norms and saw truth as a value statement.[33] The "fairness" concept has become an implicit ethical norm, implying, in general, that accounting statements have not been subject to undue influence or bias. Fairness generally implies that the preparers of accounting information acted with good faith, good business practice, and good accounting judgment. "Fairness" is merely a value statement variously applied in accounting. Patillo ranked fairness as a basic standard to be used for the evaluation of other standards because it is the only one that implies "ethical considerations."[34] Spacek went one step further in asserting the primacy of the fairness concept:

> A discussion of assets, liabilities, revenue and costs is premature and meaningless until the basic principles that will result in a *fair* presentation of the facts in the form of financial accounting and financial reporting are determined. This fairness of accounting and reporting must be

[30]Ijiri, *Theory of Accounting Measurement*, p. 28.

[31]S. C. Yu, *The Structure of Accounting Theory* (Gainesville: The University Presses of Florida, 1976), p. 20

[32]D. R. Scott, "The Basis for Accounting Principles," *The Accounting Review* (December 1941), pp. 341–49.

[33]S. C. Yu, *The Structure of Accounting Theory*.

[34]J. W. Patillo, *The Foundations of Financial Accounting* (Baton Rouge: Louisiana State University Press, 1965), p. 11.

for and to people, and these people represent the various segments of our society.[35]

Whatever it may connote, fairness has become one of the basic objectives of accounting. The Committee on Auditing Procedures refers to the criteria of "fairness of presentation" as (1) conformity with generally accepted accounting principles, (2) disclosure, (3) consistency, and (4) comparability.[36] In an unqualified report, the auditor not only states compliance with generally accepted accounting principles and generally accepted auditing standards, but also expresses an opinion with the words "present fairly." Thus, the conventional auditor's report reads as follows:

> We have examined the consolidated balance sheet of XYZ, Inc. as of June 30, 1978 and the consolidated statements of income, retained earnings, and changes in financial position for the year then ended. Our examination was made in accordance with generally accepted auditing standards, and accordingly, included such tests and other procedures as we considered necessary in the circumstances.
>
> In our opinion, these consolidated financial statements *present fairly* the financial position of the company as of June 30, 1978 and the results of its operations and the changes in financial position for the year then ended in accordance with generally accepted accounting principles applied on a basis consistent with that of the preceding year.

On close examination of this standard auditor's report, we see that the statement "present fairly" is included in addition to the auditor's expressing compliance with generally accepted accounting principles and generally accepted auditing standards. This may be seen as psychologically desirable because it may increase the users' confidence. On the other hand, it may imply a double standard, for the concept of "fairness" is substituted for the the tests of generally accepted accounting principles and generally accepted auditing standards.

"Fairness" is a desirable objective in the construction of an accounting theory if whatever is asserted on its basis is logically or empirically verified and if it is made operational by an adequate definition and identification of its properties.

Sociological Approach

The **sociological approach** to the formulation of an accounting theory emphaasizes the social effects of accounting techniques. It is an ethical approach that centers on a broader concept of fairness, that is, social welfare. According to the sociological approach, a given accounting principle or technique will be evaluated for acceptance on the basis of its reporting effects on all groups in society. Also implicit in this approach is the expectation that accounting data will be useful for social welfare judgments. To accomplish its objectives, the sociological approach assumes the existence of "established social values" that may be used as criteria for the determination of accounting theory.[37] A strict application of the sociologi-

---

[35]"Comments of Leonard Spacek," in R. T. Sprouse and M. Moonitz, *Accounting Research Study No. 3*, "A Tentative Set of Broad Accounting Principles for Business Enterprises" (New York: AICPA, 1962), p. 78.

[36]AICPA Committee on Auditing Procedures, *Statement on Auditing Procedure No. 33*, "Auditing Standards and Procedures," (New York: AICPA, 1963), pp. 69–74.

[37]A. Rappaport, "Establishing Objectives for Published Corporate Accounting Reports," *The Accounting Review* (October 1964), pp. 954–61.

cal approach to accounting theory construction may be difficult to find because of the difficulties associated with both determining acceptable "social values" to all people and identifying the information needs of those who make welfare judgments. We may, however, identify cases in which accounting is expected to serve a useful social role. Belkaoui, and Beams and Fertig,[38] among others, referred to the necessity of "internalizing" the social costs and social benefits of the private activities of business firms. Ladd, and Littleton and Zimmerman[39] made several assertions that accounting should serve the public interest and evolve in anticipation, through public inputs, minority viewpoints, and even disagreements among groups. Bedford goes one step further by arguing that the maximization of social well-being is related to a measure of income determination that is *best* for society. The measurement of operational income, Bedford says,

> plays the role of a lubricant, facilitating the functioning of society in an operational sense. Specifically, measured income is used as a computed amount to accomplish objectives necessary for the operation of society.[40]

The sociological approach to the formulation of an accounting theory has contributed to the evolution of a new accounting subdiscipline, known as **socioeconomic accounting.** The main objective of socioeconomic accounting is to encourage the business entities functioning in a free market system to account for the impact of their private production activities on the social environment through measurement, internalization, and disclosure in their financial statements. Over the years, interest in this subdiscipline has increased as a result of the social responsibility trend espoused by organizations, the government, and the public. Social-value–oriented accounting, with its emphasis on "social measurement," its dependence on "social values," and its compliance to a "social welfare criterion," will probably play a major role in the future formulation of accounting theory.

Economic Approach

The **economic approach** to the formulation of an accounting theory emphasizes controlling the behavior of macroeconomic indicators that result from the adoption of various accounting techniques. While the ethical approach focuses on a concept of "fairness" and the sociological approach on a concept of "social welfare," the economic approach focuses on a concept of "general economic welfare." According to this approach, the choice of different accounting techniques depends on their impact on the national economic good. Sweden is the usual example of a country that aligns its accounting policies to other macroeconomic policies.[41] More explicitly, the choice of accounting techniques will depend on the particular economic situation. For example, last in, first out (LIFO) will be a more attractive

---

[38]A. Belkaoui, "The Whys and Wherefores of Measuring Externalities," *The Certified General Accountant* (January–February 1975), pp. 29–32; and F. A. Beams and P. E. Fertig, "Pollution Control Through Social Cost Conversion," *The Journal of Accountancy* (November 1971), pp. 37–42.

[39]D. R. Ladd, *Contemporary Corporate Accounting and the Public* (Homewood, Ill.: Richard D. Irwin, 1963), p. ix; and A. C. Littleton and V. K. Zimmerman, *Accounting Theory: Continuity and Change* (New York: Prentice-Hall, 1962), pp. 261–62.

[40]N. M. Bedford, *Income Determination Theory: An Accounting Framework* (Reading, Mass.: Addison-Wesley, 1965), p. 18.

[41]G. G. Mueller, *International Accounting*, pp. 27–30.

accounting technique in a period of continuing inflation. During inflationary periods, LIFO is assumed to produce a lower annual net income by assuming higher, more inflated costs for the goods sold than under the first in, first out (FIFO) or average cost methods.

The general criteria used by the macroeconomic approach are (1) accounting policies and techniques should reflect "economic reality,"[42] and (2) the choice of accounting techniques should depend on "economic consequences."[43] "Economic reality" and "economic consequences" are the precise terms being used to argue in favor of the macroeconomic approach.

Until the advent of the Financial Accounting Standards Board (FASB), the economic approach and the concept of "economic consequences" were not much in use in accounting. The professional bodies were encouraged to resolve any standard-setting controversies within the context of traditional accounting. Few people were concerned with the economic consequences of accounting policies. In one case, the accounting treatment of the investment tax credit generated a debate among the Accounting Principles Board, the industry representatives, and the administrations of Presidents Kennedy, Johnson, and Nixon. The government contested the use of the deferral method on the basis that it diluted the incentive effect of an instrument of fiscal policy.[44] The economic approach and the concepts of economic consequences and economic reality have been revived since the creation of the FASB.[45] Most of the questions examined during the short life of the FASB have been the subject of a critical examination in terms of the economic consequences of possible recommendations. Some examples are accounting for research and development, self insurance and catastrophe reserves, development-stage companies, foreign currency fluctuations, leases, the restructuring of troubled debt, inflation accounting, and accounting in the petroleum industry.

In setting accounting standards, therefore, the considerations implied by the economic approach are more economic than operational. While in the past, reliance has been on technical accounting considerations, the tenor of the times suggests that standard setting encompasses social and economic concerns.

The Eclectic Approach to the Formulation of an Accounting Theory

In general, the formulation of an accounting theory and the development of accounting principles have followed an **eclectic approach** rather than only one of the approaches presented above. By "eclectic approach," we mean a combination of

---

[42]L. L. Brooks, Jr., "Accounting Policies Should Reflect Economic Reality," *The Canadian Chartered Accountant Magazine* (November 1976), pp. 39–43.

[43]A. S. Zeff, "The Rise of 'Economic Consequences,' " *The Journal of Accountancy* (December 1978), pp. 56–63.

[44]M. Moonitz, "Some Reflections on the Investment Credit Experience," *Journal of Accounting Research* (Spring 1966), pp. 47–61.

[45]*Conference on the Economic Consequences of Financial Accounting Standards* (Stamford, Conn.: FASB, 1978).

approaches. The eclectic approach is mainly the result of numerous attempts by individuals and professional and governmental organizations to participate in the establishment of concepts and principles in accounting. Before discussing these attempts, we shall identify the organizations that have been involved in this process.

Entities Concerned with Accounting Principles

Individual and Public Accounting Firms   Individual and public accounting firms are responsible through their auditors for independently certifying that corporate financial statements present fairly and accurately the results of business activities. The most influencial of these firms, which make up most of the accounting establishment, are the "big eight firms." Listed alphabetically, they are:

Arthur Andersen and Co.
Arthur Young and Co.
Coopers and Lybrand
Ernst and Whinney
Price Waterhouse Co.
Deloitte, Haskins and Sells
Peat, Marwick, Mitchell and Co.
Touche Ross and Co.

Independent auditors are expected to be truly independent of the interests of their corporate clients. The work of the public accounting firms consists principally of the performance of auditing, accounting, tax, and management advisory services. The accounting and auditing services consist of assisting in the design of reliable record-keeping systems, periodically checking the systems to ensure their effectiveness, preparing financial statements that convey accurate information, and certifying financial statements for accuracy. The tax services consist of assisting in preparing tax reports that conform to the regulations and provisions of federal, state, local, and foreign tax laws and in achieving maximum benefits for their clients. Finally, through their management advisory services, public accounting firms assist clients in the management of their businesses by providing consulting services in such areas as financial management, executive recruitment, and product analysis. In some cases, management advisory services have impaired the independence of the individual and public accounting firms. By getting involved in their client's affairs, public accounting firms have created an interest that is fundamentally inconsistent with their commitment and responsibility to remain truly independent.

The American Institute of Certified Public Accountants   The American Institute of Certified Public Accontants (AICPA) is the professional coordinating organization of practicing *certified public accountants* in the United States. Its two important senior technical committees, the Accounting Standards Executive Committee (AcSec) and the Auditing Standards Committee (AuSec), are empowered to speak for the AICPA in the areas of financial and cost accounting and auditing, respectively. These committees issue Statements on Positions ("SOPs") on accounting issues. The SOPs clarify and elaborate on controversial accounting issue and should be followed as guides if they do not contradict existing FASB pronouncements. Through its monthly publication, *The Journal of Accountancy*, the AICPA communicates with its members on controversial accounting problems and solutions. In fact, since its inception in 1887, the AICPA has taken the lead in developing accounting principles. In 1938, it formed the *Committee on Accounting Procedure* (CAP) to "narrow the areas of difference in corporate reporting" by eliminating undesirable practices. Rather than developing a set of generally accepted accounting principles, the CAP adopted an ad hoc and pragmatic approach to controversial problems. Over a period of twenty years, through 1958, the CAP issued 51 *Accounting Research Bulletins*, suggesting accounting treatments for various items and transactions. At the time, the *Accounting Research Bulletins* were supported by the SEC and the stock exchanges and, consequently, represented the only source of "generally accepted accounting principles" in the United States. After World War II, the coexistence of many alternative accounting treatments, the new tax laws, and the new financing techniques and complex capital structures, such as business combinations, leasing, convertible debts, and investment tax credit, created the need for a new approach to the development of accounting principles. In 1959, the AICPA created a new body, the Accounting Principles Board (APB), "to advance the written expression of what constitutes generally accepted accounting principles." In addition, the AICPA appointed a director of accounting research and a permanent staff. Between 1959 and 1973, the APB issued opinions, intended to be used as guidelines for accounting practices unless superseded by *FASB Statements*. In addition to the opinions, the APB published four statements and a series of *Accounting Interpretations* intended to expand on the opinions or communicate recommendations on accounting problems. The statements are:

1. *APB Statement No. 1* is a report on the receipt of *Accounting Research Studies* No. 1 and No. 3.

2. *APB Statement No. 2*, "Disclosure of Supplementary Financial Information by Diversified Companies," was issued in September 1967.

3. *APB Statement No. 3*, "Financial Statements Restated for General Price-Level Changes," was issued in June 1969.

4. *APB Statement No. 4*, "Basic Concepts and Accounting Principles Underlying Financial Statements of Business Enterprises," was issued in October 1970.

To stimulate discussion of controversial topics before the APB acts on them, the research division of the AICPA has commissioned research studies by independent investigators or by members of the research staff under the guidance of the director of research and an advisory committee. *Accounting Research Study No. 1*, titled "The Basic Postulates of Accounting," and *Accounting Research Study No. 3*, titled "A Tentative Set of Broad Accounting Principles for Business Enterprises," were published in 1961 and 1962, respectively. Moonitz and Sprouse used a deductive approach in both studies. In the first study, the authors supported exit value accounting; in the second study, they suggested that it might be necessary to account for both general and specific price-level changes. As might have been expected at the time, the AICPA rejected both studies, claiming that they were radically different from generally accepted accounting practices and therefore unacceptable. A new study was commissioned to review existing accounting principles. Thus, *Accounting Research Study No. 7*, by Paul Grady, titled "Inventory of Generally Accepted Accounting Principles for Business Enterprises," was nothing more than an inventory of existing accounting principles, practices, and methods of the APB and the CAP, that is, ARBs and APB opinions. After the AICPA's rejection of *Accounting Research Studies No. 1* and *No. 3*, the remaining studies reflected the assumptions and findings of the particular researcher who did the study. The APB opinions did not, in general, follow the recommendations of *Accounting Research Studies No. 1* and *No. 3*. The other twelve studies are:

1. *ARS No. 2*, "Cash Flow Analysis and the Funds Statement," by Perry Mason, published in 1961.
2. *ARS No. 4*, "Reporting of Leases in Financial Statements," by John H. Myers, published in 1962.
3. *ARS No. 5*, "A Critical Study of Accounting for Business Combinations," by Arthur B. Watt, published in 1963.
4. *ARS No. 6*, "Reporting the Financial Effects of Price-Level Changes," by the staff of the Research Division, published in 1963.
5. *ARS No. 8*, "Accounting for the Cost of Pension Plans," by Ernest L. Hicks, published in 1965.
6. *ARS No. 9*, "Interperiod Allocation of Corporate Income Taxes," by Hower A. Black, published in 1966.
7. *ARS No. 10*, "Accounting for Goodwill," by George R. Catlett and Norman O. Olson, published in 1968.
8. *ARS No. 11*, "Financial Reporting in the Extractive Industries," by Robert R. Field, published in 1970.
9. *ARS No. 12*, "Reporting Foreign Operations of U.S. Companies in U.S. Dollars," by Leonard Lorenson, published in 1972.
10. *ARS No. 13*, "The Accounting Basis of Inventories," by Horace G. Barden, published in 1973.
11. *ARS No. 14*, "Accounting for R & D Expenditures," by Oscar S. Gellein and Maurice S. Newman, published in 1973.
12. *ARS No. 15*, "Stockholders' Equity," by Beatrice Melcher, published in 1973.

The American Accounting Association   The American Accounting Association is an organization of accounting academics and any individuals interested in the betterment of accounting practice and theory. Its quarterly journal, the *Accounting Review*, is devoted to the exchange of ideas and results among accounting researchers. The AAA serves as a forum within which academicians express their views on various accounting topics and issues, either individually or through the organization's special appointed committees. In fact, the AAA has attempted through such special committees to provide a framework for corporate financial statements. These efforts, which have met with varying degrees of success, comprise the following studies:

1. *A Tentative Statement of Accounting Principles Underlying Corporate Financial Statements*, published in 1936 and revised successively in 1941 and 1948, with eight supplementary statements prepared between 1950 and 1954 that clarify or expand on the 1948 statement, then revised again in 1957 with five supplementary statements appearing between 1957 and 1964.
2. *An Introduction to Corporate Accounting Standards*, by Paton and Littleton, published in 1940.
3. *An Inquiry into the Nature of Accounting*, by Louis Golberg, published in 1964.
4. *A Statement of Basic Accounting Theory*, published in 1966.

5. *A Statement on Accounting Theory and Theory Acceptance*, published in 1977.

Initially based on an inductive approach, these attempts by the AAA to develop an accounting framework gradually shifted to a deductive approach with a 1957 revision, titled "Accounting and Reporting Standards for Corporate Financial Statements—1957 Revision." The members of the AAA, who are mostly college and university teachers, play one of the greatest roles in the formulation of accounting theory through continuous innovative research and active participation in the principal standard-setting bodies. The enthusiasm of AAA members is indicated by their research output appearing in the various accounting journals.[46]

The Financial Accounting Standards Board   The Financial Accounting Standards Board (FASB) replaced the APB in 1973 as the body responsible for establishing accounting standards. The APB was brought down by a crisis due mainly to the following factors: (1) the continuing existence of alternative accounting treatments that allowed companies to show higher earnings per share, especially as a result of corporate mergers and acquisitions; (2) the lack of adequate accounting treatments for such new accounting problems as the investment tax credit, accounting for the franchising industries, the land development business, and long-term leases; (3) the disclosure of a number of cases of fraud and lawsuits implicating the accounting methods, which failed to disclose relevant information in a number of cases;[47] and (4) the failure of the APB to develop a conceptual accounting framework. After investigating the situation, a committee appointed by the AICPA, known as the Wheat Committee, proposed a new structure for establishing accounting standards. The proposed new structure consisted of nonprofit organizations, The Financial Accounting Foundation (FAF), that would operate the FASB and would be cosponsored by five interest groups: The Financial Executive Institute, the National Association of Accountants, the American Accounting Association, the Financial Analysts Federation, and the Security Industry Association. Exhibit 1–1 illustrates the FASB structure adopted in 1973.

The FASB is the authoritative independent body charged with establishing and improving financial accounting and reporting standards—that is, those standards concerned with recording meaningful information about economic events and transactions in a useful manner in financial statements. The members of the FASB are assumed to represent most parties interested in financial accounting. More specifically, four members are CPAs in public practice, and three members are from areas related to accounting, for example, government, industry, and education. While the APB members were able to retain their positions with firms, companies, and institutions, FASB members must sever all such ties. Finally, the FASB members are well-paid, full-time members appointed for renewable five-

---

[46]For example, AAA members have published in *The Accounting Review, The Journal of Accounting Research, The Accounting Journal, Accounting Organizations and Society, The Journal of Business Finance and Accounting, Abacus, The Journal of Accountancy, Cost and Management, The Certified General Accountant, The Canadian Chartered Accountant Magazine, Management Accounting, Financial Management, Accounting and Business Research,* and *The Journal of Business.*

[47]See, for example, the cases of Wester, Mill Factors, Equity Funding, Student Marketing, Penn Central, Four Seasons Nursing Homes, Continental Vending, Revenue Properties, Black Watch Farms, and Investors Overseas Services.

EXHIBIT 1-1

Structure of the FASB

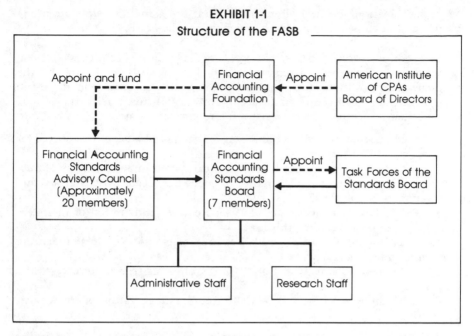

SOURCE: American Institute of Certified Public Accountants, *Report of the Study on Establishment of Accounting Principles* (New York: AICPA, 1972).

year terms. Because of such characteristics—broader representation, increased independence, and smaller full-time remunerated memberships—the FASB should have better success than the APB.

The accounting profession's relationship to the FASB was clarified by Rule 203 of the AICPA's Code of Professional Ethics, which holds that a member of the AICPA may not express an opinion that financial statements are presented fairly in comformity with generally accepted accounting principles if the statements depart from an *FASB Statement* or *Interpretation* or an *APB Opinion* or *Accounting Research Bulletin*, unless the member can demonstrate that, due to unusual circumstances, the financial statements would be otherwise misleading. Rule 203 constitutes an endorsement of the FASB, although with the reservation that recognizes that, in unusual circumstances, literal compliance with presumptively binding, generally accepted accounting principles issued by a recognized standard-setting body may not invariably ensure that financial statements are presented fairly.

Since its inception, the FASB has adopted the following method of operation:

1. A problem is identified and a task force is appointed.
2. A discussion memorandum exposing the various alternatives is issued.
3. A public hearing is staged during which various viewpoints are presented to the board.
4. An exposure draft, which may be followed by a revised exposure draft is issued.
5. A standard is promulgated.

Public participation does not alter the fact that the actual decisions regarding accounting standards are made by the members of the FASB.

The Securities and Exchange Commission   Created by an act of Congress in 1934, the Securities and Exchange Commission (SEC) is primarily responsible for the administration of various laws intended to regulate securities and to ensure proper financial reporting and disclosure by American firms. Briefly, the various acts and their respective general registration requirements are:

1. Securities Act of 1933: Requires registration of new securities offered for public sales.
2. Securities Exchange Act of 1934: Requires continuous reporting of publicly owned companies and registration of securities, security exchanges, and certain brokers and dealers.
3. Public Utility Holding Act of 1935: Requires registration of interstate holding companies covered by this law.
4. Trust Indenture Act of 1939: Requires registration of trust indenture documents and supporting data.
5. Investment Company Act of 1940: Requires registration of investment companies.
6. Investment Advisers Act of 1940: Requires registration of investment advisers.[48]

The Securities Acts of 1933 and 1934 give the SEC the power to determine accounting standards. As Horngren explains, the SEC was the top management and the APB was the lower management.[49] Although the SEC has the power to regulate accounting practices and disclosure, it has in general relied on the accounting profession, using its power to set constraints and exert veto power. John Burton better expressed this situation while he was chief accountant of the SEC:

> We are in partnership and our best interests are served in an atmosphere of mutual nonsurprise.

> The SEC does not view itself as being in a position of absolute authority and the FASB working for it.[50]

Thus, the SEC has generally concurred with the profession's pronouncements, APB opinions and FASB statements. Nevertheless, it has retained its right to express its views in the following five ways:

1. Regulation S-X, which prescribes the form and content of the reports filed with the SEC. (The most important of these SEC corporate reports are the 10-K annual report, the 10-Q quarterly report, and the 8-K report of unscheduled material events or corporate changes of interest to shareholders or the SEC.)

---

[48]For more information, see Leroy Ainsworth and Johnny S. Turner, Jr., *An Overview of the SEC with a Guide to Researching Accounting-Related SEC Problems* (Provo, Utah: Brigham Young University Press, 1971), p. 11.

[49]Charles T. Horngren, "Accounting Principles: Private or Public Sector?" *Journal of Accountancy* (May 1972), p. 38.

[50]The first statement is from "Paper Shuffling and Economic Reality," an interview with John C. Burton, *Journal of Accountancy* (January 1973), p. 26; the second statement is from John C. Burton, "Some General and Specific Thoughts on the Accounting Environment," *Journal of Accountancy* (October 1973), p. 41.

2. *Accounting Series Releases*, which are pronouncements on accounting matters.

3. SEC Decisions and Reports.

4. SEC Annual Report.

5. Speeches and articles by members of the commission and its staff.

The SEC has not always concurred with the accounting profession's pronouncements. Some of its *Accounting Series Releases* on accounting, auditing, and financial matters have been in conflict with or have in fact amended or superseded, standards set by the standard-setting bodies. Three notorious examples are (1) *ASR No. 96*, in which the SEC rejected *APB Opinion No. 2*, and gave acceptance to several methods of handling the investment credit; (2) *ASR No. 147*, in which the SEC characterized leasee disclosures required by *APB No. 31* as inadequate, and imposed additional disclosure requirements of its own; and (3) *ARS No. 146*, in which the SEC provided an interpretation of *APB Opinion No. 16* which prompted a CPA firm to sue the SEC.

After the failure of the APB and the creation of the FASB, the SEC issued a policy statement—*Accounting Series Release No. 150*—which specifically endorsed the FASB as the only standard-setting body whose standards will be accepted by the SEC as satisfying the requirements of the federal securities laws. The release states that "principles, standards and practices promulgated by the FASB will be considered by the Commission as having substantial authoritative support, and those contrary to such FASB promulgations will be considered to have no such support." It also states, however, that "the Commission will continue to identify areas where investor information needs exist and will determine the appropriate methods of disclosure to meet these needs." The SEC continues to permit the establishment of accounting standards by the private sector, and the commission's intervention as the federal government's major participant in the accounting standard-setting process is in the form of cooperation, advice, and sometimes pressure, rather than in the form of rigid controls. In other words, the SEC endorses the FASB with some reservations, in that it has not delegated any of its authority or given up any right to reject, modify, or supersede FASB pronouncements through its own rule-making procedures.

Other Professional Organizations Although the previously cited organizations have been traditionally involved with the development of accounting theory, other organizations have recently shown some active participation in the United States and abroad, in particular; (1) The Cost Accounting Standards Board, (2) The National Association of Accountants, (3) The Financial Executive Institute, (4) The Institute of Chartered Accountants in England and Wales, (5) The Canadian Institute of Chartered Accountants, (6) The Society of Management Accountants in Canada, (7) the Certified General Accountants Association of Canada, (8) The Institute of Chartered Accountants in Australia, (9) The Australian Society of Accountants, (10) The International Accounting Standards Committee, (11) The Inter-American Accounting Conferences, (12) The Union d'Experts Comptables in Europe, and (13) The Confederation of Asian and Pacific Accountants. Each of these organizations is actively involved in setting accounting standards in its respective country and furthering the basic foundations of accounting.

Users of Financial Statements The different groups interested in the results of the activities of a profit-oriented organization have been classified as **direct users** and

indirect users.[51] Direct users include: (1) the *owners* of a corporation and its shareholders, (2) the *creditors* and *suppliers*, (3) the *management* of a firm, (4) the *taxing authorities*, (5) the *laborers* in an organization, (6) the *customers*. The indirect users include: (1) the *financial analysts* and *advisers*, (2) the *Stock Exchanges*, (3) *lawyers*, (4) *regulatory or registration authorities*, (5) the *financial press and reporting agencies*, (6) *trade associations*, (7) *labor unions*, (8) *competitors*, (9) *the general public*, and (10) *other government departments*.

Direct and indirect users have diverse and conflicting sets of objectives. Basically, they have different information needs. Three kinds of financial statements may be prepared:

1. *General-purpose financial statements* meet the common needs of the users. In designing the financial statements presented in most annual reports, accountants assume the reports will meet the common needs of users.
2. *Specific-purpose financial statements* meet the need of specific user groups.
3. *Differential disclosure* present different figures for the user to select.

Whatever kind of financial statement is used, most users act as pressure groups to influence the development of accounting principles in such a way that their objectives are met.

Development of Accounting Principles

Through the groups we discussed earlier in the chapter using a mix of the approaches identified, accounting theory has been subject to a constant reexamination and critical analysis. Three phases of this process may be identified: In the first phase, management had almost complete control over the selection of financial information disclosed in annual reports (1900–1933); in the second phase, the professional bodies played a significant role in developing principles (1933–1973); and in the third phase, which continues to the present, the FASB and various pressure groups are moving toward a politicization of accounting.

Management Contribution Phase (1900–1933)   The influence of management in the formulation of accounting principles arose from the dominant economic role played by industrial corporations after 1900 and the increasing number of shareholders. The diffusion of stock ownership gave management complete control over the format and content of accounting disclosures. The intervention of management may be best characterized by the adoption of ad hoc solutions to urgent problems and controversies. The consequences of this dependence of management initiative include the following:

1. Given the pragmatic character of the solutions adopted, most accounting techniques lacked theoretical support.
2. The focus was on the determination of taxable income and the minimization of income taxes.
3. The techniques adopted were motivated by the desire to smooth earnings.
4. Complex problems were avoided and expedient solutions adopted.

---

[51]*APB Statement No. 4.*

5. Different firms adopted different accounting techniques for the same problem.[52]

This situation generated dissatisfaction during the 1920s. Two men, William Z. Ripley and J. M. B. Hoxley, were particularly outspoken in arguing for an improvement in financial reporting.[53] Similarly, Adolph A. Berle, Jr., and Gardiner C. Means pointed to the corporate wealth and power of industrial corporations and called for the protection of investors.[54]

Professional Contribution Phase (1933–1973)   The second pahse of accounting theory formulation, from 1933 to 1973, was marked by the organization of various societies and agencies to regulate accounting practices. Government intervention came in the form of the Securities Acts of 1933 and 1934. The American Institute of Certified Public Accountants acted through the *Accounting Research Bulletins* published by the *Committee on Accounting Procedure* until 1959 and through the *APB Opinions* published by the *Accounting Principles Board* until 1973. The American Accounting Association also participated in the process through several research studies and attempts to develop an integrated statement of basic accounting theory. The intervention of professional associations and agencies in the formulation of an accounting theory was spurred by the effort to eliminate undesirable techniques and codify acceptable techniques. Again, dependence on such associations and agencies has not been without consequences, which include the following:

1.   The associations and agencies did not rely on any established theoretical framework.
2.   The authority of the statements was not clear-cut.
3.   The existence of alternative treatments allowed flexibility in the choice of accounting techniques.

The dissatisfactions with the results of professional intervention, as expressed in the writings of Briloff, were quite effective in bringing to the attention of the general public the accounting abuses dominating certain annual reports.[55]

Politicization Phase (1973–present)   The limitations of both professional associations and management in the formulation of an accounting theory led to the adoption of a more deductive approach as well as politicization of the standard-setting process. This situation is created by the generally accepted view that the accounting numbers affect economic behavior and, consequently, accounting rules should be made in the political arena. In the same view, Charles Horngren states:

The setting of accounting standards is as much a product of political

---

[52]Skinner, *Accounting Principles*, p. 314.

[53]W. Z. Ripley, *Railroads, Finance and Organization* (New York: Longmans, Green & Co., 1915); and "Stop, look, listen!" *Atlantic Monthly* (September 1926); see also *Main Street and Wall Street* (Boston: Little, Brown and Co., 1927); J. M. B. Hoxley, "Accounting for Investors," *Journal of Accountancy* (October 1930), pp. 251–84.

[54]Adolph A. Berle and Gardiner C. Means, *The Modern Corporation and Private Property* (New York: Macmillan, 1933).

[55]Abraham J. Briloff, *Unaccountable Accounting* (New York: Harper & Row, 1972).

action as of flawless logic or empirical findings. Why? Because the setting of standards is a social decision. Standards place restrictions on behavior; therefore, they must be accepted by the affected parties. Acceptance may be forced or voluntary or some of both. In a democratic society, getting acceptance is an exceedingly complicated process that requires skillful marketing in a political arena.[56]

Since its inception, the FASB has adopted a deductive and a quasi-political approach to the formulation of accounting principles. The FASB conduct is better marked by, first, an effort to develop a theoretical framework or accounting constitution and, second, by the emergence of various interest groups, the contribution of which is required for the "general" acceptance of new standards. The standard setting process, therefore, has a political aspect. The following statement by the FASB indicates its awareness of this new situation:

> The process of setting accounting standards can be described as democratic because like all rule-making bodies the board's right to make rules depends ultimately on the consent of the ruled. But because standard setting requires some perspective it would not be appropriate to establish a standard based solely on a canvass of the constituents. Similarly, the process can be described as legislative because it must be deliberative and because all views must be heard. But the standard setters are expected to represent the entire constituency as a whole and not be representatives of a specific constituent group. The process can be described as political because there is an educational effort involved in getting a new standard accepted. But it is not political in the sense that an accommodation is required to get a statement issued.[57]

That the process of formulating accounting standards is becoming political is better expressed by a report released by the Senate Subcommittee on Reports, Accounting and Management, titled "The Accounting Establishment." Known as the "Metcalf Report," it charged that the "big eight" accounting firms monopolize auditing of large corporations and control the standard-setting process. Exhibit 1–2 shows the relationship of the major organizations that suggests the big eight accounting firms and the AICPA have control over accounting standards approved by the SEC. After emphasizing the need for the federal government to ensure that publicly owned corporations are properly accountable to the public, the report made the following recommendations aimed at enhancing corporate accountability:

1. Congress should exercise stronger oversight of accounting practices promulgated or approved by the Federal Government, and more leadership in establishing proper goals and policies. . . .
2. Congress should establish comprehensive accounting objectives for the Federal Government to guide agencies and departments in performing their responsibilities. . . . A comprehensive set of Federal accounting objectives should encompass such goals as uniformity, consistency, clarity, accuracy, simplicity, meaningful presentation,

---

[56]Charles T. Horngren, "The Marketing of Accounting Standards," *The Journal of Accountancy* (October 1973), p. 61.

[57]Structure Committee, *The Structure of Establishing Financial Accounting Standards* (Stamford, Conn.: FAF, April 1977), p. 15.

EXHIBIT 1-2

Control of the "Big Eight" Accounting Firms and the AICPA over Accounting Standards Approved by the SEC

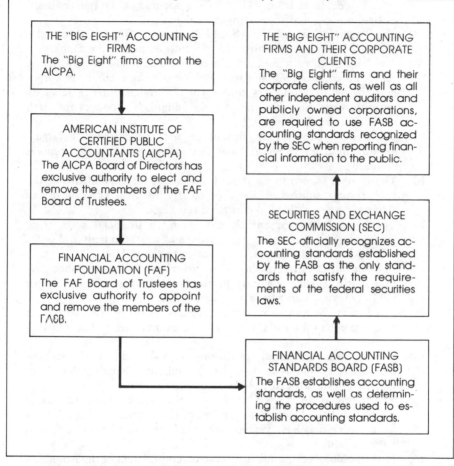

THE "BIG EIGHT" ACCOUNTING FIRMS
The "Big Eight" firms control the AICPA.

AMERICAN INSTITUTE OF CERTIFIED PUBLIC ACCOUNTANTS (AICPA)
The AICPA Board of Directors has exclusive authority to elect and remove the members of the FAF Board of Trustees.

FINANCIAL ACCOUNTING FOUNDATION (FAF)
The FAF Board of Trustees has exclusive authority to appoint and remove the members of the FASB.

THE "BIG EIGHT" ACCOUNTING FIRMS AND THEIR CORPORATE CLIENTS
The "Big Eight" firms and their corporate clients, as well as all other independent auditors and publicly owned corporations, are required to use FASB accounting standards recognized by the SEC when reporting financial information to the public.

SECURITIES AND EXCHANGE COMMISSION (SEC)
The SEC officially recognizes accounting standards established by the FASB as the only standards that satisfy the requirements of the federal securities laws.

FINANCIAL ACCOUNTING STANDARDS BOARD (FASB)
The FASB establishes accounting standards, as well as determining the procedures used to establish accounting standards.

SOURCE: Subcommittee on Reports, Accounting and Management of the Committee on Government Operations United States Senate, *Summary of the Accounting Establishment, A Staff Study*, December 1976, Rpt. New York: National Association of Accountants, p. 3.

and fairness in application. In addition, Congress should establish specific policies abolishing such "creative accounting" techniques as percentage of completion income recognition, inflation accounting, "normalized" accounting, and other potentially misleading accounting methods. . . .

3. Congress should amend the Federal Securities laws to restore the right of damaged individuals to sue independent auditors for negligence under the fraud provisions of the securities laws. . . .

4. Congress should consider methods of increasing competition among accounting firms for selection as independent auditors for major corporations. . . .

5. The Federal Government should establish financial accounting standards for publicly owned corporations. . . .
6. The Federal Government should establish auditing standards used by independent auditors to certify the accuracy of corporate financial statements and supporting records. . . .
7. The Federal Government should itself periodically inspect the works of independent auditors for publicly owned corporations. . . .
8. The Federal Government should restore public confidence in the actual independence of auditors who certify the accuracy of corporate financial statements under the Federal Securities laws by promulgating and enforcing strict standards of conduct for such auditors. . . .
9. The Federal Government should require the nation's 15 largest accounting firms to report basic operational and financial reports annually. . . .
10. The Federal Government should define the responsibilities of the independent auditors so that they clearly meet the expectations of Congress, the public, and courts of law. . . .
11. The Federal Government should establish financial accounting standards, cost accounting standards, auditing standards and other accounting practices in meetings open to the public. . . .
12. The Federal Gvernment should act to relieve excessive concentration in the supply of auditing and accounting services to major publicly owned corporations. . . .
13. The Federal Government should retain accounting firms which act as independent auditors only to perform auditing and accounting services. . . .
14. The Securities and Exchange Commission should treat all independent auditors equally in disciplinary and enforcement proceedings under the Federal securities laws. . . .
15. The Membership of the Cost Accounting Standards Board should not be dominated by representatives of the industry and accounting firms which may have vested interests in the standards established by the board. . . .
16. Federal employees should not serve on committees of the American Institute of Certified Public Accountants or similar organizations that are assigned to directly or indirectly influence accounting policies and procedures of the Federal Government. . . .[58]

Conclusions

The traditional approach to the formulation of an accounting theory has used either a normative or a descriptive methodology, a theoretical or a nontheoretical approach, a deductive or an inductive line of reasoning, and focused on a concept

---

[58]Subcommittee on Reports, Accounting and Management of the Committee on Government Operations, United Senate, *Summary of the Accounting Establishment, A Staff Study* (December 1976; Rpt. New York: National Association of Accountants, 1976), pp. 20–24.

of "fairness," "social welfare," or "economic welfare." The traditional approach has evolved into an eclectic and political approach. Above all, an accounting theory needs confirmation to be accepted.

References

Theory Construction and Verification

American Accounting Association. "Report of the Committee on Foundations of Accounting Measurement." *The Accounting Review*, supplement to vol. 46 (1971), pp. 37–45.

AAA. "Report of the Committee Accounting Theory Construction and Verification." *The Accounting Review*, suplement to vol. 46 (1971), pp. 53–79.

Buckley, John W., Paul Kircher, and Russel L. Mathews. "Methodology in Accounting Theory." *The Accounting Review* (April 1968), pp. 274–83.

Gonedes, Nicholas J. "Perception, Estimation and Verifiability." *International Journal of Accounting Education and Research* (Spring 1969), pp. 63–73.

McDonald, Daniel L. *Comparative Accounting Theory*. Reading, Mass.: Addison-Wesley, 1972.

Schrader, William J., and Robert E. Malcolm. "Note on Accounting Theory Construction and Verification." *Abacus* (June 1973), pp. 93–98.

Sterling, Robert R. "An Explication and Analysis of the Structure of Accounting, Part One." *Abacus* (December 1971), pp. 137–52 and "Part Two." *Abacus* (December 1972), pp. 145–62.

Sterling, Robert R. "On Theory Construction and Verification." *The Accounting Review* (July 1970), pp. 444–57.

Williams, Thomas H., and Charles H. Griffin. "On the Nature of Empirical Verification in Accounting." *Abacus* (December 1969), pp. 143–78.

Nontheoretical Approach

Cowan, T. K. "A Pragmatic Approach to Accounting Theory." *The Accounting Review* (January 1968), pp. 94–100.

Beams, Floyd A. "Indications of Pragmation and Empiricism in Accounting Thought." *The Accounting Review* (April 1968), pp. 382–397.

Fremgen, James M. "Utility and Accounting Principles." *The Accounting Review* (July 1967), pp. 457–67.

Geijsbeek, J. B. *Ancient Double Entry Bookkeeping: Luca Pacioli's Treatise*. Denver: University of Colorado, 1914.

Mueller, Gerhard G. "Accounting and Conventional Business Practices." *International Accounting*. New York: Macmillan, 1967, pp. 60–63.

Prince, T. R. *Extensions of the Boundaries of Accounting Theory*. Cincinnati: South-Western, 1963.

Deductive, Inductive, and Axiomatic Approaches

Bedford, N. M., and N. Dopuch. "Research Methodology and Accounting Theory: Another Perspective." *The Accounting Review* (July 1972), pp. 351–61.

Demski, Joel S. "The General Impossibility of Normative Accounting Standards." *The Accounting Review* (October 1973), pp. 718–23.

Devine, Carl Thomas. "Research Methodology and Accounting Theory Formation." *The Accounting Review* (July 1960), pp. 387–99.

Hakansson, Nils H. "Normative Accounting Theory and the Theory of Decision," *International Journal of Accounting Education and Research* (Spring 1969), pp. 33–47.

Langenderfer, Harold Q. "A Conceptual Framework for Financial Reporting." *Journal of Accountancy* (July 1973), pp. 45–55.

Mattessich, R. *Accounting and Analytical Methods.* Homewood, Ill.: R. D. Irwin, 1964.

Mattessich, R. "Methodological Preconditions and Problems of a General Theory of Accounting." *The Accounting Review* (July 1972), pp. 469–87.

Moonitz, Maurice. "Why Do We Need 'Postulates' and 'Principles'?" *The Journal of Accountancy* (December 1963), pp. 42–46.

Pellicelli, Georgio. "The Axiomatic Method in Business Economics: A First Approach." *Abacus* (December 1969), pp. 119–31.

Vernon, Kam. "Judgment and Scientific Trend in Accounting." *Journal of Accountancy* (February 1973), pp. 57–67.

Ethical Approach

Arnett, Harold E. "The Concept of Fairness." *The Accounting Review* (April 1967), pp. 291–97.

Burton, John C., ed. *Corporate Financial Reporting: Ethical and Other Problems.* New York: AICPA, 1972, pp. 17–27, ff.

Patillo, James W. *The Foundations of Financial Accounting.* Baton Rouge: Louisiana State University Press, 1965.

Scott, D. R. "The Basis for Accounting Principles." *The Acconting Review* (December 1941), pp. 341–49.

Spacek, Leonard. *A Search for Fairness in Financial Reporting to the Public.* Chicago: Arthur Andersen & Co., 1965, pp. 38–77, and 349–56.

Sociological Approach

Alexander, Michael O. "Social Accounting, If You Please!" *Canadian Chartered Accountant* (January 1973), pp. 23–27.

AAA. "Report of the Committee on Measures of Effectiveness for Social Programs." *The Accounting Review,* supplement to vol. 47 (1972), pp. 337–98.

AICPA. *Social Measurement.* New York: AICPA, 1972.

Andrews, Frederick. "Puzzled Businessmen Ponder New Methods of Measuring Success." *Canadian Chartered Accountant* (March 1972), pp. 58–61.

Beams, Floyd A., and Paul E. Fertig. "Pollution Control Through Social Cost Conversion." *Journal of Accountancy* (November 1971), pp. 37–42.

Belkaoui, A. "The Whys and Wherefores of Measuring Externalities." *The Certified General Accountant* (January–February 1975), pp. 29–32.

Estes, Ralph W. "Socio-Economic Accounting and External Diseconomies." *The Accounting Review* (April 1972), pp. 284–90.

Gambling, Trevor. *Societal Accounting.* London: Allen and Unwin, 1974.

Ladd, D. R. *Contemporary Corporate Accounting and the Public.* Homewood, Ill. Richard D. Irwin, 1963.

Mobley, Sybil C. "The Challenges of Socio-Economic Accounting." *The Accounting Review* (October 1970), pp. 762–68.

Economic Approach

Brooks, L. L., Jr. "Accounting Policies Should Reflect Economic Reality." *The Canadian Chartered Accountant Magazine* (November 1976), pp. 39–43.

Conference on the Economic Consequences of Financial Accounting Standards. Stamford, Conn.: FASB, 1978.

Enthoven, Adolf J. H. *Accountancy and Economic Development Policy.* New York: American Elsevier Publishing Co., 1973.

Moonitz, M. "Some Reflections on the Investment Credit Experience." *Journal of Accounting Research* (Spring 1966), pp. 47–61.

Mueller, Gerhard G. "Accounting Within a Macroeconomic Framework." *International Accounting.* New York: Macmillan, 1967.

Zeff, A. S. "The Rise of 'Economic Consequences.'" *The Journal of Accountancy* (December 1978), pp. 56–63.

Legislative and Political Approach

Buckley, John. "FASB and Impact Analysis." *Management Accounting* (April 1976), pp. 13–17.

Horngren, Charles T. "The Marketing of Accounting Standards." *The Journal of Accountancy* (October 1973), pp. 61–66.

May, R. G., and G. L. Sundern. "Research for Accounting Policy: An Overview." *The Accounting Review* (October 1976), pp. 747–63.

Solomons, David. "The Politicization of Accounting." *The Journal of Accountancy* (November 1978), pp. 65–72.

Sterling, Robert R. "Accounting Research, Education and Practice." *The Journal of Accountancy* (September 1973), pp. 44–52.

Structure Committee. *The Stucture of Establishing Financial Accounting Standards.* Stamford, Conn.: FAF, April 1977.

Watts, R., and Jerold L. Zimmerman. "Toward a Positive Theory of the Determination of Accounting Standards." *The Accounting Review* (January 1978), pp. 112–34.

Questions

1–1 Define *accounting* and identify its fields of applications.

1–2 What is meant by "generally accepted accounting principles"?

1–3 What is the difference between accounting theory construction and verification?

1–4 What is the main difference between the traditional and new approaches to accounting theory construction and verification?

1–5 What is an accounting theory?

1–6 Define a middle-range accounting theory.

1–7 Elaborate on the differences between a descriptive and a normative methodology for the formulation of an accounting theory.

1–8 What is the main difference between a theory of accounting and a theory for accounting?

1–9 Define and evaluate the following approaches to the formulation of an accounting theory:

a. Deductive approach
b. Inductive approach
c. Nontheoretical approach
d. Theory of accounts approach
e. Axiomatic approach
f. Sociological approach
g. Ethical approach
h. Economic approach
i. Eclectic approach
j. Political approach

1–10   Discuss the development of accounting principles by the AICPA.
1–11   Discuss the role of the SEC in the development of accounting principles.
1–12   What is the role of the AAA in the development of accounting principles?
1–13   Does the FASB face the same problems as the APB? Explain.
1–14   Contrast general-purpose financial statements, specific-purpose financial statement, and differential disclosure.
1–15   The following statements were made by George J. Benston in *Corporate Financial Disclosure in the UK and the USA* (London: Saxon House, D.C. Heath Ltd., 1976), p. 150:

> In a fine society, government ought not to require private companies or persons to do anything unless, at the very least, the requirement resulted in a net benefit to society. Why, then, should financial disclosure be required of privately owned companies?

What might be some possible benefits to society of financial disclosure?
1–16   The following statements are made by S. C. Yu in *The Structure of Accounting Theory* (Gainesville: The University Presses of Florida, 1976), p. 45:

> In one sense, a discipline may mean a body of specific instructions and exercises designed to train to proper conduct, behavior, or action; or it may mean a set of established rules and regulations and guiding or controlling action or performance. Alternatively, a discipline may be viewed as a branch of learning requiring the use of proper methodology.

Which of the above definitions applies to accounting?
1–17   The following statements were made by Arthur H. Woolf in *A Short History of Accountants and Accountancy* (London: Gee & Co., 1912), pp. xxix–xxx:

> In one important respect, bookkeeping differs from other sciences, in that it is not in the least theoretical, but essentially and fundamentally practical. It is based on expediency,and upon the actual needs and requirements of everyday life. It was invented because man wanted it, because he found that he could not get on without it. It is essentially utilitarian. It is not the result of the work of *dilletanti*, of men who conceived some theory and labored to prove the truth of it.

Do you agree with the above statements? Why or why not?
1–18   The following statements were made by R. Chatov in an article titled "Should the Public Sector Take Over the Function of Determining Gener-

ally Accepted Accounting Principles?" in *The Accounting Journal* (Spring), p. 119:

> I suggest that what is needed is a national commission to develop a comprehensive accounting code for industrial corporations within the United States. You may shudder with horror at my assertion that this accounting code ought to provide several things: (1) it ought to provide for uniformity in accounting treatment; (2) it ought to provide the elimination of alternative treatments of accounting; (3) it ought to provide for comparability among the financial reports of different corporations, which should result if the first two objectives are met. Only in this way will investors be able to rely upon corporate financial reports and upon making comparison between them. Only in this way will the government have reliable financial information which it will be able to appraise on the basis of knowing specifically what is in the reports and their aggregations. And only in this way can we look forward to intelligent and meaningful public policy decisions to be made by government, based on consistent, aggregatable corporate financial data.

Do you think that the standard setting should be transferred to the public sector?

1–19   The following statements were made by David Solomons in "The Politicization of Accounting," *The Journal of Accountancy* (November 1978), p. 70:

> Information cannot be neutral—it cannot therefore be reliable—if it is selected or presented for the purpose of producing some chosen effect on human behavior. It is this quality of neutrality which makes a map reliable; and the essential nature of accounting, I believe, is cartographic. Accounting is financial mapmaking. The better the map, the more completely it represents the complex phoenomena that are being mapped.

What are the strengths and limitations of the analogy with cartography?

1–20   The following four statements have been taken directly or with some modification from the accounting literature. All are taken out of context, involve circular reasoning, or contain one or more fallacies, half-truths, erroneous comments or conclusions, or inconsistencies (internally or with generally accepted principles or practices).

Statement 1: Accounting is a service activity. Its function is to provide quantitative financial information that is intended to be useful in making economic decisions about and for economic entities. Thus, the accounting function might be viewed primarily as a tool or device for providing quantitative financial information to management to facilitate decision making.

Statement 2: Financial statements that were developed in accordance with generally accepted accounting principles, which apply the conservatism convention, can be free from bias (or can give a presentation that is fair with respect to continuing and prospective stockholders as well as to retiring stockholders).

Statement 3: When a company changes from the LIFO to the FIFO method of valuing ending inventories, and this change results in a $1 million increase both in income after taxes and in income taxes for the year of change, the increase would stem from the elimination of LIFO reserves established in prior years.

Statement 4: If the value of an enterprise were to be determined by the method that computes the sum of the present values of the marginal (or incremental) expected net receipts of individual tangible and intangible assets, the resulting valuation would tend to be less than if the value of the entire enterprise had been determined in another way, such as by computing the present value of total expected net receipts for the entire enterprise (that is, the resulting valuation of parts would sum to an amount that was less than that for the whole). This would be true even if the same pattern of interest or discount rates were used for both valuations.

Required: Evaluate each of the above statements as follows:

a. List the fallacies, half-truths, circular reasoning, erroneous comments or conclusions, and inconsistencies;

b. Explain by what authority or on what basis each item listed in (a), above, may be considered fallacious, circular, inconsistent, a half-truth, or an erroneous comment or conclusion. If the statement or portion of it is merely out of context, indicate the context(s) in which the statement would be correct.

(AICPA adapted)

chapter two

New Approaches to the Formulation of an Accounting Theory

I_n Chapter 1, we stated that accounting theory arises from the need to provide a rationale for what accountants expect to do, and that to be complete, the construction of an accounting theory should be followed by theory verification. We also presented the traditional approaches to the formulation of an accounting theory as those aimed at developing an accounting framework but characterized, in general, by the absence of a rigorous process of verification. Because an accounting theory should result from both processes, new approaches have been developed or revised recently, the aims of which are to verify as well as construct an accounting theory. Such new approaches are not yet generally accepted by the various interest groups or by the accounting profession in particular. They represent new streams of accounting research that use both conceptual and empirical reasoning to formulate and verify a conceptual accounting framework. Among the new approaches, we may distinguish (1) the "events" approach, (2) the "behavioral" approach, and (3) the "predictive" approach.

Each approach generated new research methodologies and interests and employed unique ways at looking at accounting problems. Because the interests and the methodologies were unique, each of these approaches evolved to take on the attributes of a distinctive paradigm, causing accounting to become a multi-paradigmatic science in a constant state of crisis. In a state of dissatisfaction with competing paradigms, each theorist will use a particular approach to provide a theoretical framework for the accounting field.

Consequently, our purpose in this chapter is first, to elaborate on each of the new approaches—the events, the behavioral, and the predictive approach—emphasizing the contribution of each one to accounting theory construction; and, second, to explain the resulting paradigmatic status of accounting.

The Events Approach

The Nature of the Events Approach

The **events** approach was first explicitly stated after a divergence of opinion among the members of the committee of the American Accounting Association, which issued *A Statement of Basic Accounting Theory* in 1966. The majority of the committee members favored the "value" approach to accounting. Only one member, accounting professor George Sorter, favored the "events" approach.[1]

The "value" school, which Sorter also called the "user need" school, considered that needs of users are known sufficiently to allow the deduction of an accounting theory that provides optimal input to the specified decision models. In fact, however, input values cannot be optimal for all uses. An exhaustive list of all normative and descriptive decision models is lacking.

The events approach, on the contrary, suggests that the "purpose of accounting is to provide information about relevant economic events that might be useful in a variety of possible decision models."[2] *It is up to the accountant to provide information about the events and leave to the user the task of fitting the events to their decision models. It is up to the user to aggregate and assign weights and*

---

[1]G. H. Sorter, "An 'Events' Approach to Basic Accounting Theory," *The Accounting Review* (January 1969), pp. 12–19.

[2]*Ibid.*, p. 13.

values to the data generated by the event in conformity with his or her own utility function. The user rather than the accountant transforms the event into accounting information suitable to the user's own individual decision model.

"Event" refers to any action that may be portrayed by one or more basic dimensions or attributes. According to Johnson, "event" will mean *feasible observation of specified characteristics of an action in regard to which a reporter could say, 'I foresaw that and saw it happen myself'.*[3]

Thus, the characteristics of an event may be directly observed and are of economic significance to the user.[4] Given the number of characteristics and the number of events susceptible to observation that might be relevant for the decision models of all users, the "events" approach suggests a tremendous expansion of the accounting data presented in financial reports. Characteristics of an event other than just monetary values may have to be disclosed. The events approach also assumes that the level of aggregation and evaluation of accounting data are decided by the user, given the user's loss function. If the user aggregates and evaluates data on events, measurement errors, biases, and information losses generated by the accountant's attempt to match, to assign weights, to generate values, and to aggregate information into an income statement is avoided. Under the events approach because of a disaggregation of the data provided to users, the data are expanded.[5]

Financial Statements and the Events Approach

What would be the consequence of the events approach to conventional annual reports?

While in the value approach, the balance sheet is perceived as an indicator of the financial position of the firm at a given point in time, in the events approach, it is perceived as an *indirect* communication of all accounting events relevant to the firm since its inception. Sorter proposes the following operational definition for the construction of a balance sheet under the events approach:

A balance sheet should be so constructed as to maximize the reconstructibility of the events to be aggregated.[6]

Sorter's definition implies that all aggregated figures in the balance sheet may be disaggregated to show all the events that have occurred since the inception of the firm.

While in the value approach, the income statement is perceived as an indicator of the financial performance of the firm for a given period, in the events approach, it is perceived as a *direct* communication of the operating events occurring during period. Again, Sorter proposes the following operational rule for the construction of the income statement under the events approach:

Each event should be described in a manner facilitating the forecasting of that same event in a future time period given exogeneous changes.[7]

---

[3]O. Johnson, "Towards an 'Events' Theory of Accounting," *The Accounting Review* (October 1970), pp. 641–53.

[4]C. S. Calantoni, R. P. Manes, and A. Whinston, "A Unified Approach to the Theory of Accounting and Information Systems," *The Accounting Review* (January 1971), p. 91.

[5]L. Revsine, "Data Expansion and Conceptual Structure," *The Accounting Review* (October 1970), pp. 704–11.

[6]Sorter, "An 'Events' Approach to Basic Accounting Theory," p. 15.

[7]*Ibid.*, p. 16.

In the value approach, the funds statement is perceived as an expression of the changes in working capital. In the events approach, however, it is better perceived as an expression of financial and investment events. In other words, an event's relevance rather than its impact on the working capital determines the reporting of an event in the funds statement.

The Normative Events Theory of Accounting

The *normative events* theory of accounting has been tentatively summarized as follows:

> In order for interested persons (shareholders, employees, manager, suppliers, customers, government agencies, and charitable institutions) to better forecast the future of social organizations (households, businesses, governments, and philanthropies), the most relevant attributes (characteristics) of the crucial events (internal, environmental, and transactional) which affect the organizations are aggregated (temporally and sectionally) for periodic publication free of inferential bias.[8]

Thus, the objective of the normative events theory of accounting is to maximize the forecasting accuracy of accounting reports by focusing on the most *relevant* attributes of events *crucial* to the users. One way to meet this objective is to structure an events-accounting information system as a concept of a common data base. Such a data base will include primarily raw data stored in a way that allows easy retrieval and adaptation by users. An events-accounting information system will have the following components:

   i.   Mass Data Base containing a record of all events in some generalized format.
   ii. User-Defined Structure providing for each user his own conceptual structure (and aggregation levels) of the events.
   iii. User-Defined Functions, or operations, for manipulating the data.[9]

The events approach suffers from the following limitations:

   1.   Information overload may result from the attempt to measure the *relevant* characteristics of all *crucial* events affecting a firm.
   2.   An adequate criterion for the choice of the *crucial* events has not been developed.
   3.   Measuring all the characteristics of an event may prove to be difficult, given the state of the art in accounting.

The Behavioral Approach

The Nature of the Behavioral Approach

Most traditional approaches to the construction of an accounting theory have failed to take into consideration user behavior, in particular, and behavioral assumptions, in general. In 1960, Devine made the following critical remark:

---

[8] Johnson, "Towards an 'Events' Theory of Accounting," p. 680.

[9] A. Z. Lieberman and A. B. Whinston, "An Event-Accounting Information System," *The Accounting Review* (April 1975), p. 249.

Let us now turn to . . . the psychological reactions of those who consume accounting output or are caught in its threads of control. On balance it seems fair to conclude that accountants seem to have waded through their relationships to the intricate psychological network of human activity with a heavy-handed crudity that is beyond belief. Some degree of crudity may be excused in a new discipline, but failure to recognize that much of what passes as accounting theory is hopelessly entwined with unsupported behavior assumptions is unforgivable.[10]

The behavioral approach to the formulation of accounting theory emphasizes the relevance to decision making of the information communicated—*a communication–decision orientation*—and on the individual and group behavior caused by the communication of the information—a *decision–maker orientation*. Accounting is assumed to be action oriented—its purpose is to influence action, that is, behavior, directly through the informational content of the message conveyed and indirectly through the behavior of accountants. Because accounting is considered to be a behavioral process,[11] the behavioral approach to the formulation of an accounting theory applies behavioral science to accounting. The overall objective of this approach is similar to that of behavioral science. The American Accounting Association's Committee on Behavioral Science Content of the Accounting Curriculum provides the following view of the objective of behavioral science, which may also apply to behavioral accounting:

> The objective of behavioral science is to understand, explain and predict human behavior; that is, to establish generalizations about human behavior that are supported by empirical evidence collected in an impersonal way by procedures that are completely open to review and replication and capable of verification by other interested scholars. Behavioral science, thus, represents the systematic observation of man's behavior for the purpose of experimentally confirming specific hypotheses by reference to observable changes in behavior.[12]

The behavioral approach to the formulation of an accounting theory is concerned with human behavior as it relates to accounting information and problems. In this context, the choice of an accounting technique must be evaluated with reference to the objectives and behavior of the users of financial information.

Although relatively new, the behavioral approach has generated in accounting research an enthusiasm and a new impetus focusing on the behavioral structure within which accountants function. We have seen recently a new multidisciplinary area in the field of accounting conveniently labeled "behavioral accounting." Behavioral accounting's basic objective is to explain and predict human behavior in all possible accounting contexts. Research studies in behavioral accounting have relied on experimental, field, or correlational techniques. Most studies have made little attempt to formulate a theoretical framework that would support the problems or hypotheses to be tested. Instead, the studies generally have focused on the behavioral effects of accounting information or on the problems of human information processing. The results of both

---

[10]C. T. Devine, "Research Methodology and Accounting Theory Formation," *The Accounting Review* (July 1960), pp. 387–99.

[11]"Report of The Committee on Behavior Science Content of the Accounting Curriculum," *The Accounting Review* (Supplement 1971), p. 247.

[12]*Ibid.*, p. 394.

kinds of studies may provide an understanding of the behavioral environment of accounting and guide in the formulation of an accounting theory. We shall examine each group of studies and then evaluate the behavioral accounting approach.

Behavioral Effects of Accounting Information

That accounting information, in terms of its content and format, may have an impact on individual decision making, although evident and easily accepted, suggests avenues of research for the improvement of accounting and reporting systems. Accordingly, research studies in this area have examined alternative reporting models and disclosure practices to assess the available choices in terms of relevance and impact on behavior. Because an agreed-upon general theoretical framework is lacking, however, it is difficult to classify these studies. Several writers have attempted to provide classification schemes.[13] A more recent and exhaustive attempt, made by Dyckman, Gibbins, and Swieringa,[14] will be used in this section to illustrate the nature of the studies of the behavioral effects of accounting information.

We may divide these studies into five general classes: (1) the adequacy of disclosure, (2) the usefulness of financial statement data, (3) attitudes about corporate reporting practices, (4) materiality judgments, and (5) the decision effects of alternative accounting procedures.[15]

Three approaches were used to examine the adequacy of disclosure. The first approach examined the patterns of use of data with a view to resolving controversial issues concerning the inclusion of certain information.[16] The second approach examined the perceptions and attitudes of different interest groups.[17] The third approach examined the extent to which different informational items were disclosed in annual reports and the determinants of any significant differences in the adequacy of financial disclosure among companies.[18] The research on disclo-

---

[13]J. G. Birnberg and R. Nath, "Implications of Behavioral Science for Managerial Accounting," *The Accounting Review* (January 1975), pp. 81–98; T. R. Hofstedt, "Some Behavioral Parameters of Financial Analysis," *The Accounting Review* (October 1972), pp. 679–92; J. G. Rhode, "Behavioral Science Methodologies with Application for Accounting Research: References and Source Materials," Chapter 7 of "Report of the Committee on Research Methodology in Accounting," *The Accounting Review* (Supplement 1972), pp. 494–504.

[14]T. R. Dyckman, M. Gibbins, and R. J. Swieringa, "Experimental and Survey Research in Financial Accounting: A Review and Evaluation," *The Impact of Accounting Research in Financial Accounting and Disclosure on Accounting Practice*, ed. A. R. Abdel-Khalik and T. F. Keller (Durham, N.C.: Duke University Press, 1978), pp. 48–89.

[15]We shall present a brief overview of the studies included in each class to provide an outlook of the research topics and methodologies used by behavioral accountant researchers to conduct their inquiry. For a full examination of these studies see Dyckman, Gibbins, and Swieringa's survey.

[16]C. T. Horngren, "Security Analysis and the Price Level," *The Accounting Review* (October 1955), pp. 575–81, and "The Funds Statement and Its Use by Analysts," *Journal of Accountancy* (January 1956), pp. 55–59.

[17]R. D. Bradish, "Corporate Reporting and the Financial Analyst," *The Accounting Review* (October 1965), pp. 757–66; W. W. Ecton, "Communication Through Accounting—Banker's Views," *Journal of Accountancy* (August 1969), pp. 79–81.

[18]A. R. Cerf, *Corporate Reporting and Investment Decisions* (Berkeley, Calif.: Institute of Business and Economic Research, 1961); S. S. Singhvi and H. B. Desai, "An Empirical Analysis of the Quality of Corporate Financial Disclosure," *The Accounting Review*

sure adequacy and use showed a general acceptance of the adequacy of available financial statements, a general understanding and comprehension of these financial statements, that the differences in disclosure adequacy among the financial statements were due to such variables as company size, profitability, size of the auditing firm and the listing status.

Three approaches were used to examine the usefulness of financial statement data. The first approach examined the relative importance to investment analysis of different information items to both users and preparers of financial information.[19] The second approach examined the relevance of financial statements to decision making using laboratory experimentation.[20] The third approach examined the effectiveness of the communication of financial statement data in terms of readability and meaning to users in general.[21] The overall conclusions of these studies are (1) that some consensus exists between users and preparers on the relative importance of the information items disclosed in financial statements, and (2) that users do not rely solely on financial statements for their decisions.

Two approaches were used to examine attitudes about corporate reporting practices. The first approach examined preferences for alternative accounting techniques.[22] The second approach examined the attitudes about general reporting issues, such as about how much information should be available, how much

---

(January 1971), pp. 129–38; S. L. Buzby, "Selected Items for Information and their Disclosure in Annual Reports," *The Accounting Review* (July 1974), pp. 423–35; A. Belkaoui and A. Kahl, *Corporate Financial Disclosure in Canada*, CCGAA Research Monograph #1 (Vancouver, B.C.: Canadian Certified General Accountants Association, 1978).

[19]H. K. Baker and J. A. Haslem, "Information Needs of Individual Investors," *The Journal of Accountancy* (November 1973), pp. 64–69; G. Chandra, "A Study of the Consensus on Disclosure Among Public Accountants and Security Analysts," *The Accounting Review* (October 1974), pp. 733–42; A. Belkaoui, A. Kahl, and J. Peyrard, "Information Needs of Financial Analysts: An International Comparison," *Journal of International Education and Research in Accounting* (Fall 1977), pp. 19–27; A. Belkaoui, "Consensus on Disclosure," *The Canadian Chartered Accountant Magazine* (June 1979), pp. 44–46.

[20]H. Falk and T. Ophir, "The Effect of Risk on the Use of Financial Statements by Investment Decision Makers: A Case Study," *The Accounting Review* (April 1973), pp. 323–38, and "The Influence of Differences in Accounting Policies on Investment Decision," *The Journal of Accounting Research* (Spring 1973), pp. 108–16; R. Libby, "The Use of Simulated Decision Makers in Information Evaluation," *The Accounting Review* (July 1975), pp. 475–89, and "Accounting Ratios and the Prediction of Failure: Some Behavioral Evidence," *Journal of Accounting Research* (Spring 1975), pp. 150–61.

[21]F. J. Soper and R. Dolphin, Jr., "Readability and Corporate Annual Reports," *The Accounting Review* (April 1964), pp. 358–62; J. E. Smith and N. P. Smith, "Readability: A Measure of the Performance of the Communication Function of Financial Reporting," *The Accounting Review* (July 1971), pp. 552–61; A. A. Haried, "The Semantic Dimensions of Financial Statements," *Journal of Accounting Research* (Autumn 1972), pp. 376–91, and "Measurement of Meaning in Financial Reports," *Journal of Accounting Research* (Spring 1973), pp. 117–45; B. L. Oliver, "The Semantic Differential: A Device for Measuring the Interprofessional Communication of Selected Accounting Concepts," *Journal of Accounting Research* (Autumn 1974), pp. 299–316; A. Belkaoui, "The Interprofessional Linguistic Communication of Accounting Concepts: An Experiment in Sociolinguistics," *The Journal of Accounting Research* in press.

[22]K. Nelson and R. H. Strawser, "A Note on APB Opinion No. 76," *Journal of Accounting Research* (Autumn 1970), pp. 284–89; V. Brenner and R. Shuey, "An Empirical Study of Support for APB Opinion No. 16," *Journal of Accounting Research* (Spring 1972), pp. 200–208.

information is available, and the importance of certain items.[23] These research studies showed the extent to which some accounting techniques proposed by the authoritative bodies are accepted, and brought to light some attitudinal differences among professional groups concerning reporting issues.

Two approaches were used to examine the materiality judgments. The first approach examined the main factors that determine the collection, classification, and summarization of accounting data.[24] The second approach focused on what people consider material.[25] This second approach sought to determine how great a difference in accounting data is required before the difference is perceived as material. These studies indicate that several factors appear to affect materiality judgments and that these judgments differ among individuals.

Finally, the decision effects of various accounting procedures were examined primarily in the context of the use of different inventory techniques, of price-level information, and of nonaccounting information.[26] The results indicate that alternative accounting techniques may influence individual decisions and that the extent of the influence may depend on the nature of the task, the characteristics of the users, and the nature of the experimental environment.

Human Information Processing

The interest in human information processing arose from a desire to improve the information set presented to users of financial data and the ability of users to use the information. Theories and models from human information processing

---

[23]R. M. Copeland, A. J. Francia, and R. H. Strawser, "Students as Subjects in Behavioral Business Research," *The Accounting Review* (April 1973), pp. 365–74; L. B. Godurn, "CPA and User Opinions on Increased Corporate Disclosure," *The CPA Journal* (July 1975), pp. 31–35.

[24]S. M. Woolsey, "Materiality Survey," *The Journal of Accountancy* (September 1973), pp. 91–92; J. Dyer, "A Search for Objective Materiality Norms in Accounting and Auditing," Diss. University of Kentucky, 1973; J. A. Boatsman and J. C. Robertson, "Policy-Capturing on Selected Materiality Judgments," *The Accounting Review* (April 1974), pp. 342–52; J. W. Pattilo, "Materiality: The (Formerly) Elusive Standard," *Financial Executive* (August 1975), pp. 20–27; J. W. Patillo and J. D. Siebel, "Materiality in Financial Reporting," *Financial Executive* (October 1973), pp. 27–28.

[25]J. Rose et al., "Toward an Empirical Measure of Materiality," *Journal of Accounting Research*, supplement to vol. 8, (1970), pp. 138–56; J. W. Dickhaut and I. R. C. Eggleton, "An Examination of the Processes Underlying Comparative Judgments of Numerical Stimuli," *Journal of Accounting Research* (Spring 1975), pp. 38–72.

[26]A. Belkaoui and A. Cousineau, "Accounting Information, Nonaccounting Information, and Common Stock Perception," *The Journal of Business* (July 1977), pp. 334–42; C. T. Horngren, "Security Analysts and the Price Level," *The Accounting Review* (October 1955), pp. 575–81; T. R. Dyckman, "On the Investment Decision," *The Accounting Review* (April 1976), pp. 258–95; and *Accounting Research Study #1*, "Investment Analysis and General Price Level Adjustments: A Behavioral Study" (Sarasota, Fla.: AAA, 1969); R. E. Jensen, "An Experimental Design for Study of Effects of Accounting Variations in Decision Making," *Journal of Accounting Research* (Autumn 1966); John L. Livingston, "A Behavioral Study of Tax Allocation in Electric Utility Regulations," *The Accounting Review* (July 1967), pp. 544–52; Adbellatif Khemakhem, "A Simulation of Management-Decision Behavior: 'Funds' and Income," *The Accounting Review* (July 1968), pp. 522–34; M. E. Barrett, "Accounting for Intercorporate Investments: A Behavioral Field Experiment," *Journal of Accounting Research*, supplement to vol. 9 (1971), pp. 50–92; N. Elias, "The Effects of Human Asset Statements on the Investment Decision: An Experiment," *Journal of Accounting Research*, supplement to vol. 10 (1972), pp. 215–40; T. R. Hofstedt, "Some Behavioral Parameters of Financial Analysis," *The Accounting Review* (October 1972), pp. 679–92; N. Dopuch and

psychology provide a tool for transforming accounting issues into generic information-processing issues.[27] There are three main components of an information-processing model: input, process, and output. Studies of the information set focus on the variables that are likely to affect the way people process information for decision making. The variables examined are (1) the scaling characteristics of individual cues, (2) the statistical properties of the information set, (3) the information content, (4) the method of presentation, (5) the context, and (6) the task characteristics. Studies of the process component focus on variables likely to affect the way the decision maker processes information. The variables examined in the studies are (1) judge characteristics (personality characteristics, task-related characteristics, number of decision makers, human or mechanical) and (2) characteristics of the decision rule. Finally, studies of the output component focus on variables related to the judgment or prediction decision likely to affect the way the user processes information. The variables examined are (1) the qualities of the judgment and (2) self-insight.

The different emphasis on any of three components of an information processing model led to the use of three different approaches: (1) *the lens model*, (2) *the probabilistic judgment*, and (3) *cognitive style*.

The Brunswick's Lens Model[28] allows explicit recognition of the interdependence of environmental and individual-specific variables. It is used primarily to assess human judgmental situations in which people make judgments on the basis of a set of explicit cues from the environment. The model emphasizes the similarities between the environment and subject response. The right side of the model describes the relationships between the subject responses or judgments (y_s) and the level of cues (x_j) in terms of their correlation (r_{is}). The left side of the model describes the relationships between the actual criterion or event (y_e) and the level of cues (x_j). The analysis relies on a regression model when the cues are continuous and on an analysis of variance (ANOVA) model when the cues take on categorical values. This model allows us to investigate the impact of the information set on decision rule form, stability or learning, cue usage, and decision accuracy, reliability, and predictability of these variables. Various studies relied on the ANOVA models when actual values of cues are not used.[29] Various other studies

J. Ronen, "The Effects of Alternative Inventory Valuation Methods: An Experimental Study," *Journal of Accounting Research* (Autumn 1973), pp. 191–211; D. F. Hawkins and M. M. Wehle, *Accounting for Leases* (New York: Financial Executives Research Foundation, 1973); R. Libby, "The Use of Simulated Decision Makers in Information Evaluation," *The Accounting Review* (July 1975), pp. 475–89; R. F. Ortman, "The Effect of Investment Analysis of Alternative Reporting Procedure for Diversified Firms," *The Accounting Review* (April 1974), pp. 298–304.

[27]An excellent review of human information processing literature in accounting is in R. Libby and Barry L. Lewis, "Human Information Processing Research in Accounting: The State of the Art," *Accounting Organizations and Society* (1977), pp. 245–68.

[28]E. Brunswick, *The Conceptual Framework of Psychology* (Chicago: The University of Chicago Press, 1972).

[29]P. Slovic, "Analyzing the Expert Judge: A Descriptive Study of a Stockbroker's Decision Process," *Journal of Applied Psychology* (August 1969), pp. 255–63; P. Slovic, D. Fleissner, and W. S. Bauman, "Analyzing the Use of Information in Investment Decision Making: A Methodological Proposal," *Journal of Business* (April 1972), pp. 283–301; R. Ashton, "An Experimental Study of Internal Control Judgments," *Journal of Accounting Research* (Spring 1974), pp. 143–57; T. Hofstedt and G. Hughes, "An Experimental Study of the Judgment Element in Disclosure Decisions," *The Accounting Review* (April 1977), pp. 379–95.

relied on regression and discriminant analysis following the use of the actual values of cues.[30]

The probabilistic judgment approach allows an investigation of the ways people form subjective judgments. Using the normative model of Bayes' theorem, the approach also relied on heuristics and biases as criteria or to measure cue usages. Various studies relied on a Bayesian framework to integrate prior probabilities and new information.[31] Other studies relied on heuristics and biases as expressions of the limited information processing capacities of individuals[32]

The cognitive style approach focuses on the impact of variables likely to affect the decision maker's decision. More specifically, the approach examines the impact of various cognitive characteristics of the decision maker and various information structures on cue usage, information search, quality of decisions and learning.[33]

Evaluation of the Behavioral Approach

Most of the behavioral accounting research that we have discussed in the preceding sections attempts to establish generalizations about human behavior in relation to accounting information. The implicit objective of all these studies is to develop and verify the behavioral hypotheses relevant to accounting theory, which are hypotheses on the adequacy of disclosure, the usefulness of financial statement data, attitudes about corporate reporting practices, materiality judgments, the decision effects of alternative accounting procedures, and components of an information processing model—input, process, and output. This implicit objective has not yet been reached, however, because most of the experimental and survey research in behavioral accounting suffers from a lack of theoretical and methodological rigor.

---

[30]R. Barefield, "The Effects of Aggregation on Decision Making Success: A Laboratory Study," *Journal of Accounting Research* (Autumn 1972), pp. 229–42; J. Boatsman and J. Robertson, "Policy Capturing on Selected Materiality Judgments," *The Accounting Review* (April 1974), pp. 342–52; R. Libby, "The Use of Simulated Decision Makers in Information Evaluation," *The Accounting Review* (July 1975), pp. 475–89; and "Accounting Ratios and the Prediction of Failure: Some Behavioral Evidence," *Journal of Accounting Research* (Spring 1975), pp. 150–61; W. Wright, "Cognitive Information Processing Models: An Empirical Study," *The Accounting Review* (July 1977), pp. 676–89.; J. Dickhaut, "Alternative Information Structures and Probability Revision," *The Accounting Review* (January 1973), pp. 61–79.

[31]R. Barefield, "The Effect of Aggregation on Decision Making Success: A Laboratory Study"; H. Kennedy, "A Behavioral Study of the Usefulness of Four Financial Ratios," *Journal of Accounting Research* (Spring 1975), 97–116.

[32]R. Swieringa et al., "Experiments in the Heuristics of Human Information Processing," *Studies on Human Information Processing Accounting,* supp. to *Journal of Accounting Research,* (1976) 159–87; W. Uecker and W. Kinney, "Judgmental Evaluation of Sample Results: A Study of the Type and Severity of Errors Made by Practicing CPAs," Working Paper (Iowa City, Iowa: University of Iowa, 1976); J. Ronen, "Some Effects of Sequential Aggregation in Accounting on Decision Making," *Journal of Accounting Research* (Autumn 1971), pp. 307–32; J. Dickhaut and J. Eggleton, "An Examination of the Process Underlying Comparative Judgments of Numerical Stimuli," *Journal of Accounting Research* (Spring 1975), pp. 38–72.

[33]T. Mock, T. Estrin, and M. Vasarhelyi, "Learning Patterns, Decision Approach and Value of Information," *Journal of Accounting Research* (Spring 1972), pp. 129–53; J. Dermer, "Cognitive Characteristics and the Perceived Importance of Information," *The Accounting*

Behavioral accounting research has been done mostly without explicit formulation of a theory. This lack of a theory imposes limitations on an acceptable and meaningful evaluation and interpretation of the results. Some of the studies, however, have borrowed theoretical constructs from other disciplines. To the growing body of research based on theories and models from the psychology of information processing and the linguistic relativism hypothesis,[34] we may add, for example Abdel-Khalik's and Ronen and Falk's attempts to use entropy concepts to study the aggregation problem in accounting; Rose, Dickhaut and Eggleton's attempt to use Weber's law from psychophysics to study judgments of numerical data;[35] Ritt's attempt to use dissonance theory to explain compliance with APB opinions;[36] and Ijiri, Jaedicke, and Knight's use of "functional fixity" to explain the decision maker's inability to adjust the decision process to a change in the accounting process.[37]

Laboratory experimentation is generally favored in behavioral accounting research because it can isolate variables and effects to provide unambiguous evidence about causation and allow better control over extraneous variables. As stated by Hofstedt and Kinard, "A problem is stripped of nonessential factors through abstraction, allowing observation and control of the one or few critical variables which remain."[38] The failure to ensure validity, however, causes significant problems with laboratory experiments. Cook and Campbell have distinguished four general types of validity, namely, internal validity, external validity, construct validity, and statistical conclusion validity.[39] With the exception of internal validity, the nature of the subject studied and the nature of the experiment as a social situation may threaten the other types of validity.

The problems concerning the nature of the subject sample arise from the reluctance of business people to cooperate and the relatively high cost of field studies. In general, therefore, students have been used as surrogates of business people. But do students and business people react similarly to stimuli? Several

Review (July 1973), pp. 511–19; M. Driver, and T. Mock, "Human Information Processing, Decision Style Theory, and Accounting Information Systems," *The Accounting Review* (July 1975), pp. 490–511; J. G. San Miguel, "Human Information Processing and Its Relevance to Accounting: A Laboratory Study," *Accounting Organization and Society No. 4* (1976), pp. 357–73.

[34]A. Belkaoui, "Linguistic Relativism in Accounting," *Accounting Organizations and Society*, 3, No. 2 (1978), 97–104.

[35]R. A. Abdel-Khalik, "The Effect of Aggregating Accounting Reports on the Lending Decision: An Empirical Investigation," *Journal of Accounting Research,* supplement to vol. 12 (1973), pp. 791–93; J. Ronen and G. Falk, "Accounting Data and the Entropy Measure: An Experimental Approach," *The Accounting Review* (October 1973), pp. 697–717; J. W. Dickhaut and I. R. C. Eggleton, "An Examination of the Process Underlying Comparative Judgments of Numerical Stimuli"; J. Rose et al., "Toward an Empirical Measure of Materiality," *Journal of Accounting Research,* supplement to vol. 8 (1970), pp. 138–56.

[36]Blaine A. Ritts, "A Study of the Impact of the APB Opinions on Practicing CPAs," *Journal of Accounting Research* (Spring 1974), pp. 93–111.

[37]Y. Ijiri, R. K. Jeadicke, and K. E. Knight, "The Effect of Accounting Alternatives on Management Decisions," in *Research in Accounting Measurement,* ed. R. K. Jaedicke et al., (New York: AAA, 1966), pp 186–99.

[38]T. R. Hofstedt and J. Kinard, "A Strategy for Behavioral Accounting Research," *The Accounting Review* (January 1970), pp. 38–54.

[39]T. D. Cook and D. T. Campbell, "The Design and Conduct of Quasi-Experiments and the Experiments in Field Settings," in *Handbook of Industrial and Organizational Research,* ed. M. D. Dunette (New York: Rand McNally, 1976), pp. 223–326.

studies have examined the surrogation problem without any conclusive results.[40]

Similarly, the experiment as a social contract implies a role relationship between the subject and the experimenter. Some aspects of this relationship may threaten the validity of the experiment.

The Predictive Approaches

The Nature of the Predictive Approach

The predictive approach arose from the difficult problem of evaluating alternative methods of accounting measurement and from the search for a criterion on which to base the choice between measurement alternatives. The predictive approach to the formulation of an accounting theory uses the criterion of predictive ability. Predictive ability means that the choice among different accounting options should depend on the particular method's ability to predict events of interest to users. More specifically, "the measure with the greatest predictive power with respect to a given event is considered to be the 'best' method for that particular purpose."[41]

The criterion of "predictive ability" follows from the emphasis on "relevance" as the primary criterion of financial reporting.[42] *Relevance* connotes a concern with information about future events. Relevant data, therefore, are characterized by an ability to predict future events.

The criterion of predictive ability is also well accepted in the natural and physical sciences as a method of choosing among competing hypotheses. Beaver et al.,[43] by showing that alternative accounting measures have the properties of competing hypotheses, rationalized the use of predictive ability in accounting. An obvious advantage of the predictive approach is that it allows us *empirically* to evaluate alternative accounting measurements and to make a clear choice on the basis of a *discriminatory* criterion.

Predictive ability is also a purposive criterion, easily related to one of the purposes of gathering accounting data—the facilitation of decision making. The accounting literature has always held that accounting data must facilitate decision making. As soon as "facilitation of decision making" is introduced, however, two problems arise. First, it is difficult to identify and define all the decision models employed by accounting information users. Most of the models are descriptive rather than normative. Second, even if the decision model was well defined, a criterion for the choice of relevant information was missing. Intended to resolve this second problem, the "predictive ability" criterion allows us to

---

[40]J. W. Dickhaut, G. L. Livingstone, and David J. Watson, "On the Use of Surrogates in Behavioral Experimentation," in "Report of the Committee on Research Methodology in Accounting," *The Accounting Review*, supplement to vol. 48 (1972), pp. 455–70; R. A. Abdel-Khalik, "On the Efficiency of Subject Surrogation in Accounting Research," *The Accounting Review* (October 1974), pp. 443–50.

[41]W. H. Beaver, J. W. Kennelly, and W. M. Voss, "Predictive Ability as a Criterion for the Evaluation of Accounting Data," *The Accounting Review* (October 1968), p. 675.

[42]*A Statement of Basic Accounting Theory*, Ch. 3 (New York: AAA, 1966).

[43]Beaver, "Predictive Ability as a Criterion for the Evaluation of Accounting Data," p. 676.

determine which accounting measure produces the better decisions. Let us note here the fundamental distinction between prediction and decision. *It is possible to predict without making a decision, but it is not possible to make a decision without a prediction.*

It appears then that the predictive method may suffer from failure to identify and define the decision models of users and the types of events that ought to be predicted. Even if a given theoretical structure were developed to identify items or events that ought to be predicted, the problem remains of specifying a theory that will link those events to the accounting measures in terms of an explanatory and predictive relationship.

A growing body of empirical accounting research has evolved from the predictive approach. Two streams may be identified: one concerned with the ability of accounting data to explain and predict economic events, and the other with the ability of accounting data to explain and predict market reaction to disclosure.

Prediction of an Economic Event

One general objective of accounting is to provide information useful for the prediction of business events. In the perspective of the predictive approach to the formulation of an accounting theory, alternative accounting measurements should be evaluated on the basis of their ability to predict economic or business events.

Ability to Predict Earnings   The first manifestation of the predictive approach is the concern with the prediction of earnings as one of the major accounting tasks: An accountant should choose the accounting technique that most accurately predicts the firm's earnings. Frank examined the respective predictive ability of traditionally calculated accounting income and a measure incorporating current cost for a sample of 76 firms.[44] A linear regression model and a moving average smoothing model were used to evaluate the relative predictive ability of both measures. Simmons and Gray also examined the predictive ability of three income concepts based on historical cost, general price-level-adjusted cost, and replacement cost by using a simulation technique.[45] Neither study gave any credence to the widely held belief that current-costs income series are a better predictor than historical cost income series.

Predictive Ability of Interim Reporting   The predictive approach was also used to analyze the predictive power of interim reports. Because costs and revenues must be matched, the shorter the period, the more severe the measurement and accuracy problems.[46]

A broad range of information is disclosed by interim reports, however, which leads one to question their relevance and predictive ability. Although some of the

[44]W. Frank, "A Study of the Predictive Significance of the Income Measures," *Journal of Accounting Research* (Spring 1969), pp. 123–36.

[45]J. K. Simmons and J. Gray, "An Investigation of the Effects of Differing Accounting Frameworks on the Prediction of Net Income," *The Accounting Review* (October 1969), pp. 757–76.

[46]D. Green, Jr., "Toward a Theory of Interim Reports," *Journal of Accounting Research*, (Spring 1963), pp. 35–49.

evidence is conflicting, most empirical studies support the contention that interim reports are useful and may be used to predict annual financial data.[47]

Corporate Failure Prediction   The most relevant applications of the predictive approach are attempts made by practicing auditors to predict corporate failure on the basis of available accounting ratios. Both univariate models and multivariable models have been used to help an auditor determine when a firm is approaching default. In Beaver's univariate study[48] testing a set of accounting ratios to predict corporate failure, the ratios were categorized in six broad categories: cash flow, net income, debt to total asset, liquid asset to total asset, liquid asset to current debt, and turnover. The most noticeable result was the superior predictive ability of the cash flow to total debt ratio, followed by net income to total assets. Among the multivariate studies, Altman's use of a multiple discriminant analysis for the prediction of corporate failure[49] resulted in a discriminant model that contained the following five variables: (1) working capital/total assets (liquidity), (2) retained earnings/total assets (age of firm and cumulative profitability), (3) earnings before interest and taxes/total assets (profitability), (4) market value of equity/book value of debt (financial structure), and (5) sales/total assets (capital turnover). Altman was able to classify correctly more than 90 percent of the firms in his sample. The discriminant analysis technique for the prediction of corporate failure has been used successfully in other studies.[50]

The major limitation of the research on corporate distress prediction arises from the absence of a general theory of corporate failure with which to specify the variables to be included in the models. In addition, the results of the superior predictive ability of some accounting ratios may not be generalized to allow the formulation of an accounting theory based on consistent predictors of corporate failure.

Prediction of Bond Premium and Bond Ratings   The following four factors are assumed to create bond risks and consequently to affect the yields to maturity of bonds!

1. *Default risk*—the inability of a firm to meet part or all of the bond interest and principal payments.

---

[47]D. Green, Jr., and J. Segall, "The Predictive Power of First-Quarter Earnings Reports," *Journal of Business* (January 1970), pp. 44–55; P. Brown and V. Niederhoffer, "The Predictive Content of Quarterly Earnings," *Journal of Business* (October 1968), pp. 488–97; R. Coates, "The Predictive Content of Interim Reports—A Time Series Analysis," *Empirical Research in Accounting: Selected Studies, 1972,* Supplement to vol. 10, *Journal of Accounting Research*, pp. 132–44; P. Brown and J. W. Kennelly, "The Informational Content of Quarterly Earnings: An Estimation and Further Evidence," *Journal of Business* (July 1972), pp. 403–15.

[48]W. H. Beaver, "Financial Ratios and Predictors of Failure," *Empirical Research in Accounting: Selected Studies, 1966,* Supplement to vol. 4, *Journal of Accounting Research*, pp. 71–127.

[49]E. Altman, "Predicting Railroad Bankruptcies in America," *Bell Journal of Economics and Management Science* (Spring 1973), pp. 184–211.

[50]M. P. Blum, *The Falling Company Doctrine.* Columbia University, 1969; R. O. Edmister, "An Empirical Test of Financial Ratio Analysis for Small Business Failure Prediction," *Journal of Financial and Quantitative Analysis* (March 1972), pp. 1477–93; E. Deakin, "A Discriminant Analysis of Business Failure," *Journal of Accounting Research* (Spring 1972), pp. 167–79.

2. *Marketability risk* — the possibility of learning to dispose of the bonds at a loss.

3. *Purchasing power risk* — the loss incurred by bond holders due to changes in the general price level.

4. *Interest rate risk* — the effect of unexpected changes in the interest rates on the market value of bonds.

Fisher examined the power of a four-factor model to explain differences in the risk premiums of industrial corporate bonds.[51] The following four variables are included in the model:

1. Earnings variability, measured as the coefficient of variation on after-tax earnings of the most recent nine years.

2. Solvency, or reliability in meeting obligations, measured as the length of time since the latest of the following events occured: the firm was founded, the firm emerged from bankruptcy, or a compromise was made in which creditors settled for less than 100 percent of their claims.

3. Capital structure, measured by market value of the firm's equity/par value of its debt.

4. Total value of the market value of the firm's bonds.

The first three variables represented different proxies for default risk, while the fourth variable represented a proxy for marketable risk. The four variables acounted for 75 percent of the variation in the risk premiums on bonds.

The bonds ratings issued by the three rating agencies in the United States (Fitch Investors Service, Moody's Investors' Service, and Standard and Poor's Corporation) are judgments about the investment quality of long-term obligations. Each rating is an aggregation of default probability. In spite of the claim by these agencies that their ratings cannot be empirically explained and predicted, various studies have attempted to develop models to predict the ratings categories assigned to industrial bonds,[52] electric utility bonds,[53] and general obligation municipal bonds.[54] Most of the studies used a discriminant analysis of bond raters without reaching any conclusive result. As in the case of corporate failure prediction, these models suffered from the lack of a theory of bond ratings specifying the variables to be included.

Prediction of Takeovers   The prominence of takeovers has caused the predictive approach to be used in several studies attempting to identify financial characteristics of acquired firms. Chambers saw the underevaluation of assets — as a

---

[51]L. Fisher, "Determinants of Risk Premium on Corporate Bonds," *The Journal of Political Economy* (June 1959), pp. 217–37.

[52]J. O. Horrigan, "The Determination of Long Term Credit Standing with Financial Ratios," *Empirical Research in Accounting: Selected Studies, 1966,* Supplement to vol. 4, *Journal of Accounting Research*, pp. 44–62; G. E. Pinches and K. E. Mingo, "A Multivariate Analysis of Industrial Bond Ratings," *Journal of Finance* (March 1973), pp. 1–18; A. Belkaoui, "Industrial Bond Ratings: A Discriminant Analysis Approach," *Financial Management* in press.

[53]E. I. Altman and S. Katz, "Statistical Bond Rating Classification Using Financial and Accounting Data," in *Proceedings of the Conference on Topical Research in Accounting,* ed. M. Schiff and G. Porter (New York: New York University Press, 1976), pp. 205–39.

[54]J. J. Horton, "Statistical Classification of Municipal Bonds," *Journal of Bank Research* (Autumn 1970), pp. 29–40.

result of conservative accounting policies—as a key factor in predicting take-overs. This finding was rejected by Taussig and Hayes.[55] Both Chamber's and Taussig and Hayes' studies were univariate in nature in the sense that they considered only undervaluation of assets as the key factor in takeover bids. Various other studies developed multivariate models for the prediction of takeovers in the United States, the United Kingdom, and Canada.[56] All these studies point to the relevance of certain accounting ratios for the prediction of takeovers. The limitations of these studies are similar to those of the studies on the prediction of corporate failures.

Predictive Ability of the Information Decomposition Measures   Information theory concerns the problem of measuring changes in knowledge.[57] Theil applied information theory and the related entropy concept to develop a set of measures for financial statement analysis.[58] These measures, labeled "information decomposition measures" were assumed to express the degree of stability over time in financial statement decomposition. Studies investigating the predictive ability of these information decomposition measures reported results in which the measures were found to be associated with the event of corporate bankruptcy[59] and corporate takeover.[60] The initial results point to the usefulness of the entropy concept in financial analysis and suggest opportunities for future research.

Prediction of Market Reaction

Capital Markets and External Accounting   According to one interpretation of the predictive approach, the observations of capital market reaction may be used as a guide for the evaluation and choice among various accounting measurements. For example, Gonedes contends that:

> Observation of the market reactions of recipients of accounting outputs should govern evaluations of the actual information content of accounting numbers produced via a given set of procedures and the informational content of accounting numbers produced via an alternative set of accounting procedures.[61]

[55]R. J. Chambers, "Finance Information and the Securities Market," *Abacus* (September 1965), pp. 4–30.

[56]R. A. Taussig and Samuel L. Hayes, III, "Cash Takeovers and Accounting Valuation," *The Accounting Review* (January 1968), pp. 68–72; D. L. Stevens, "Financial Characteristics of Merged Firms: A Multivariate Analysis," *Journal of Financial and Quantitative Analysis* (March 1973), pp. 149–58; J. Tzoannos and J. M. Samuels, "Mergers and Takeovers: the Financial Characteristics of Companies Involved," *Journal of Business Finance* (Spring 1972), pp. 5–16; A. Belkaoui, "Financial Ratios as Predictors of Canadian Takeovers," *Journal of Business Finance* (Spring 1978), pp. 93–107.

[57]S. Kullback, *Information Theory and Statistics* (New York: John Wiley and Sons, 1959), p. 7.

[58]H. Theil, "On the Use of Information Theory Concepts in the Analysis of Financial Statements," *Management Science* (May 1969), pp. 459–80.

[59]B. Lev, "Accounting and Information Theory," *Accounting Research Study No. 2* (Evanston, Ill.: AAA, 1969), pp. 18–34.

[60]A. Belkaoui, "The Entropy Law, Information Decomposition Measures and Corporate Takeover," *Journal of Business Finance and Accounting* (Autumn 1976), pp. 41–52.

[61]N. J. Gonedes, "Efficient Capital Markets and External Accounting," *The Accounting Review* (January 1972), p. 12.

Beaver and Dukes favor the predictive approach when they state that:

> The method which produces earnings numbers having the highest association with security prices is the most consistent with the information that results in an efficient determination of security prices. . . . It is the method that ought to be reported.[62]

In other words, the predictive approach favors the adoption of the accounting numbers with the highest association with market prices. It calls for an evaluation of the usefulness of accounting numbers transmitted to capital market transactors viewed as an "aggregate." "Aggregate," in this case, means the focus is on the reaction of the "securities market" rather than the individual investors making up the market.

The roles of the securities market and of information in the securities market justify the use of the prediction of market reaction for the formulation of an accounting theory. The role of the securities market is to provide an orderly exchange market whereby investors may exchange claims to present and future consumption on a continuous basis. The role of information is twofold: "(1) to aid in establishing a set of security prices, such that there exists an optimal allocation of securities among investors, and (2) to aid the individual investor, who faces a given set of prices, in the selection of an optimal portfolio of securities."[63] For this reason, the relevance of accounting information and the choice of accounting measurement procedures may be examined in terms of market reactions. Some major arguments exist against the use of the predictive approach with capital markets. First, it has been argued that users individually or in aggregate react because they have been conditioned to react to accounting data rather than because the data have any information content. Accordingly, observations of users' reactions should not guide the formulation of an accounting theory. Sterling contends that:

> If the response of receivers to accounting stimuli is to be taken as evidence that certain kinds of accounting practices are justified, then we must not overlook the possibility that those responses were conditioned. Accounting reports have been issued for a long time, and their issuance has been accompanied by a rather impressive ceremony performed by the managers and accountants who issue them. The receivers are likely to have gained the impression that they ought to react and have noted that others react, and thereby have become conditioned to react.[64]

It may also be argued that the recipients of accounting information react when they "should" not react or should not react the way they did.

Both arguments lose their validity when we see that the predictive approach is based on the theory and evidence of the efficient market model.

The Efficient Market Model   It is generally assumed that the securities market is efficient. A *perfectly efficient market* is in *continuous equilibrium*, so the intrinsic values of securities *vibrate randomly* and market prices always equal

---

[62]W. H. Beaver and R. E. Dukes, "Interperiod Tax Allocation, Earnings Expectations, and External Accounting," *The Accounting Review* (April 1972), p. 321.

[63]W. Beaver, "The Behavior of Security Prices and Its Implications for Accounting Research (Methods)," *The Accounting Review* (Supplement 1972), p. 408.

[64]R. Sterling, "On Theory Construction and Verification," *The Accounting Review* (July 1970), p. 453.

underlying intrinsic values at every instant in time.[65] Applied to the securities market, this assumption implies that (1) market prices "fully reflect" all publicly available information and, by implication, (2) market prices react instantaneously and without bias to new information. A mathematical formulation of this model, called the "expected-returns model" or "fair game model," was suggested by Fama[66] and is given by:

$$Z_{i,t+s} = (r_{i,t+s}/\lambda_{t+1}, \Phi) - E(r_{i,t+1}/\Phi)$$

$$E(Z_{i,t+1}/\lambda_{t+1}, \Phi) = 0$$

where

λ_{t+1} = any trading scheme implemented in the interval t to $t + 1$, given the information set Φ_t

$Z_{i,t+1}$ = the excess return for security i in period $t + 1$ (that is, the difference between the observed return and the equilibrium expected return)

$(r_{i,t+1}/\lambda_{t+1}, \Phi_t)$ = the observed return for security i in period $t + 1$, conditional upon trading scheme λ_{t+1} and information Φ_t, and

$E(r_{i,t+1}/\Phi_t)$ = the equilibrium expected return, which is the return that fully reflects the information available in period $t (\Phi_t)$.

In other words, the rate of return series $(r_{i,t+1})$ is "a fair game" relative to the information series (Φ_t). By defining the information set (Φ_t) in three different ways, Fama distinguishes three levels of market efficiency: the weak, the semistrong, and the strong form.[67]

The *weak form of the efficient market hypothesis* states that the equilibrium expected returns (prices) "fully reflect" the sequence of past returns (prices). In other words, historical price and volume data for securities contain no information that may be used to earn a profit superior to a simple "buy-and-hold" strategy. This form of the hypothesis began with the theory that price changes follow a true "random walk" (with an expected value of zero). This school of thought is challenged by "technical analysts" or "chartists," who believe that their rules based on past information can earn greater-than-normal profits. Filter rules, serial correlation, and run tests have tested the weakly efficient market hypothesis. The results support the hypothesis, particularly for returns longer than a day.

The *semistrong form of the efficient markets hypothesis* states that the equilibrium expected returns (prices) fully reflect all publicly available information. In other worfs, no trading rule based on available information may be used to earn an excess return. The semistrong form is most relevant to accounting because publicly available information includes financial statements. Tests of the semistrong hypothesis were concerned with the speed with which prices adjusted

---

[65]P. Samuelson, "Proof that Properly iscounted Present Values of Assets Vibrate Randomly," *Bell Journal of Economics and Management Science* (Autumn 1973), pp. 369–74.

[66]E. Fama, "Efficient Capital Markets: A Review of Theory and Empirical Work," *Journal of Finance* (May 1970), pp. 383–447.

[67]*Ibid.*, p. 383.

to specific kinds of events. Some of the events examined were stock splits, announcements of annual earnings, large secondary offerings of common stocks, new issues of stocks, announcements of changes in the discount rate, and stock dividends. The results again support the efficient markets hypothesis in the sense that prices adjust rather quickly after the first public announcement of information. Needless to say, the list of events examined is not exhaustive, and further empirical research is warranted to prove this hypothesis, which is of extreme importance to accounting.

The strong form of the equilibrium hypothesis states that the equilibrium expected returns (prices) fully reflect all information (not just publicly available information). In other words, no trading rule based on any information including *inside information* may be used to earn an excess return. Evidence on the strong form of the efficient market hypothesis is not conclusive. While Jensen[68] was able to show that mutual funds do not have any superior consistent performance over time, given a presumed access to special information, Niederhoffer and Osborne[69] argued for the possibility of superior returns, given an access to the *Specialists' book.*

The Capital Asset Pricing Model and the Market Model   The efficient markets hypothesis requires the use of "expected returns" and assumes that securities are properly priced. A theory is needed to specify the relationship between the individual stock's expected returns and prices. One such theory is the Sharpe, Lintner and Mossin[70] capital asset pricing model, which relates asset returns to asset risk as follows:

$$E(R_{it}) = R_{ft} + [E(R_{mt}) - R_{ft}]\beta$$

where

$$
\begin{aligned}
E(R_{it}) &= \text{the expected return of security } i \text{ in period } t \\
R_{ft} &= \text{the return on a riskless asset in period } t \\
E(R_{mt}) &= \text{the expected return on the market portfolio in period } t \\
\sigma(R_{it}, R_{mt}) &= \text{the covariance between } R_{it} \text{ and } R_{mt} \\
\sigma^2(R_{mt}) &= \text{the variance of the return on the market portfolio}
\end{aligned}
$$

$$\beta = \frac{\sigma(R_{it}, R_{mt})}{\sigma^2(R_{mt})} = \text{risk coefficient}$$

Given certain assumptions, the capital asset pricing model asserts that there is a linear relationship between an individual security and its systematic risk.

---

[68]M. Jensen, "Risk, the Pricing of Capital Assets, and the Evaluation of Investment Portfolios," *Journal of Business* (April 1969), p. 170.

[69]Victor Niederhoffer, and M. F. M. Osborne, "Market Making and Reversal on the Stock Exchange," *Journal of the American Statistical Association*, 61 (December 1966), 897–916.

[70]W. F. Sharpe, "Capital Asset Prices: A Theory of Market Equilibrium Under Conditions of Risk," *Journal of Finance* (September 1964), pp. 425–42; John Lintner, "The Valuation of Risky Assets and the Selection of Risky Investments in Stock Portfolios and Capital Budgets," *Review of Economics and Statistics* (February 1965), pp. 13–37; J. Mossin, "Equilibrium in a Capital Asset Market," *Economica* (October 1966), pp. 768–83.

The capital asset pricing model does not lead to easy testing of the efficient market hypothesis. Instead, the market model of Markovitz and Sharpe[71] is used for the purpose. It defines the stochastic process generating security price as follows:

$$R_{it} = \alpha_i + \beta_i R'_{mt} + u_{it}$$

where

$$E(u_{it}) = 0,$$
$$\sigma(R'_{mt}, u_{it}) = 0,$$
$$\sigma(u_{it}, u_{jt}) = 0,$$

R_{it} = the return of security i in period t,

α_i, β_i = intercept and slope of the linear relationship between R_{it} and R_{mt},

R'_{mt} = the market factor in period t, and,

u_{it} = stochastic portion of individualistic component of R_{it}.

The market model asserts that the return on each security is linearly related to the market return. More specifically, it states that the total return R_{it} *can be separated into a systematic component,* $\beta_i R'_{mt}$, which reflects the extent of common movement of security's i return with the average return on all other securities in the market. β_i, the systematic risk, reflects the response of security i to economywide events reflected in the market factor, and u_{it} reflects the response to the class of events having an impact on security i only. Thus, the isolation of the individualistic component of a security i, u_{it}, allows an evaluation of the effect of specific information items or measurements. This model has been used in most studies evaluating the announcement effect of several types of information items and measurements.

Information Content of Financial Accounting Numbers   Using theory and evidence regarding the efficient market hypothesis and the methodologies provided mainly by the capital asset pricing model, portfolio theory, and the market model, the predictive approach proceeded with the evaluation of accounting numbers and techniques on the basis of the capital market reactions. To date, a number of interesting results have been obtained:

1.   Various studies reported results consistent with the hypothesis that earning reports convey information in the sense of leading to changes in equilibrium prices.[72]

---

[71]H. Markovitz, "Portfolio Selection," *Journal of Finance* (March 1952), pp. 77–91; W. F. Sharpe, "A Simplified Model for Portfolio Analysis," *Management Science* (January 1963), pp. 277–93.

[72]R. Ball and P. Brown, "An Empirical Evaluation of Accounting Income Numbers," *Journal of Accounting Research* (Autumn 1968), pp. 159–78; N. Gonedes, "Capital Market Equilibrium and Annual Accounting Numbers: Empirical Evidence," *Journal of Accounting Research* (Spring 1974), pp. 26–62; V. Niederhoffer and P. Reagan, "Earning Changes, Analysts' Forecasts, and Stock Prices," *Financial Analysts Journal* (May–June 1972), pp. 65–71; D. W. Collins, "SEC Product Line Reporting and Market Efficiency," *Journal of Financial Economics* (June 1975), pp. 167–79; W. Beaver, "The Information Context of Annual Earnings Announcement," *Empirical Research in Accounting: 1968*, Supplement to vol. 6, *Journal of Accounting Research*, pp. 87–92; P. Brown and J. W. Kennelly, "The Informational Content of Quarterly Earnings: An Extension and Some Further Evidence," *Journal of Business* (July 1972), pp. 403–15.

2. Various studies reported results consistent with the hypothesis that information from accounting numbers may be used to form expectations about the systematic risk of a security.[73]

3. Various studies reported results consistent with the hypothesis that company forecasts and socioeconomic accounting information provide useful in-. formation to investors.[74]

4. Various studies reported results consistent with the hypothesis that accounting changes had no impact on stock prices, with the immediate assumption that investors are able to see through the numbers created by changes in the reporting methods and recognize economic reality.[75]

5. Various studies reported results consistent with the hypothesis that the most preferred option is the one presenting the highest association with stock price changes.[76]

The efficient market hypothesis was contested by Gonedes and Dopuch[77] on the grounds that stock price associations are not sufficient for evaluation of alternative information systems, and social welfare considerations are needed. More specifically, Gonedes and Dopuch identified two assertions used in the predictive approach for the evaluation of alternative accounting procedures:

A.1. Capital market efficiency, taken by itself, provides justification for using prices of (or rates of return on) firms' ownership shares in assessing the *desirability* of alternative accounting procedures of regulations.

A.2. Capital market efficiency, taken by itself, provides sufficient justification for using prices of (or rates of return on) firms' ownership

---

[73]W. Beaver, P. Kettler, and M. Scholes, "The Association Between Determined and Accounting Determined Risk Measures," *The Accounting Review* (October 1970), pp. 654–82; N. Gonedes, "Evidence on the Information Content of Accounting Messages: Accounting-Based and Market-Based Estimates of Systematic Risk," *Journal of Financial and Quantitative Analysis* (July 1973), pp. 407–44; W. Beaver and J. Marregold, "The Association Between Market Determined and Accounting Determined Measures of Systematic Risk," *Journal of Financial and Quantitative Analysis* (June 1975), pp. 231–84; N. Gonedes, "A Note on Accounting-Based and Market-Based Estimates of Systematic Risk," *Journal of Financial and Quantitative Analysis* (June 1975), pp. 115–20.

[74]R. W. Ingram, "An Investigation of the Information Content of (Certain) Social Responsibility Disclosures," *Journal of Accounting Research* (Autumn 1978, pp. 270–85; A. Belkaoui, "The Impact of the Disclosure of the Environmental Effects of Organizational Behavior on the Market," *Financial Management* (Winter 1976), pp. 26–31.

[75]R. Kaplan and R. Roll, "Investor Evaluation of Accounting Information: Some Empirical Evidence," *Journal of Business* (April 1972), pp. 225–57; R. Ball, "Changes in Accounting Techniques and Stock Prices," *Empirical Research in Accounting: 1972*, supplement to vol. 10, *Journal of Accounting Research*, pp. 1–38; S. Sunder, "Stock Price and Risk Related to Accounting Changes in Inventory Valuation," *The Accounting Review* (April 1975), pp. 305–15.

[76]W. Beaver and R. E. Dukes, "Interpolated Tax Allocation, Earnings Expectations, and the Behavior of Security Prices," *The Accounting Review* (April 1972), pp. 320–32; R. E. Dukes, "An Investigation of the Effects of Expensing Research and Development in Security Prices," *Proceedings of the Conference on Topical Research in Accounting, 1975* (New York: New York University Press, 1976), pp. 147–93; George Foster, "Accounting Earnings and Stock Prices of Insurance Companies," *The Accounting Review* (October 1975), pp. 686–89.

[77]N. Gonedes and N. Dopuch, "Capital Market Equilibrium Information Production, and Selecting Accounting Techniques: Theoretical Framework and Review of Empirical Work," *Studies on Financial Accounting Objectives: 1974*, Supplement to vol. 12, *Journal of Accounting Research*, pp. 48–129.

shares in assessing the *effects* of alternative accounting procedures or regulations.[78]

Gonedes and Dopuch argue that the contemporary institutional setting allowed a "free rider" effect that caused the desirability assertion (A.1) to be logically invalid, although the effects assertion (A.2) was held to be valid.

The Paradigmatic Status of Accounting

Evolution or Revolution in Accounting

So far, in the first two chapters, we have presented an array of approaches used to formulate an accounting theory. Given the advantages and flaws of each approach, we may expect that the situation will lead to a fruitful debate and a unified theory of accounting. This view may be advanced by anyone believing that progress in accounting will proceed through accumulation of ideas or evolution. Such a view allows acceptance of most proposed approaches as likely to make a contribution to the final, unified, or comprehensive, theory of accounting.

The prevailing and more logical view, however, is that accounting, like most social and natural sciences, progresses through revolution rather than evolution. The notion of revolution in accounting is taken from Kuhn's "The Structure of Scientific Revolutions"[79] and proposed successively by Wells[80] and the American Accounting Association's *Statement on Accounting Theory and Theory Acceptance*[81] Kuhn's model of revolution comprises the following steps:

1. A science at any given time is dominated by a specific *paradigm*.
2. The science goes through a period of accumulation of knowledge during which researchers work on and expand the *dominant* paradigm; during this period, it is known as a *normal science*.
3. *Anomalies* may develop that cannot be explained by the existing paradigm.
4. A *crisis* stage is reached, beginning with the search for new paradigms and ending with a *revolution* and the overthrow of the *dominant* paradigm by a *new reigning paradigm*.

After using the term paradigm in at least 21 different ways and being criticized for vagueness, Kuhn offered the following definition of *paradigm:*

> The concrete puzzle solutions which when employed as models or examples, can replace explicit rules as a basis for the solution of the remaining puzzles of normal science.[82]

---

[78]*Ibid.*, p. 50.

[79]T. S. Kuhn, "The Structure of Scientific Revolutions," *International Encyclopedia of Unified Science*, 2nd enlarged Ed. (Chicago: University of Chicago Press, 1970).

[80]M. C. Wells, "A Revolution in Accounting," *The Accounting Review* (July 1976), pp. 471–82.

[81]Committee on Concepts and Standards for External Financial Reports, *Statement on Accounting Theory and Theory Acceptance* (Sarasota, Fla.: AAA, 1977).

[82]T. S. Kuhn, "The Structure of Scientific Revolutions," p. 105.

Given this narrow definition, Ritzer, in a pioneering article in sociology, offered a more operational definition of *paradigm:*

> *A paradigm is a fundamental image of the subject matter within a science. It serves to define what should be studied, what questions should be asked, how they should be asked, and what rules should be followed in interpreting the answer obtained. The paradigm is the broadest unit of consensus within a science and serves to differentiate one scientific community (or subcommunity) from another. It assumes, defines and interrelates the exemplars, theories, methods, and instruments that exist within it.*[83]

A paradigm, therefore, may be identified by three basic components: (1) a major article explicating the idea or exemplar, (2) theories, and (3) methods and techniques.

We may easily argue that accounting is currently in the *crisis stage*, given the general dissatisfaction with the old matching-attaching approach to specifying the content of annual reports.

Accounting: A Multiparadigmatic Science

If accounting is in the crisis stage, then it may be possible to identify competing paradigms. In other words, accounting is a multiple paradigmatic science, with each of its paradigms competing for hegemony within the discipline. Following Ritzer's definition of paradigm, each existing accounting paradigm will contain its own exemplar, theories, and methods. In other words, the approaches to the formulation of an accounting theory presented in the first two chapters result from the attempt by each of the accounting paradigms to resolve accounting questions. More specifically, "Each of the currently competing accounting paradigms tends to specify a different empirical domain over which an accounting theory ought to apply.[84]

An examination of the existing accounting literature allows us to identify the following basic accounting paradigms:

1. *The anthropoligical paradigm*, which specifies accounting practices as the domain of accounting.

2. *The behavior of the markets paradigm*, which specifies the capital market reaction as the domain of accounting.

3. *The economic event paradigm*, which specifies the prediction of economic events as the domain of accounting.

4. *The decision process paradigm*, which specifies the decision theories and the decision processes of individuals as the domain of accounting.

5. *The ideal income paradigm*, which specifies the measurement of performance as the domain of accounting.

6. *The information economics paradigm*, which specifies the evaulation of information as the domain of accounting.

7. *The users' behavior paradigm*, which specifies the information recipients' behavior as the domain of accounting.

We shall examine each of these paradigms in Chapter 9.

---

[83]G. Ritzer, "Sociology: A Multiparadigm Science," *The American Sociologist* (August 1975), p. 157.

[84]*Statement on Accounting Theory and Theory Acceptance*, p. 47.

Conclusions

The new approaches to the formulation of an accounting theory differ from the traditional approaches in terms of their novelty, their less general acceptance, and their reliance on verification. They present innovative and more empirically oriented methods of resolving accounting issues. The influence of the new approaches is manifested in the accounting literature of the last decade.

Both the new and the traditional approaches to the formulation of an accounting theory may be perceived as emanating from different accounting paradigms competing in a period of crisis for the domination of accounting thought. It may be assumed that some of the approaches to the formulation of an accounting theory and their respective paradigms will likely be replaced in the future by other paradigms. The attempts for theoretical closure may lead to an "infinite regress" caused by continuous reappraisal of the nature and scope of the field of accounting.

References

The Events Approach

Calantoni, C. S., R. P. Manes, and A. Whinston. "A Unified Approach to the Theory of Accounting and Information Systems." *The Accounting Review* (January 1971), pp. 90–102.

Johnson, O. "Towards an 'Events' Theory of Accounting." *The Accounting Review* (October 1970), pp. 641–53.

Lieberman, A. Z., and A. B. Whinston. "An Event-Accounting Information System." *The Accounting Review* (April 1975), pp. 246–58.

Revsine, L. "Data Expansion and Conceptual Structure." *The Accounting Review* (October 1970), pp. 704–11.

Sorter, G. H. "An 'Events' Approach to Basic Accounting Theory." *The Accounting Review* (January 1969), pp. 12–19.

The Behavioral Approach

Belkaoui, A. "Linguistic Relativism in Accounting." *Accounting, Organizations and Society*, 3, no. 2 (October 1978), 97–104.

Birnberg, J. G., and R. Nath. "Implications of Behavioral Science for Managerial Accounting." *The Accounting Review* (January 1975), pp. 81–89.

Demski, J. S. "Choice among Financial Reporting Alternatives." *The Accounting Review* (April 1974), pp. 221–32.

Dickhaut, J. W., G. L. Livingstone, and D. J. Watson. "On the Use of Surrogates in Behavioral Experimentation: Report of the Committee on Research Methodology in Accounting." *The Accounting Review*, supplement to vol. 48 (1972), pp. 455–70.

Dyckman, T. R., M. Giblins, and R. J. Swieringa. "Experimental and Survey Research in Financial Accounting." *The Impact of Accounting Research in Financial Accounting and Disclosure on Accounting Practice.* Ed. A. R. Abdel-Khalik and T. F. Keller (Durham, N. C.: Duke University Press, 1978), pp. 48–89.

Einhorn, H. J. "A Synthesis: Accounting and Behavioral Science." *Journal of Accounting Research* (Supplement, 1976), pp. 196–206.

Hawkins, D. F. "Behavioral Implication of Generally Accepted Accounting Principles." *California Management Review* (Winter 1969), pp. 13–21.

Hofstedt, T. R. "Some Behavioral Parameters of Financial Analysis." *The Accounting Review* (October 1972), pp. 679–92.

Libby, R., and B. L. Lewis. "Human Information Processing Research in Accounting: The State of the Art." *Accounting, Organizations and Society* (September 1977) pp. 245–68.

Rhode, J. G. "Behavioral Science Methodologies with Application for Accounting Research: References and Source Materials," Chapter VII of "Report of the Committee on Research Methodology in Accounting." *The Accounting Review* (Supplement 1972), pp. 494–504.

The Predictive Approach

Abdel-Khalik, A. R. "The Efficient Market Hypothesis and Accounting Data: A Point of View." *The Accounting Review* (October 1972), pp. 791–93.

American Accounting Association. "Report of the Committee on Corporate Financial Reporting." *The Accounting Review*, supplement to vol. 47 (1972), pp. 525–28.

Ashton, R. H. "The Predictive Ability Criterion and User-Prediction Models." *The Accounting Review* (October 1974), pp. 719–32.

Beaver, W. H., J. W. Kennelly, and W. M. Voss. "Predictive Ability as a Criterion for the Evaluation of Accounting Data." *The Accounting Review* (October 1968), pp. 675–83.

Beaver, William H. "The Behavior of Security Prices and Its Implications for Accounting Research (Methods)." In American Accounting Association "Report on the Committee on Research Methodology in Accounting." *The Accounting Review*, supplement to vol. 47 (1972), pp. 407–37. Also in *Research Methodology in Accounting*. Edited by Robert R. Sterling. Lawrence, Kans.: Scholars Book Co., 1972, pp. 9–37.

Beaver, William H. "Implications of Security Price Research for Accounting: A Reply to Bierman." *The Accounting Review* (July 1974), pp. 563–71.

Bierman, Harold, Jr. "The Implications to Accounting of Efficient Markets and the Capital Asset Pricing Model." *The Accounting Review* (July 1974), pp. 557–62.

Downes, David, and Thomas R. Dyckman. "A Critical Look at the Efficient Market Empirical Research Literature as It Relates to Accounting Information." *The Accounting Review* (April 1973), pp. 300–17.

Fama, E. "Efficient Capital Markets: A Review of Theory and Empirical Work." *Journal of Finance* (May 1970), pp. 383–447.

Gonedes, N., and N. Dopuch. "Capital Market Equilibrium, Information Production, and Selecting Accounting Techniques: Theoretical Framework and Review of Empirical Work." In *Studies on Financial Accounting Objectives: 1974*, supplement to vol. 12, *Journal of Accounting Research*, pp. 48–129.

Gonedes, Nicholas J. "Efficient Capital Markets and External Accounting." *The Accounting Review* (January 1972), pp. 11–21.

Greenball, M. N. "The Predictive-Ability Criterion: Its Relevance in Evaluation of Accounting Data." *Abacus* (June 1971), pp. 1–7.

Kaplan, R. S. "The Information Content of Financial Accounting Numbers: A

Survey of Empirical Evidence." *The Impact of Accounting Research in Financial Accounting and Disclosure on Accounting Practice,* Eds. A. R. Abdel-Khalik and T. F. Keller (Durham, N. C.: Duke University Press, 1978), pp. 134–73.

Keane, Simon M. "Portfolio Theory, Corporate Objectives and the Disclosure of Accounting Data." *Accounting and Business Research* (Summer 1974), pp. 210–19.

May, Robert G., and Gary L. Sundem. "Cost of Information and Security Prices: Market Association Tests for Accounting Policy Decisions." *The Accounting Review* (January 1973), pp. 80–94.

The Paradigmatic Status of Accounting

Committee on Concepts and Standards for External Financial Reports. *Statement on Accounting Theory and Theory Acceptance* (Sarasota, Fla.: AAA, 1977).

Hakansson, Nils H. "Where We Are in Accounting: A Review of Statement on Accounting Theory and Theory Acceptance." *The Accounting Review* (July 1978), pp. 717–25.

Kuhn, T. S. "The Structure of Scientific Revolutions," *International Encyclopedia of Unified Science,* 2nd enlarged Ed. Chicago: The University of Chicago Press, 1970.

Wells, M. C. "A Revolution in Accounting." *The Accounting Review* (July 1976), pp. 471–82.

Questions

2–1 Define and explain the "events" approach to theory construction and verification.

2–2 Define and explain the "behavioral" approach to theory construction and verification.

2–3 Define and explain the "predictive" approaches to theory construction and verification.

2–4 Elaborate on the paradigmatic status of accounting.

2–5 What are some of the basic criticisms of the value approach?

2–6 Compare the role of the accountant and that of the user under the "events" approach to basic accounting theory.

2–7 What type of accounting reports are appropriate to the "events" approach?

2–8 What do we mean by the word "event"?

2–9 Orace Johnson made the following statement in "Towards an 'Events' Theory of Accounting," *The Accounting Review* (October 1970), p. 653:

> The major issue between the events observation approach and the value inference approach to accounting theory is whether the receivers are better served by the limited range of forecasts possible with inferences, or by the wider range possible with observation.

Do you agree? Why or why not?

2–10 A. Z. Lieberman and A. B. Whinston made the following statement in "A Structuring of an Event: Accounting Information System," *The Accounting Review* (April 1975), pp. 247–48:

A problem that too often is not recognized is that each figure on the financial statements represents the aggregation of many events. For example, the revenue derived by selling a company's many products is summed into the sales account balance. A computer accounting system designed around the value approach would report only a total dollar value of sales on an income statement. Hence the meaning of the figure is lost; the information concerning the many events that took place to create the total are not saved by the system, and breaking down these aggregated figures could be a very difficult process. The value system will aggregate events as deemed necessary to achieve predetermined goals of reporting and not take into consideration that another accounting function—perhaps in the future—will need the data broken down differently. (If the sales department of the firm desires a sales analysis, it is often required to keep its own set of data corresponding to individual sales; data are generally shared by users.)

Do you agree with this defense of an events-accounting information system?

2–11 What are the similarities between SPR (security price research) and BAR (behavioral accounting research)?

2–12 Ahmed Belkaoui made the following statement in "Linguistic Relativity in Accounting," *Accounting Organizations and Society* (October 1978), p. 102:

> Given the existence of the components identified: symbols and grammatical rules, accounting may be defined *a priori* as a language. Consequently, according to the "Sapir-Whorf Hypothesis," both its lexical and grammatical characteristics will shape the world view held by users of accounting: that accounting influences thinking may be supported by the "linguistic relativity" paradigm.

What are the implications of the "linguistic relativity" paradigm for the construction of an accounting theory?

2–13 T. R. Hofstedt and J. C. Kinard asked the following questions in "A Strategy for Behavioral Accounting Research," *The Accounting Review* (January 1970), pp. 38–54.

> Is it "proper" for accountants to conduct research on human behavior? . . . is it an issue worthy of research?

Answer each of these questions.

2–14 In their review article on behavioral accounting research cited earlier in the chapter, Dyckman, Giblins, and Swieringa reached the following conclusions:

> The impact of behavioral research on accounting practice has been almost nonexistent. While the pronouncements of the AOB and now the FASB may have reflected behavioral considerations, there is no clear tie-in to the behavioral research we have examined. The changes we have seen in recent years and those being considered by policy makers at this time do not reflect the findings of behavioral research nor do the official prouncements indicate any reliance on the existing

behavioral literature. The thinking of senior and influencial practitioners as expressed in their writings and speeches gives little evidence of a
behavioral research impact. Operating rules and requirements of major
government bureaus and organizations involved with accounting reports also do not appear to reflect any behavioral research findings
(p. 87).

What are the reasons for this situation?

2–15 Ijiri, Jeadicke, and Knight were the first to suggest that the reason for a
decision maker's inability to adjust the decision process to a change in the
accounting process was "functional fixation." They made the following
statements in "The Effects of Accounting Alternatives on Management
Decisions," *Research in Accounting Measurement*, edited by R. K.
Jaedicke et al. (New York: American Accounting Association, 1966), p.
194:

> Psychologists have found that there appears to be "functional fixation"
> in most human behavior in which the person attaches a meaning to a
> title or object (e.g., manufacturing cost) and is unable to see alternative
> meanings or uses. People intuitively associate value with an item
> through past experience, and often do not recognize that the value of
> the item depends, in fact, upon the particular moment in time and may
> be significantly different from what it was in the past. Therefore, when
> a person is placed in a new situation, he views the object or term as used
> previously. . . . If the outputs from different accounting methods are
> called by the same name, such as profit, cost, etc., people who do under-
> stand accounting well tend to neglect the fact that alternative methods
> may have been used to prepare the outputs. In such cases, a change in
> the accounting process clearly influences the decision.

What are the implications of "functional fixity" for the construction of an
accounting theory?

2–16 What are some of the problems associated with the behavioral approach to
the construction and verification of an accounting theory?

2–17 W. H. Beaver, J. W. Kennelly, and W. M. Voss made the following statements in "Predictive Ability as Criterion for the Evaluation of Accounting
Data," *The Accounting Review* (October 1968), p. 680:

> Because prediction is an inherent part of the decision process, know-
> ledge of the predictive ability of alternative measures is a prerequisite
> to the use of the decision-making criterion. At the same time, it per-
> mits tentative conclusions regarding alternative measures, subject to
> subsequent confirmation when the decision models eventually become
> specified. The use of predictive ability as a purposive criterion is more
> than merely consistent with accounting's decision-making orientation.
> It can provide a body of research that will bring accounting closer to its
> goal of evaluation in terms of a decision-making criterion.

Do you agree with this evaluation of the predictive approach for the
formulation of an accounting theory? Why or why not?

2–18 What economic events may be predicted by accounting data? Support your
answer by empirical results from the literature.

2–19 N. Gonedes made the following statement in "Efficient Capital Markets and External Accounting," *The Accounting Review* (January 1972), p. 19:

> The markets' reactions (e.g., anticipatory price reactions) to accounting numbers provide reliable indicants of accounting numbers' informational content. It might be added that one who seeks a market based evaluation of accounting numbers' informational content need not use only direct reactions to particular accounting numbers, with respect to income numbers. One might also attempt to evaluate the informational content of accounting numbers by examining their predictive ability in regard to accounting numbers from which market reactions have been documented.

Do you agree with this evaluation of the predictive approach for the formulation of an accounting theory?

2–20 W. H. Beaver made the following statement on the findings of security price research in "The Behavior of Security Prices and Its Implications for Accounting Research (Methods)," *The Accounting Review* (supplement to vol. 47, 1972), p. 407:

> The nature of the findings is two-fold. (1) Evidence is provided regarding the efficiency of the market in processing accounting information. (2) The evidence indicates an association exists between accounting data and security prices both in the context of returns and risk measures. The implication is that the market acts as if it uses accounting data in setting equilibrium prices. Alternatively stated, accounting data are consistent in many respects with the underlying information set used by the market. The consistency reflects either or both of two possible states of the world. The market literally uses accounting data, or the market uses other sources of information where these sources and accounting data reflect the same underlying relationships.

What are the implications of these findings for the formulation of an accounting theory?

2–21 What is a fair game model?

2–22 Explain the various degrees of market efficiency.

2–23 Does functional fixation imply market inefficiency?

2–24 Briefly explain the market model and the capital asset pricing model.

2–25 E. H. Caplan made the following statement in an article titled "Accounting Research as an Information Source for Theory Construction," *The Accounting Review* (supplement to vol. 47, 1972), p. 113:

> We have an abundance of opinions in accounting. Unfortunately, these opinions are often called theories, and so we may tend to mistakenly believe that we have an abundance of theory. This does not mean that opinions are unimportant to theory formulation. Indeed the first step in developing theory is to have an idea or opinion on the subject. But meaningful progress in theory construction requires that some method be available for identifying those opinions which are valid and for selecting the appropriate opinion from among views on a particular issue. Because accounting is pragmatic and can be justified only in terms of its usefulness in the real world, the test of what is valid and

appropriate in accounting must relate to real world phenomena and behavior. In turn, the relationship between such phenomena and behavior and various accounting concepts and procedures can only be determined by empirical research.

Do you agree with this view of accounting theory construction? Why or why not?

2-26 What is meant by the word *paradigm*?

2-27 Do you think Kuhn's notion of a revolution can be applied to accounting?

2-28 Identify existing paradigms in financial accounting.

2-29 J. S. Kuhn made the following statement in "The Structure of Scientific Revolutions," *International Encyclopedia of Unified Science*, 2nd enlarged Edition (Chicago: University of Chicago Press, 1970), p. 150:

> Practicing in different worlds, the two groups of scientists see different things when they look from the same point in the same direction. Again, that is not to say that they can see anything they please. Both are looking at the world, and what they look at has not changed. But in some areas they see different things, and they see them in different relations one to the other. That is why a law that cannot even be demonstrated to one group of scientists may occasionally seem intuitively obvious to another.

How does this statement apply to the different approaches to the construction of an accounting theory?

2-30 The following statement was made in the "Statement on Accounting Theory and Theory Acceptance," by the Committee on Concepts and Standards for External Reports (Sarasota, Florida: American Accounting Association, 1977), p. 51:

> The central message to policy makers is that *until consensus paradigm acceptance occurs, the utility of accounting theories in aiding policy decisions is partial.* Competing theories merely provide a basis for forming opinions on what must remain inherently subjective judgments. While it is true that consensus will frequently develop on certain points, usually this consensus only narrows the range of disagreement; it often does not resolve the basic issue that gives rise to the underlying problem. That is, consensus about peripheral improvements may occasionally emanate from applying a theory, but the basic underlying choice issues continue to be disputatious.

Discuss the above statement and explain its importance for accounting theory construction.

chapter three

The Nature
of the Objectives
# of Financial Accounting

Classification and Conflicts of Interests

The Objectives
of Financial Statements
as Stated in APB Statement No. 4

Report of the Study Group
on the Objectives
of Financial Statements

Methodology Used

The Objectives of Financial Statements
as Expressed in the "Trueblood Report"

Qualitative Characteristics of Reporting

The Corporate Report

From the Objectives
to a Possible Accounting Constitution

Phase I:
Tentative Conclusions on the Objectives
Phase II:
Conceptual Framework Issues
Phase III:
The Objectives of Financial Reporting
by Business Enterprises
Phase IV:
Qualitative Characteristics:
Criteria for Selecting and Evaluating
Financial Accounting and Reporting Policies
Phase V:
Objectives of Financial Reporting
by Nonbusiness Organizations

Conclusions

References

Questions

We established in Chapter 1 that accounting theory constitutes a frame of reference on which will be based the development of accounting techniques. This frame of reference, in turn, is based primarily on the establishment of accounting concepts and principles. Of vital importance to the accounting discipline is that the accounting profession and other interest groups accept these concepts and principles. Thus, to guarantee such a consensus, a statement of the reasons or objectives that motivated the establishment of the concepts and principles must be the first step in the formulation of an accounting theory. A statement of the objectives of financial statements has always been recognized as urgent and essential if debate over alternative standards and reporting techniques is to be resolved by reason and logic. For example, in 1960, Devine argued that

the first order of business in constructing a theoretical system for a service function is to establish the purpose and the objectives of the function. The objectives and purposes may shift through time, but for any period they must be specified or specifiable.[1]

Watts and Zimmerman noted that financial accounting theory has had little substantive, direct impact on accounting theory and practice and offered the following explanation:

Often the lack of impact is attributed to basic methodological weaknesses in the research. Or, the prescriptions offered are based on explicit or implicit objectives which frequently differ among writers. Not only are the researchers unable to agree on the objectives of financial statements, but they also disagree over the methods of deriving the prescriptions from the objectives.[2]

Aware of the importance of objectives, the accounting professions in the United States, the United Kingdom, and Canada have made various attempts to formulate the objectives of financial statements. In the United States, the importance of the development of financial statement objectives was first expressed by the report of the Study Group on the Objectives of Financial Statements,[3] highlighted by the FASB attempts to develop a conceptual framework or constitution,[4] and finally promulgated in the *FASB Statement of Accounting Concepts No. 1.*[5] In the United Kingdom, the importance of the objectives was highlighted by the publication of *The Corporate Report*[6] by the Institute of Chartered Accountants in England and Wales. In Canada, interest in the subject led the Canadian Institute of Chartered Accounts to appoint a task force on the objectives of financial statements. Although relatively recent, all these efforts are directly influenced to a great extent by Chapter 4 of *APB Statement No. 4.*[7]

---

[1]C. Devine, "Research Methodology and Accounting Theory Formulation," *The Accounting Review* (July 1960), p. 399.

[2]R. L. Watts and J. L. Zimmerman, "The Demand and Supply of Accounting Theories: The Market for Excuses," *The Accounting Review* (April 1979), pp. 273–305.

[3]*Objectives of Financial Statements* (New York: AICPA, 1973).

[4]*FASB Discussion Memorandum,* "Conceptual Framework for Financial Accounting and Reporting: Elements of Financial Statements and Their Measurement" (Stamford, Conn.: FASB, 1976).

[6]The Accounting Standards Steering Committee, *The Corporate Report* (London: The Institute of Chartered Accountants in England and Wales, 1975).

[7]*APB Statement No. 4,* "Basic Concepts and Accounting Principles Underlying Financial Statements of Business Enterprises" (New York: AICPA, 1970).

In this chapter, we shall elaborate on the various attempts to formulate the objectives of financial statements as a first and necessary step in the formulation of a conceptual framework for financial accounting and reporting.

Classification and Conflicts of Interests

Formulating the objectives of accounting depends on resolving the conflicts of interest that exist in the information market. More specifically, financial statements result from the interaction of three groups: firms, users, and the accounting profession.[8]

Firms are the main party engaged in the accounting process. By their operational, financial, and extraordinary (that is, nonoperational) activities, they justify the production of financial statements. Their existence and behavior produce financial results partly measurable by the accounting process. Firms are also the "preparers" of accounting information.

Users are the second group, influencing by their interests and needs the production of accounting information. Although a complete list of users is not possible, a list would include shareholders, financial analysts, creditors, and governmental agencies.

The accounting profession constitutes the third group that may affect the information to be included in financial statements. Accountants act principally as "auditoro" in charge of verifying that financial statements conform to generally accepted accounting principles.

Following Cyert and Ijiri's analysis, the interaction between the three groups may be represented by a Venn diagram, as shown in Exhibit 3–1. Circle U represents the interests of the users in the information deemed useful for their economic decision making. Circle C represents the set of information that the corporation publishes and discloses, whether or not it is within the boundaries of generally accepted accounting principles. Finally, circle P represents the set of information that the accounting profession is capable of producing and verifying.

The area labeled I represents the set of information that is acceptable to the three groups. In other words, these data are disclosed by the firm, accountants are capable of producing and verifying them, and they are perceived as relevant by users. Areas II through VII represent areas of conflict of interests.

Given these conflicts, Cyert and Ijiri considered three possible approaches to the formulation of accounting objectives. The first approach considers the set of information that the firm is ready to disclose and attempts to find the best means of measuring and verifying it. In other words, circle C is kept fixed and circles P and U are moved toward it. The second approach considers the information that the profession is capable of measuring and verifying and attempts to accommodate users and firms through various accounting options. In other words, circle P is kept fixed and circles C and U are moved toward it. Under the third approach, the set of information deemed relevant by users is considered central, the profes-

---

[8]R. M. Cyert and Y. Ijiri, "Problems of Implementing the Trueblood Objectives Report," in *Studies on Financial Accounting Objectives: 1974,* Supplement to vol. 12, *Journal of Accounting Research,* p. 29.

EXHIBIT 3-1

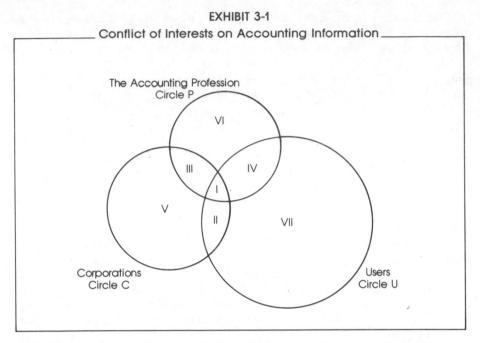

Conflict of Interests on Accounting Information

SOURCE: R. M. Cyert and Y. Ijiri, "Problems of Implementing the Trueblood Objectives Report," in *Studies on Financial Accounting Objectives: 1974*, Supplement to vol. 12, *Journal of Accounting Research*, pp. 29–42.

sion and firms are encouraged to produce and verify that information. In other words, circle U is kept fixed and circles P and C are moved toward it.

Stated simply, the first approach is firm-oriented, the second approach is profession-oriented, and the third approach is user-oriented. Needless to say, given the dominance of the political and legislative approach to the formulation of an accounting theory, as we saw in Chapter 1, the user-oriented approach will prevail in the future when the objectives of financial statements are formulated. In fact, the user-oriented approach is used by both the study group on the objectives of financial statements in the United States and the Corporate Report in the United Kingdom, while the other approaches were used for *APB Statement No. 4.*

The Objectives
of Financial Statements
as Stated in APB Statement No. 4

As indicated in Chapter 1, the Accounting Research Division of the Accounting Principles Board was created to motivate research on the basic postulates and principles of accounting. *ARS Nos. 1* and *3* were rejected, however, and, although *ARS No. 7* was accepted, it did not lead to a statement of broad principles of accounting. Subsequently, the APB recommended that the objectives of accounting be defined and the basic concepts, principles, and terminology known as generally accepted accounting principles be enumerated and described. This recommendation resulted in the publication of *APB Statement No. 4*, "Basic Concepts and Accounting Principles Underlying Financial Statements of Business Enterprises." Although it was basically descriptive, which diminished its chances of providing the first accounting conceptual framework, the statement did influence most subsequent attempts to formulate the objectives of financial statements and to develop a basic conceptual framework for the field of accounting. Chapter 4 of *APB Statement No. 4* classified objectives as particular, general, and qualitative and placed them under a set of constraints. These objectives may be summarized as follows:

1. The *particular* objectives of financial statements are to present fairly, and in conformity with generally accepted accounting principles, financial position, results of operations, and other changes in financial position.
2. The *general* objectives of financial statements are
    a. To provide reliable information about economic resources and obligations of a business enterprise in order to (1) evaluate its strengths and weaknesses, (2) show its financing and investment, (3) evaluate its ability to meet its commitments, and (4) show its resource base for growth.
    b. To provide reliable information about changes in net resources resulting from a business enterprise's profit-directed activities in order to (1) show to investors expected dividend return; (2) show the operation's ability to pay creditors and suppliers, provide jobs for employees, pay taxes, and generate funds for expansion; (3) provide management with information for planning and control; and (4) show its long-term profitability.
    c. To provide financial information useful for estimating the earnings potential of the firm.
    d. To provide other needed information about changes in economic resources and obligations.
    e. To disclose other information relevant to statement users' needs.
3. The *qualitative* objectives of financial accounting are the following:
    a. Relevance, which means selecting the information most likely to aid users in their economic decisions.
    b. Understandability, which implies not only that the selected information must be intelligible but also that the users can understand it.
    c. Verifiability, which implies that the accounting results may be corroborated by independent measurers using the same measurement methods.
    d. Neutrality, which implies that the accounting information is directed toward the common needs of users rather than the particular needs of specific users.
    e. Timeliness, which implies an early communication of information to avoid delays in economic decision making.
    f. Comparability, which implies that differences should not be the result of different financial accounting treatments.
    g. Completeness, which implies that all the information that "reasonably" fulfills the requirements of the other qualitative objectives should be reported.

The objectives as expressed by *APB Statement No. 4* appear to provide a rationale for the form and content of conventional financial reports. The statement even admits that the particular objectives are stated in terms of accounting principles that are generally accepted at the time the financial statements are prepared. The general objectives fail to identify the informational needs of users. The statement implicitly recognizes these limitations when it admits that "the objectives of financial accounting and financial statements are at least partially achieved at present." In spite of these limitations, *APB Statement No. 4* was a necessary step toward the development of a more consistent and comprehensive structure of financial accounting and of more useful financial information. As we shall see, it has directly influenced both the "Trueblood Report" (discussed in the following sections) and *The Corporate Report* in their search for the objectives of financial statements and the FASB's attempts to develop a conceptual framework for financial accounting and reporting.

Report of the Study Group on the Objectives of Financial Statements

Methodology Used

In response to the criticisms of corporate financial reporting and the realization that a conceptual framework of accounting is urgently needed, the board of directors of the American Institute of Certified Public Accountants announced in April 1971 the formation of two study groups. The study group on the establishment of accounting principles known as the "Wheat Committee," was charged with the task of improving the standard-setting process. Its report resulted in the formation of the Financial Accounting Standards Board (FASB). A second study group, known as the "Trueblood Committee," was charged with the development of the objectives of financial statements. It was charged with determining:

1. Who needs financial statements.
2. What information they need.
3. How much of the needed information can be provided by accounting.
4. What framework is required to provide the needed information.

The Trueblood Committee was composed of nine members representing the accounting profession, the academic world, industry, and the Financial Analysts Federation. A team of academicians, practitioners, and consultants served as advisors. The committee conducted meetings and interviews to assess the informational needs of various interested groups from all sectors of the business and professional communities and government. Relevant literature in accounting, economics, and finance provided the basic conceptual foundations. On the basis of the empirical and conceptual data gathered, the study group issued two reports. The first and most important, *Report of the Study Group on the Objectives of Financial Statements*, contains the principal conclusions and the stated objectives of financial statements. The second report contains a selection of articles by the team of advisors that were considered by the study group in forming the conclusions and objectives in the first report.[9]

The Objectives of Financial Statements as Expressed in the "Trueblood Report"

Although the 12 objectives in the study group's report were intended to be equal, there is a justifiable tendency to distinguish a definite hierarchical structure of the objectives.[10] Differences in emphasis and the relative dependency among the objectives justify such a hierarchy. Accordingly, Exhibit 3–2 illustrates a hierarchical structure of the objectives of accounting, with the basic objective at the top and specific recommendations below it. The following six levels may be derived from the report:

1. The basic objective (No. 1).
2. Four objectives (Nos. 2, 3, 11, and 12) that specify the diverse users and uses of accounting information.
3. Two objectives (Nos. 4 and 5) that specify enterprise earning power and management ability (accountability) as the type of information needed.
4. One objective (No. 6) that specifies the nature of the needed information as factual and interpretive.
5. Four objectives (Nos. 7, 8, 9, and 10) that describe the financial statements required to meet objective No. 6.
6. A number of specific recommendations for the financial statements are made in order to meet each of the preceding objectives (Nos. 7, 8, 9, and 10).

We shall analyze each of the objectives.

No. 1: The basic objective of financial statements is to provide information for making economic decisions.

The first objective clearly and directly links accounting to decision making. The emphasis again is directed to the usefulness of accounting information. Decisions are characterized as "economic" in the sense that they refer to resource allocation. In other words, there is a direct link between the relevance of accounting information and the efficient allocation of resorces.

No. 2: An objective of financial statements is to serve primarily those users who have limited authority, ability, or resources to obtain information and who rely on financial statements as their principal source of information about an enterprise's economic activity.

Objective No. 2 seems to designate a "primary audience" for financial statements. This audience consists of those who have limited access to the information and therefore must rely on accounting reports. If we interpret the objective literally, the primary users of accounting information are those shareholders who depend on financial statements for information about a firm's financial position,

---

[9]J. J. Crammer, Jr., and G. H. Sorter, eds., *Objectives of Financial Statements: Selected Papers* (New York: AICPA, 1974).

[10]G. H. Sorter and M. S. Gans, "Opportunities and Implications of the Report on Objectives of Financial Statements," in *Studies on Financial Accounting Objectives: 1974*, Supplement to vol. 12, *Journal of Accounting Research*, pp. 1–12.

EXHIBIT 3-2

Classification of the Objectives of Accounting

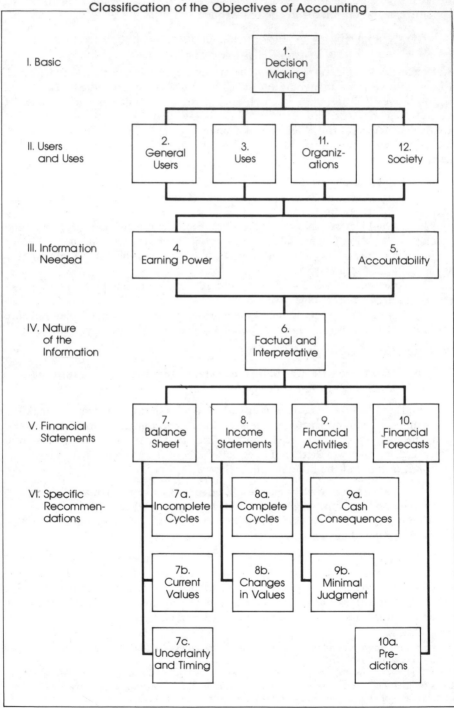

I. Basic

II. Users and Uses

III. Information Needed

IV. Nature of the Information

V. Financial Statements

VI. Specific Recommen- dations

1. Decision Making

2. General Users

3. Uses

11. Organiz- ations

12. Society

4. Earning Power

5. Accountability

6. Factual and Interpretative

7. Balance Sheet

8. Income Statements

9. Financial Activities

10. Financial Forecasts

7a. Incomplete Cycles

8a. Complete Cycles

9a. Cash Consequences

7b. Current Values

8b. Changes in Values

9b. Minimal Judgment

7c. Uncertainty and Timing

10a. Pre- dictions

performance, and changes in financial position. It may appear, therefore, that accountants should present a set of financial statements that, standing alone, contain relevant information for shareholders.

No. 3: An objective of financial statements is to provide information useful to investors and creditors for predicting, comparing, and evaluating potential cash flows to them in terms of amount, timing, and related uncertainty.

Objective No. 3 identifies two important users: investors and creditors. The basis of their interest in financial statements is the cash flow from the enterprise, and no mention is made of net income. The decision models of both investors and creditors involve the tasks of prediction, comparison, and evaluation of cash flows. The characteristics of cash flows of interest to investors and creditors pertain to amount, timing, and degree of uncertainty. One may perceive an emphasis on the stochastic nature of the accounting information in general and cash flow in particular.

No. 4: An objective of financial statements is to provide users with information for predicting, comparing and evaluating enterprise earning power.

While objective No. 3 specifies the information and the decision model of investors and creditors, objective No. 4 accomplishes the same task for all users. While the decision model is still expressed in terms of the activities of prediction, comparison, and evaluation, the information needed is specified in terms of "earning power." This objective is important because it identifies earning power rather than accounting income as the information primarily needed by users. Earning power is perceived as the ability to bring in cash rather than as the ability to produce earnings. The emphasis on earning power, and consequently on cash flows, is a shift in emphasis from traditional accounting objectives.

No. 5: An objective of financial statements is to supply information useful in judging management's abiity to utilize enterprise resources effectively in achieving the primary enterprise goal.

To cash flows and earning power specified by objectives 3 and 4 as the information needed, objective No. 5 adds management ability. This implies that accounting data may be used to evaluate the economic behavior of management. This economic behavior includes the fiduciary stewardship function, or safekeeping of assets to prevent their loss. It goes beyond the stewardship function, however, to include all of management's decisions regarding the use of assets. Objective No. 5 assumes that accounting data can measure management's ability to use resources effectively in achieving the primary enterprise goal.

No. 6: An objective of financial statements is to provide factual and interpretive information about transactions and other events which is useful for predicting, comparing, and evaluating enterprise earning power. Basic underlying assumptions with respect to matters subject to interpretation, evaluation, prediction, or estimation should be disclosed.

Objective No. 6 expands the scope of accounting measurement to include not only factual, or objective, information but also interpretative, or subjective, information. The prediction, comparison, and evaluation of enterprise earning power rest not only on objective and verifiable information but also on subjective information, which may be subject to interpretation. Such factual and interpretative information is the result of both transactions and events. We may interpret objective No. 6 as an application of the events approach, which we presented in Chapter 2. Because information may be interpretative rather than factual and because it may result from events rather than transactions, objective No. 6 specifically recommends that the accountant disclose the assumptions made to derive the information. Such disclosure will facilitiate the interpretation, evaluation, prediction, or estimation on the basis of factual and interpretive information about transactions and events.

No. 7: An objective is to provide a statement of financial position useful for predicting, comparing and evaluating enterprise earning power. This statement should provide information concerning enterprise transactions and other events that are part of incomplete earnings cycles. Current values should also be reported when they differ significantly from historical cost. Assets and liabilities should be grouped or segregated by the relative uncertainty of the amount and timing of prospective realization or liquidation.

Objective No. 7 refers to a concept of a balance sheet or a statement of financial position. The objective specifically recommends that the balance sheet or statement of financial position include transactions and events of incomplete earning cycles, the possible reporting of current values, and the criteria for grouping or segregating assets and liabilities. Objective No. 7 distinguishes between a completed earning cycle (a chain of events whose impact on earning power lies in the past); an incomplete cycle (a chain of events that has commenced but is not yet complete); and a prospective cycle (a chain of events that lies wholly in the future). Thus, a statement of financial position reports on transactions and events that are not yet complete. More specifically, an "earnings cycle is defined as incomplete (1) when a realized sacrifice or a benefit has occurred, but the related benefit or sacrifice has not been realized; (2) when both sacrifice and benefit are not realized; or (3) when the effort has not taken place."[11]

With this objective, a timid step is made toward the disclosure of current values. The uncertainty of the amount and timing of prospective realization or liquidation seems to call for probabilistic values.

No. 8: An objective is to provide a statement of periodic earnings useful for predicting, comparing, and evaluating enterprise earning power. The net result of completed earnings cycles and enterprise activities resulting in recognizable progress toward completion of incomplete cycles should be reported. Changes in the values reflected in successive statements of financial position should also be reported, but separately, since they differ in terms of their certainty of relization."

Objective No. 8 refers to a concept of profit and loss statement or a statement of periodic earnings. The objective specifically recommends that the profit and loss statement or statement of periodic earnings include transactions and events of completed earnings cycles, results of the progress of incomplete cycles, and changes in values. Specifically, reporting transactions and events that are com-

---

[11]*Objectives of Financial Statements*, p. 29.

plete and the progress of incomplete cycles is recommended. "For an earnings cycle to be defined as completed, three conditions should be fulfilled: (1) a *realized sacrifice* (an actual or highly probable disbursement of cash), (2) a related *realized benefit* (an actual or highly probable receipt of cash), and (3) no further related substantive effort."[12] The objective states that the inclusion of unrealized value changes in earnings is both desirable and practical as long as they are disclosed separately to emphasize the uncertainty of their realization.

No. 9: An objective is to provide a statement of financial activities useful for predicting, comparing, and evaluating enterprise earning power. This statement should report mainly on factual aspects of enterprise transactions having or expected to have significant cash consequences. This statement should report data that require minimal judgment and interpretation by the preparer.

The statement refers to a concept of funds statement or statement of financial activities. The objective specifically recommends reporting transactions that establish highly probable receipts and disbursements of cash and factual information with minimal intervention by the preparer. While the statement of earnings shows *progress and results* and the statement of financial position shows *status*, the statement of financial activities shows *conduct*. It is merely a summary of the enterprise's financial transactions, during the period, that are presumed to have cash consequences. While the statement of earnings involves reporting the relationship between sacrifices and benefits of different periods through matching and allocation procedures, the statement of financial activities reports only the benefits and sacrifices made during the period with likely cash consequences.

No. 10: An objective of financial statements is to provide information useful for the predictive process. Financial forecasts should be provided when they will enhance the reliability of users' predictions.

Again, the objective emphasizes the importance of predicting and forecasting in the economic decision-making process. Publication of explicit forecasts of enterprise activities is deemed an important objective of financial statements. Specifically, the objective recommends that, in order to be published, these forecasts enhance the relative accuracy of users' predictions.

No. 11: An objective of financial statement for governmental and not-for-profit organizations is to provide information useful for evaluating the effectiveness of the management of resources in achieving the organization's goals. Performance measures should be quantified in terms of identified goals.

Objective No. 11 expands the scope of financial accounting to the measurement of the performance and goal attainment of governmental and not-for-profit organizations. Because the measurement of potential or actual benefits and sacrifices of not-for-profit organizations is rather difficult and because the goals of such organizations are primarily nonmonetary, performance measures should be expressed in terms of the not-for-profit organization goals.

No. 12: An objective of financial statements is to report on those activities of the enterprise affecting society which can be determined and

---

[12]*Ibid.*, p. 28.

described or measured and which are important to the role of the enterprise in its social environment.

Objective No. 12 adds a socioeconomic dimension to the scope of financial accounting. It recognizes the possible interactions between the private goals of the enterprise and its social goals. There may be reciprocal or direct interactions when the enterprise derives social benefits, such as fire and police protection, in exchange for tax payments or private costs. In the case of direct and reciprocal interactions, therefore, the firm enjoys benefits and incurs costs. Interactions may also be nonreciprocal or indirect. Examples are situations which a firm contributes to the social welfare, which is a social benefit, or when the firm imposes a burden on society, which is a social cost. Objective No. 12 seems to call for reporting both the sacrifices and benefits accruing to a firm that result from direct and reciprocal interactions and nonreciprocal and indirect interactions. One may perceive the stewardship function as including not only the safeguard of assets of the firm but also the safeguard of the social welfare.

Qualitative Characteristics of Reporting

To satisfy users' needs, information contained in financial statements must meet certain characteristics. The "Trueblood Report" mentions seven qualitative characteristics of reporting: (1) relevance and materiality, (2) form and substance, (3) reliability, (4) freedom from bias, (5) comparability, (6) consistency, and (7) understandability.

In the report's words:

> The qualitative characteristics of financial statements should be based largely upon the needs of users of the statements. Information should be as free as possible from any biases of the preparer. In making decisions, users should not only understand the information presented, but also should be able to assess its reliability and compare it with information about alternative opportunities and previous experience. In all cases, information is more useful if it stresses economic substance rather than technical form.[13]

The Corporate Report

In July 1976, the Accounting Standards Steering Committee of the Institute of Chartered Accountants in England and Wales published *The Corporate Report* as a discussion paper intended as a first step toward a major review of users, purposes, and methods of modern financial reporting in the United Kingdom. The report represented the efforts of an eleven-member working party, working with the following frame of reference:

> The purpose of this study is to reexamine the scope and aims of published financial reports in the light of modern needs and conditions.

---

[13]*Ibid.*, p. 60.

It will be concerned with the public accountability of economic entities of all kinds, but especially business enterprises.

It will seek to establish a set of working concepts as a basis for financial reporting. Its aims will be to identify the persons or groups for whom published financial reports should be prepared, and the information appropriate to their interests.

It will consider the most suitable means of measuring and reporting the economic position, performance and prospects of undertakings for the purposes and persons identified above.[14]

How well the report lives up to its stated aims is evidenced by its major findings and recommendations.

First, the basic philosophy and starting point of *The Corporate Report* is that financial statements should be appropriate to their expected use by the potential users. In other words, they should attempt to satisfy the informational needs of their users.

Second, the report assigned responsibility for reporting to the "economic entity" having an impact on society through its activities. The economic entities are itemized as: limited companies, listed and unlisted; pension schemes, charitble and other trusts, and not-for-profit organizations; noncommercially oriented central government departments and agencies; partnerships and other forms of unincorporated business enterprises; trade unions and trade and professional associations; local authorities; and nationalized industries and other commercially oriented public sector bodies.[15]

Third, the report defined users as those having a reasonable right to information and whose information needs should be recognized by corporate reports. The users are identified as: the equity investor group, the loan creditor group, the employee group, the analyst-advisor group, the business contact group, the government, and the public.[16]

Fourth, to satisfy the fundamental objectives of annual reports set by the basic philosophy, seven desirable characteristics are cited, namely, that the corporate report be relevent, understandable, reliable, complete, objective, timely, and comparable.

Fifth, after documenting the limitations of current reporting practices, the report suggests the need for the following additional statements:

1. *A statement of value added,* showing how the benefits of the efforts of an enterprise are shared among employees, providers of capital, the state, and reinvestment. Exhibit 3–3 is an example of a statement of value added.

2. *An employment report,* showing the size and composition of the work force relying on the enterprise for its livelihood, the work contribution of employees, and the benefits earned.

3. *A statement of money exchange with government,* showing the financial relationship between the enterprise and the state.

---

[14]*The Corporate Report,* p. 10.
[15]*Ibid.,* p. 16.
[16]*Ibid.,* p. 17.

EXHIBIT 3–3
A Manufacturing Company Statement of Value

	Year to Dec. 31, 1974		Preceding Year
	(thousands of pounds)		(thousands of pounds)
Turnover	£103.9		£102.3
Brought-in material and services	67.6		72.1
Value Added	£ 36.3		£ 30.2
Applied the following way:			
To Pay Employees			
Wages, pensions, and fringe benefits	25.9		17.3
To Pay Providers of Capital			
Interest on loans	0.8	0.6	
Dividends to shareholders	0.9	0.9	
	1.7		1.5
To Pay Government			
Corporation tax payable	3.9		3.1
To Provide for Maintenance and Expansion of Assets			
Depreciation	2.0	1.8	
Retained profits	2.8	6.5	
	4.8		
Value Added	£ 36.3		£ 30.2

SOURCE: The Accounting Standards Steering Committee, *The Corporate Report* (London: The Institute of Chartered Accountants in England and Wales, 1975), p. 50.

4. *A statement of transactions in foreign currency*, showing the direct cash dealings between the United Kingdom and other countries.

5. *A Statement of future prospects*, showing likely future profit, employment, and investment levels.

6. *A statement of corporate objectives*, showing management policy and medium-term strategic targets.

Finally, after assessing six measurement bases (historical cost, purchasing power, replacement cost, net realizable value, value to the firm, and net present value) against three criteria (theoretical acceptability, utility, and practicality), the report rejected the use of historical cost in favor of current values accompanied by the use of general index adjustment.

In conclusion, a comparison of the principal findings and recommendations of *The Corporate Report* and the "Trueblood Report" cannot be made without considering the different economic and political environments in Great Britain and the United States. In general, *The Corporate Report* expresses a more pronounced concern for statements useful for improving both the social and economic welfare of society.

From the Objectives
to a Possible Accounting
Constitution

Phase I:
Tentative Conclusion on the Objectives

The "Trueblood Report" specified twelve objectives and seven qualitative characteristics of financial reporting. Since its inception, the FASB has recognized the
importance of the objectives of financial statements for the adoption of financial
accounting standards. On June 6, 1974, therefore, the FASB issued a discussion
memorandum concerned with objectives of financial statements and the qualitative characteristics of financial reporting.[17] The memorandum raised four general
questions:

    1.   Which, if any, of the objectives and qualitative characteristics set forth in
the *Report of the Study Group on the Objectives of Financial Statements* should
the FASB adopt at this time?
    2.   Which, if any, of the objectives and qualitative characteristics should the
FASB subject further to study and consideration before deciding whether to adopt?
    3.   Should the FASB defer further consideration of any of the objectives and
qualitative characteristics set forth in the *Report of the Study Group on the
Objectives of Financial Statements?* If so, which?
    4.   Are there objectives or qualitative characteristics other than those set
forth in the *Report on the Study Group on the Objectives of the Financial Statements* that the FASB should consider?

    The discussion memorandum also raised the following specific questions on
each of the twelve objectives in the report:
    1.   What should be included in the term "financial statements"?
    2.   Are guidelines needed to determine which information should be pro-
vided by financial statements rather than by some other medium?
    3.   If a primary audience is critical, how should it be discovered?
    4.   Is the ability to obtain information more critical than the ability to
assimilate it?
    5.   Should "financial" be defined in cash-flow terms, and if so, what are the
implications for financial statements?
    6.   What role should management have in preparing financial statements to
be used to evaluate management?
    7.   Is there a valid distinction between "factual" and "interpretive" in-
formation?
    8.   How should "current value" be reported?
    9.   How can "uncertainty" be communicated?
    10.   Should the articulation of financial statements be abandoned?
    11.   What role should the "statement of financial activities" play?

---

    [17]*FASB Discussion Memorandum*, "Conceptual Framework for Accounting and Report-
ing: Consideration of the Report of the Study Group on the Objectives of Financial Statements" (Stamford, Conn.: FASB, 1974).

12.   Can the qualitative characteristics of the "Trueblood Report" serve as the attributes of useful information?

In addition, an appendix to the memorandum discussed a hierarchial arrangement of the various elements of a conceptual framework. The hierarchy, presented in Exhibit 3–4, attempts to integrate all the elements of accounting

EXHIBIT 3-4

Hierarchy of Elements in a Conceptual Framework for Financial Accounting and Reporting

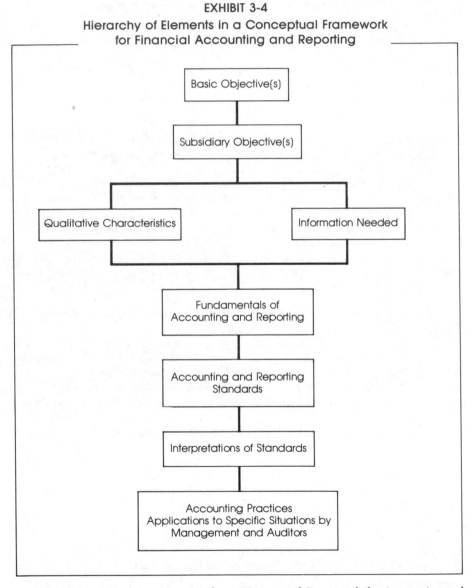

SOURCE: *FASB Discussion Memorandum,* "Conceptual Framework for Accounting and Reporting: Consideration of the Report of the Study Group on the Objectives of Financial Statements" (Stamford, Conn.: FASB, 1974), p. 15.

in a whole to be called the conceptual framework for financial accounting and reporting.

The basic and subsidiary objectives are at the first and second levels of the hierarchy, serving as the first important step for the development of the remainder of the elements of the conceptual framework. Below these objectives, we find the qualitative characteristics to be met and the information needed in terms of number, format, and content of financial statements.

On the fourth level of the hierarchy, we find the fundamentals of accounting and reporting. By this we mean the definitions of assets, liabilities, capital, earnings, revenue and expense, and valuation bases in accounting.

Next—the fifth and sixth levels—accounting and reporting standards and interpretations of standards serve as a guide to accounting practice. Finally, accounting practices, applications to specific situations by management and auditors function as the final means of achieving the objectives of accounting.

The memorandum identifies the crucial parts of the conceptual framework project and justifies the step-by-step process adopted by the FASB for the accomplishment of a task with the hope of succeeding where prior authoritative accounting bodies have not.[18]

Phase II:
Conceptual Framework Issues

The FASB continued its efforts to establish a conceptual framework of accounting with a thorough examination of each of the elements of the framework. This is clearly evident in the published documents titled *Tentative Conclusions on Objectives of Financial Statements of Business Enterprises,*[19] *the Scope and Implications of the Conceptual Framework Project,*[20] and the *Conceptual Framework for Financial Accounting and Reporting: Elements of Financial Statements and their measurement.*[21]

The Objective Issues   After consideration of the *Report of the Study Group,* the relevant literature dealing with that report, and the responses to the discussion memorandum on the report, the FASB issued tentative conclusions about the objectives of financial statements. The FASB examined three issues as background and rationale for its conclusions: (1) the role of investment decisions in a private enterprise economy; (2) the traditional and modern views of the informational needs of investor and creditors, and (3) the links between cash flows and investors and creditors, between cash flows and the enterprise, and between enterprise resources and obligations and changes in them.

---

[18]This refers to the efforts by the Committee on Accounting Procedure and the Accounting Principles Board to Develop a Conceptual Framework for financial accounting and reporting. For more information see the following studies: J. L. Casey, *The Rise of the Accounting Profession,* vol. 2 (New York: AICPA, 1970); M. Moonitz, *Studies in Accounting Research No. 8,* "Obtaining Agreement on Standards in the Accounting Profession" (Sarasota, Fla.: AAA, 1974); and S. Zeff, *Forging Accounting Principles in Five Countries: A History and an Analysis of Trends* (Champaign, Ill.: Stripes Publishing Company, 1972).

[19]*Tentative Conclusions on Objectives of Financial Statements of Business Enterprises* (Stamford, Conn.: FASB, 1976).

[20]*The Scope and Implications of the Conceptual Framework Project* (Stamford, Conn.: FASB, 1967).

[21]*Conceptual Framework for Financial Accounting and Reporting: Elements of Financial Statements and their Measurement* (Stamford, Conn.: FASB, 1976).

The FASB tentatively concluded that financial statements of business enterprises should provide: (1) Information, within the limits of financial accounting, that is useful to current and potential investors and creditors in making rational investment decisions and that is comprehensible to those having a reasonable comprehension of financial affairs; (2) information that helps investors and creditors assess the prospects of receiving cash from dividends or interest and from proceeds from the sale, redemption, or maturity of securities or loans; and (3) information about economic resources, obligations, and earnings, which represent prospective sources and uses of cash.

Two obsevations deserve careful attention: First, compare these tentative conclusions with the objectives stated by *APB Statement No. 4* in 1970:

> The basic purpose for financial accounting and financial statements is to provide financial information about individual business enterprises that is useful in making economic decisions. . . . General and qualitative objectives aid in fulfilling this basic purpose and provide means for evaluating present and proposed accounting principles.
>
> General objectives determine the appropriate content of accounting information. These objectives are to present reliable financial information about enterprise resources and obligations, economic progress, and other changes in resources and obligations, to present information in *estimating earnings potential*, and to present other financial information needed by users, particularly owners and creditors.[22]

We may conclude that the FASB is unwilling to depart from the propositions contained in *APB Statement No. 4*. Also, the FASB was careful to absolve financial statements from the obligation to adapt their elements to the stated objectives. For instance, the board asserts:

> Financial statements may aid investors, security analysts, and others in estimating the earning power of an enterprise, but accrual accounting measures periodic earnings, not enterprise earning power. Earning power is a financial analysis concept used to assess whether or not a stock is undervalued or overvalued by the stock market. It is an estimate of a "representative" amount of earnings, obtained by steps such as averaging or normalizing reported earnings over several periods and ignoring or averaging out the financial effects of "non-representative" transactions and events.[23]

This assertion implies that it is up to the user to adapt reported earnings to particular decision needs and a particular model. In other words, while cash flows and earning power are still perceived as the most important decision parameters of users, investors, and creditors, the accountant will limit his or her function to the measurement and reporting of earnings. An inconsistency exists between the stated objectives and the earnings measurements.

The Elements of the Conceptual Framework   Having stated tentative conclusions regarding the objectives of financial statements that are fairly consistent with those of the study group, the FASB published its discussion memorandum on

---

[22]*APB Statement No. 4*, pars. 21 and 22.

[23]*Tentative Conclusions on Objectives of Financial Statements of Business Enterprises*, p. 58.

the elements of financial statements and their measurements. First, the board acknowledged the erosion of the credibility of financial reporting in recent years, criticizing the following existing situations:

- Two or more methods of accounting are accepted for the same facts.
- Less conservative accounting methods are being used rather than the earlier, more conservative methods.
- Reserves are used to artificially smooth earning fluctuations.
- Financial statements fail to warn of impending liquidity crunches.
- Deferrals are followed by "big bath" write-offs.
- Unjustified optimism exists in estimates of recoverability.
- Off-balance-sheet financing (that is, disclosure in the notes to the financial statements) is common.
- An unwarranted assertion of immateriality has been used to justify non-disclosure of unfavorable information or departure from standards.
- Form is elevated over substance.[24]

The FASB described its project as follows:

A conceptual framework is a constitution, a coherent system of interrelated *objectives* and *fundamentals* that can lead to consistent standards and that prescribes the nature, function, and limits of financial accounting and financial statements. The *objectives* identify the goals and the purposes of accounting. The *fundamentals* are the underlying concepts of accounting, concepts that guide the selection of events to be accounted for, the measurement of those events, and the means of summarizing and communicating them to interested parties. Concepts of that type are fundamental in the sense that other concepts flow from them and repeated reference to them will be necessary in establishing, interpreting, and applying accounting and reporting standards.[25]

The conceptual framework, therefore, is intended to act as a constitution for the standard-setting process. Its purpose is to guide in resolving disputes in the standard-setting process by narrowing the question to whether specific standards conform to the conceptual framework. The constitution specifies both objectives and fundamentals. Given that the tentative conclusions on the objectives of accounting stressed resources, obligations, and earnings, the FASB discussion memorandum on the conceptual framework proposed to identify and provide operational definitions of these elements. It defined eight elements of financial statements of business enterprises that are directly related to measuring the performance of an enterprise.[26] These definitions were concerned with the essential characteristics of items that qualify as elements. More precisely, to be included in financial statements, an item must qualify as an element, but it must also meet criteria for recognition and have the relevant attribute capable of reasonably reliable measurement or estimate. Nine issues are presented for discussion and resolution.

---

[24]*The Conceptual Framework for Financial Accounting and Reporting: Elements of Financial Statements and Their Measurement*, p. 4.

[25]*Ibid.*, p. 2.

[26]*Elements of Financial Statements of Business Enterprises*, Revision of Exposure Draft (Stamford, Conn.: FASB, December 29, 1977).

Issue 1. Which View of Earnings Should Be Adopted?　　Three distinct views about measuring earnings are identified: the asset/liability view, the revenue/ expense view, and the nonarticulated view. For both the asset/liability view and the revenue/expense view, the statement of earnings "articulates" with the statement of financial position in the sense that they are both part of the same measurement process. The differences between revenues and expenses are also equivalent to the increase in net capital.

The **asset/liability view**, also called the balance-sheet or capital-maintenance view, holds that revenues and expenses result only from changes in assets and liabilities. Revenues are increases in assets and decreases in liabilities, while expenses are decreases in assets and increases in liabilities. Some increases and decreases in net assets are excluded from the definition of earnings, namely capital contributions, capital withdrawals, correction of earnings of prior periods, and holding gains and losses. The asset/liability view should not be interpreted as an abandonment of the matching principle. In fact, matching revenues and expenses results from a good definition of assets and liabilities.

The **revenue/expense view**, also called the income statement or matching view, holds that revenues and expenses result from the need for a proper matching. Earnings are merely the difference between revenues of a period and the expenses of earning those revenues. Matching, the fundamental measurement process in accounting, comprises two steps: (1) revenue recognition or timing through the realization principle, and (2) expense recognition in three possible ways: (a) *associating cause and effect,* such as for cost of goods sold; (b) *systematic and rational allocation,* such as for depreciation; and (c) *immediate recognition,* such as for selling and administrative costs. Thus, contrary to the asset/ liability view, the revenue/expense view primarily emphasizes measuring the earnings of the firm and not the increase or decrease in net capital. Assets and liabilities, including deferred charges and credits, are considered residuals that must be carried to future periods in order to ensure proper matching and avoid distortion of earnings.

The **nonarticulated view** is based on the belief that articulation leads to redundancy "since all events reported in the income statement are also reported in the balance sheet, although from a different perspective."[27] According to this view, the definition of assets and liabilities may be critical in the presentation of financial position, and the definitions of revenues and expenses may dominate the measurement of earnings. The two financial statements have independent existences and meanings; therefore, different measurement schemes may be used for them. An example of the nonarticulated view would be the use of LIFO in the income statement and the use of FIFO in the balance sheet. The nonarticulated view has gained some ground recently. In fact, the American Accounting Association's *Statement of Basic Accounting Theory* criticized articulation:

> We find no logical reason why external financial reports should be expected to "balance" or articulate with each other. In fact, we find that forced balancing and articulation have frequently restricted the presentation of relevant information. The important guide should be the dis-

---

.　　[27]G. H. Sorter, "The Partitioning Dilemma," *Objectives of Financial Statements; Selected Papers,* vol. 2, compiled and edited by J. J. Cramer, Jr., and G. H. Sorter (New York: AICPA, 1974), p. 117.

closure of all relevant information with measurement procedures that meet the other standards suggested in ASOBAT (A Statement of Basic Accounting Theory).[28]

Which view of earnings should be adopted as the basis of a conceptual framework for financial accounting and reporting? If articulation could be proved not only necessary but advantageous, then the choice is between the asset/liability view and the revenue/expense view. The choice between these two views rests on which constitutes the fundamental measurement process: (1) measurement of the attributes of assets and liabilities and changes in them, or (2) the matching process. If measurement of the attributes of assets and liabilities and changes in them is deemed the fundamental measurement process—as in the asset/liability view—then earnings are only the consequence and the result of certain changes in assets and liabilities. On the other hand, if the matching process is deemed the fundamental measurement process—as in the revenue/expense view—then changes in assets and liabilities are merely the consequences and results of revenues and expenses. This latter view led to the recognition in the statement of financial position of such items as "deferred charges," "deferred credits" and "reserves," which do not represent economic resources and obligations but which are necessary to ensure a proper matching and income determination. The asset/liability view would reject the deferral method of intraperiod tax allocation in favor of either the so-called liability or net-of-tax methods. By rejecting these new items in the balance sheet, the asset/liability view faces a major criticism, which concerns its unwillingness to recognize as revenues and expenses anything but current changes in economic resources and obligations to transfer resources making it incapable of dealing with the complexities of the modern business world.

The choice between these views is not only important for providing a basis underlying a conceptual framework for financial accounting and reporting but also for a definition of the elements of financial statements. Each view affects the definitions of the elements of financial statements.

Issues 2 through 7. What are the Definitions of Assets, Liabilities, Earnings, Revenues, Expenses, Gains and Losses? A definition of each these elements may be provided under both the asset/liability view and the revenue/expense view.

Under the asset/liability view, **assets** are the economic resources of a firm; they represent future benefits expected to result directly or indirectly in a net cash inflow. Alternatively, we may exclude from the definition of assets economic resources not having the characteristics of exchangeability or severability. In either case, under the asset/liability view assets are restricted to those representing economic resources of the firm. The economic resources of the firm are: (1) productive resources of the enterprise, (2) contractual rights to productive resources, (3) products, (4) money, (5) claims to receive money, (6) ownership interests in other enterprises.[29]

Under the revenue/expense view, assets may be defined to include not only assets as defined in the asset/liability view but also all items that do not represent economic resources but are required for a proper matching and income determination.

A third view of assets arises from the perception of the balance sheet not as a

---

[28]*A Statement of Basic Accounting Theory* (Evanston, Ill.: AAA, 1966), p. 118.
[29]*APB Statement No. 4*, par. 57.

statement of financial position but as "a statement of the sources and composition of company capital."[30] Under this view, assets constitute the "present composition of invested capital."

If we exclude the problem of "deferred charges," the definitions of assets presented under the different views have the following common characteristics:

1. An asset represents potential cash flows to a firm.
2. Potential benefits are obtainable by the firm.
3. The legal concept of property *may* affect the accounting definition of assets.
4. The way an asset is acquired *may* be part of the definitions; it may have been acquired in a past or current transaction or event; the event includes either an exchange transaction, a nonreciprocal transfer from owners or nonowners, or a windfall and *may* exclude executory contracts.
5. Exchangability *may* be an essential characteristic of assets.

Which of the above definitions or modifications of definitions should compose the substance of a definition of assets for a conceptual framework for financial accounting and reporting? What is needed is a definition that contains the generality of application required for a conceptual framework. Such a definition should take into account the following characteristics:

1. An asset represents only economic resources and does not include "deferred charges."
2. An asset represents potential cash flows to a firm.
3. Potential benefits are obtainable by the firm.
4. An asset represents the legal binding right to a particular benefit, results from a past or current transaction, and includes all commitments, as in wholly executory contracts.
5. Exchangeability is not an essential characteristic of assets except for the deferred charges, in order to keep most intangibles as assets and exclude deferred charges.

The FASB opted finally for the following definition of an asset:

> Assets are probably future economic benefits obtained or controlled by a particular enterprise as a result of past transactions or events affecting the enterprise.

An asset has three essential characteristics:

1. A probable future benefit exists involving a capacity, singly or in combination with other assets, to contribute directly or indirectly to future net cash inflows.
2. The enterprise can obtain the benefit and control others' access to it. Legal enforceability of a claim to benefit is not a prerequisite for an asset.
3. The transaction or other event giving rise to the enterprise's claim to or control of the benefit has already occurred.[31]

---

[30]R. P. Marple, "The Balance Sheet: Capital Sources and Composition," *The Journal of Accountancy* (November 1962), pp. 57–60. Reprinted in R. P. Marple, ed., *Toward a Basic Accounting Philosophy* (New York: National Association of Accountants, 1964), pp. 69–74.

[31]*Elements of Financial Statements of Business Enterprises,* Revision of Exposure Draft, p. 8.

Once acquired, an asset continues as an asset until the enterprise collects it, transfers it to another entity, or uses it, or another event or circumstance destroys the future benefit or removes the enterprise's ability to obtain it.

The second element to be defined is *liabilities*. Under the asset/liability view, **liabilities** are the obligations of the firm to transfer economic resources to other entities in the future. We may expand this definition to exclude items that do not represent binding obligations to transfer economic resources to other entities in the future.

Under the revenue/expense view, liabilities comprise not only the same items as under the asset/liability view but also certain deferred credits and reserves that do not represent obligations to transfer economic resources but are required for proper matching and income determination. A third view of liabilities arises from the perception of the balance sheet as "a statement of the sources and composition of company capital." Under this view, liabilities constitute sources of capital and include certain deferred credits and reserves that do not represent obligations to transfer economic resources.

If we disregard the problem of deferred credits, the definitions of liabilities presented under the different views have the following characteristics in common:

1. A liability is a future sacrifice of economic resources.
2. A liability represents an obligation of a particular enterprise.
3. A liability *may* be restricted to legal debt.
4. A liability results from past or current transactions or events.

APB Statement No. 4 summarized these characteristics of liabilities in paragraph 58:

The economic obligations of an enterprise at any time are its present responsibilities to transfer economic resources or provide services to other entities in the future. Obligations usually arise because the enterprise has received resources from other entities through purchases or borrowings. Some obligations, however, arise by other means, for example, through the imposition of taxes or through legal action. Obligations are general claims against the enterprise rather than claims to specific resources of the enterprise unless the terms of the obligation or applicable legal rules provide otherwise.

Which of the above definitions or modifications of definitions should compose the substance of a definition of liabilities for a conceptual framework for financial accounting and reporting? As in the case of assets, what is needed is a definition of liabilities that contains the generality of application required for a conceptual framework.

The FASB opted finally for the following definition of a liability:

Liabilities are probable future sacrifices of economic benefits stemming from present legal, equitable, or constructive obligations of a particular enterprise to transfer assets or provide services to other entities in the future as a result of past transactions or events affecting the enterprise.

A liability has three essential characteristics:

1. A legal, equitable, or constructive duty or responsibility entails satis-

faction of settlement by future transfer or use of assets at a specified event, or on demand.

2. The duty or responsibility obligates a particular enterprise, leaving it little or no discretion to avoid the future sacrifice. Legal enforceability is not a prerequisite for an obligation to qualify as a liability.

3. The transaction or other event obligating the enterprise has already happened.[32]

Once incurred, a liability continues as a liability until the enterprise settles it, or another event or circumstance discharges it or removes the enterprise's responsibility to settle it.

The third element to be defined is *earnings*. Under the asset/liability view, **earnings** result from the net assets of the firm other than "capital" changes. Under the revenue/expense view, earnings result from the matching of revenues and expenses and, perhaps, from the gains and losses. Gains and losses, therefore, may be distinguished from the revenues and expenses or they may be considered part of them. Each possible component of earnings (revenues, expenses, gains and losses) may be defined as follows:

1. Revenues and expenses

Under the asset/liability view, **revenues,** which encompass gains and losses, are defined as increases in the assets or decreases in the liabilities other than those affecting capital. Similarly, **expenses,** which encompass gains and losses, are defined as decreases in the assets or increases in the liabilities arising from the use of economic resources and services during a given period.

Under the revenue/expense view, revenues, which encompass gains and losses, result from the sale of goods and services and include gains from the sale and exchange of assets other than inventories, interest and dividends earned on investments, and other increases in owners' equity during a period, other than capital contributions and adjustments. Similarly, expenses comprise all the expired costs that correspond to the revenues of the period. If gains and losses are defined as a separate element of earnings, however, revenues are defined as measures of enterprise outputs that result from production or delivery of goods and rendering of services during a period. Similarly, expenses are the expired costs corresponding to the revenues of the period.

Which of these definitions of earnings should compose the substance of definitions of revenues and expenses for a conceptual framework for financial accounting and reporting? In other words, which definition contains the generality of application needed for a conceptual framework?

The definitions under the revenue/expense view rely on a listing of all items that may be perceived as revenues or expenses. First, such a list is not necessarily exhaustive, and second, the items in the list may change. As a result, the revenue/expense view of earnings and the ensuing definitions of revenues and expenses lack the generality of application needed for a conceptual framework.

The FASB opted, finally, for the following definitions of revenues and expenses:

Revenues are inflows or other enhancements of assets of an enterprise or settlements of its liabilities (or a combination of both) during a period

---

[32]*Ibid.*, pp. 9–10.

from delivering or producing goods, rendering services, or other activities that constitute the enterprise's ongoing major or central operations.

Revenues are accomplishments of the earning process of a business enterprise during a period. They represent actual or expected cash inflows that have occurred or will eventuate as the result of the enterprise's ongoing major or central operations during the period.[33]

Expenses are outflows or other using up of assets or incurrences of liabilities (or a combination of both) during a period from delivering or producing goods, rendering services, or carrying out other activities that constitute the enterprise's ongoing major or central operations.

Expenses represent actual or expected cash outflows that have occurred or will eventuate as a result of the enterprise's ongoing major or central operations during the period.[34]

2. Gains and losses

Under the asset/liability view, **gains** are defined as increases in net assets other than from revenues or from changes in capital. Similarly, **losses** are defined as decreases in net assets other than from expenses or from changes in capital. Thus, gains and losses constitute that part of earnings not explained by revenues and expenses.

Under the revenue/expense view, gains are defined as the excess of proceeds over the cost of assets sold, or as windfalls and other benefits obtained at no cost or sacrifice. Similarly, losses are defined as the excess over related proceeds, if any, of all or an appropriate portion of the cost of assets sold, abandoned, or wholly or partially destroyed by casualty (or otherwise written off), or as costs that expire without producing revenues. Thus, under the revenue/expense view, gains and losses are independent from the definitions of the other elements of financial statements.

Which of the definitions of gains and losses contain the generality of application needed for a conceptual framework? Under the revenue/expense view, the definitions are independent of the definitions of the other elements and may for that reason be considered as lacking generality of application. Under the asset/liability view, the definitions are derived from the other definitions and emphasize the incidental nature of gains and losses. They appear to contain the generality of application needed for a conceptual framework.

In any case, gains and losses may be either gains and losses from exchanges, "holding" gains and losses resulting from a change in the value of assets and liabilities held by the firm, or gains and losses from nonreciprocal transfers. The FASB opted, finally, for the following definitions of gains and losses:

Gains (or other appropriately descriptive terms) are increases in owners' equity (net assets) from peripheral or incidental transactions of an enterprise and from all other transactions and other events and circumstances affecting the enterprise during a period except those that result from revenues or investments in the enterprise by owners.

Losses (or other appropriately descriptive terms) are decreases in owners' equity (net assets) from peripheral or incidental transactions of an enterprise and from all other transactions and other events and circumstances

---

[33]*Ibid.*, p. 29.
[34]*Ibid.*, p. 30.

affecting the enterprise during a period except those that result from revenues or investments in the enterprise by owners.[35]

3. Relations Between Earnings and Its Components
Three major relations exist between earnings and the conponent of earnings:

Earnings = Revenues − Expenses + Gains − Losses
Earnings = Revenues − Expenses
Earnings = Revenues (including gains) − Expenses (including losses)

In the first relation, each component is separate and essential for a definition of earnings. The different sources of earnings are distinguished, thereby providing greater flexibility in the classification and analysis of a firm's performance.

In the second relation, gains and losses are not separate and not essential for the definition of earnings. All increases and decreases are treated similarly as either revenues or expenses. Such a definition, however, does not fit all the gains and losses from nonreciprocal transfers, windfalls, casualties, and holding gains and losses.

In the third relation, although gains and losses are separate concepts, they are part of revenues and expenses. Such a definition has the same advantages as the first relation and avoids the disadvantages of the second relation. The definitions of revenues and expenses, however, must mix different items and may require a complete identification and listing of the items making up revenues, expenses, gains and losses.

The first relation appears to present the least disadvantage under both the asset/liability view and the revenue/expense view. It allows identification and disclosure of the three kinds of gains and losses: gains and losses from exchanges, holding gains and losses, and gains and losses from nonreciprocal transfers, windfalls, and casualties.

The FASB opted, finally, for the following definitions of comprehensive income:

> Comprehensive income is the change in owners' equity (net assets) of an enterprise during a period from transactions and other events and circumstances from nonowner sources.[36]

With regard to the sources and components of comprehensive income, the FASB exposure draft states:

> Comprehensive income of an enterprise equals its cash receipts less its cash outlays (excluding those from investments by owners) over the life of the enterprise.

> Comprehensive income is the amount by which an enterprise is better or worse off at the end of a period than at the beginning as a result of all transactions and other events and circumstances affecting it during the period except for investments by and distributions to owners.[37]

Specifically, comprehensive income results from:

---

[35]*Ibid.*, p. 31.
[36]*Ibid.*, p. 18.
[37]*Ibid.*, pp. 19–20.

- Exchange transactions and other transfers, excluding owners
- Productive efforts
- Price changes, casualties
- Other effects of interaction between an enterprise and its total environment (economic, legal, social, political, and physical)

Comprehensive income includes revenues, expenses, gains and losses.

4. Accrual Accounting

The elements of financial statements are accounted for and included in financial statements through the use of accrual accounting procedures. Accrual accounting rests on the concepts of accrual, deferral, allocation, amortization, realization, and recognition.

The FASB opted for the following definitions of these concepts:

1. Accrual is the accounting process of recognizing noncash events and circumstances as they occur; specifically, accrual entails recognizing revenues and related increases in assets and expenses and related increases in liabilities for amounts expected to be received or paid, usually in cash, in the future. . . .

2. Deferral is the accounting process of recognizing a liability for a current cash receipt or an asset for a current cash payment (or current incurrence of a liability) with an expected future impact on revenues and expenses. . . .

3. Allocation is the accounting process of assigning or distributing an amount according to a plan or a formula. It is a broader term than amortization—that is, amortization is an allocation process. . . .

4. Amortization is the accounting process of systematically reducing an amount by periodic payments or write-downs. . . .

5. Realization is the process of converting noncash resources and rights into money and is most precisely used in accounting and financial reporting to refer to sales of assets for cash or claims of cash. The related terms, realized and unrealized, therefore identify revenues or gains and losses on assets sold and unsold, respectively. . . .

6. Recognition is the process of formally recording or incorporating an item in the accounts and financial statements of an enterprise. Thus, an element may be recognized (recorded) or unrecognized (unrecorded). "Realization" and "recognition" are not used as synonyms, as they sometimes are in accounting and financial literature.[38]

Issue 8. Which Capital Maintenance or Cost Recovery Concepts Should be Adopted for a Conceptual Framework for Financial Accounting and Reporting? The concept of capital maintenance allows a distinction between the return on capital, or earnings, and the return of capital, or cost recovery. Earnings follow from recovery or maintenance of capital. Two concepts of capital maintenance exist: the financial capital concept and the physical capital concept. Both concepts use measurements in terms of units of money or units of the same general purchasing power, resulting in four possible concepts of capital maintenance: (1) financial capital measured in units of money, (2) financial capital mea-

---

[38]*Ibid.*, pp. 35–37.

sured in units of the same general purchasing power, (3) physical capital measured in units of money, and, (4) physical capital measured in units of the same general purchasing power.

We shall examine the conceptual and operational differences among these concepts in Chapters 5, 6, and 7. Note, however, that the comprehensive income, as defined by the FASB, is a return on financial capital as distinguished from a return on physical capital. The essential difference in the two concepts is that "holding gains and losses" are included in income under the financial capital concept but are treated as "capital maintenance adjustments" under the physical capital concept.

Issue 9. Which Measurement Method Should be Adopted? The issue of measurement method concerns the determination of both the unit of measure and the attribute to be measured. As far as the unit of measure is concerned, the choice is between actual dollars and general purchasing-power-adjusted dollars. As far as the particular attribute to be measured is concerned, we have five options: (1) historical cost method, (2) current cost, (3) current exit value, (4) expected exit value, and (5) present value of expected cash flows. Issue 9 will also be the subject of Chapters 5, 6, and 7.

Phase III:
The Objectives of Financial Reporting by Business Enterprises

The FASB began its effort to develop a "constitution" for financial accounting and reporting by issuing in November 1978 authoritative, broadly based guidelines spelling out the objectives of financial reporting in *Statement of Accounting Concepts No. 1*, "Objectives of Financial Reporting by Business Enterprises." The statement was not limited to the contents of financial statements. "Financial reporting," the statement said, "includes not only financial statements but also other means of communicating information that relates, directly or indirectly, to the information provided by the accounting system—that is, information about an enterprise's resources, obligations, earnings, etc."[39]

The objectives of financial reporting are summarized in the following excerpts from the statement:

Financial reporting should provide information that is useful to present and potential investors and creditors and other users in making rational investment, credit, and similar decisions. The information should be comprehensible to those who have a reasonable understanding of business and economic activities and are willing to study the information with reasonable diligence [paragraph 34].

Financial reporting should provide information to help present and potential investors and creditors and other users in assessing the amounts, timing, and uncertainty of prospective cash receipts from dividends or interest and the proceeds from the sale, redemption, or maturity of securities or loans. The prospects for those cash receipts are affected by an enterprise's ability to generate enough cash to meet its obligations when due and its other cash operating needs, to reinvest in operations, and to

---

[39]*Statement of Accounting Concepts No. 1*, par. 7.

pay cash dividends and may also be affected by perceptions of investors and creditors generally about that ability, which affect market prices of the enterprise's securities. Thus financial reporting should provide information to help investors, creditors, and others assess the amount, timing, and uncertainty of prospective net cash inflows to the related enterprise [paragraph 37].

Financial reporting should provide information about the economic resources of an enterprise, the claims to those resources (obligations of the enterprise to transfer resources to other entities and owners' equity), and the effects of transactions, events, and circumstances that change resources and claims to those resources [paragraph 40].

Financial reporting should provide information about an enterprise's financial performance during a period. Investors and creditors often use information about the past to help in assessing the prospects of an enterprise. Thus, although investment and credit decisions reflect investors' and creditors' expectations about future enterprise performance, those expectations are commonly based at least partly on evaluations of past enterprise performance [paragraph 42].

The primary focus of financial reporting is information about an enterprise's performance provided by measures of earnings and its components [paragraph 43].

Financial reporting should provide information about how an enterprise obtains and spends cash, about its borrowing and repayment of borrowing, about its capital transactions, including cash dividends and other distributions of enterprise resources to owners, and about other factors that may affect an enterprise's liquidity or solvency [paragraph 49].

Financial reporting should provide information about how management of an enterprise has discharged its stewardship responsibility to owners (stockholders) for the use of enterprise resources entrusted to it [paragraph 50].

Financial reporting should provide information that is useful to managers and directors in making decisions in the interests of owners [paragraph 52].

The statement also points out that:

- Financial reporting is not an end in itself but is intended to provide information that is useful in making business and economic decisions.
- The objectives of financial reporting are not immutable—they are affected by the economic, legal, political, and social environment in which financial reporting takes place.
- The objectives are also affected by the characteristics and limitations of the kind of information that financial reporting can provide.
- The objectives in this statement are those of general purpose external financial reporting by business enterprises.
- The terms "investor" and "creditor" are used broadly and apply not only to those who have or contemplate having a claim to enterprise resources but also to those who advise or represent them.

- Although investment and credit decisions reflect investors' and creditors' expectations about future enterprise performance, such expectations are commonly based at least partly on evaluations of past enterprise performance.
- The primary focus of financial reporting is information about earnings and its components.
- Information about enterprise earnings based on accrual accounting generally provides a better indication of an enterprise's present and continuing ability to generate favorable cash flows than information limited to the financial effects of cash receipts and payments.
- Financial reporting is expected to provide information about an enterprise's financial performance during a period and about how management of an enterprise has discharged its stewardship responsibility to owners.
- Financial accounting is not designed to measure directly the value of a business enterprise, but the information it provides may be helpful to those who wish to estimate its value.
- Investors, creditors, and others may use reported earnings and information about the elements of financial statements in various ways to assess the prospects for cash flows. They may wish, for example, to evaluate management's performance, estimate "earning power," predict future earnings, assess risk, or to confirm, change, or reject earlier predictions or assessments. Although financial reporting should provide basic information to aid them. Users do their own evaluating, estimating, predicting, assessing, confirming, changing, and rejecting.
- Management knows more about the enterprise and its affairs than investors, creditors, or other "outsiders" and, accordingly many often increase the usefulness of financial information by identifying certain events and circumstances and explaining their financial effects on the enterprise.

After issuing this statement on the objectives of financial reporting, the FASB is in a better position to evaluate existing standards that are inconsistent with the stated objectives and to complete the remaining phases of the conceptual framework project, namely, to determine (1) the qualitative characteristics, (2) the elements of financial statements, (3) the attributes of the elements of financial statements and capital maintenance, and (4) the unit of measure.

Phase IV:
Qualitative Characteristics:
Criteria for Selecting and Evaluating
Financial Accounting and Reporting Policies

The objectives of financial reporting stated in the FASB *Statement of Accounting Concepts, No. 1* are a starting point for judgments about the quality of financial information. The natural next step would be to establish the characteristics of the information needed to attain these objectives. Accordingly, on August 9, 1979, the FASB issued an exposure draft on qualitative characteristics.[40] The proposed statement establishes criteria by which financial accounting and reporting policies and procedures are to be judged. These policy issues arise whenever alternative accounting or disclosure treatments are possible. The FASB presented

---

[40]*Qualitative Characteristics: Criteria for Selecting and Evaluating Financial Accounting and Reporting Policies* (Stamford, Conn.: FASB, August 9, 1979).

the characteristics of financial information as a hierarchy of qualities, with usefulness for decision making at its head. The hierarchy includes decision usefulness, benefits and costs, relevance, reliability, neutrality, verifiability, representational faithfulness, comparability, timeliness, understandability, completeness, consistency, and materiality.

From this hierarchy, we may draw some general conclusions. (1) The best choice among available information is the one most useful for decision making. (2) The relevant information is that capable of making a difference to the decision maker by changing the assessment of the probability of occurrence of some event relating to the attainment of a goal. (3) Timely information is available when it is needed. A trade-off may exist between timeliness and precision. (4) Information understood by those for whom it is intended is relevant to them. (5) Reliable information allows the user to depend on it to represent the economic conditions or events that it purports to represent. (6) "Verifiable financial accounting information provides results that would be substantially duplicated by independent measurers using the same measurement methods."[41] (7) The measure must have representational faithfulness in the sense that it should represent what it purports to represent. (8) Like all other commodities, desirable information must present benefits exceeding its costs. (9) Material information is significant to the decision-making process.

Phase V:
Objectives of Financial Reporting by Nonbusiness Organizations

Organizations   Nonbusiness organizations differ from business organizations in at least two respects: (1) Nonbusiness organizations have no indicator of performance comparable to a business enterprise's profit, and (2) nonbusiness organizations are not generally subject to the test of competition in markets.

The major distinguishing characteristics of nonbusiness organizations are: (1) significant amounts of resources are received from resource providers who do not expect to receive either repayment or economic benefits proportionate to the resources provided; (2) operating purposes are primarily other than to provide goods or services at a profit or profit equivalent; and (3) there are no defined ownership interests that can be sold, transferred, or redeemed, or that convey entitlement to a share of a residual distribution of resources in the event of liquidation of the organization. On the basis of this definition, the FASB exposure draft on the *Objectives of Financial Reporting by Nonbusiness Organizations*, issued September 15, 1980, cites examples of nonbusiness organizations, which include private nonprofit and philanthropic organizations, such as colleges and universities, hospitals, health and welfare agencies, churches, and foundations; state and local governmental units; and such membership organizations as trade and professional associations. Examples of organizations that do not possess all the distinguishing characteristics of nonbusiness organizations are membership clubs in the transferrable equity interests, investor-owned hospitals and educational institutions, mutual insurance companies, and types of mutual and cooperative organizations that provide dividends, lower costs, or economic benefits directly to their owners, members, or participants.

---

[41]*APB Statement No. 4*, par. 90.

Four particular groups are especially interested in the information provided by the financial reporting of a nonbusiness organizations. They are:

1. The resource providers—lenders, suppliers, employees, taxpayers, members, and contributors.
2. The constituents who use and benefit from the services rendered by the organization.
3. The governing and oversight bodies who are responsible for setting policies and overseeing and appraising the managers of nonbusiness organizations.
4. The managers.

To meet the needs of these particular users of information provided by nonbusiness organizations, the FASB exposure draft presents the following objectives:

1. *Information useful in making resource allocation decisions.* Financial reporting by nonbusiness organizations should provide information that is useful to resource providers in making rational decisions about the allocation of resources to those organizations.
2. *Information useful in assessing services and ability to provide services.* Financial reporting by nonbusiness organizations should provide information that is useful to present and potential resource providers in assessing the services that a nonbusiness organization provides and its ability to continue to provide those services.
3. *Information useful in assessing management stewardship and performance,* Financial reporting by nonbusiness organizations should provide information that is useful to present and potential resource providers in assessing how managers of a nonbusiness organization have discharged their stewardship responsibilities and about other aspects of their performance. Information about an organization's performance should be the focus for assessing the stewardship, or accountability, of managers. Information about departures from such spending mandates as formal budgets and donor restrictions on the use of resources that may impinge on an organization's financial performance or its ability to provide a satisfactory level of services is also important in assessing how well managers have discharged their stewardship responsibilities.
4. *Information about economic resources, obligations, net resources, and changes in them.* Financial reporting should provide information about the economic resources and interests in those resources.
5. *Organization performance.* Financial reporting by nonbusiness organizations should provide information about the peformance of an organization during a period. Periodic measurement of the changes in the amount and nature of the net resources of a nonbusiness organization and information about the service efforts and acomplishments of an organization together represent the information most useful in assessing its performance.
6. *Liquidity.* Financial reporting by nonbusiness organizations should provide information about how an organization obtains and spends cash, about its borrowing and repayment of borrowing, and about other factors that may affect an organization's liquidity.
7. *Managers' explanations and interpretations.* Financial reporting by nonbusiness organizations should include explanations and interpretations to help resource providers and other users understand the financial information they receive. Because managers usually know more about an organization and its af-

fairs than do resource providers or others outside the organization, they can often increase the usefulness of financial reporting information by identifying certain transactions, events, and circumstances that affect the organization and explaining their financial impact.

Conclusions

Logically, the formulation of an accounting theory entails a sequential process starting with developing the objectives of financial statements and ending with the derivation of a conceptual framework or constitution to be used as a guide to accounting techniques. Such a process has started and is manifested by (1) *APB Statement No. 4*, (2) The "Trueblood Report," (3) *The Corporate Report*, (4) the discussion memorandum on the conceptual framework, (5) *FASB Statement of Accounting Concepts No. 1* on the objectives of financial reporting by business enterprises, and reporting policies, (6) The FASB exposure drafts on the qualitative characteristics or criteria for selecting and evaluating financial accounting and reporting policies, and on the elements of financial statements.

The FASB must succeed where previous authoritative accounting bodies have not. The accounting standard-setting process needs a constitution or conceptual framework that will facilitate resolving disputes in the standard-setting process. In order to be effective, this constitution must gain general acceptance, represent collective behavior, and protect the public interest in areas in which it is affected by financial reporting. Can this be achieved in a democratic society without violation or sacrifice of individual rights? The answer to this question may depend on one's view of the benefits and costs of regulation versus a free market mechanism.

References

Accounting Standards Steering Committee. *The Corporate Report*. London: Institute of Chartered Accountants in England and Wales, 1975.

American Instititue of Certified Public Accountants. *Accounting Principles Board Statement No. 4*, "Basic Concepts and Accounting Principles Underlying Financial Statements of Business Enterprises." New York: AICPA, 1970.

Anton, Hector R. "Objectives of Financial Accounting: Review and Analysis," *Journal of Accountancy* (January 1976), pp. 40–51.

Beaver, William H., and Joel S. Demski. "The Nature of Financial Objectives: A Summary and Synthesis." In *Studies in Financial Accounting Objectives: 1974*. Supplement to vol. 12, *Journal of Accounting Research*, pp. 170–87.

Beaver, William H. "What Should Be the FASB's Objectives?" *Journal of Accountancy* (August 1973), pp. 49–56.

Chastain, Clark E. "Accounting Objectives and User Needs: A Behavioral View." *National Public Accountant* (May 1974), pp. 24–27, and "Part II," *National Public Accountant* (June 1974), pp. 26–31.

Chen, Rosita S. "Social and Financial Stewardship." *The Accounting Review* (July 1975), pp. 533–43.

Climo, Tom. "What's Happening in Britain?" *Journal of Accountancy* (February 1976), pp. 55–59.

Clinton, Raymond P. "Objectives of Financial Statements." *Journal of Accountancy* (November 1972), pp. 56–58, f.

Cramer, Joe J., Jr., and George H. Sorter, eds. *Objectives of Financial Statements: Selected Papers.* Vol. 2. New York: AICPA, 1973.

Cyert, Richard M., and Yuji Ijiri. "Problems of Implementing the Trueblood Objectives Report." In *Studies on Financial Accounting Objectives: 1974,* Supplement to vol. 12, *Journal of Accounting Research,* pp. 29–42.

Dopuch, Nicholas, and Shyam Sunder. "FASB's Statement on Objectives and Elements of Financial Accounting: A Review." *The Accounting Review* (in press).

FASB. *Tentative Conclusion on Objectives of Financial Statements.* Stamford, Conn.: FASB, 1976.

FASB. *Scope and Implications for the Conceptual Framework Project.* Stamford, Conn.: FASB, 1976.

FASB. *Conceptual Framework for Financial Accounting and Reporting: Elements of Financial Statements and Their Measurement.* Stamford, Conn.: FASB, 1976.

Goetz, B. E., and J. G. Birnberg. "A Comment on the Trueblood Report."

Harrison, R. B. "Corporate Report: A Critique." *Chartered Accountant Magazine* (December–January 1976), pp. 27–33.

Kenley, W. J. and G. J. Stausbus. *Objectives and Concepts of Financial Statements.* Melbourne, Australia: Accountancy Research Foundation, 1972.

Mautz, R. K. "Accounting Objectives—The Conservative View." *CPA Journal* (September 1973), pp. 771, 774–777.

Most, K. S. and A. L. Winters. "Focus on Standard Setting: From Trueblood to the FASB." *Journal of Accountancy* (February 1977), p. 67–75.

Objectives of Financial Statements. New York: AICPA, 1974.

Schattke, R. W. "Accounting Principles Board Statement No. 4—Promise for the Future." *CPA Journal* (July 1972), pp. 552–56.

Sorter, George H., and Martin S. Gans. "Opportunities and Implications of the Report on Objectives of Financial Statements." In *Studies on Financial Accounting Objectives: 1974,* Supplement to vol. 12, *Journal of Accounting Research,* pp. 1–12.

Staubus, George J. *A Theory of Accounting to Investors.* Berkeley: University of California Press, 1961.

Trueblood, Robert M. *Memorial Conference Studies on Financial Accounting Objectives: 1974.* Chicago: The Institute of Professional Accounting, Graduate School of Business, University of Chicago, 1974.

Williams, Robert Jan. "Differing Opinions on Accounting Objectives." *CPA Journal* (August 1973), pp. 651–56.

Questions

3–1 Why is it important to know the objectives of accounting in order to construct an accounting theory?

3–2 List the various attempts to develop the objectives of accounting in the United States, Canada, and the United Kingdom.

3–3 Describe the conflicts of interest in the information market and the impact of such conflicts on the methodology for the development of accounting objectives.

3–4 Evaluate the methodology used by the Trueblood committee.

3–5 List and discuss the twelve objectives of financial statements contained in the "Trueblood Report."

3–6 List and discuss the seven qualitative characteristics of reporting contained in the "Trueblood Report."

3–7 What economic entities are identified in *The Corporate Report*?

3–8 List and and explain the different financial statements advocated by *The Corporate Report*.

3–9 What is meant by an "accounting constitution"?

3–10 Explain the different views about measuring earnings.

3–11 Recently, the accounting profession has shown substantial interest in delineating the objectives and principles of accounting. For example, *APB Statement No. 4*, "Basic Concepts and Accounting Principles Underlying Financial Statements of Business Enterprises" (1) discusses the nature of financial accounting, the environmental forces that influence it, and the potential and limitations of financial accounting in providing useful information, (2) sets forth the objectives of financial accounting and financial statements, and (3) presents a description of present generally accepted accounting principles.

Required:

a. Discuss the basic purpose of financial accounting and financial statements.

b. Identify and discuss each of the general and each of the qualitative objectives of financial accounting and financial statements.

(AICPA adapted)

3–12 In "Opportunities and Implications of the Report on Objectives of Financial Statements," in *Studies on Financial Accounting Objectives 1974*, supplement to volume 12 of the *Journal of Accounting Research*, pp. 1–2, G. H. Sorter and M. S. Gans made the following statement on the importance of the "Trueblood Report" and the objectives suggested:

> The Report's mere existence and acknowledgment can have profound implications for the development of accounting standards and the resolution of accounting problems. No longer should it be possible to legislate accounting standards by fiat; no longer should it be possible to thunder "Thou shalt" without continuing with "because." If the existence of explicit objectives is acknowledged then each proposed accounting standard should be evaluated in terms of how the standard relates to and furthers the objectives. Disagreement relating to alternative standards should be analyzed and resolved in terms of what standard relates to and furthers the objectives. In other words, for something to be a part of the recognized body of generally accepted accounting principles, it should be demonstrated to be right because it is the best available means for executing the objectives.

In your opinion, how valid is this implication?

3–13 What are the differences between complete and incomplete earning cycles?

3–14 What is meant by earning power?

3–15 Explain the differences among the three distinct views about measuring earnings: the asset/liability view, the revenue/expense view, and the nonarticulated view.

3–16 Should the asset/liability view, the revenue/expense view, or the non-articulated view be adopted as the basis for a conceptual framework for financial accounting and reporting? Discuss.

3–17 Explain the differences in the definitions of assets, liabilities, revenues, expenses, and gains and losses under the asset/liability view and the revenue/expense view. Which of the alternative definitions should make up the substance of a definition of assets, liabilities, revenues, expenses, and gains and losses for a conceptual framework for financial accounting and reporting?

3–18 What are the arguments for articulation? What are the arguments for non-articulation?

3–19 Evaluate the three different formulations of the relation between earnings and its compoents.

3–20 List the different concepts of capital maintenance. How do they differ from one another?

3–21 Discuss the objectives of financial reporting by business enterprises.

3–22 Discuss the nature and purpose of the qualitative criteria for selecting and evaluating financial accounting and reporting policies.

3–23 In "Recommendations on Accounting Theory," in *Studies in Accounting Theory* (edited by W. T. Baxter and S. Davidson, Sweet and Maxwell, 1962), p. 427, W. T. Baxter made the following statement:

> Recommendations by authority on matters of accounting theory may in the short run seem unmixed blessings. In the end, however, they will probably do harm. They are likely to yield little fresh knowledge. . . . They are likely to weaken the education of accountants; the conversion of the subject into cut-and-dried rules, approved by authority and not to be lightly questioned, threatens to reduce its value as a subject of liberal education almost to *nil*. They are likely to narrow the scope of individual thought and judgment; and a group of men who resign their hard problems to others must eventually give up all claim to be a learned profession.

Does this statement apply to the FASB's effort to develop a conceptual framework? Explain.

chapter four

The Structure of Accounting Theory

The Nature of the Structure
of Accounting Theory

The Nature of Accounting Postulates,
Theoretical Concepts, and Principles

The Accounting Postulates

The Entity Postulate
The Going Concern Postulate
The Unit-of-Measure Postulate
The Accounting Period Postulate

The Theoretical Concepts of Accounting

The Proprietary Theory
The Entity Theory
The Fund Theory

The Accounting Principles

The Cost Principle
The Revenue Principle
The Matching Principle
The Objectivity Principle
The Consistency Principle
The Full Disclosure Principle
The Conservatism Principle
The Materiality Principle
The Uniformity and
Comparability Principles

Conclusions

References

Questions

A full appreciation of the current and future scope of accounting depends on an understanding not only of accounting techniques but also of the structure of accounting theory from which the techniques are derived. The development of a structure of accounting theory to better justify the existing rules and techniques began with Paton's examination of the basic foundations of accounting.[1] The effort was continued by a number of authors using either a deductive approach[2] or an inductive approach.[3] The primary objective was to codify the postulates and principles of accounting and to formulate a coherent accounting theory to enable accountants to improve the quality of financial reporting.

Although the resulting theories differ in terms of who uses accounting information, what constitutes "use" of accounting data, and the nature of the environment assumed by users and preparers of accounting data, they all provide a frame of reference, or a *structure of accounting theory*, within which the adequacy of specific methods may be judged. While the elements of the structure may differ according to the methodologies used and the assumptions made, a consensus exists in the literature and in practice on the primacy of certain of the elements as essential foundations of accounting. Accordingly, in this chapter, we shall discuss the principal elements of the broad structure of accounting theory.

The Nature of the Structure of Accounting Theory

Whatever approaches and methodologies are used for the formulation of an accounting theory—deductive or inductive, normative or descriptive—the resulting structure, or frame of reference, is based on a set of elements and relationships that govern the development of accounting techniques. As shown in Exhibit 4–1, the structure of an accounting theory contains the following elements:

1. A statement of the objectives of financial statements.
2. A statement of the postulates and theoretical concepts of accounting dealing with the environmental assumptions and the nature of the accounting

---

[1]William A. Paton, *Accounting Theory* (New York: The Ronald Press, 1922).

[2]Henry W. Sweeney, *Stabilized Accounting* (New York: Harper & Brothers, 1936); Kenneth MacNeal, *Truth in Accounting* (Philadelphia: University of Pennsylvania Press, 1939); Edgar O. Edwards and Philippe W. Bell, *The Theory and Measurement of Business Income* (Berkeley: University of California Press, 1961); Maurice Moonitz, *Accounting Research Study No. 1*, "The Basic Postulates of Accounting" (New York: AIPCA, 1961); Robert T. Sprouse and Maurice Moonitz, *Accounting Research Study No. 3*, "A Tentative Set of Broad Accounting Principles for Business Enterprises " (New York: AICPA, 1962); John B. Canning, *The Economics of Accountancy* (New York: The Ronald Press, 1929); Sidney S. Alexander, "Income Measurement in a Dynamic Economy," *Five Monographs on Business Income* (New York: AICPA, 1950).

[3]Henry Hatfield, *Accounting: Its Principles and Problems* (New York: D. Appleton & Company, 1927); Stephen Gilman, *Accounting Concepts of Profits* (New York: The Ronald Press, 1939); William A. Paton and A. C. Littleton, *An Introduction to Corporate Accounting Standards*, Monograph No. 3 (Columbus, Ohio: AAA, 1940); A. C. Littleton, *Structure of Accounting Theory*, Monograph No. 5 (Iowa City: AAA, 1953); Yuji Ijiri, *Studies in Accounting Research No. 10*, "Theory of Accounting Measurement" (Sarasota, Fla.: AAA, 1975); R. M. Skinner, *Accounting Principles* (Toronto: Canadian Institute of Chartered Accountants, 1973).

EXHIBIT 4-1

Hierarchy of the Elements of Structure of Accounting Theory

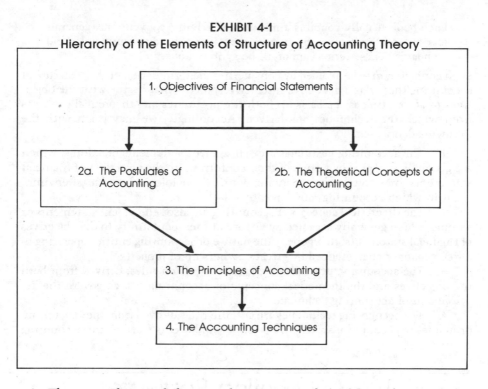

1. Objectives of Financial Statements

2a. The Postulates of Accounting

2b. The Theoretical Concepts of Accounting

3. The Principles of Accounting

4. The Accounting Techniques

unit. These postulates and theoretical concepts are derived from the stated objectives.

3. A statement of the basic accounting principles based on both the postulates and theoretical concepts.

4. A body of accounting techniques derived from the accounting principles.

We discussed the first element—the formulation of the objectives of financial statements—in Chapter 3. Recall the importance of the objectives for the development of a structure of accounting theory. The last element—a body of knowledge or techniques for accountants—is the subject of other technique-oriented courses, and we shall not cover it here. In the rest of this chapter, therefore, we shall discuss the following three elements of an accounting theory: (1) the postulates of accounting, (2) the theoretical concepts of accounting, and (3) the principles of accounting.

The Nature of Accounting Postulates, Theoretical Concepts, and Principles

The development of the postulates, theoretical concepts, and principles of accounting has always been one of the most challenging and difficult tasks in accounting. The lack of a precise terminology, which has been recognized by most authors, has compounded the problem. A. C. Littleton referred to this problem when he stated that:

Each book usually contains a mixture of axioms, conventions, generalizations, methods, rules, postulates, practices, procedures, principles and standards. These terms cannot all be synonymous.[4]

Such confusion may be avoided by considering the formulation of the structure of accounting theory as a deductive interactive process that begins with the objectives of accounting as the basis for both the postulates and theoretical concepts from which the techniques are derived. Accordingly, we may begin with the following definitions:

1. The accounting **postulates** are self-evident statements or axioms, which are generally accepted by virture of their conformity to the objectives of financial statements, that portray the economic, political, sociological, and legal environment in which accounting must operate.

2. The **theoretical concepts** of accounting are also self-evident statements or axioms, which generally accepted by virture of their conformity to the objectives of financial statements, that portray the nature of accounting entities operating in a free economy characterized by private ownership of property.

3. The accounting **principles** are general decision rules, derived from both the objectives and the theoretical concepts of accounting, which govern the development of accounting techniques.

4. The accounting **techniques** are specific rules derived from the accounting principles to account for specific transactions and events faced by the accounting entity.

The Accounting Postulates

The Entity Postulate

Accounting measures the results of the operations of specific **entities,** which are separate and distinct from its owners. The **entity postulate** holds that each enterprise is an accounting unit separate and distinct from its owners and others firms. The postulate defines the accountant's area of interest and limits the number of objects, events, and their attributes that are to be included in financial statements. The transactions of the enterprise are to be reported rather than the transactions of the enterprise's owners. The postulate therefore enables the accountant to distinguish between personal and business transactions. It also recognizes the fiduciary responsibility of management to stockholders. The entity concept applies to partnerships, sole proprietorships, corporations (incorporated and unincorporated), and small and large enterprises. It may also apply to a segment of a firm, such as a division, or several firms, such as when interrelated firms are consolidated.

One way to define an accounting entity is to define the economic unit responsible for the economic activities and administrative control of the unit. This view is held by Moonitz in *ARS No. 1* and by the study group at the University of Illinois.[5] Thus, postulate A2 of *ARS No. 1* states that "economic activity is carried

---

[4]A. C. Littleton, "Tests for Principles," *The Accounting Review* (March 1938), p. 16.

[5]Moonitz, *ARS No. 1*, p. 22; Study Group at the University of Illinois, "A Statement of Basic Accounting Postulates and Principles" (Urbana: Center for International Education and Research in Accounting, University of Illinois, 1964).

on through specific units or entities."[6] This approach is better exemplified by the consolidated reporting of different entities as a single economic unit, regardless of their legal differences.

Another way to define an accounting entity is in terms of the economic interests of various users rather than the economic activities and administrative control of the unit. This approach is user oriented rather than firm oriented. The interests of the users rather than the economic activities of the firm define the boundaries of the accounting entity and the information to be included in the financial statements. This view was held by the American Accounting Association's 1964 Concepts and Standards Research Study Committee on the Business Entity Concept, which stated, "the boundaries of such an economic entity are identifiable (1) by determining the interested individual or group, and (2) by determining the nature of that individual's or that group's interest."[7] This second approach justifies the possible data expansion that may result from the new scope of accounting as it attempts to meet all the potential informational needs of users. For example, information generated by the possible adoption of human resource accounting, socioeconomic accounting, accounting for the cost of capital, and reporting financial forecasts may be more easily included in the financial reports under the user rather than the firm approach to the definition of an accounting entity.

The Going Concern Postulate

The **going concern postulate,** or continuity postulate, holds that the business entity will continue its operations long enough to realize its projects, commitments, and ongoing activities. The postulate assumes either that the entity is not expected to liquidate in the foreseeable future or that it will continue for an indefinite period of time. Such a hypothesis of stability reflects the expectations of all parties interested in the entity. Thus, the financial statements provide a tentative view of the financial situation of the firm and are only part of a series of continuous reports. Except for the case of liquidation, the user will interpret the information as computed on the basis of the assumption of the continuity of the firm. Accordingly, if an entity has a limited life, the corresponding reports will specify the terminal date and the nature of the liquidation.

The going concern postulate justifies the valuation of assets on a nonliquidation basis and forms the basis for depreciation accounting. First, because neither current values nor liquidation values are appropriate for asset valuation, the going concern postulate calls for the use of historical cost for many valuations. Second, the fixed assets and intangibles are amortized over their useful life rather than over a shorter period in expectation of early liquidation.

The going concern postulate may also be used to support the "benefit theory." Expectations of future benefits give managers a forward-looking direction and motivate investors to commit capital to an enterprise. The going concern—that is, an indefinite continuance of the accounting entity—is essential for the justification of the benefit theory.

Many accounting theorists consider the going concern postulate as a necessary and essential accounting convention. Paton and Littleton simply state that

---

[6]Moonitz, *ARS No. 1*, p. 22.

[7]Concepts and Standards Research Study Committee on the Business Entity Concept, "The Entity Concept," *The Accounting Review* (April 1965), pp. 358–67.

"the possibility of abrupt cessation of activity cannot afford a foundation for accounting."[8]

All accounting theorists do not share this interpretation of the going concern postulate. Storey and Sterling separately argued that the going concern postulate does not provide justification for valuing inventories at cost.[9] Storey argued that "it is the realization convention and not the going concern convention which requires valuation of inventories at cost."[10] Sterling argued that assuming an accounting entity has an indefinite life does not justify the use of liquidation value, but it is also not a sufficient reason for using historical cost when other relevant valuation alternatives exist. Furthermore, if the going concern postulate is to be retained, it should be perceived as a prediction.

Some accounting theorists prefer not to include the going concern postulate in the structure of accounting theory. Chambers views a going concern as an entity that is in a continuous state of orderly liquidation rather than one in forced liquidation.[11] This interpretation of a going concern conforms with the use of the "current cash equivalent" proposed by Chambers as a valuation base. Other theorists do not include the going concern postulate because they assume it is irrelevant to a structure of accounting theory.[12]

All these objections point to the necessity of reinterpreting the going concern postulate. The postulate may be considered a judgment on continuity based on actual evidence to that effect. Fremgen offers a definition consistent with the view that the going concern postulate is a conclusion or judgment rather than an assumption. He states that "the entity is viewed as remaining in operation indefinitely" *in recognition of evidence to that effect*, not "in the absence of evidence to the contrary."[13]

The Unit-of-Measure Postulate

A unit of exchange and of measurement is necessary to account for the transactions of firms in a uniform manner. The common denominator chosen in accounting is the monetary unit. The exchangeability of goods, services, and capital is measured in terms of money. The **unit-of-measure postulate** holds that accounting is a measurement and communication process of the activities of the firm that are measurable in monetary terms.

The **monetary unit postulate** implies two principal limitations of accounting. First, accounting is limited to the production of information expressed in terms of a monetary unit; it does not record and communicate other relevant but non-monetary information. Accounting information is perceived as essentially

---

[8]Patton and Littleton, *An Introduction to Corporate Accounting Standards*, p. 9.

[9]R. K. Storey, "Revenue Realization, Going Concern and Measurement of Income," *The Accounting Review* (April 1959), pp. 232–38; R. R. Sterling, "The Going Concern: An Examination," *The Accounting Review* (July 1968), pp. 481–502.

[10]Storey, "Revenue Realization," p. 238.

[11]R. J. Chambers, *Accounting, Evaluation and Economic Behavior* (Englewood Cliffs, N.J.: Prentice-Hall, 1966), p. 218.

[12]R. R. Sterling, "Elements of Pure Accounting Theory," *The Accounting Review* (January 1967), pp. 62–73; Y. Ijiri, "Axioms and Structures of Conventional Accounting Measurement," *The Accounting Review* (January 1965), pp. 36–53.

[13]J. M. Fremgen, "The Going Concern Assumption: A Critical Appraisal," *The Accounting Review* (October 1968), pp. 649–56.

monetary and quantified, while nonaccounting information is nonmonetary and nonquantified. This view leads us to define accounting information as "quantitative, formal, structured, audited, numerical and past oriented" and nonaccounting information as "qualitative, informal, narrative, unaudited and future oriented.[14] These definitions show, however, that although accounting is a discipline concerned with measurement and communication of monetary activities, it has been expanding into areas previously viewed as qualitative in nature. In fact, a number of empirical studies refer to the relevance of nonaccounting information compared with accounting information.[15]

The limitation implied by the monetary unit postulate concerns the limitations of the monetary unit itself as a unit of measure. The primary characteristic of the monetary unit—purchasing power, or the quantity of goods or services that money can acquire—is of concern. Unlike the meter, which is invariably 100 centimeters long, the purchasing power of the monetary unit, which is the dollar, is subject to changes. Conventionally accounting theory has dealt with this problem by stating that the unit-of-measure postulate is also a "stable monetary postulate" in the sense that the postulate assumes either that the purchasing power of the dollar is stable over time or that the changes are not significant. While still accepted for current financial reporting, the stable monetary postulate is the object of continuous and persistent criticisms. The accounting profession faces the challenging choice between units of money and units of general purchasing power as the unit of measurement.

The Accounting Period Postulate

Although the going concern postulate holds that the firm will exist for an indefinite time, a variety of information about the financial position and performance of a firm is needed by users for short-term decision making. In response to this constraint imposed by the user environment, the **accounting period postulate** holds that financial reports depicting the changes in wealth of a firm should be disclosed periodically. Although the periods vary, income tax laws, which require income determination on an annual basis, and traditional business practice result in the period usually being a year. Although most companies use an accounting period that corresponds to the calendar year, some companies use a fiscal or "natural" business year. When the business cycle does not correspond to the calendar year, it is more meaningful to end the accounting period when the business activity has reached its lowest point. Because of the need for more timely, relevant, and frequent information, most companies also issue interim reports that provide financial information on a quarterly or monthly basis. Empirical studies on stock market reactions to the issuance of interim reports and their impact on users' investment decisions indicate the usefulness of interim reports. To ensure the credibility of interim reports, the Accounting Principles Board issued *APB Opinion No. 28*, which requires interim reports to be based on the same accounting principles and practices used for the preparation of annual reports.

---

[14]T. Hofstedt, "Some Behavioral Parameters of Financial Analysis," *The Accounting Review* (October 1972), p. 681 and 680.

[15]*Ibid.*, pp. 679–92; Ahmed Belkaoui and Alain Cousineau, "Accounting Information, Nonaccounting Information, and Common Stock Perception," *Journal of Business* (July 1977), pp. 334–42.

By requiring the entity to provide periodic short-term financial reports, the accounting period postulate imposes the use of accruals and deferrals, the application of which is the principal difference between accrual accounting and cash accounting. Each period, accruals and deferrals are necessary for the preparation of the financial position of the firm in terms of prepaid expenses, uncollected revenues, unpaid wages, and depreciation expense. The accountant may have to rely on experience and judgment to reconcile the postulate of continuity with the necessity for accruals and deferrals. Although short-term financial reports may be arbitrary and imprecise, such drawbacks are overridden by their significance to users, which dictates that the accounting process continue to produce them.

The Theoretical Concepts of Accounting

The Proprietary Theory

Under the **proprietary theory**, the entity is the "agent, representative, or arrangement through which the individual entrepreneurs or shareholders operate.[16] That the viewpoint of the proprietor group is the center of interest is reflected in the way that accounting records are kept and the financial statements are prepared. The primary objective of the proprietary theory is the determination and analysis of the proprietor's net worth. Accordingly, the accounting equation is viewed as:

$$\text{Assets} - \text{Liabilities} = \text{Proprietor's Equity}$$

In other words, the proprietor owns the assets and liabilities. If the liabilities may be considered negative assets, the proprietary theory may be said to be asset centered and, consequently, balance-sheet oriented. Assets are valued and balance sheets are prepared in order to measure the changes in the proprietary interest or wealth. Revenues and expenses are as increases or decreases, respectively, in proprietorship not resulting from proprietary investments or capital withdrawals by the proprietor. Thus, net income is an increase in the proprietor's wealth to be added to capital. Losses, interest on debt, and corporate income taxes are expenses, while dividends are withdrawals of capital.

While the theory is generally held to be adapted best to such closely held corporations as proprietorships and partnerships, the influence of the proprietary theory may be found in some of the accounting techniques and terminology used by widely held corporations. For example, the corporate concept of income, which is arrived at after treating interest and income taxes as expenses, represents "net income to the stockholders" rather than to all providers of capital. Similarly, terms such as "earnings per share," "book value per share," and "dividend per share" connote a proprietary emphasis. The equity method of accounting for nonconsolidated investments in subsidiaries recommends that the firm's share of the unconsolidated subsidiary net income be included in the net income. This practice also implies a proprietary concept.

16J. W. Coughlan, *Guide to Contemporary Theory of Accounts* (Englewood Cliffs: Prentice-Hall, 1965), p. 155.

The proprietary theory has at least two forms, which differ on the basis of who is considered to be included in the proprietary group. In the first form, only the common stockholders are part of the proprietor group, and preferred stockholders are excluded.[17] Thus, preferred dividends are deducted when calculating the earnings of the proprietor. This narrow form of the proprietary theory is identical to the "residual equity" concept put forward by Staubus.[18] Consistent with this form of the proprietary theory, the net income is extended to deduct preferred dividends and arrive at net income to the residual equity on which will be based the computation of earnings per share. In the second form of the proprietary theory, both the common stock and preferred stock are included in the proprietor's equity.[19] Under this wider view, the focus of attention becomes the shareholder's equity section in the balance sheet and the amount to be credited to all shareholders in the income statement.

The Entity Theory

Under the **entity theory,** the entity is viewed as something separate and distinct from those who provided capital to it. Simply stated, the business unit rather than the proprietor is the center of accounting interest. It owns the resources of the enterprises and is liable to both the claims of the owners and the claims of the creditors. Accordingly, the accounting equation is:

$$Assets = Equities$$

or

$$Assets - Liabilities + Stockholders' Equity$$

Assets are rights accruing to the entity, while equities represent sources of the assets, consisting of liabilities and the stockholders' equity. Both the creditors and the stockholders are equity holders, although they have different rights with respect to income, risk, control, and liquidation. Thus, income earned is the property of the entity until distributed as dividends to the shareholders. Because the business unit is held responsible for meeting the claims of the equity holders, the entity theory is said to be income centered and, consequently, income-statement oriented. Accountability to the equity holders is accomplished by measuring the operating and financial performance of the firm. Accordingly, income is an increase in the stockholders' equity after the claims of other equity holders are met—for example, interest on long-term debt and income taxes. The increase in stockholders' equity is considered income to the stockholders only if a dividend is declared. Similarly, undistributed profits remain the property of the entity because they represent the "corporation's proprietary equity in itself."[20] Note that strict adherence to the entity theory would dictate that interest on debt and income taxes be considered distributions of income rather than expenses. The

---

[17]G. R. Husband, "The Entity Concept in Accounting," *The Accounting Review* (October 1954), p. 561.

[18]G. J. Staubus, "The Residual Equity Point of View in Accounting," *The Accounting Review* (January 1959), p. 12.

[19]A. N. Lorig, "Some Basic Concepts of Accounting and Their Implications," *The Accounting Review* (July 1964), p. 565.

[20]G. R. Husband, "The Entity Concept in Accounting," p. 554.

general belief and interpretation of the entity theory, however, is that interest and income taxes are expenses.

The entity theory is most applicable to the corporate form of business enterprise, which is separate and distinct from its owners. The impact of the entity theory may be found in some of the accounting techniques and terminology used in practice. First, the entity theory favors the adoption of LIFO inventory valuation rather than FIFO because LIFO achieves a better income determination. (Because of its better inventory valuation on the balance sheet, FIFO may be considered a better technique under the proprietary theory.) Second, the common definition of revenues as product of an enterprise and expenses as goods and services consumed to obtain this revenue is consistent with the entity theory's preoccupation with an index of performance and accountability to equity holders. Third, the preparation of consolidated statements and the recognition of a class of minority interest as additional equity holders is also consistent with the entity theory. Finally, both the entity theory, with its emphasis on proper determination of income to equity holders, and the proprietary theory, with its emphasis on proper asset valuation, may be perceived to favor the adoption of current values or valuation bases other than historical costs.

The Fund Theory

Under the **fund theory,** the basis of accounting is neither the proprietor nor the entity but a group of assets and related obligations and restrictions governing the use of the assets called a "fund."[21] Thus, the fund theory views the business unit as consisting of economic resources (funds) and related obligations and restrictions in the use of these resources. The accounting equation is viewed as:

$$\text{Assets} = \text{Restriction of Assets}$$

The accounting unit is defined in terms of assets and the uses to which these assets are committed. Liabilities represent a series of legal and economic restrictions on the use of the assets. The fund theory is therefore asset centered in the sense that it places primary focus on the administration and appropriate use of assets. Neither the balance sheet nor the financial statement is the primary objective of financial reporting, but the statement of sources and uses of funds is most important. This statement reflects the conduct of the operations of the firm in terms of sources and dispositions of funds.

The fund theory is useful primarily to government and nonprofit organizations. Hospitals, universities, cities, and governmental units, for example, are engaged in multifaceted operations that warrant separate funds. Each self-balanced fund produces its separate reports through its separate accounting system and proper set of accounts. A fund may be defined as:

> an independent fiscal and accounting entity with a self-balancing set of accounts recording cash and/or other resources together with all related liabilities, obligations, reserves, and equities which are segregated for the purpose of carrying on specific activities or attaining certain objectives in accordance with special regulations, restrictions, or limitations.[22]

---

[21]W. J. Vatter, *The Fund Theory of Accounting and Its Implications for Financial Reports* (Chicago: The University of Chicago Press, 1947).

[22]National Committee on Governmental Accounting, *Governmental Accounting, Auditing, and Financial Reporting* (Chicago: Municipal Finance Officers Association of the United States and Canada, 1968), pp. 6–7.

The number of funds used by any nonprofit institution will depend on the number and type of their activities for which legal restrictions are imposed in the use of the assets entrusted to them. For instance the following eight major funds are suggested for the sound financial administration of a governmental unit:

(1) The General Fund to account for all financial transactions not properly accounted for in another fund;
(2) Special Revenue Funds to account for the proceeds of specific revenue sources (other than special assessments) or to finance specified activities as required by law or administrative regulation;
(3) Debt Service Funds to account for the payment of interest and principle on long-term debt other than special assessment and revenue bonds;
(4) Capital Projects Funds to account for the receipt and disbursement of moneys used for the acquisition of capital facilities other than those financed by special assessment and enterprise funds;
(5) Enterprise Funds to account for the financing of services to the general public where all or most of the costs involved are paid in the form of charges by users of such services;
(6) Trust and Agency Funds to account for assets held by a governmental unit as trustee or agent for individuals, private organizations, and other governmental units;
(7) Intragovernmental Service Funds to account for the financing of special activities and services performed by a designated organization unit within a government jurisdiction for other organization units within the same governmental jurisdiction, and
(8) Special Assessment Funds to account for special assessments levied to finance public improvements or services deemed to benefit the properties against which the assessments are levied.[23]

The fund theory is also relevant to profit-oriented organizations, which use funds for such diverse activities as: sinking funds, accounting for bankruptcies and estates and trusts, branch or divisional accounting, segregation of assets between current and fixed assets, and in consolidation.

The Accounting Principles

The Cost Principle

According to the **cost principle,** the acquisition cost, or historical cost, is the appropriate valuation basis for recognition of the acquisition of all goods and services, expenses, costs, and equities. In other words, an item is valued at the exchange price at the date of acquisition and shown in the financial statements at that value or an amortized portion of it. Accordingly, *AICPA Accounting Terminology Bulletin No. 4* defines the term "cost" as follows:

Cost is the amount, measured in money, of cash expended or other property transferred, capital stock issued, services performed, or a liability

---

[23]*Ibid.*, pp. 7–8.

incurred, in consideration of goods or services received or to be received. Costs can be classified as unexpired or expired. Unexpired costs (assets) are those which are applicable to the production of future revenues. . . . Expired costs are not applicable to the production of future revenues, and for that reason are treated as deduction from current revenues or are charged against retained earnings.[24]

Cost represents the exchange price or monetary consideration given for the acquisition of goods or services. If the consideration comprises nonmonetary assets, the exchange price is the cash equivalent of the asset or services given up. The cost principle is equally applicable to the measurement of liabilities and capital transactions.

The cost principle may be justified both by its objectivity and by the going concern postulate. First, acquisition cost is objective, verifiable information. Second, the going concern postulate assumes that the entity will continue its activities indefinitely and, consequently, eliminates the necessity of using current values or liquidation values for asset valuation.

The precarious validity of the unit-of-measure postulate, which assumes that the purchasing power of the dollar is stable, is a major limitation to the use of the cost principle. Historical cost valuation may produce erroneous figures if changes in the values of assets over time are ignored. Similarly, the values of assets acquired at different times over a period during which the purchasing power of the dollar is changing cannot be added together in the balance sheet and provide meaningful results.

The Revenue Principle

The **revenue principle** specifies (1) the nature and components of revenue, (2) the measurement of revenue, and (3) the timing of revenue recognition. Each facet raises interesting and controversial issues for accounting theory.

The Nature and Components of Revenue   **Revenue** has been interpreted as (1) an inflow of net assets resulting from the sales of goods or services,[25] (2) an outflow of goods or services from the firm to its customers,[26] and (3) product of the firm resulting from the mere creation of goods or services by an enterprise during a given period of time.[27] Hendriksen considered, first, that the product concept is superior to the outflow concept, which is superior to the inflow concept, and second, that the product concept is neutral with respect to both the measurement (amount) and timing (date of recognition) of revenue, while the inflow concept confuses both measurement and timing with the revenue process.[28]

The different interpretations of the nature of revenue are compounded by different views on what should be included in revenue. Basically, two views exist

---

[24] American Institute of Certified Public Accountants, *APB Statement No. 4* (New York: AICPA), p. 57.

[25] American Institute of Certified Public Accountants, *Professional Standards* (Chicago: Commerce Clearing House, 1975), p. 7248.

[26] G. J. Staubus, "Revenue and Revenue Accounts," *The Accounting Review* (July 1956), pp. 284–94.

[27] Paton and Littleton, *An Introduction to Corporate Accounting Standards,* p. 46.

[28] E. S. Hendriksen, *Accounting Theory,* 3rd ed. (Homewood, Ill.: R. D. Irwin, 1977), pp. 177–78.

on the components of revenue. Under a broad or comprehensive view, revenue includes all the proceeds from business and investment activities. This view identifies as revenue all changes in the net assets resulting from the revenue-producing activities and other gains or losses from the sale of fixed assets and investments. Applying this view, *Accounting Terminology Bulletin No. 2* defines the term "revenue" as follows:

> *Revenue* results from the sale of goods and the rendering of services and is measured by the charge made to customers, clients or tenants for goods and services furnished to them. It also includes gains from the sale or exchange of assets (other than stock in trade) interest and dividends earned on investments, and other increases in the owners' equity except those arising from the capital contributions and capital adjustments.[29]

Under the narrower view, only the results of the revenue-producing activities are included in revenue, and investment income and gains and losses on disposal of fixed assets are excluded. This view calls for a clear distinction between revenue and gains and losses. Adopting this view, the American Accounting Association in its 1957 statement defined "net income" as:

> the excess or deficiency of revenue compared with related expired cost and (2) other gains and losses to the enterprise from sales, exchanges, or other conversion of assets.[30]

The Measurement of Revenue   Revenue is measured by the value of the product or services exchanged in an arm's-length transaction. This value represents either the net cash equivalent or present discounted value of the money received or to be received in exchange for the products or services transferred by the enterprise to its customers. Two primary interpretations arise from this concept of revenue:

(1) Cash discounts, and any reductions in the billed prices, such as bad debt losses, are adjustments necessary to compute the true net cash equivalent or present discounted value of the money claims and, consequently, should be deducted when computing revenue. Such an interpretation conflicts with the view that cash discounts and bad debt losses should be considered expenses.

(2) For noncash transactions, the exchange value is set equal to the fair market value of the consideration given or received, whichever is more easily and clearly computed.

The Timing of Revenue Recognition   It is generally admitted that revenues and income are earned throughout all stages of the operating cycle, that is, during order reception, production, sale, and collection. Given the difficulties of allocating revenues and income to the different stages of the operating cycle, accountants have relied on the *realization principle* to select a "critical event" in the cycle for the timing of revenue and the recognition of income. The critical event is chosen to indicate when certain changes in assets and liabilities may be appropriately accounted for. An early definition of the realization principle is:

---

[29]*Accounting Terminology Bulletin No. 2*, "Proceeds, Revenue, Income, Profit and Earnings" (New York: AICPA, 1955), p. 2.

[30]AAA Committee on Accounting Concepts and Standards, *Accounting and Reporting Standards for Corporate Financial Statements and Preceding Statements and Supplements* (Columbus, Ohio: AAA, 1957), p. 5.

The essential meaning of realization is that a change in asset or liability has become sufficiently definite and objective to warrant recognition in the accounts. This recognition may rest on an exchange transaction between independent parties, or on established trade practices, or on the terms of a contract performance of which is considered to be virtually certain.[31]

Because of its broad nature, this statement led accountants to search for specific rules or considerations necessary to the recognition of certain asset and liability changes. Naturally, the realization concept and the corresponding criteria for the recognition of asset and liability changes were the subject of different interpretations.[32] As reported by the 1973–74 AAA Committee on Concepts and Standards—External Reporting, the specific criteria for recognition are:

1. Earned, in some sense or another,
2. In distributable form,
3. The result of a conversion brought about in a transaction between the enterprise and someone external to it,
4. The result of a legal sale or similar process,
5. Severed from Capital,
6. In the form of liquid assets,
7. Both its gross and net effects on shareholder equity had to be estimable with a high degree of reliability.[33]

The committee tied the realization principle to a concept of a reliable income measurement. The realization principle is an expression of the level of certainty of the profit impact of an event reported as revenue. More explicitly, the committee defined realization as follows:

Income must always be in existence before the question of realization can arise. Realization is not a determinant in the concept of income; it only serves as a guide in deciding when events, otherwise resolved as being within the concept of income, can be entered in the accounting records in objective terms; that is, when the uncertainty has been reduced to an acceptable level.[34]

Given these different interpretations of the realization principle and of the criteria to be used for the recognition of asset and liability changes, reliance on the realization principle may be misleading.[35] In general, revenue is recognized on an accrual basis or a "critical event" basis.

---

[31]*Ibid.*, p. 3.

[32]F. W. Windal, *The Accounting Concept of Realization*, Occasional Paper No. 5, Bureau of Business and Economic Research, Graduate School of Business Administration (East Lansing: Michigan State University, 1961); J. H. Myers, "The Critical Event and Recognition of New Profit," *The Accounting Review* (October 1959), pp. 528–32; AAA Committee on Concepts and Standards Research Study, "The Realization Concept," *The Accounting Review* (April 1965), pp. 312–33.

[33]"Report of the 1973–74 Committee on Concepts and Standards—External Reporting," *The Accounting Review*, supplement to vol. 40 (1974), pp. 207–8.

[34]*Ibid.*, p. 209.

[35]H. E. Arnett, "Recognition as a Function of Measurement in the Realization Concept," *The Accounting Review* (October 1963), pp. 733–41.

The Accrual Basis for the Reporting of Revenue   The **accrual approach** to revenue recognition may imply that revenue should be reported during production (in which case the profit may be computed proportionally to the work done or service performed), at the end of production, upon sale of goods, or upon collection of sale. Revenue is generally recognized during production in the following situations:

1. Rent, interest, and commission revenue are recognized as earned, given the existence of a prior agreement or contract specifying the gradual increase in the claim against the customer.

2. An individual or a firm rendering professional or similar services might better use an accrual basis for the recognition of revenues, given that the nature of the claim against the customer is a function of the proportion of services rendered.

3. Revenues on long-term contracts are recognized on the basis of the progress of construction or "percentage-of-completion." The percentage of completion is computed as either (a) the engineering estimates of the work performed to date compared with the total work to be completed in terms of the contract or (b) the total costs incurred to date compared with the total costs estimated for the total project in the contract.

4. Revenues on "cost plus fixed-fee contracts" are better recognized on the accrual basis.

5. Finally, asset changes due to accretion give rise to revenue, for example, when liquor or wines age, timber grows, or livestock matures. While in these examples, a transaction must occur before revenue is recognized, accretion revenue relies on making comparative inventory valuations.

The "Critical Event" Basis   Under the **critical event approach,** the recognition of revenue is triggered by a crucial event in the operating cycle. That event may be (1) the time of sale, (2) the completion of production, (3) receipt of payment subsequent to sale.

1. The sales basis for the recognition of revenue is justified because (a) the price of the product is then known with certainty, (b) the exchange has been finalized by delivery of goods, leading to an objective knowledge of the costs incurred, and (c) in terms of realization, a sale constitutes a crucial event.

2. The completion-of-production basis for the recognition of revenue is justified when a stable market and a stable price exist for a standard commodity. The production process rather than sale, therefore, constitutes the crucial event for the recognition of revenue. This rule is primarily applicable to "precious metals that have a fixed selling price and insignificant market prices."[36] The completion-of-production treatment is appropriate for gold, silver, and other precious metals. Agricultural and mineral products meeting the required criteria may also be appropriate.

3. The cash basis for the recognition of revenue is justified when the sales will be made and when a reasonably accurate valuation cannot be placed on the product transferred. This method, which amounts to a mere deferral of revenues, is primarily identified with the "installment method" of recognizing revenue.

---

[36] AICPA *Professional Standards*, p. 7301.

The Matching Principle

The **matching principle** holds that expenses should be recognized in the same period as the associated revenues. That is, revenues are recognized in a given period according to the revenue principle, and then the related expenses are recognized. The association is best accomplished when it reflects the "cause and effect" relationship between costs and revenues. Operationally, it consists of a two-stage process for accounting for expenses. First, costs are capitalized as assets representing bundles of service potential or benefits. Second, these assets are written off as expenses to recognize the proportion of the asset's service potential that has expired in the generation of the revenues during this period. Thus, accrual rather than cash basis accounting is implied by the matching principle in the form of capitalization and allocation.

The association between revenues and expenses depends on one of four criteria. The first applicable criterion is applied:

1. Direct matching of expired cost with a revenue (for example, cost of goods sold matched with related sale),

2. Direct matching of expired cost with the period (for example, president's salary for the period),

3. Allocation of costs over periods benefited (for example, depreciation), or

4. Expensing all other costs in the period incurred, unless it can be shown that they have future benefit (for example, advertising expense).

Unexpired costs (that is, assets) not meeting one of the four criteria for expensing in the current period are chargeable to future periods and may be classified under different categories according to their different uses in the firm. Such different uses may justify differences in the application of the matching principles.

The major asset and cost categories and the corresponding rules for the time of expenses are discussed in the following paragraphs.

Costs of Producing Finished Goods for Sale   The costs of producing finished goods for sale generally include raw materials, direct labor, and factory overhead. These costs are accounted for using a two-stage process: inventory valuation, or the determination of the product costs that attach to the product, and income determination, or the matching of product costs with revenues. When determining the inventory valuation amount, the problem is to decide which costs are product costs (because they benefit future periods and should be inventoried) and which costs are period costs (because they benefit only the current period and should be charged against current income). The absorption, or full, costing method and the direct, or variable, costing method produce different answers.

Under the absorption costing method, all production costs are treated as product costs. They are attached to the product, carried forward, and only released as period costs at the time of sale. Under the direct costing method, only the variable production costs are treated as product costs. All the fixed manufacturing overhead costs are treated as period costs. The choice between these two methods has been a major controversy in the accounting literature for a great number of years. Neither method has emerged as a major victor.[37] It is generally admitted,

---

[37] A. M. Fekrat, "The Conceptual Foundations of Absorption Costing," *The Accounting Review* (April 1972), pp. 351–55; J. M. Fremgen "The Direct Costing Controversy: An Identification of Issues," *The Accounting Review* (January 1964), pp. 43–51; David G.

however, that direct costing is more relevant for internal decision making. The separate reporting of fixed and variable costs is assumed to facilitate incremental profit analysis and remove from income the impact of inventory changes.

Depreciable Operating Assets   Depreciable operating assets are also referred to as "wasting capital assets." Assumed to benefit more than one period, a depreciable operating asset is capitalized at its acquisition cost, which is then allocated on some logical basis over the asset's useful life. This allocation process is known as **depreciation** for such tangible assets as building, equipment, tools, and furniture, **depletion** for assets represented by a *natural resource,* such as mineral deposits and timber tracts, and **amortization** for such intangible assets as *special rights* or benefits (for example, patents, copyrights, franchises, trademarks, goodwill, deferred charges, research and development costs, organization costs, and leaseholds). Depreciation accounting has been defined as follows:

> *Depreciation accounting* is a system of accounting which aims to distribute the cost or other basic value of tangible capital assets, less salvage (if any), over the estimated useful life of the unit (which may be a group of assets) in a systematic and rational manner. It is a process of allocation, not of valuation. *Depreciation for the year* is the portion of the total charge under such a system that is allocated during the year. Although the allocation may properly take into account occurrences during the year, it is not intended to be a measurement of the effect of all such occurrences.[38]

A number of depreciation methods have been developed, each of which is based on different patterns of depreciation charges over the life of the tangible asset. A depreciation method may be based on (1) time such as the straight-line method; (2) output, such as the service-hours method and the unit-of-output method; (3) reducing depreciation charge, such as the sum-of-the-years' digits method, the fixed percentage on declining base amount method, the declining rate on cost method, and the double declining-balance method; and finally, (4) investment and interest concepts, such as the annuity method and the sinking fund method.[39]

Nondepreciable Operating Assets   The third major asset and cost category consists of nondepreciable operating assets, which are also referred to as permanent capital assets, because they are assumed not to be consumed while the operations of the business are being conducted. Their value is not affected by production activities, and they have no impact on income determination until they are sold or revalued. Accordingly, the matching principle is not applicable to nondepreciable operating assets.

Green, Jr., "A Moral to Direct Costing Controversy," *The Journal of Business* (July 1960), pp. 218–26; C. T. Horngren and G. H. Sorter, "The Effects of Inventory Costing Methods on Full and Direct Costing," *Journal of Accounting Research* (Spring 1965), pp. 63–74; G. J. Staubus, "Direct, Relevant or Absorption Costing?" *The Accounting Review* (January 1963), pp. 64–75.

[38] *Accounting Terminology Bulletin No. 1* (New York: AICPA, 1955), p. 100.

[39] G. A. Welsh, C. T. Zlatkovitch, and J. A. White, *Intermediate Accounting* (Homewood, Ill.: R. D. Irwin, 1976), pp. 547–48.

Costs of Selling and Administration   The costs of selling and administration are all the nonmanufacturing costs necessary to maintain a basic selling and adminis-trative organization. They are treated as period costs in the period in which they are incurred under either the direct or absorption costing method.

The Objectivity Principle

The next principle we shall discuss is known as the **objectivity principle.** The usefulness of financial information depends heavily on the *reliability* of the mea-surement procedure used. Because ensuring maximum reliability is frequently difficult, accountants have employed the principle of objectivity to justify the choice of a measurement or a measurement procedure. The principle of objectiv-ity, however, has been subject to different interpretations:

1. An objective measurement is an "impersonal" measure in the sense that it is free from the personal bias of the measurers. "In other words, objectivity refers to the external reality that is independent of the persons who perceive it.[40]
2. An objective measurement is a verifiable measurement in the sense that it is based on an evidence.[41]
3. An objective measurement is the result of a *"consensus* among a given group of observers or measures."[42] This view also implies that objectivity will depend on the given group of measurers.
4. Finally, the size of the dispersion of the measurement distribution may be used as an indicator of the degree of objectivity of a given measurement system.

Ijiri and Jaedicke used the fourth interpretation of objectivity.[43] Specifically objectivity (V) was defined to be:

$$V = \frac{1}{n} \sum_{i=1}^{n} (x_i - \bar{x})^2$$

where

n = number of measures in the reference group,

x_i = the quantity that the ith measurer reports,

$\bar{x}$ = average of x_i's over all measurers in the reference group.

In other words, between accounting measurement techniques resulting in two measurement distributions, the technique resulting in the smaller variance is

---

[40]Y. Ijiri and R. K. Jaedicke, "Reliability and Objectivity of Accounting Measurements," *The Accounting Review* (July 1966), p. 476.

[41]Paton and Littleton, *An Introduction to Corporate Accounting Standards*, p. 18.

[42]Ijiri and Jaedicke, "Reliability and Objectivity of Accounting Measurements," p. 476.

[43]*Ibid.*, p. 477.

the most objective. This is shown by the following two measurement techniques yielding the same average value.

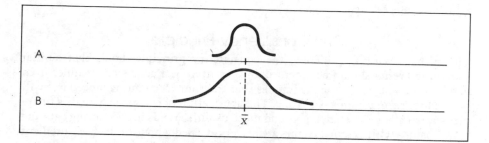

Measurement technique A is more objective than measurement technique B because it has a narrower dispersion of values around the mean. As mentioned earlier, however, objectivity does not measure reliability, which is a more useful concept for accountants. Ijiri and Jaedicke suggests the use of the mean square error as a measure of reliability.[44] Specifically, reliability (R) was defined to be

$$R = \frac{1}{n} \sum_{i=1}^{n} (x_i - x^*)^2,$$

(1)

where $x^* =$ alleged value or

$$R = \frac{1}{n} \sum_{i=1}^{n} (x_i - \bar{x})^2 + (\bar{x} - x^*)^2$$

(2)

From the second expression of reliability, Ijiri and Jaedicke stated that the degree of reliability is equal to the degree of objectivity (first term) plus a "reliance bias" (second term). Notice that the reliance bias is equal to the difference between the mean value and the alleged value of the measurement.

The application of this reliability measure is shown by the following two measurement procedures, which yield different average values although they have similar alleged values:

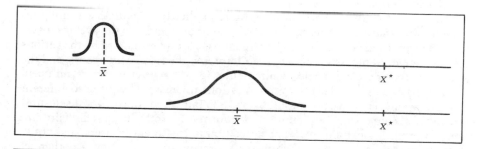

---

[44]*Ibid.*, p. 481.

From the above analysis, we may conclude that the accounting profession ought to find a trade-off between objectivity and bias that leads to acceptable levels of reliability. This is only possible when a consensus exists on the alleged values to be measured.

The Consistency Principle

The fifth accounting principle, the **consistency principle,** holds that similar economic events should be recorded and reported in a consistent manner from period to period. The principle implies that the same accounting procedures will be used for similar items over time. The application of consistency makes financial statements more comparable and more useful. Trends in accounting data and relationships with external factors are better revealed when similar measurement procedures are used. Similarly, distortion of income and balance sheet amounts and possible manipulation of financial statements are avoided by consistency in the use of accounting procedures over time. Therefore, consistency is a user constraint intended to facilitate a user's decision by ensuring comparable presentation of financial statements of a given firm over time, thereby enhancing the statements' utility. Consistency is a major concern of accountants when auditing financial statements. In the standard opinion, the CPA recognizes the consistency principle by noting whether or not the financial statements were prepared in conformity with generally accepted accounting principles applied on a basis "consistent with that of the preceding year."

The consistency principle does not preclude a firm's changing accounting procedures when justified by changing circumstances or if the alternative procedure is preferable (rule of preferability). According to *APB Opinion No. 20,* changes that justify a change in procedure are: (1) a change in accounting principle, (2) a change in accounting estimate, and (3) a change in reporting entity. These changes are to be reflected in the accounts and reported on the financial statements retroactively for a change in accounting entity, prospectively for a change in accounting estimate, and generally, currently for a change in accounting principle.

The Full Disclosure Principle

There is a general consensus in accounting that there should be a "full," "fair," and "adequate" disclosure. **Full disclosure** requires that financial statements be designed and prepared to portray accurately the economic events that affected the firm for the period and to contain information sufficient to make them useful and not misleading to the average investor. More explicitly, the full disclosure principle implies that no information of substance or of interest to the average investor will be omitted or concealed. The principle is further reinforced by the various disclosure requirements set by the *APB Opinions,* the *FASB Statements,* and the *SEC Accounting Releases* and requirements. It is, however, a broad and open-ended construct, which leaves several questions unanswered or open to different interpretations. First, what is meant by "full," "fair," and "adequate" disclosure? "Adequate" connotes a minimum set of information to be disclosed; "fair" implies an ethical constraint dictating an equitable treatment of users; and "full" refers to complete and comprehensive presentation of information. Another accepted position is to view "fairness" as the central objective and trade-off between full and adequate disclosure. Hence, under the heading "Fair Presentation in

Conformity with Generally Accepted Accounting Principles," *APB Statement No. 4* states that fair presentation is met when "a proper balance has been achieved between the conflicting needs to disclose important aspects of financial positions and results of operations in accordance with conventional aspects and to summarize the voluminous underlying data into a limited number of financial statement captions and supporting notes." Second, what are the data that should be disclosed so that a "prudent average investor" will not be misled? Should they be essentially accounting information? Should they include novel information and such additions as human asset accounting, socioeconomic accounting, inflation accounting, and segment reporting? The answers to these questions rest on a proper determination of the users, their needs, their level of sophistication, and, more importantly, their information processing capabilities, given the risks of information overload caused by data expansion. Skinner has drawn attention to some matters that should be the subject of full disclosure:

(a) Details of accounting policies and methods, particularly where judgment is required in the application of an accounting method, the method is peculiar to the reporting entity, or alternative accounting methods could be used;

(b) Additional information to aid in investment analysis or to indicate the rights of various parties having claims upon the reporting entity;

(c) Changes from the preceding year in accounting policies or methods of applying them and the effect of such changes;

(d) Assets and liabilities, costs and revenues arising out of transactions with parties such as controlling interests, or directors or officers, that have a special relationship to the reporting entity;

(e) Contingent assets, liabilities and commitments;

(f) Financial or other nonoperating transactions after the balance sheet date which have a material effect on the financial position shown by the year-end statement.[45]

The Conservatism Principle

The **conservatism principle** is an exception or modifying principle in the sense that it acts as a constraint to the presentation of relevant and reliable accounting data. The conservatism principle holds that when choosing among two or more acceptable accounting techniques, some preference is shown for the option that has the least favorable impact on stockholders' equity. More specifically, it implies that the lowest values of assets and revenues and the highest values of liabilities and expenses preferably should be reported. The conservatism principle, therefore, dictates a general pessimistic attitude from the accountant when choosing accounting techniques for financial reporting. To accomplish the objectives of understating current income and assets, the conservatism principle may lead to treatments that constitute a departure from acceptable or theoretical treatment. For example, the adoption of the "lower of cost or market" concept conflicts with the historical principle. Although LIFO and accelerated depreciation are generally perceived as counterinflationary measures, they may be viewed as resulting from the adoption of the conservatism principle. Thus, Chatfield maintains that:

---

[45]Skinner, *Accounting Principles*, p. 234.

Both [LIFO and accelerated depreciation] reinforced an older tradition of balance sheet conservatism, so much so that taxpayers are still not allowed to use LIFO together with lower of cost or market inventory valuation. Both gave precedence to management's need for cash retention and asset replacement, even at the expense of the accountant's desire for more precise asset valuation.[46]

Conservatism has been used in the past as a way of dealing with uncertainty in the environment, the possible overoptimism of managers and owners, and also as a way of protecting creditors against an unwarranted distribution of the firm's assets as dividends. Conservatism was a more highly esteemed virutue in the past than today. It led to arbitrary and inconsistent treatment in the form of rapid asset write-offs or creation of excessive provisions for liabiities or both.

Sterling calls conservatism "the most ancient and probably the most pervasive principle of accounting valuation."[47] Today, the emphasis on objective and fair presentation and the primacy of the investor as user has lessened the reliance on conservatism. It is perceived more as a guide for extraordinary situations than as a general rigid rule to apply in all circumstances. Conservatism is still applied in some situations that require an accountant's judgment, such as choosing the estimated useful life and residual value of an asset for depreciation accounting and the corollary rule of applying "lower of cost or market" in valuing inventories and marketable equity securities. Because it is essentially the manifestation of the accountant's intervention that may result in the introduction of bias, errors, possible distortions, and misleading statements, the present view of conservatism is bound to disappear as an accounting principle.

The Materiality Principle

Like conservatism, the **materiality principle** is an exception or modifying principle. The principle holds that transactions and events having an insignificant economic effect may be handled in the most expeditious manner, whether or not in conformity with generally accepted accounting principles, and need not be disclosed. Materiality is an implicit guide for the accountant in deciding what should be disclosed in the financial reports. The accountant may decide, therefore, what is not important or what does not matter on the basis of record-keeping cost, accuracy of financial statements, and relevance to the user.

In general, the accounting bodies have left the application of materiality to the accountant's judgment, while at the same time stressing its importance. According to *APB Statement No. 4*, materiality implies that "financial reporting is only concerned with information that is significant enough to affect evaluations or decisions."[48] *APB Opinion No. 30* relied on an undefined concept of materiality to describe extraordinary items. Similarly, *APB Opinion No. 22* recommended the disclosure of all the policies or principles that materially affect the financial position, results of operations, and changes in the financial position. More re-

---

[46]M. Chatfield, *A History of Accounting Thought* (New York: The Dryden Press, 1974), p. 244.

[47]R. R. Sterling, "Conservatism: The Fundamental Principle of Valuation in Traditional Accounting," *Abacus* (December 1967), p. 110.

[48]*APB Statement No. 4*, p. 48.

cently, the FASB issued a *Discussion Memorandum* on the materiality issue, indicating the importance of this principle.[49]

The materiality principle lacks an operational definition. Most definitions of materiality stress the accountant's role in interpreting what is and what is not material. For example, Frishkoff defines materiality as the "relative, quantitative importance of some piece of financial information, to a user, in the context of a decision to be made."[50]

A recent study by the Accountants' International Study Group characterizes materiality as follows:

> Materiality is essentially a matter of professional judgment. An individual item should be judged material if the knowledge of that item could reasonably be deemed to have influence on the users of the financial statements.[51]

Guidelines or criteria to be used in determining materiality are urgently needed. Two basic criteria have been recommended. The first, referred to as the *size approach*, relates the size of the item to another relevant variable such as net income. For example, Berstein suggests a border zone of 10–15 percent of net income after taxes as the point of distinction between what is and what is not material.[52] Similarly, the *FASB Discussion Memorandum* on materiality suggested criteria based on the size approach, as follows:

> If the amount of its current or potential effect equals or exceeds 10 percent of a pertinent financial statement amount, the matter should be presumed to be material.

> If its amount or current or potential effect is between 5 and 10 percent of a pertinent financial statement amount, the materiality of the matter depends on the surrounding circumstances.[53]

The second criterion, referred to as the *change criterion approach*, evaluates the impact of an item on trends or changes between periods. This approach is advocated primarily by Rappaport, who contends that materiality criteria can be stated in terms of financial averages, trends, and ratios that express significant analytic relationships for accounting information.[54] The change criterion approach influenced the Accountants' International Study Group, as shown by the following exerpt from *Materiality in Accounting*:

> An amount is not material solely by reason of its size; other factors including those set out below must be considered in making decisions as to materiality:

---

[49]*APB Opinion No. 30*, "Reporting the Results of Operations" (New York: AICPA, 1973), para. 24; *APB Opinion No. 22*, "Disclosure of Accounting Policies" (New York: AICPA, 1972), para. 12; *FASB Discussion Memorandum*, "An Analysis of Issues Related to Criteria for Determining Materiality" (Stamford, Conn.: FASB, March 21, 1975).

[50]P. Frishkoff, "An Empirical Investigation of the Concept of Materiality in Accounting," *Empirical Research in Accounting: Selected Studies, 1970, Journal of Accounting Research*, p. 116.

[51]Accountants' International Study Group, *Materiality in Accounting* (1974), p. 30.

[52]L. A. Berstein, "The Concept of Materiality," *The Accounting Review* (January 1967), p. 93.

[53]*FASB Discussion Memorandum*, p. 50.

[54]D. Rappaport, "Materiality," *The Journal of Accountancy* (April 1964), p. 48.

A. The nature of the item, i.e., whether it is:
    (1) a factor entering into the determination of net income
    (2) unusual or extraordinary
    (3) contingent upon an event or condition
    (4) determinable based upon existing facts and circumstances
    (5) required by statute or regulation.

B. The amount itself, in relation to:
    (1) the financial statements taken as a whole
    (2) the total of the accounts of which it forms, or should form, a part
    (3) related items
    (4) the corresponding amount in previous years or the expected amount in future years.[55]

The Uniformity and Comparability Principles

While the consistency principle refers to the use of the same procedures for related items by a given firm over time, the **uniformity principle** refers to the use of the same procedures by different firms. The desired objective is to reach comparability of financial statements by reducing the diversity created by the use of different accounting procedures by different firms. In fact, a constant debate has taken place over whether flexibility or uniformity should prevail in accounting and financial reporting.

The principal supports for uniformity are claims that: (1) it would reduce the diversity in the use of accounting procedures and the inadequacies and "horror stories" of accounting practices; (2) it would allow meaningful comparisons of the financial statements of different firms; (3) it would restore the confidence of users in the financial statements; and (4) it would lead to government intervention and regulation of accounting practice. The main supports for flexibility are the claims that: (1) uniformity in the use of accounting procedures for the same item occurring in many cases runs the risk of concealing important differences among cases; (2) comparability is a utopian goal; "it cannot be achieved by the adoption of firm rules that do not take adequate account of different factual situations";[56] and (3) "differences in circumstances" or "circumstantial variables" call for different treatments so that corporate reporting can respond to circumstances in which transactions and events occur. The circumstantial variables were defined as

> environmental conditions which vary among companies and which influence (1) the feasibility of accounting methods and/or (2) the objectivity of the measures resulting from applying the accounting methods.[57]

The implicit objective of both uniformity and flexibility is to protect the user and present the user with meaningful data. Both fail because of their extreme positions on the issue of financial reporting. Uniformity per se does not lead to comparability—an admittedly unfeasible goal. Flexibility evidently leads to confusion and mistrust. A trade-off solution may be provided by encouraging unifor-

---

[55] *Materiality in Accounting*, p. 30.

[56] T. F. Keller, "Uniformity versus Flexibility: A Review of the Rhetoric," *Law and Contemporary Problems* (Autumn 1965), p. 637.

[57] G. M. Cadenhead, "Differences in Circumstances: Fact or Fantasy?" *Abacus* (September 1970), p. 72.

mity by narrowing the diversity of accounting practices and, at the same time, allowing a proper recognition of market and economic events peculiar to a given firm and a given industry by a proper association of certain economic circumstances with related accounting techniques. This middle position calls for an operational definition of "differences in circumstances" and better guidelines for relating differences in circumstances to various accounting procedures.[58]

Conclusions

Existing accounting rules and techniques are based on foundations of accounting theory. These foundations are composed of hierarchial elements that function as a frame of reference or theoretical structure. In this chapter, we have viewed the formulation of such theoretical structure as a deductive interactive process consisting of the successive formulation of the objectives, the postulates, the concepts, the principles, and the techniques of accounting. An understanding of these elements and relationships of accounting theory guarantees understanding the rationale behind actual and future practices. The financial statements presented in the formal accounting reports are merely a reflection of the application of the theoretical structure of accounting. Improving the content and format of financial statements is definitely linked to improving the theoretical structure of accounting. Foremost on the agenda of accounting bodies should be the formulation of the elements of accounting theory, namely the objectives of accounting, the environmental postulates, the theoretical concepts, and the principles.

References

Postulates, Concepts, and Principles

American Accounting Association. *A Statement of Basic Accounting Theory.* New York: AAA, 1966.

Burton, John C. "Some General and Specific Thoughts on the Accounting Environment." *Journal of Accountancy* (October 1973), pp. 40–46.

Byrne, Gilbert R. "To What Extent Can the Practice of Accounting Be Reduced to Rules and Standards?" *Journal of Accountancy* (November 1937), pp. 364–79.

Chambers, R. J. "The Anguish of Accountants." *Journal of Accountancy* (March 1972), pp. 68–74.

Deinzer, Harvey T. *Development of Accounting Thought.* New York: Holt, Rinehart, & Winston, 1965, Chapters 8 and 9.

Grady, Paul. "Inventory of Generally Accepted Accounting Principles in the United States of America." *The Accounting Review* (January 1965), pp. 21–30.

Hicks, Ernest L. "APB: The First 3600 Days." *Journal of Accountancy* (September 1969), pp. 56–60.

Higgins, Tomas S., and Herman Bevis. "Generally Accepted Accounting Prin-

---

[58]J. F. Dewhirst, "Is Accounting Too Principled?" *The Canadian Chartered Accountant Magazine* (July 1976), pp. 44–49.

ciples—Their Definition and Authority." *The New York Certified Public Accountant* (February 1964), pp. 93–94.

Horngren, Charles T. "Accounting Principles: Private or Public Sector?" *Journal of Accountancy* (May 1972), pp. 37–41.

Husband, G. R. "The Entity Concept in Accounting." *The Accounting Review* (October 1954), pp. 560–62.

Lambert, Samuel Joseph, III. "Basic Assumptions in Accounting Theory Construction." *Journal of Accountancy* (February 1974), pp. 41–48.

Lorig, A. N. "Some Basic Concepts of Accounting and Their Implications." *The Accounting Review* (July 1964), pp. 563–73.

Mautz, Robert K. "The Place of Postulates in Accounting." *Journal of Accountancy* (January 1965), pp. 46–49.

May, George O. "Generally Accepted Principles of Accounting." *Journal of Accountancy* (January 1958), p. 26.

Metcalf, Richard W. "The Basic Postulates in Perspective." *The Accounting Review* (January 1964), pp. 16–21.

Popoff, Boris. "Postulates, Principles and Rules." *Accounting and Business Research* (Summer 1972), pp. 182–93.

Staubus, G. J. "The Residual Equity Point of View in Accounting." *The Accounting Review* (January 1959), pp. 11–15.

Storey, Reed K. *The Search for Accounting Principles—Today's Problems in Perspective.* New York: AICPA, 1964.

Vatter, W. J. *The Fund Theory of Accounting and Its Implications for Financial Reports.* Chicago: The University of Chicago Press, 1947.

Zeff, Stephen A. *Forging Accounting Principles in Five Countries: A History and an Analysis of Trends.* Champaign, Ill.: Stipes Publishing Co., 1971.

Going Concern

Devine, C. T. "Entity, Continuity, Discount, and Exit Values." *Essays in Accounting Theory*, 3 (1971), pp. 111–35.

Fremgen, J. M. "The Going Concern Assumption: A Critical Appraisal." *The Accounting Review* (October 1968), pp. 649–56.

Sterling, R. R. "The Going Concern: An Examination." *The Accounting Review* (July 1968), pp. 481–502.

Storey, R. K. "Revenue Realization, Going Concern and Measurement of Income." *The Accounting Review* (April 1959), pp. 232–38.

Van Seventer, A. "The Continuity Postulate in the Dutch Theory of Business Income." *International Journal of Accounting, Education and Research* (Spring 1969), pp. 1–19.

Yu, S. C. "A Reexamination of the Going Concern Postulate." *International Journal of Accounting, Education and Research* (Spring 1971), pp. 37–58.

Revenue Principle

AAA Committee on Concepts and Standards Research Study. "The Realization Concept." *The Accounting Review* (April 1965), pp. 312–22.

Arnett, H. E. "Recognition as a Function of Measurement in the Realization Concept." *The Accounting Review* (October 1963), pp. 733–41.

Horngren, C. T. "How Should We Interpret the Realization Concept?" *The Accounting Review* (April 1965), pp. 323–33.

Myers, J. H. "The Critical Event and the Recognition of Net Profit." *The Accounting Review* (October 1959), pp. 528–32.

Staubus, G. J. "Revenue and Revenue Accounts." *The Accounting Review* (July 1956), pp. 284–94.

Matching Principle

Fekrat, A. M. "The Conceptual Foundations of Absorption Costing." *The Accounting Review* (April 1972), pp. 351–55.

Fremgen, J. M. "The Direct Costing Controversary: An Indentification of Issues." *The Accounting Review* (January 1964), pp. 43–51.

Green, David, Jr. "A Moral to Direct Costing Controversy?" *Journal of Business* (July 1960), pp. 218–26.

Horngren, Charles T., and George H. Sorter. "The Effects of Inventory Costing Methods on Full and Direct Costing." *Journal of Accounting Research* (Spring 1965), pp. 63–74.

Staubus, G. J. "Direct, Relevant or Absorption Costing." *The Accounting Review* (January 1963), pp. 64–75.

Materiality

Barlev, B. "On the Measurement of Materiality." *Accounting and Business Research* (Summer 1972), pp. 194–97.

Barnes, D. P. "Materiality—An Illusive Concept." *Management Accounting* (October 1976), pp. 19–20.

Berstein, L. "The Concept of Materiality." *The Accounting Review* (January 1967), pp. 86–95.

FASB Discussion Memorandum, "An Analysis of Issues Related to Criteria for Determining Materiality." Stamford, Conn.: FASB, March 21, 1975.

FASB. *An Analysis of Issues Related to Criteria for Determining Materiality* Stamford, Conn.: FASB, March 22, 1975.

Frishkoff, P. "An Empirical Investigation of the Concept of Materiality in Accounting." *Empirical Research in Accounting: Selected Studies, 1970, Journal of Accounting Research,* pp. 138–53.

Hicks, E. L. "Some Comments on Materiality." *The Arthur Young Journal* (April 1958), pp. 15–18.

Holmes, W. "Materiality—Through the Looking Glass." *Journal of Accountancy* (February 1972), pp. 44–49.

Leitch, R. A., and J. R. Williams. "Materiality in Financial Statement Disclosure." *The Canadian Chartered Accountant Magazine* (December 1975/January 1976), pp. 53–58.

Rappaport, D. "Materiality." *Journal of Accountancy* (April 1964), pp. 45–52.

Rose, J., W. Beaver, and G. Sorter. "Toward an Empirical Measure of Materiality." *Empirical Research in Accounting: Selected Studies, 1970, Journal of Accounting Research,* pp. 138–53.

Woolsey, S. "Approach to Solving the Materiality Problem." *Journal of Accountancy* (March 1973), pp. 47–50.

Woolsey, S. "Materiality Survey." *Journal of Accountancy* (September 1973), pp. 91–92.

Conservatism

Devine, C. T. "The Rule of Conservatism Reexamined." *Journal of Accounting Research* (Autumn 1963), pp. 137–38.

Landry, M. "Le Conservatism en Compatabilite—Essai d'Explication." *The Canadian Chartered Accountant Magazine* (November 1970), pp. 321–24 and (January 1970), pp. 44–49.

Sterling, R. R. "Conservatism: The Fundamental Principle of Valuation in Traditional Accounting." *Abacus* (December 1967), p. 110.

Reliability, Objectivity, Freedom from Bias

Arnett, H. E. "What Does Objectivity Mean to Accountants?" *Journal of Accountancy* (May 1961), pp. 65–70.

Ijiri, Y., and R. K. Jaedicke. "Reliability and Objectivity of Accounting Measurements." *The Accounting Review* (July 1966), pp. 474–83.

McFarland, W. B. "Concept of Objectivity." *Journal of Accountancy* (September 1961), pp. 25–32.

Murphy, G. J. "A Numerical Representation of Some Accounting Conventions." *The Accounting Review* (April 1976), pp. 277–86.

Consistency, Uniformity, and Comparability Principles

Bedford, Norton, and Iino Toshio. "Consistency Reexamined." *The Accounting Review* (July 1968), pp. 453–58.

Cadenhead, Gary M. "Differences in Circumstances: Fact or Fantasy." *Abacus* (September 1970), pp. 71–80.

Chasteen, Lanny G. "An Empirical Study of Differences in Economic Circumstances as a Justification for Alternative Inventory Pricing Methods." *The Accounting Review* (July 1971), pp. 504–8.

Frishkoff, Payl. "Consistency in Auditing and APB Opinion No. 20." *Journal of Accountancy* (August 1972), pp. 64–70.

Hendriksen, Eldon S. "Toward Greater Comparability through Uniformity of Accounting Principles." *CPA Journal* (February 1967), pp. 105–15.

Keller, Thomas F. "Uniformity versus Flexibility: A Review of the Rhetoric." *Law and Contemporary Problems* (Autumn 1965), pp. 637–51.

Mautz, Robert K. "An Approach to the Uniformity-Flexibility Issues in Accounting." *Financial Executive* (February 1971), pp. 14–19.

Revsine, Lawrence. "Toward Greater Comparability in Accounting Reports." *Financial Analysts Journal* (January–February 1975). pp. 45–51.

Simmons, John K. "A Concept of Comparability in Financial Reporting." *The Accounting Review* (October 1967), pp. 680–92.

Sterling, Robert R. "A Test of the Uniformity Hypotheses." *Abacus* (September 1969), pp. 37–47.

Questions

4–1 Define the structure of accounting theory.

4–2 Explain briefly the following elements of the structure of accounting theory:

a. accounting objectives
b. accounting postulates
c. accounting theoretical concepts
d. accounting principles
e. accounting techniques

4–3 Name the three accounting theoretical concepts and briefly explain each.

4–4 Name the four accounting postulates and briefly explain each.

4–5 Name the nine accounting principles and briefly explain each.

4–6 What are the primary sources of accounting techniques?

4–7 What is meant by the term "generally accepted accounting principles"?

4–8 Professor R. R. Sterling made the following statement in "The Going Concern: An Examination," in *The Accounting Review* (July 1968), p. 481:

> Thus, the going concern is one of the most important concepts in accounting. Such status would lead one to believe that the concept would be well defined, its necessity as an axiom thoroughly discussed, and its connection to historical cost demonstrated. Anyone with such expectations is due for disappointment.

Do you agree with Professon Sterling's statement? Why or why not?

4–9 Professor L. A. Berstein made the following statement in "The Concept of Materiality," in *The Accounting Review* (January 1967), p. 90:

> In a profession where objectivity is a consideration of cardinal importance, materiality seems to be its "Achilles' Heel." If materiality is really such an important concept, and it certainly does play a dominant role in a number of pronouncements, then how is the profession to attain any semblance of consistent or uniform treatment in this area? How are new entrants to the profession to be trained? What are they to be told about the judgment processes leading up to materiality decisions?

Suggest some solutions to these questions.

4–10 As the CPA responsible for an "opinion" audit engagement, you are requested by the client to organize the work to provide him at the earliest possible date with some key ratios based on the final figures appearing on the comparative financial statements. This information is to be used to convince creditors that the client business is solvent and to support the use of going concern valuation procedures in the financial statements. The client wishes to save time by concentrating on only these key data.

The data requested and the computations taken from the financial statements are:

	Last Year	This Year
Current ratio	2.0:1	2.5:1
Quick (acid-test) ratio	1.2:1	0.7:1
Property, plant, and equipment to owners' equity	2.3:1	2.6:1
Sales to owners' equity	2.8:1	2.5:1
Net income	Down 10%	Up 30%
Earnings per common share	$2.40	$3.12
Book value per common share	Up 8%	Up 5%

Required:

a. The client asks that you prepare a list of brief comments stating how each of these items supports the solvency and going concern potential of his business. He wishes to use your comments to support the presentation of data to his creditors. Prepare the comments as requested, giving the implications and the limitations of each item separately and then the collective inference one may draw from them about the client's solvency and going concern potential.

b. Prepare a brief listing of additional ratio-analysis data for this client that you think his creditors are going to ask for to supplement the data provided in part a. Explain why you think the additional data will be helpful to these creditors in evaluating the client's solvency.

c. What warnings should you offer creditors about the limitations of ratio analysis for the purpose stated here?

(AICPA adapted)

4–11. The concept of the accounting entity often is considered to be the most fundamental of accounting concepts, one that pervades all of accounting.

a. (1) What is an accounting entity? Explain.
   (2) Why is the accounting entity concept so fundamental that it pervades all of accounting?

b. For each of the following, indicate whether or not the accounting concept of entity is applicable; discuss and give illustrations.
   (1) a unit created by or under law
   (2) the product-line segment of an enterprise
   (3) a combination of legal units and product-line segments
   (4) all the activities of an owner or a group of owners
   (5) an industry
   (6) the economy of the United States

(AICPA adapted)

4–12 After the auditor's report on the examination of the financial statements is presented to the board of directors of the Savage Publishing Company, one of the new directors is surprised that the income statement assumes that an equal proportion of the revenue is earned with the publication of every issue of the company's magazine. The director feels that the "crucial event," that is, the most difficult task, in the process of earning revenues in the magazine business is the cash sale of subscriptions. He does not understand why, other than for the smoothing of income, most revenue cannot be "realized" in the period of the sale.

Discuss the propriety of timing the recognition of revenue in the Savage Publishing Company's account with:

a. the cash sale of the magazine subscription.

b. the publication of the magazine every month.

c. both events, by recognizing a portion of the revenue with the cash sale of the magazine subscription and a portion of the revenue with the publication of the magazine every month.

(AICPA adapted)

4–13 Revenue is usually recognized at the point of sale. Under special circumstances, however, bases other than the point of sale are used for the timing of revenue recognition.

Disregarding the special circumstances when bases other than the point of sale are used, discuss the merits of each of the following objections to the sales basis of revenue recognition:

a. It is too conservative because revenue is earned throughout the entire process of productions.

b. It is not conservative enough because accounts receivable do not represent disposable funds; sales returns and allowances may be made; and collection and doubtful account expenses may be incurred in a later period.

(AICPA adapted)

4–14 On May 5, 19X1, Sterling Corporation signed a contract with Stony Associates under which Stony agreed (1) to construct an office building on land owned by Sterling, (2) to accept responsibility for procuring financing for the project and finding tenants, and (3) to manage the property for 50 years. The annual profit from the project, after debt service, was to be divided equally between Sterling Corporation and Stony Associates. Stony was to accept its share of future profits as full payment for its services in construction, obtaining finances and tenants, and management of the project.

By April 30, 19X2, the project was nearly completed and tenants had signed leases to occupy 90 percent of the available space at annual rentals aggregating $2,600,000. It is estimated that, after operating expenses and debt service, the annual profit will amount to $850,000. The management of Stony Associates believed that the economic benefit derived from the contract with Sterling should be reflected on its financial statements for the fiscal year ended April 30, 19X2, and directed that revenue be accrued in an amount equal to the commercial value of the services Stony had rendered during the year, that this amount be carried in contracts receivable, and that all related expenditures be charged against the revenue.

Required:

a. Explain and justify why revenue is often recognized as earned at the time of sale.

b. In what situations would it be appropriate to apply the accretion concept (recognizing revenue as the productive activity takes place or as values increase)?

c. At what times, other than those in parts a and b, above, may it be appropriate to recognize revenue? Explain.

(AICPA adapted)

4–15 A business enterprise recognizes the earning of revenue for accounting purposes when the transaction is recorded. In some situations, revenue is recognized approximately as it is earned in the economic sense. In other situations, however, accountants have developed guidelines for recognizing revenue by other criteria, such as the point of sale.

Required:

a. Explain and justify why revenue is often recognized as earned at the time of sale.

b. In what situations would it be appropriate to apply the accretion concept (recognizing revenue as the productive activity takes place or as values increase)?

c. At what times, other than those in parts (a) and (b), above, may it be appropriate to recognize revenue? Explain.

(AICPA adapted)

4–16 You are engaged in the audit of the Smith Corporation, which opened its first branch office in 1974. During the audit, the president of Smith raises the question of the accounting treatment of the operating loss of the branch office for its first year, which is material in amount.

The president proposes to capitalize the operating loss as a "starting-up" expense to be amortized over a five-year period. He states that branch offices of other firms engaged in the same field generally suffer a first-year operating loss that is invariably capitalized, and you are aware of this practice. He argues, therefore, that the loss should be capitalized so that the accounting will be "conservative"; further, he argues that the accounting must be "consistent" with established industry practice.

Required:
Discuss the president's use of the words "conservative" and "consistent" from the standpoint of accounting terminology. What accounting treatment would you recommend and why?

(AICPA adapted)

4–17 An accountant must be familiar with the concepts involved in determining earnings of a business entity. The amount of earnings reported for a business entity depends on the proper recognition, in general, of revenue and expense for a given time period. In some situations, costs are recognized as expenses at the time of product sale; in other situations, guidelines have been developed for recognizing costs as expenses or losses by other criteria.

Required:
a. Explain the rationale for recognizing costs as expenses at the time of product sale.
b. What is the rationale for treating costs as expenses of a period, instead of assigning the cost to an asset? Explain.
c. In what general circumstance would it be appropriate to treat a cost as an asset instead of as an expense? Explain.
d. Some expenses are assigned to specific accounting periods on the basis of systematic and rational allocation of asset cost. Explain rationale for this procedure.
e. Under what conditions would it be appropriate to treat a cost as a loss?

(AICPA adapted)

4–18 Current accounting theory is based on the assumption that the "value of money" is relatively stable. If there is a significant change in the price level or in the purchasing power of the dollar, problems arise in interpreting income data determined under conventional accounting procedures.

Required:
State and explain briefly the nature of such problems as they concern inventories and fixed assets. You need not attempt to offer specific solutions to these problems.

(AICPA adapted)

4–19 In auditing a corporation, you find certain liabilities, such as taxes, which appear to be overstated. Also, some partially obsolete inventory items seem to be undervalued, and the tendency is to expense rather than to capitalize as many items as possible.

In talking with management about the policies, you are told that "the company has always taken a very conservative view of the business and its future prospects." The managers suggest that they do not wish to weaken the company by reporting any more earnings or paying any more dividends than are absolutely necessary, since they do not expect business to continue to be good. They point out that the undervaluation of assets, for example, does not lose anything for the company and creates reserves for "hard times."

Required:

Discuss fully whether the policies followed by the company are appropriate and comment on each of the arguments presented by management.

(AICPA adapted)

4–20 What is your understanding of the meaning of consistency in the application of accounting principles, for example, as used in the standard form of an independent public accountant's report?

(AIPCA adapted)

4–21 Accountants frequently refer to a concept of "conservatism." What is meant by conservatism in accounting? To what extent is it possible to follow accounting procedures that will result in consistently conservative financial statements over a considerable number of years? Give an example of an application of conservatism in accounting.

(AICPA adapted)

4–22 The general manager of the Cumberland Manufacturing Company received from the controller an income statement, which covered the calendar year. The general manager said to the controller, "This statement indicates that a net income of only $100,000 was earned last year. You know the value of the company is much more than it was this time last year."

"You're probably right," replied the controller. "You see, there are factors in accounting that sometimes keep reported operating results from reflecting the change in the fair market value of the company."

Required:

Present a detailed explanation of the accounting theories and principles to which the controller referred.

(AICPA adapted)

4–23 The general ledger of Enter-tane, Inc., a corporation engaged in the development and production of television programs for commercial sponsorship, contains the following accounts before amortization at the end of the current year:

Account	Balance (debit)
Sealing Wax and Kings	$51,000
The Messenger	36,000
The Desperado	17,500
Shin Bone	8,000
Studio Rearrangement	5,000

An examination of contracts and records revealed the following information:

(1) The first two accounts listed above represent the total cost of completed programs that were televised during the accounting period just ended. Under the terms of an existing contract, "Sealing Wax and Kings" will be rerun during the next accounting period at a fee equal to 50 percent of the fee for the first televising of the program. The contract for the first run produced $300,000 of revenue. The contract with the sponsor of "The Messenger" provides that at the sponsor's option, the program can be rerun during the next season at 75 percent of the fee on the first televising of the program.

(2) The balance in "The Desparado" account is the cost of a new program that has just been completed and is being considered by several companies for commercial sponsorship.

(3) The balance in the "Shin Bone" account represents the cost of a partially completed program for a projected series that has been abandoned.

(4) The balance of the Studio Rearrangement account consists of payments made to a firm of engineers that prepared a report concerning the more efficient use of existing studio space and equipment.

Required:

a. State the general principle (or principles) of accounting applicable to the first four accounts.

b. How would you report each of the first four accounts in the financial statements of Enter-tane, Inc.? Explain.

c. In what way, if at all, does the Studio Rearrangement account differ from the first four? Explain.

(AICPA adapted)

4–24 At the completion of the Smith Store audit, the president asks about the meaning of the phrase "in conformity with generally accepted accounting principles" that appears in your audit report on the management's financial statements. He observes that the meaning of the phrase must include more than what he thinks of as "principles."

Required:

a. Explain the meaning of the term "accounting principles" as used in the audit report.

b. The president wants to know how you determine whether or not an accounting principle is generally accepted. Discuss the sources of evidence for determining whether an accounting principle has substantial authoritative support.

c. The president believes that diversity in accounting practice always will exist among independent entities despite continual improvements in comparability. Discuss the arguments that support his belief.

(AICPA adapted)

4–25 Select the best answer for each of the following items.

(1) Determining periodic earnings and financial position depends on measuring economic resources and obligations and changes in them as these changes occur. This explanation pertains to

a. disclosure
b. accrual accounting
c. materiality
d. the matching concept

(2) Lower-of-cost-or-market accounting is an example of which concept?
   a. consistency
   b. conservatism
   c. realization
   d. matching

(3) Which of the following is not a theoretical basis for the allocation of expenses?
   a. systematic allocation
   b. cause and effect
   c. profit maximization
   d. immediate recognition

(4) The concept of objectivity is complied with when an accounting transaction occurs that
   a. involves an arm's length transaction between two independent interests
   b. furthers the objectives of the company
   c. is promptly recorded in a fixed amount of dollars
   d. allocates revenues or expense items in a rational and systematic manner

(5) Which accounting concept justifies the use of accruals and deferrals?
   a. going concern
   b. materiality
   c. consistency
   d. stable monetary unit

(6) What is the underlying concept supporting the immediate recognition of a loss?
   a. matching
   b. consistency
   c. judgment
   d. conservatism

(7) An accrued expense can best be described as an amount
   a. paid and currently matched with earnings
   b. paid and not currently matched with earnings
   c. not paid and not currently matched with earnings
   d. not paid and currently matched with earnings

(8) Which of the following principles best describes the conceptual rationale for the methods of matching depreciation expense with revenues?
   a. associating cause and effect
   b. systematic and rational allocation
   c. immediate recognition
   d. partial recognition

(9) What is the basic difference between direct costing and absorption costing?
   a. Direct costing always produces less taxable earnings than absorption costing.
   b. Direct closing recognizes fixed costs as a period cost and absorption costing recognizes fixed costs as a product cost.
   c. Direct costing cannot use standards, whereas standards may be

used with absorption costing.

    d. Direct costing may be used only in situations in which production is essentially homogeneous but absorption costing may be used under any manufacturing condition.

(10) What factor, related to manufacturing costs, causes the difference in net earnings computed using absorption costing and net earnings computed using direct costing?

    a. Absorption costing considers all costs in the determination of net earnings, whereas direct costing considers only direct costs.

    b. Absorption costing "inventories" all direct costs for the period in ending finished goods inventory, but direct costing considers direct costs to be period costs.

    c. Absorption costing "inventories" all fixed costs for the period in ending finished goods inventory, but direct costing expenses all fixed costs.

    d. Absorption costing allocates fixed costs between cost of goods sold and inventories, and direct costing considers all fixed costs to be period costs.

(11) Why is direct costing not in accordance with generally accepted accounting principles?

    a. Fixed manufacturing costs are assumed to be period costs.

    b. Direct costing procedures are not well known in industry.

    c. Net earnings are always overstated when using direct costing procedures.

    d. Direct costing ignores the concept of lower of cost or market when valuing inventory.

(AICPA adapted)

4–26 The following problem consists of 22 alternatives disclosures or treatments. For each case, specify whether the treatment is supported by the proprietary theory or the entity theory.

(1) A company maintains a qualified pension plan. In prior years, the related pension provision has been included in the determination of corporate net income. In accounting for the costs related to qualified pension plans, ignore pension-related activities in the accounts of the company that maintains the pension plan.

(2) For the same situation as described in (1), record pension-related activities in the accounts of the company that maintains the pension plan.

(3) Report earnings per share in external financial statements.

(4) Do not report earnings per share in external financial statements.

(5) Report income tax payments as distribution of income (that is, not included in the determination of net income).

(6) Report income tax payments as expenses in the determination of net income.

(7) Two autonomous and independent entities effect a plan of business combination in which the voting equity securities are exchanged for substantially all the common stock interests of each of the combining companies. The surviving company does not plan to dispose of a substantial part of the assets of the formerly separate companies with-

in the next several years. Account for this combination as a purchase.

(8)   Account for the combination described in (7) as a pooling of interests.

(9)   A parent company holds all the outstanding voting equity securities of another company. The products of each company are homogeneous and it is reasonably anticipated that the parent company will maintain continuity of control over the other company. The treatment is not to combine the accounts of the two companies.

(10) Combine the accounts of the two companies described in (9).

(11) An investor company purchases 25 percent of the outstanding voting equity securities of another company, the investee. The investor has the ability to exercise significant influence over the investee. In accounting for the income or loss of an investee in the accounts of the investor, record an appropriate amount of the investee's income or loss in the accounts of the investor.

(12) For the situation described in (11), ignore the investee's income or loss in the accounts of the investor.

(13) A company issues convertible debt securities that can be converted by the holder into voting equity securities at a specified price. Attached to the convertible securities are detachable warrants that may be traded separtely from the debt instrument. In accounting for the proceeds from the sale of convertible debt securities that have detachable stock purchase warrants, assign all the proceeds to debt.

(14) For the situation described in (13), allocate the proceeds to debt and equity.

(15) A company issues a stock dividend to common shareholders. The stock dividend is in an amount equal to the par value of the related common shares. In determining whether stock dividends at par represent net income to recipients, do not treat stock dividend at par as income to recipients.

(16) For the situation described in (15), treat stock dividends at par as income to recipients.

(17) No special standards of financial accounting and reporting should be applied to development-stage companies.

(18) Special standards of financial accounting and reporting should be applied to development-stage companies.

(19) A company has sustained heavy losses over a period of time resulting in a significant deficit in Retained Earnings. Furthermore, the carrying values of certain assets are significantly overstated. In accounting for quasi-reorganizations, effect the quasi-reorganization.

(20) For the situation described in (19), do not effect the quasi-reorganization.

(21) A company reports its inventory or stock-in-trade at cost or market, whichever is lower. Departures from historical cost to reflect inventory prices in excess of historical cost dictates to report inventory at the lower of cost or market.

(22) For the situation described in (21), report inventory at current values. (Adapted from an article by David N. Ricchiute, "Standard Setting and the Entity-Proprietary Debate," *Accounting, Organizations and Society* [January 1980], pp. 67–76.)

chapter five

Current-Value Accounting

Relevance
of the Income Concept

The Traditional
Accounting Concept of Income

A Description of Accounting Income
Advantages of Accounting Income
Disadvantages of Accounting Income

The Nature
of the Economic Concept of Income

Concepts
of Capital Maintenance

Concepts
of Current Value

Capitalization
Current Entry Price
Current Exit Price
Other Notions of Current Values

Conclusions

References

Questions

The theory and measurement of **business income** occupy a central place in the literature of financial and managerial accounting. Despite the proliferation of articles on its merits and measurement methods, however, the income concept remains the subject of different interpretations and schools of thought, each claiming practical or conceptual superiority to the others. Basically, four schools of thought exist concerning the better measurement of business income.

The **classical school** is characterized primarily by adherence to the unit of measure postulate and the historical cost principle. Generally known as "historical cost accounting" or "conventional accounting," the classical school regards "accounting income" as business income.

The **neoclassical school** is characterized primarily by its abandonment of the unit of measure postulate, the recognition of the changes in the general price level, and adherence to the historical cost principle. Generally known as "general price-level adjusted historical cost accounting," the neoclassical school's concept of business income is the "general price-level adjusted accounting income."

The **radical school** is characterized by its choice of current value as the valuation base. This school takes two forms. In one form, the current-value–based financial statements are not adjusted for changes in the general price level. Generally known as "current-value accounting," this school's concept of business income is "current income." In the second form of the radical school, the current-value–based financial statements are adjusted for changes in the general price level. Generally known as "general price-level adjusted current-value accounting," this school uses "adjusted current income" as its concept of income.

In this chapter, our purpose is, first, to rationalize the existence of these four schools of thought by examining some of the features of the income concept in accounting and economics and introducing the concept of capital maintenance and, second, to elaborate on the conceptual and operational problems associated with the implementation of current-value accounting. We shall examine the other schools of thought in subsequent chapters.

Relevance
of the Income Concept

Why measure income? Arguments in favor of measuring income could be extended *ad infinitum*. Income is a basic and important item of financial statements—it has various uses in various contexts. Income is generally perceived as a basis for taxation, a determinant of dividend payment policy, a guide for investment and decision making, and an element in prediction.

First, income has been considered a basis for taxation and redistribution of wealth among individuals. For such a task, a version of income—known as "taxable income"—is computed according to rules specified by governmental fiscal legislation. Two other bases for taxation, however, have been suggested as superior to income. The possession of resources, for example, may be a more equitable basis for taxing economic entities. Also, it may be argued that individuals should be taxed on the basis of their expenditures rather than on the basis of their income.[1]

---

[1] N. Kaldor, *An Expenditure Tax* (London: Allen & Unwin, 1955), pp. 54–78.

The second way in which income has been perceived is a guide to a firm's dividend and retention policy. The income recognized is an indicator of the maximum amounts to be distributed as dividends and retained for expansion or plowed back. Because of the differences between accrual accounting and cash accounting, however, a firm may recognize an amount of income and at the same time have insufficient funds to pay dividends. Thus, the recognition of income per se does not guarantee that dividends will be paid. Liquidity and investment prospects are necessary additional variables for the determination of dividend policy.

Third, income is considered a guide for investment and decision making in general. It is generally hypothesized that investors seek to maximize the return on capital invested, commensurate with an acceptable degree of risk. For example, the American Accounting Association's Committee on External Reporting defined a normative stockholders' valuation model centering on: (1) the future dividends per share flows to be derived from an investment and (2) the risk associated with these flows. The model is as follows:[2]

$$V_{0k} = \left(\sum_{i=1}^{m} \frac{(\alpha_{ik})\,(D_{ik})\,(m_{ik})}{\prod_{i=1}^{i}\,[1 + \beta_j\,(m_{jk})]} \right) + \left(\frac{(I_{nk} - CG_{nk})\,(\alpha_{nk})}{\prod_{i=1}^{m}\,[1 + \beta_j\,(m_{jk})]} \right) - I_0$$

where

V_{0k} = the net subjective present value of the gain that can be obtained by an investor (k) at time period (0) from buying one share at the market price I_0,

D_{ik} = the expected value of cash flows (dividends per share) during each period (i),

I_{nk} = the expected transaction price of the stock at period (n) as projected by investor (k), less commission and other direct outlays,

CG_{nk} = the expected capital gain tax to be paid by the investor (k) when the securities are sold in period (n),

β_j = the before-tax opportunity rate for a riskless investment. The rate may change over time (j).

n_k = the discrete time period used by the investor,

α_{ik} = a "certainty equivalent" factor that adjusts the expected cash flows to a value such that a given investor is indifferent between D_{ik} and a cash-flow that is certain to be paid. This factor is determined by each investor's utility preference for risk.

$m_{ik}(m_{jk})$ = one minus the expected marginal tax rate for each cash flow for each investor (k) and for each time period (i) or (j),

I_0 = the transaction price at the time of decision.

[2]Report of the 1966–68 Committee on External Reporting, *An Evaluation of External Reporting Practices* (Evanston, Ill.: AAA, 1969), p. 81.

The AAA Committee on External Reporting also suggested that a firm's ability to pay dividends is a function of the following variables: (1) net cash flows from operations, (2) nonoperating cash flows, (3) cash flows from changes in the level in investment by stockholders and creditors, (4) cash flows arising from investment in assets, (5) cash flows from priority claims, (6) cash flows from random events, (7) management attitudes regarding stocks of resources, and (8) cash dividend policy.[3] It is doubtful, however, that accounting income could be used to predict most of these variables. Besides, there has been a gradual shift of emphasis from the income concept to a cash flow concept. For example, the "Trueblood Report" (see Chapter 3) expressed the following objective:

> An objective of financial statements is to provide information useful to investors and creditors for predicting, comparing and evaluating potential cash flows to them in terms of amount, timing and related uncertainty.[4]

Fourth, income is perceived as a predictive device. It aids in the prediction of future incomes and future economic events. In fact, past values of income, based on historical cost and on current value, were found to be useful in predicting future values of both versions of income.[5] Income consists of both operational results, or ordinary income, and nonoperational results, or extraordinary gains and losses, the sum of which is equal to net income. Ordinary income is assumed to be current and repetitive, while extraordinary gains and losses are not. Research findings show that, as a predictor of future earnings, ordinary income is superior to net income.[6] Because such findings imply that the behavior of net income might be erratic and of no use to investors' decision making, there is some reason to use a measure of income that is conducive to accurate predictions. In other words, "income smoothing" may be justified by the need for good predictive ability and may be intended by management to show plausible forms of trends over time to outside users of financial statements.[7] Income smoothing has been defined as the "*intentional* dampening of fluctuations about some level of earnings that is currently *considered* to be normal for a firm."[8] This definition implies that a choice must be made among a number of accounting procedures and measurements to minimize the cyclical behavior of accounting income. Income smoothing is motivated by the desire to enhance the reliability of prediction based on income and reduce the risk surrounding the accounting numbers.[9] A recent study focuses more precisely on the reduction of systematic risk through the impact of income smoothing on reducing the covariance of the firm's returns with the market returns.[10] Three smoothing dimensions may be identified,

---

[3]*Ibid.*, pp. 83–88.

[4]*Ibid.*, p. 81.

[5]Werner Frank, "A Study of the Predictive Significance of Two Income Measures," *Journal of Accounting Research* (Spring 1969), pp. 123–33.

[6]J. Ronen and S. Sadan, "Extraordinary Items and the Predictive Ability of Income Number," Vincent C. Ross Institute of Accounting Research, Working Paper 74-3 (New York: New York University, 1974).

[7]Carl R. Beidleman, "Income Smoothing: The Role of Management," *The Accounting Review* (October 1973), pp. 653–667.

[8]*Ibid.*, p. 654.

[9]A. Barnea, J. Ronen, and S. Sadan, "Classificatory Smoothing of Income with Extraordinary Items," *The Accounting Review* (January 1976), pp. 110–22.

[10]Beidleman, "Income Smoothing," p. 654.

namely: (1) smoothing through the occurence and/or recognition of events, (2) smoothig through allocation over time, and (3) smoothing through classification.[11]

The fifth way that income may be perceived is as a measure of efficiency. Income is both a measure of management's stewardship of an entity's resources and of management's efficiency in conducting the affairs of a firm. This concern is well expressed in the FASB's Report of the Study Group on the Objectives of Financial Statements, which maintained that "an objective of financial statements is to supply information useful in judging management's ability to utilize enterprise resources effectively in achieving the primary enterprise goal," and "the earning process consists of effort and performance directed at reaching the primary enterprise goal of returning, over time, the maximum amount of cash to its owners."[12] Management's primary goal is assumed to be to maximize earnings per share. In fact, the stockholders' welfare maximization model (SWM) may be challenged by the management welfare maximization (MWM) model. The management welfare maximization model implies that managers may try to increase their remunerations by maximizing sales or assets, the firm's rate of growth, or managerial utility.[13] As a result, Findly and Whitmore make the following contention with respect to earnings:

> SWM assumes that earnings are objectively determined to reveal the time position of the business to its owners and the capital market. . . .
>
> MWM presumes management manipulation or avoidance within the legality of full disclosure in order to present the firm's operations in the most favorable light.[14]

Thus, management welfare maximization casts doubt on income as a measure of efficiency.

In conclusion, income has a role to play in various areas, but its usefulness may be subject to a number of limitations, as indicated by the five cases we have discussed.

The Traditional Accounting Concept of Income

A Description of Accounting Income

Accounting income is operationally defined as the difference between the *realized revenues* arising from the transactions of the *period* and the *corresponding historical costs*. This definition suggests five characteristics of accounting income.

---

[11]Barnea, Ronen, and Sadan, "Classifactory Smoothing," p. 111.

[12]*Objectives of Financial Statements* (New York: AICPA, 1974), p. 26.

[13]W. Baumol, *Business Behavior, Value and Growth* (New York: Macmillan, 1959); R. Marris, *The Economic Theory of "Managerial Capitalism,"* (London: Macmillan, 1964); A. Papandreou, "Some Basic Issues in the Theory of the Firm," in *Survey of Contemporary Economics,* Ed. B. Haley (Homewood, Ill.: R. D. Irwin, 1952), pp. 250–62; M. Chapman Findlay, III, and G. A. Whitmore, "Beyond Shareholder Wealth Maximization," *Financial Management* (Winter 1974), pp. 25–35.

[14]*Ibid.,* p. 30.

First, accounting income is based on the actual transaction entered into by the firm, primarily revenues arising from the sales of goods or services minus the costs necessary to achieve these sales. The accounting profession conventionally has used a transaction approach to income measurement. The transactions may be explicit (or external) and implicit (or internal). Explicit, or external, transactions result from the acquisition of goods or services by a firm from other entities. Implicit, or internal, transactions result from the use or allocation of assets within a firm. While external transactions are explicit because they are based on objective evidence, internal transactions are implicit because they are based on less objective evidence such as the use and passage of time.

Second, accounting income is based on the **period postulate.** Accounting income refers to the financial performance of the firm for a given period.

Third, accounting income is based on the **revenue principle.** Accounting income requires the definition, measurement, and recognition of revenues. In general, "realization" is the test for the recognition of revenues and, consequently, for the recognition of income. There are exceptions in specific circumstances, however, as suggested in Chapter 4.

Fourth, accounting income requires the measurement of expenses in terms of the **historical cost** to the enterprise; constituting a strict adherence to the cost principle. Assets are accounted for at their acquisition cost until a sale is realized, at which time any change in value is recognized. Thus, expenses are expired assets or expired acquisition costs.

Fifth, accounting income requires that the realized revenues of the period be related to appropriate or corresponding relevant costs. Accounting income, therefore, is based on the **matching princple.** Basically, certain costs or period costs are allocated or matched with revenues and the others are reported and carried forward as assets. Costs allocated and matched with period revenues are those assumed to have an expired service potential.

Advantages of Accounting Income

The use of accounting income has not been without defenders and strong defenses. Among the important and most spirited defenders of accounting income are Kohler, Littleton, Ijiri, and Mautz.[15] We shall discuss four of their principal arguments.

The first argument in favor of accounting income is that it has survived the test of time. Most users of accounting data believe that accounting income is useful and that it constitutes a determinant of the practices and patterns of thought of decision makers. To support this argument, Mautz states that:

Accounting is what it is today not so much because of the desire of accountants as because of the influence of businessmen. If those who make management and investment decisions had not found financial

---

[15]Eric L. Kohler, "Why Not Retain Historical Cost?" *The Journal of Accountancy* (October 1963), pp. 35–41; A. C. Littleton, "The Significance of Invested Cost," *The Accounting Review* (April 1952), pp. 167–73; Yuji Ijiri, "A Defense of Historical Cost Accounting," in *Asset Valuation and Income Determination,* ed. R. R. Sterling (Lawrence, Kansas: Scholars Book Co., 1971), pp. 1–14; Robert K. Mautz, "A Few Words for Historical Cost," *Financial Executive* (January 1973), pp. 93–98.

reports based on historical cost useful over the years, changes in accounting would long since have been made.[16]

Second, because it is based on actual and factual transactions, accounting income is measured and reported objectively and is therefore basically verifiable. Objectivity is generally reinforced by the belief of advocates of the use of accounting income that accounting should report fact rather than value. As Kohler states: "Accounting has never been a device for 'measuring (current) value,' 'changes in value' or the present worth of an asset or asset group."[17]

Third, by relying on the realization principle for the recognition of revenue, accounting income meets the criterion of conservatism. In other words, reasonable caution is taken in the measurement and reporting of income by ignoring value changes and recognizing only realized gains.

Fourth, accounting income is considered useful for control purposes and especially in reporting on stewardship, that is, management's use of resources entrusted to it. Accounting income conveys the background of the story of the way in which management has met its responsibilities.

Disadvantages of Accounting Income

In addition to being strongly defended, accounting income has also been severely criticized in the literature for its various limitations. Basically, the arguments against the use of accounting income question its relevance to decision making. Let us examine some of these arguments.

Accounting income fails to recognize unrealized increases in values of assets held in a given period because of the application of the historical cost and the realization principles. This prevents useful information from being disclosed and allows disclosure of a heterogeneous mix of gains from the prior and current periods. The net result does not correspond effectively to the income of the current period.

The reliance of accounting income on the historical cost principle makes comparability difficult, given the different acceptable methods of computing "cost" (for example, the different inventory costing methods) and the different acceptable methods of cost allocation deemed arbitrary and incorrigible.[18]

Reliance on accounting income or the realization principle, historical cost principle, and conservatism may lead to misleading and misunderstood data or data that is irrelevant to the users. A case in point is the lack of usefulness of ratios based on financial statements prepared in conformity with the above principles.

Reliance on the historical cost principle may give the impression to users that the balance sheet represents an approximation of value rather than merely a statement of unallocated cost balances. Besides, the emphasis on an income determination led to a resolution of controversial issues based on their impact on the income statement, thereby creating in the balance sheet a mixture of items that are quite hard to define, for example, deferred tax allocation debits and credits.

---

[16]Eric L. Kohler, "Why Not Retain Historical Costs?" p. 36.

[17]*Ibid.*, p. 32.

[18]Arthur L. Thomas, *Accounting Research Study No. 3*, "The Allocation Problem in Financial Accounting" (Evanston, Ill.: AAA, 1969) and *Accounting Research Study No. 9*, "The Allocation Problem: Part 2" (Sarasota, Fla.: AAA, 1974).

The Nature of the Economic
Concept of Income

The concept of income has always been an important point of interest to economists. Adam Smith was the first economist to define income as an increase in wealth.[19] Most classicists—Alfred Marshall in particular—followed Smith in the concept of income and linked its conceptualization to business practices.[20] For example, they separated fixed and circulating (that is, working) capital, separated physical capital and income, and emphasized realization as a test of income recognition. Toward the end of the nineteenth century, the understanding that income is more than cash was expressed by the theories of capital and income of Bohm Bawerk.[21] Bawerk attempted to develop a nonmonetary concept of income in spite of the monetary movement dominating economic analysis at the time.[22]

At the beginning of the twentieth century, ideas concerning income advanced by Fisher, Lindhal, and Hicks brought a major and new outlook in the nature of the economic concept of income. Fisher defined economic income as a series of events that correspond to different stages: the enjoyment of psychic income, the real income, and the money income.[23] Psychic income is that actual personal consumption of goods and services that produces a psychic enjoyment and satisfaction of wants. While psychic income is a psychological concept that cannot be measured directly, it can be approximated by real income. Real income is an expression of the events that give rise to psychic enjoyments. Real income is best measured by the cost of living. In other words, the satisfaction created by the psychic enjoyment of profit is measured by the money payments made for the acquisition of goods and services before or after consumption. Thus, psychic income, real income, and the cost of living are three different stages of income. Finally, money income represents all the money received and intended to be used for consumption to meet the cost of living. While psychic income is the most fundamental and money income is the one most often referred to as income, the real income is perceived by Fisher as the most practical for accountants.

Lindahl introduced the notion of income as interest, referring to the continuous *appreciation* of capital goods over time. The differences between the interest and consumption anticipated for a given period are perceived as *saving*. This idea led to the generally accepted notion of economic income as consumption plus saving expected to take place during a certain period, the saving being equal to the change in economic capital. This may be expressed by the following identity

$$Y_e = C + (K_t - K_{t-1})$$

[19]Adam Smith, *An Enquiry into the Nature and Causes of the Wealth of Nations* (London: George Rontledge, 1890).

[20]Alfred Marshall, *Principles of Economics*, 8th ed. (London: Macmillan, 1947), Book II, Chs. 2 and 4, and Appendix E.

[21]Eugene Von Bohm Bawerk, *Positive Theory of Capital, Vol. 88 of Capital and Interest*, (South Holland, Ill.: Libertarian Press, 1959), pp. 16–66.

[22]J. M. Keynes, *The General Theory of Employment, Interest and Money* (London: Macmillan, 1936), Ch. 6.

[23]Irving Fisher, *The Nature of Capital and Income* (New York: Macmillan, 1912), p.38.

where

$$Y_e \quad = \text{ economic income,}$$

$$C \quad = \text{ consumption,}$$

$$K_t \quad = \text{ capital at the period } (t), \text{ and}$$

$$K_{t-1} = \text{ capital at the period } (t-1).$$

Hicks used the concepts introduced by Fisher and Lindhal to develop a general theory of economic income.[24] He defined a person's personal income as "the maximum amount he can consume during a week, and still *expect* to be as well-off at the end of the week as he was at the beginning.[25] This definition has become the basis of many discussions on the concept of income. One problem raised by such a definition, however, is the lack of consensus on the interpretation of the term "as well-off," or "welloffness." The most accepted interpretation is that of capital maintenance, in which case the "Hicksian" income is the maximum amount that may be consumed in a given period and still maintain the capital intact.

Concepts of Capital Maintenance

The concept of **capital maintenance** implies that income is recognized after capital has been maintained or costs have been recovered. *Return on capital* (income) is distinguished from *return of capital* (cost recovery). Two principal concepts of capital maintenance or cost recovery may be expressed both in terms of units of money and in terms or units of the same general purchasing power: *financial capital* and *physical capital*. We have, therefore, four concepts of capital maintenance:

1.   Financial capital measured in units of money —*money maintenance,*
2.   Financial capital measured in units of the same purchasing power— *general purchasing power money maintenance,*
3.   Physical capital measured in units of money—*productive capacity maintenance,* and
4.   Physical capital measured in units of the same purchasing power— *general purchasing power productive capacity maintenance.*

The first concept implies that the financial capital invested or reinvested by the owners is maintained. Under the money maintenance concept, income is equal to the change in net assets adjusted for capital transactions expressed in terms of dollars. Conventional accounting, as it relies on historical cost for the valuation of assets and liabilities, conforms to the money maintenance concept.

The second concept implies that the purchasing power of the financial capital invested or reinvested by the owner is maintained. Under the general purchasing power money maintenance concept, income is equal to the change in net assets

---

[24]J. R. Hicks, *Value and Capital,* 2nd ed. (Oxford: Clarendon Press, 1946).
[25]*Ibid.,* p. 122.

adjusted for capital transactions expressed in units of the same purchasing power money. General price-level adjusted historical cost financial statements conform to the general purchasing power money maintenance concept.

The third concept implies that the physical productive capacity of the firm is maintained. Different interpretations exist for the specific meaning of "productive capacity." The "Sandilands Report" in the United Kingdom interprets productive capacity as follows:

> What is meant by a company's "productive capacity" and how is it to be maintained intact? We have received various suggestions as to how this calculation should be made, which may be classified into three alternatives definitions of productive capacity:
> (a) Productive capacity should be defined as the physical assets possessed by the company, so that profit would be the amount that could be distributed after making sufficient provision to replace the physical assets held by the company as they are consumed or wear out.
> (b) Productive capacity should be defined as the capacity to produce the same *volume* of goods and services in the following year as could be produced in the current year.
> (c) Productive capacity should be defined as the capacity to produce the same *value* of goods and services in the following year as could be produced in the current year.[26]

While the first definition of productive capacity in terms of "same assets" does not take into account the technological improvements, the last two definitions in terms of "same volume of output" and "same value of output" allow technological improvements. Productive capacity maintenance is the concept of capital maintenance used in current-value accounting, in which assets and liabilities are disclosed in the financial statements at their current values.

Finally, the fourth concept of capital maintanance implies the maintenance of the physical productive capacity of the firm measured in units of the same purchasing power. General purchasing power productive capacity maintenance is the concept of capital maintenance used in general price-level adjusted current-value accounting.

The following example illustrates the impact on income statements of each of the four concepts of capital maintenance. Let us suppose that a given firm has $2,000 of net assets at the beginning and $3,000 of net assets at the end of a given period. Let us also assume that $2,500 of net assets are required to maintain the actual physical productive capacity and that the general price level increased 10 percent during the period. Income under each of the concepts of capital maintenance would be:

1. Money maintenance:

$$\$3,000 - \$2,000 = \$1,000$$

2. General purchasing power maintenance:

$$\$3,000 - (\$2,000 + 0.10 \times \$2,000) = \$800$$

---

[26]*Inflation Accounting: Report of the Inflation Accounting Committee* (London: Her Majesty's Stationery Office, 1975), p. 35.

3. Productive capacity maintenance:

$$\$3,000 - \$2,500 = \$500$$

4. General purchasing power productive capacity maintenance:

$$\$3,000 - (2,500 + 0.10 \times \$2,500) = \$250$$

The accounting income, therefore, is $1,000, the general price-level adjusted accounting income is $800, the current-value–based income is $500, and the general price-level adjusted current-value–based income is $250. In the rest of this chapter, we shall discuss current-value accounting; the other concepts will be presented in the following chapters.

Concepts of Current Value

The productive capacity maintenance concept requires the use of current values for the assets and liabilities of a firm. Several methods of calculating curent value are: (1) capitalization, or present-value method, (2) current entry price, (3) current exit price, and (4) a combination of values from the first three methods.

Capitalization

Under the capitalization method for calculating current value, the capitalized or economic value of an asset, group of assets, or total assets is the net amount of the discounted expected cash flows pertaining to the asset, group of assets, or total assets during their useful lives. To compute this capitalized value, four variables must be known: (1) the expected cash flows that may result from the use or disposal of the asset, (2) the timing of those expected cash flows, (3) the number of years of the asset's remaining life, an (4) the appropriate discount rate. If these variables may be determined in an acurate and objective manner, the capitalization or present value method may be expressed by the following formulas:

$$P_0 = \sum_{j=2}^{n} \frac{R_j}{(1+i)^j} \;, \quad P_1 = \sum_{j=2}^{n} \frac{R_j}{(1+i)^{j-1}}, \quad \text{and } I_1 = (P_1 - P_0) + R_j$$

where

P_0 = The present value or capitalized value at time 0,

P_1 = The present value or capitalized value at time 1,

I_1 = Income for the first year,

R_j = Net cash flow expected in period j,

i = Appropriate discount rate, and

n = Useful remaining life.

While the accounting income based on historical data for a specific period may be labeled *ex post* income, or periodic income, *the present-value* income is a *total pure profit income* expected to be accruing up to the firm's planning horizon.

It is an *ex ante* income, or economic income, that reflects expectations about future cash flows. Such income may be computed in the situation in which all the relevant variables are known with certainty as well as in the situation in which all the relevant variables are probabilistic.

For example, let us assume the following expected net cash flows from the total assets of a firm whose useful remaining life is four years:

Year	0	1	2	3	4
Cash Flow	—	$7,000	$8,500	$10,000	$12,000

If the appropriate discount rate is assumed to be 5 percent, the present value at the beginning of Year 1 would be $32,887, computed (using present value tables) as follows:

Capitalized value at beginning Year 1	Capitalized value at end of Year 1
$ 7,000 × .9524 = $ 6,667	$ 8,500 × .9524 = $ 8,095
$ 8,500 × .9070 = $ 7,710	$10,000 × .9070 = $ 9,070
$10,000 × .8638 = $ 8,638	$12,000 × .8638 = $10,366
$12,000 × .8227 = $ 9,872	
$32,887	$27,531

The income for the first year may be computed as follows:

	Cash flow expected from the use of the assets for Year 1	$ 7,000
+	Capitalized value of total assets at the end of Year 1	27,531
=	Total value of the firm at the end of Year 1	$34,531
−	Capitalized value of total assets at the beginning of Year 1	32,887
=	Income for the first year	$ 1,644

The present value income, or economic income, is $1,644, which represents the real increase in the value of the firm in the first year. It is equivalent to 5 percent of the starting capital of $32,887. Because most authors define the discount rate as the subjective rate of return, Edwards and Bell call the economic income of $1,644 the "subjective profit."[27] Several appropriate discount rates, however, may be used to compute capitalized value: (1) the historical rate of discount, (2) the current rate of discount, (3) the average expected rate of discount, (4) the weighted average cost of capital, and (5) the incremental borrowing rate. The FASB appropriately defined these rates as follows:

---

[27]Edgar O. Edwards and Phillippe W. Bell, *The Theory and Measurement of Business Income* (Berkeley and Los Angeles: University of California Press, 1961), pp. 38–44.

The historical rate of discount is the rate of return that is implicit in the amount of cash (or other consideration) paid to acquire an asset. More specifically, it is the rate discount that, at the date of acquisition, causes the present value of the expected cash flows from an asset to be equal to the asset's historical cost. . . .

The *current rate* of discount is the rate of return implicit in the amount of cash (or other consideration) that would have to be paid if the same asset were acquired currently. . . .

The *average expected rate* of discount is the average rate of return that is expected to be earned on similar assets during some, usually long term, future period. . . .

The *weighted average cost of capital* is based on a particular capital structure—that is, a particular ratio of long-term debt, prefered stock-holders' equity, and common stockholders' equity. . . .

The *incremental borrowing rate* is the rate of interest that would have to be paid to obtain additional borrowed capital currently. . . .[28]

The variables included in the capitalized value formula are merely expectations that are subject to changes. For example, let us suppose at the end of the first year it is found that the expected cash flows will be $10,000 a year instead of $8,500, $10,000, and $12,000. The present-value income for the first year is found as follows:

	Cash flow expected at the end of the first year	$ 7,000
+	Capitalized value at the end of Year 1 of estimated cash flows of $10,000 a year for three years	27,232
=	Total value of the firm at the end of Year 1	$34,232
−	Capitalized value of total assets at beginning of Year 1	32,887
=	Income for the year	$ 1,345

This new income for the year—$1,345—includes the following elements:

1.	Anticipated economic income (5% × $32,887)	$1,644
2.	Diminution in the capitalized value of the firm	(299)
3.	Income for the year	$1,345

While in the above analysis, we considered the diminution in the capitalized value as a loss, another point of view considers it as a mere adjustment of the original value of the firm due to the changes in expectations. In other words, the capitalized value of the firm based on the new expectations should have been $32,602 rather than $32,887. Consequently, the new income for the year—$1,345—includes instead the following elements:

---

[28]*FASB Discussion Memorandum,* "An Analysis of Issues Related to Conceptual Framework for Financial Accounting and Reporting: Elements of Financial Statements and Their Measurement" (Stamford, Conn.: FASB, December 2, 1976), pp. 206–8.

1. Economic income (5% × $32,602)		$1,630
2. Changes in the original value of the firm $32,887 less $32,602)		(285)
3. Decrease in the capitalized value		$1,345

The next question that arises pertains to the nature of the differences between the present-value, or economic, income and the accounting income. While economic income is an *ex ante* income based on future cash flow expectations, the accounting income is an *ex post*, or *periodic*, income based on historical values. In his revision of a work by Alexander, Solomons proposed the following distinction between economic income and accounting income:

> Accounting income
> + Unrealized tangible asset changes
> − Realized tangible asset changes that occurred in prior periods
> + Changes in the value of intangible assets
> = Economic income[29]

The changes in the value of intangible assets do not refer to the conventional intangible assets found in the balance sheet but to a concept called **subjective goodwill** arising from the use of expectations in the computation of economic income. Thus, using the previous example, the economic income for the four-year period is equal to $4,613, as shown in Table 5–1. Assuming an annual depreciation of $7,000, the accounting income is equal to $9,500. The difference between the economic income and the accounting income is $4,887, which is the *subjective goodwill*. A reconciliation is presented in Table 5–2.

TABLE 5–1
Computation of Economic Income

Year	Capitalized Value at the Beginning of the Year (1)	Capitalized Value at the End of the Year (2)	Cash Flow Expected for the Year (3)	Economic Profit (4) (4) = (2)+(3)−(1)
1	$32,887	$27,531	$ 7,000	$1,644
2	27,531	20,408	8,500	1,377
3	20,408	11,428.8	10,000	1,020.8
4	11,428.8	—	12,000	571.2
Total economic profit				$4,613
Total cash flow			$37,500	
Total depreciation expense (assumed)			28,000	
Accounting income			9,500	$9,500
Subjective goodwill				$4,887

---

[29]Sidney S. Alexander, "Income Measurement in a Dynamic Economy," rev. David Solomons, in *Studies in Accounting Theory*, ed. W. T. Baxter and Sidney Davidson (Homewood, Ill.: R. D. Irwin, 1962), pp. 126–27.

TABLE 5–2
Reconciliation of the Economic and Accounting Incomes

Year	Depreciation Accounting	Subjective Goodwill	Difference
1	$ 7,000	$ 5,356	($1,644)
2	7,000	7,123	123
3	7,000	8,979.2	1,979.2
4	7,000	11,428.8	4,428.8
Total	$28,000	$32,887	$4,887

The capitalized value method is deemed useful for such long-term operating decisions as capital budgeting and product development. The options yielding the highest positive capitalized values are deemed to be the best methods. Capitalized values of long-term receivables and long-term payables are also used in financial statements, as shown by *APB Opinion No. 21*, "Interest on Receivables and Payables."[30] The capitalized value is generally considered an ideal attribute of assets and liabilities, although it presents some conceptual and practical limitations. From a practical point of view, capitalized value suffers from the subjective nature of the expectations used for its computation. From a conceptual point of view, capitalized value suffers from (1) the lack of an adequate adjustment for risk preference of all users, (2) the ignorance of the contribution of other factors than physical assets to the cash flows, (3) the difficulty of allocating total cash flows to the separate factors that made the contribution, and (4) the fact that the marginal present values of physical assets used jointly in operations cannot be added together to obtain the value of the firm.[31]

Current Entry Price

Notions of Current Entry Prices   **Current entry price** represents the amount of cash or other consideration that would be required to obtain the same asset or its equivalent. The following interpretations of current entry price have been used.

Replacement cost–used is equal to the amount of cash or other consideration that would be needed to obtain an *equivalent* asset on the second-hand market having the same remaining useful life.

Reproduction cost is equal to the amount of cash or other consideration that would be needed to obtain an *identical* asset to the existing asset. Edwards and Bell have focused on the notion of replacing an existing asset with an *identical* asset:

It must be remembered that it is not the current cost of equivalent

---

[30]*APB Opinion No. 21*, "Interest on Receivables and Payables," (New York: AICPA, 1972).

[31]Arthur L. Thomas, "Discounted Services Again: The Homogeneity Problem," *The Accounting Review* (January 1964), pp. 1–11; Allan Barton, *An Analysis of Business Income Concepts*, International Center for Research in Accounting, Occasional Paper No. 7 (Lancaster, England: University of Lancaster, 1975), p. 50.

services provided by fixed assets over some time period which we wish to measure, but the current cost of using the particular fixed asset which the entrepreneur chose to adopt and is still using. It is that particular decision that the entrepeneur wishes to evaluate on the basis of accounting data. It may well be that he then may wish to compare these data with opportunity cost data relating to selling and/or replacing the fixed asset, but in order to make this decision about the future, he must have information about the actual, present and past.[32]

While both replacement cost–used and reproduction cost emphasize the replacement of existing assets, **replacement cost–new** emphasizes the replacement of the productive capacity of assets. Replacement cost–new is equal to the amount of cash or other consideration needed to replace or reproduce the productive capacity of an asset with a new asset that reflects changes in technology. For example, Paton and Paton considered the alternative of replacing an existing asset with an asset of equivalent capacity:

> It should be understood that the significant replacement cost is the cost of providing the existing capacity to produce in terms of the most up-to-date methods available. Thus it is largely a waste of time to estimate the cost of replacing an obsolete or semi-obsolete plant unit literally in kind; such an estimate will never afford a basis for a sound appraisal of the property nor furnish a useful measure of current operating cost. The fact of interest is what it would cost to replace the capacity represented in the existing asset with a machine or modern design. To put the point in another way, cost of replacing in kind is a significant basis on which to measure the economic importance of property in use only in the case of standard, up-to-date facilities.[33]

The common characteristic of the three notions of current entry prices is that they all correspond to the costs of replacing or reproducing an asset held. The issue that remains to be solved is the choice of method of measurement of current entry prices. The three most advocated methods use *quoted market prices, specific price indexes,* and *appraisals,* or management estimates. The AAA Committee on Concepts and Standards has expressed the following order of preference:

> The current cost of obtaining the same or equivalent services should be the basis for valuation subsequent to acquisition, as well as at the date of acquisition. Where there is an established market for assets of like kind and condition, quoted market prices provide the most objective evidence of current cost. Such prices may be readily available for land, buildings, and certain types of standard equipment. Where there is no established market for assets of like kind and condition, current cost may be estimated by reference to the purchase price of assets which provide equivalent service capacity. The purchase price of such substitute assets should

[32]Edwards and Bell, *The Theory and Measurement of Business Income,* p. 286.

[33]William A. Paton and William A. Paton, Jr., *Asset Accounting* (New York: Macmillan, 1952), p. 325.

be adjusted for differences in operating characteristics such as cost, capacity, and quality. In other cases, adjustment of historical cost by the use of specific price indexes may provide acceptable approximations of current cost. Appraisals are acceptable only if they are based on the above methods of estimating current costs.[34]

Accounting for Holding Gains and Losses   The valuation of assets and liabilities at current entry prices gives rise to holding gains and losses as entry prices change during a period of time when they are held or owed by a firm. They may be divided into two elements: (1) the realized holding gains and losses that correspond to the items sold or liabilities discharged and (2) the nonrealized holding gains and losses that correspond to the items still held or liabilities owed at the end of the reporting period. These holding gains and losses may be classified as income when capital maintenance is viewed solely in money terms. They may also be classified as capital adjustments, because they measure the additional elements of income that must be retained to maintain the existing productive capacity. Thus, justification for the holding gains and losses on capital adjustment may be related to a particular definition of income.

Proponents of the capital adjustment alternative favor a definition of income based on the preservation of physical capital. Such an approach would define the profit of an entity for a given period as the maximum amount that would be distributed and still maintain the operating capability at the level that existed at the beginning of the period. Because the changes in replacement cost cannot be distributed without impairing the operating capability of the entity, this approach dictates that replacement cost changes be classified as capital adjustments.

Proponents of the holding gains and losses alternative favor a definition of income based on the preservation of financial capital (money maintenance concept). Such an approach would define profit as the maximum amount that could be distributed and still maintain the financial capital invested at the level that existed at the beginning of the period. Such an approach dictates that replacement cost changes be classified as holding gains and losses. The academic literature provides two alternative arguments in support of the holding gains treatment. The first argument is that holding gains represent a "realizable cost savings" in the sense that the entity is now better off because it would now cost more to acquire the asset. The second argument is that replacement cost changes may be viewed as "surrogates" for changes in net realizable or capitalized value. Thus, the holding gains represent increases in the expected net receipts from either using or selling the asset in the future.

The following two examples demonstrate the accounting treatments of holding gains and losses for inventories and depreciable assets:

Example 1: The accounting treatment of inventories at the current entry price and the corresponding holding gains and losses.

Assume that a firm invests $6,000 in a new company on January 1. On the same date it buys 1,000 pounds of coffee at $6.00 a pound. During the year, the firm sells 600 pounds of coffee at $10.00 when the replacement cost is $8.00 per

---

[34]"Accounting for Land, Buildings, and Equipment," *The Accounting Review* (July 1964), p. 696.

pound. The replacement cost of coffee at the end of the year is $9.00 per pound. The accounting entries are as follows:

Merchandise Inventory (1,000 × $6.00)	6,000	
Cash		6,000
(To record purchase of merchandise)		
Cash	6,000	
Cost of goods sold (600 × $8.00)	4,800	
Sale (600 × $10.00)		6,000
Merchandise Inventory (600 × $8.00)		4,800
(To record sale of merchandise)		
Merchandise Inventory	2,400	
Realized Holding Gain [600 × ($8 − $6)]		1,200
Unrealized Holding Gain [400 × ($9 − $6)]		1,200
(To record the holding gains)		

Example 2: The accounting treatment of noncurrent assets at the current entry price and the corresponding holding gains and losses.

Assume that a firm purchases an asset for $2,900 with a four-year useful life and its replacement cost increases $1,000 a year. The depreciation expenses must be determined on the basis of replacement cost. Most proponents of the replacement cost method agree on the need to include added amounts in current expenses as a "catch-up," "make-up," or "backlog" depreciation if the replacement costs continue to increase over the useful life of the asset. Determination of the "backlog" depreciation is shown in the following table:

Year	1	2	3	4
Replacement cost, end of the year	$3,000	$4,000	$5,000	$6,000
Depreciation expense based on replacement cost	750	1,000	1,250	1,500
Backlog depreciation	—	250	500	750
Opening accumulated depreciation		750	2,000	3,750
Adjusted accumulated depreciation	$ 750	$2,000	$3,750	$6,000

Thus, the accounting entries in each year would be:

Year 1

Asset (replacement cost)	1,000	
Depreciation	750	
Holding gain		1,000
Accumulated depreciation		750

Year 2

Asset (replacement cost)	1,000	
Depreciation	1,000	
Backlog depreciation	250	
Holding gain		1,000
Accumulated depreciation		1,250

Year 3

Asset (replacement cost)	1,000	
Depreciation	1,250	
Backlog depreciation	500	
Holding gain		1,000
Accumulated depreciation		1,750

Year 4

Asset (replacement cost)	1,000	
Depreciation	1,500	
Backlog depreciation	750	
Holding gain		1,000
Accumulated depreciation		2,250

If, however, we assume that the value of the asset increases uniformly over the year, the depreciation expense should be computed on the basis of the average current entry price for the year. The entries for the first year result from the fact that depreciation expense is $625 (25 percent of the average asset value of $2,500) and that the holding gain will be $875 ($1,000 less a half-year depreciation on the $1,000 increase). Accordingly, the entries for each year would be:

Year 1

Asset (replacement cost)	1,000	
Depreciation	626	
Holding gain		875
Accumulated depreciation		750

Year 2

Asset (replacement cost)	1,000	
Depreciation (25% of $3,500)	875	
Holding gain		625
Accumulated depreciation		1,250

Year 3

Asset (replacement cost)	1,000	
Depreciation (25% of $4,500)	1,125	
Holding gain		375
Accumulated depreciation		1,750

Year 4

Asset (replacement cost)	1,000	
Depreciation (25% of $5,500)	1,375	
Holding gain		125
Accumulated depreciation		2,250

EXHIBIT 5–1

Smith Corporation Balance Sheet

	December 31, 19X6		December 31, 19X7	
	Debit	Credit	Debit	Credit
Cash	$ 10,000		$ 30,000	
Accounts Receivable	20,000		30,000	
Inventories	30,000	(3,000 units)	20,000	(2,000 units)
Land	40,000		40,000	
Plant (5 years' life)	50,000		50,000	
Less: Allowance for Depreciation		$ 10,000		$ 20,000
Bonds (10% interest rate)		50,000		50,000
Common Stock		50,000		50,000
Retained Earnings		40,000		50,000
	$150,000	$150,000	$170,000	$170,000

Various methods have been suggested to account for "backlog depreciation," namely: (1) charge or credit to retained earnings, (2) charge or credit to current income, and (3) adjust holding gains and losses by the amount of "backlog depreciation."

Replacement Cost Techniques Applied   Exhibit 5–1 shows the Smith Corporation balance sheet on December 31, 19X6 and 19X7. Smith Corporation's income statement appears in Exhibit 5–2.

The following additional information is available:

EXHIBIT 5–2
Smith Corporation Income Statement

Sales (5,000 units at $40 per unit)		$200,000
Cost of Goods Sold		
Beginning Inventory (3,000 units at $10 per unit)	$ 30,000	
+ Purchases (4,000 units at $12 per unit)	48,000	
Goods available	78,000	
− Ending Inventory (2,000 units at $10 per unit)	20,000	58,000
Gross Margin		$142,000
Operational Expenses		
Depreciation	10,000	
Interest	5,000	
Other Expenses	117,000	$132,000
Net Profit		$ 10,000

1. The firm uses a LIFO inventory method.
2. During 19X7, the replacement cost was $70,000 for the land and $80,000 for the plant.
3. The sales were made at the end of 19X7, when the replacement cost of inventory was $20 per unit.

The income statement of the Smith Corporation for 19X7 under the current entry price basis is shown in Exhibit 5–3. Two items deserve explanation and further attention. First, the holding gain on plant was determined by the following entry:

Plant	30,000	
Depreciation	13,000	
Accumulated depreciation		22,000
Holding gain		21,000

EXHIBIT 5–3

Smith Corporation Income Statement for 19X7

Current Entry Price Basis

Sales (5,000 units at $40)			$200,000
Cost of Goods Sold			
Beginning inventory (3,000 units at $20)		$ 60,000	
Purchases (4,000 units at $20)		80,000	
Goods Available		$140,000	
Ending Inventory (2,000 units at $20)		40,000	100,000
Gross Margin			$100,000
Depreciation (20% × $\frac{80,000 + 50,000}{2}$)		13,000	
Interest		5,000	
Other Expenses		117,000	135,000
Operating Profit before Holding Gains and Losses			(35,000)
Realizable Holding Gains			
1. On Inventory			
a. Purchases: [4,000 units × ($20 – $12)]		$ 32,000	
b. Beginning Inventory: [1,000 units × ($20 – $10)]		10,000	
2. On Depreciation: ($13,000 – $10,000)		3,000	
Unrealized Holding Gains			$ 45,000
1. On Ending Inventory: ($20 – $10) × (2,000 units)		20,000	
2. On Plant		18,000	
3. On Land: ($70,000 – $40,000)		30,000	68,000
Net Profit			$ 78,000

In other words, if the $30,000 increase in plant's value accrued uniformly over the year, the depreciation expense should be $13,000 (20 percent of the average asset value of $65,000). The holding gain is equal to $30,000 less a 1½ year's depreciation of the $30,000.

Second, the operating profit before holding gains and losses and the realized holding gains and losses are both based on the realization concept. Consequently, their sum is equal to the accounting profit. The added advantage under the current entry price basis is the dichotomy between the results of (1) the operational decisions involving the production and sales of goods and services and (2) the holding decisions involving holding assets over time in expectation of an increase in their replacement cost.

Smith Corporation's balance sheet for 19X7 under the current entry price basis appears in Exhibit 5–4.

Evaluation of Current Entry Price Based Accounting   The primary advantage of current entry price results from the breakdown and segregation of current value income into current operating profit and holding gains and losses.

First, the dichotomy between current operating profit and holding gains and losses is useful for evaluating the past performance of managers. Current operating profit and holding gains and losses constitute the separate results of holding or investment decisions and production decisions, allowing a distinction between the recurring and relatively controllable gains arising from production and the gains arising from factors that are independent of current and basic enterprise operations. Edwards and Bell state that:

EXHIBIT 5–4
Smith Corporation Balance Sheet, December 19X7
Current Entry Price Basis

Assets		
Cash		$ 30,000
Accounts Receivable		30,000
Inventories (2,000 units at $20)		40,000
Land		70,000
Plant	80,000	
Less: Accumulated Depreciation	(32,000)	48,000
Total Assets		$218,000
Equities		
Bonds		$ 50,000
Common Stock		50,000
Retained Earnings		
Beginning Balance		40,000
Operating Profit		(35,000)
Realized Holding Gain		45,000
Unrealized Holding Gain		68,000
		$218,000

These two kinds of gains are often the result of quite different sets of decisions. The business firm usually has considerable freedom in deciding what quantity of assets to hold over time at any or all stages of the production process and what quantity of assets to commit to the production process itself. . . . The difference between the forces motivating the business firm to make profit by one means rather than by another and the difference between the events on which the two methods of making profits depend require that the two kinds of gain be carefully separated if the two types of decision involved are to be meaningfully evaluated.[35]

Second, the dichotomy between current operating profit and holding gains and losses is useful for making business decisions. Such a dichotomy allows the long-run profitability of the firm to be assessed, assuming continuation of existing conditions. Because it is recurring and relatively controllable, the current operating profit may be used for predictive purposes.

Third, current operating profit corresponds to the income that contributes to the maintenance of physical productive capacity, that is, the maximum amount that the firm can distribute while maintaining its physical productive capacity intact. As such, current operating profit has been appropriately labeled "distributable or sustainable income":

An important characteristic of distributable income from operations is that it is sustainable. If the world does not change, the company maintains its physical capacity next year and have the same amount of distributable income that it had this year.[36]

Fourth, the dichotomy between current operating profit and holding gains and losses provides important information for analyzing and comparing interperiod and intercompany performance gains.

Fifth, in addition, to the dichotomy between current operating profit and holding gains and losses, the current entry price method allows the separation between realized holding gains and losses and unrealized holding gains and losses. It represents an abandonment of the realization and conservatism principles, so that holding gains and losses are recognized as they accrue rather than as they are realized.

The feasibility of financial statements based on replacement cost basis appears more and more accepted. Hence, Revsine reports the results of efforts to pepare replacement cost financial statements for an electronic equipment manufacturer as follows:

Very few implementation problems were encountered during the course of the study. In those cases where data were initially absent, it was usually possible to reconstruct the missing information or to develop some surrogate approach. One might reasonably expect that even these occasional problems would diminish were market based measures widely adopted for reporting purposes.

This study has indicated that the test company was already employing

[35]Edwards and Bell, *The Theory and Measurement of Business Income*, p. 73.

[36]Richard F. Vancil and Roman L. Weil, "Current Replacement Cost Accounting, Depreciable Assets, and Distributable Income," in *Replacement Cost Accounting: Readings on Concepts, Uses and Methods* (Glen Ridge, N.J.: Thomas Horton and Daughters, 1976), p. 58.

what is essentially a replacement cost system for internal inventory accounting. This itself indicates the practicality of the replacement cost inventory procedures more forcefully than any academic study ever could. . . .

On the basis of these results, it would appear defensible to conclude that the data necessary to prepare replacement cost financial statements were generally available. Thus, this case study did not disclose any obstacles which would impede the implementation of replacement cost reports. Whether this conclusion can be generalized to other situations is a subject for future research.[37]

There are, however, some disadvantages to the current entry price system. Each claim about the benefits to be derived from dichotomizing current value income into current operating profit and holding gains and losses has been contested.[38]

The current entry price system is based on the assumptions that the firm is a going concern and that reliable current entry price data may be easily obtained. Both assumptions have been called invalid and unnecessary.[39]

The current entry price system recognizes current value as a basis of valuation but does not account for changes in the general price level and gains and losses on holding monetary assets and liabilities.

Finally, there is the difficult of correctly specifying what is meant by current entry price. Is an asset held for use or sale to be replaced by one equivalent, identical, or new asset? A defensible argument may be made for each of the interpretations of current entry price, namely, replacement cost–used, reproduction cost, and replacement cost–new.

Current Exit Price

Notions of Current Exit Prices   **Current exit price** represents the amount of cash for which assets might be sold or liabilities refinanced. It is generally agreed that the current exit price corresponds first to the selling prices under conditions of orderly rather than forced liquidation, and second, to the selling price at the time of measurement. In case the concern is with adjusted future selling price, the notion of **expected exit value** or **net realizable value** is used instead. More specifically, expected exit value or net realizable value is the amount of cash for which assets might be expected to be sold or liabilities refinanced. Thus, expected exit value or net realizable value refers to expected future sales proceeds, whereas current exit price refers to current selling price under conditions of orderly liquidation.

The notion of current exit price was introduced by MacNeal and further

[37]Lawrence Revsine, "Replacement Cost Accounting: A Theoretical Foundation," in *Objectives of Financial Statements: Selected Papers*, Vol. 2, ed. Joe J. Cramer, Jr., and George H. Sorter (New York: AICPA, 1974), pp. 241–44.

[38]David F. Drake and Nicholas Dopuch, "On the Case for Dichotomizing Income," *The Accounting Review* (October 1965), pp. 731–41; Prem Prakash and Shyam Sunder, "The Case Against Separation of Current Operating Profit and Holding Gain," *The Accounting Review* (January 1979), pp. 1–22.

[39]Robert R. Sterling, "The Going Concern: An Examination," *The Accounting Review* (July 1968), pp. 481–502.

developed by Sterling and Chambers.[40] In fact, another embracing term for current exit price—**current cash equivalent**—was proposed by Chambers, who explains:

> At any *present* time all past prices are simply a matter of history. Only present prices have any bearing on the choice of an action. The price of a good ten years ago has no more relation to this question than the hypothetical price twenty years hence. As individual prices may change even over an interval when the general purchasing power of money does not, and as the general purchasing power of money may change even though some individual prices do not, no useful inference may be drawn from past prices which has a necessary bearing on present capacity to operate in a market. Every measurement of a financial property for the purpose of choosing a course of action—to buy, to hold, or to sell—is a measurement at a point of time, in the circumstances of the time, and in the units of currency at that time, even if the measurement process itself takes some time.

> Excluding all past prices, there are two prices which could be used to measure the monetary equivalent of any nonmonetary good in possession, the buying price and the selling price. But the buying price, or replacement price, does not indicate capacity, on the basis of present holdings, to go into a market with cash for the purpose of adapting oneself to contemporary conditions, whereas the selling price does. We propose, therefore, that the single financial property which is uniformly relevant at a point of time for all possible future actions in markets is the market selling price or realizable price of any or all goods held. Realizable price may be described as *current cash equivalent*. What men wish to know, for the purpose of adaptation, is the numerosity of the money tokens which could be substituted for particular objects and for collections of objects if money is required beyond the amount which one already holds.[41]

Under the current exit approach, all assets and liabilities are revalued at their net realizable values. Net realizable values generally obtained from market quotations adjusted for estimated selling costs and, therefore, correspond to the quoted sales price on the demand market, while the current entry prices correspond to the quoted sales price on the supply market. Whenever the net realizable value can not be estimated directly from the demand market, these two alternatives may be considered: (1) the use of specific sales price indices, whether computed by external sources or internally by the firm; and, (2) the use of appraisals by external appraisers or by management. The primary characteristic of current exit price systems is the complete abandonment of the realization principle for the recognition of revenues. Valuing all nomonetary assets at their current exit price produces an immediate recognition of all gains. Thus, operating gains are recognized at the time of production, while holding gains and losses are recognized at the

---

[40]K. MacNeal, *Truth in Accounting* (Lawrence, Kansas: Scholars Book Co., 1970); R. R. Sterling, *Theory of the Measurement of Enterprise Income* (Lawrence, Kansas: University of Kansas Press, 1970); R. J. Chambers, *Accounting, Evaluation and Economic Behavior* (Englewood Cliffs, N.J.: Prentice-Hall, 1966).

[41]*Ibid.*, pp. 91–92.

time of purchase and, consequently, whenever prices change rather than at the time of sale. The critical event in the accounting cycle becomes the point of purchase or production rather than the point of sale.

Net Realizable Value Techniques Applied   Assume the same data as in Example 1 (page 153), except that the current exit price of coffee at the end of the period is $12 per unit. The income statement, balance sheet, and relevant notes under the current exit price basis are shown in Exhibit 5–5.

EXHIBIT 5–5
Income Statement
Current Exit Price Basis

Revenues			
Sales:	600 lb. × $10	$ 6,000	
Inventory:	400 lb. × $12	4,800	
Total			$10,800
Cost			
Cost of Sales:	600 lb. × $8	4,800	
Inventory:	400 lb. × $9	3,600	8,400
Operating Profit			$ 2,400
Realized Holding Gains			
On Sales:	600 lb. × ($8 − $6)		1,200
Unrealized Holding Gains			
On inventory:	400 lb. × ($9 − $6)		1,200
Current Exit Income			$ 4,800

Balance Sheet
Current Exit Price Basis

Assets		Liabilities and Stockholders' Equity	
Cash	$10,000	Share Capital	$10,000
Inventory[a]	4,800	Retained Earnings	
		Realized[b]	2,400
		Unrealized[c]	2,400
	$14,800		$14,800

[a] The inventory at the end of the year is valued at the net realizable value at that time: 400 lb. × $12 = $4,800.

[b] The realized retained earnings include:
  (1) the realized operating profit: (sales of $6,000 less cost of goods sold at $4,800 = $1,200), and
  (2) the realized holding gains on sales: $1,200.

[c] The unrealized retained earnings include:
  (1) the unrealized operating profit: revenues on the inventory at hand of $4,800, cost of inventories at hand of $3,600 = $1,200, and
  (2) the unrealized holding gains on inventory: $1,200.

Evaluation of Current Exit Price Based Accounting   The use of current-value accounting based on current exit price presents some advantages and some disadvantages. We shall discuss first some of the advantages attributed to current exit price based accounting.

First, the current exit price and the capitalized value of an asset provide different measures of the economic concept of opportunity costs. Thus, a firm's opportunity cost is either the cash value to be derived from the sale of the asset or the present value of the benefits to be derived from the use of the asset. Both values are relevant to making decisions concerning whether a firm should continue to use or sell assets already in use and whether or not a firm should *remain* a going concern.

Second, current exit price provides relevant and necessary information to evaluate the financial adaptability and liquidity of a firm. Thus, a firm holding fairly liquid assets has more opportunity to adapt to changing economic conditions than a firm holding assets with little or no resale value.

Third, current exit price provides a better guide for the evaluation of managers in their stewardship function because it reflects current sacrifices and other choices. Chambers states:

> As financial statements include in general terms the disposition of assets and increments in assets from time to time, they are regarded as the basis upon which the performance of a company and its management may be judged. . . . If the amounts of assets from time to time were stated on any basis other than their money equivalents, there would be no firm and satisfactory basis for determining the use and disposition of assets. Since all uses and dispositions in a period entail movements of money and money equivalents, financial statements based on the money equivalents of assets provide information on which periodical performance may fairly be judged.[42]

Fourth, the use of current exit price eliminates the need for arbitrary cost allocation on the basis of the estimated useful life of the asset. More explicitly, depreciation expense for a given year is the difference between the current exit price of the asset at the begining and at the end of the period.

Finally, the feasibility of exit price financial statements appears to be more and more accepted. For example, McKeown reports the results of efforts to prepare exit price financial statements by an electronic manufacturer as follows:

> Preparation of two exit-value balance sheets and an exit-value income statement for X Company demonstrated that in this case readily available market prices could be determined at very little cost for the land and building and most of the equipment. Market prices for the rest of the equipment (mainly metal furniture) were estimated again at nominal cost by use of general guidelines suggested by used furnitue dealers. A more accurate estimate for these items might have been obtained by employing an appraiser. However, the cost of appraisal of these items would have been significant (five percent of appraised value) and would probably be incurred every three or five years if at all. This procedure of relatively infrequent appraisals should yield accurate estimates because,

---

[42]R. J. Chambers, *Accounting for Inflation, Exposure Draft* (Sydney, Australia: University of Sydney, September 1975), par 20.

according to the used furniture dealers, the resale price is determined mainly by the type and quality of the asset rather than the age. Thus, barring major changes in the used asset market, an appraisal of a particular item (possibly adjusted by a specific price index) should be valid for several years.

Measurements of items other than fixed assets were readily computed at nominal cost. The only way management would have had any effect on the exit-value figures reported would have been solicitation of special offers for particular assets. Although this activity could be called manipulation, the economic fact remains that management could realize the offered amount. Further, the effect of these offers could easily be segragated. Other than the solicitation of special offers, management cannot manipulate exit-value figures because the measurements are taken from the markets rather than management estimates. This provides less opportunity for manipulation of profit figures than is available under conventional accounting procedures (alternative depreciation methods, sale of particular fixed assets to realize an available gain or loss, etc.)

The conclusion must be reached that critics of exit value who based their opposition on lack of feasibility of implementation will find no evidence to support their position in this case. Preparation of exit-value statements for X Company was possible at a reasonable cost.[43]

There are, however, some significant disadvantages to the current exit pice system that need to be mentioned.

First, the current exit price system is relevant for assets expected to be sold and for which a market price may be determined. The current exit price may be easily determined for assets for which a second-hand market exists. It may become a harder task for the specialized, custom-designed plant and equipment with little or no alternative use. Scrap values may be the only alternative measure for such assets.

Second, the current exit price system is not relevant for assets that the firm expects to use. The disclosure of the amount of cash that would be available if the firm sold such assets to move out of its industry and move into another one is not likely to be relevant to any user interested in the actual profitability of the firm in its present industry.

Third, the valuation of certain assets and liabilities at the current exit price has not yet been adequately resolved. On the one hand, there is the general problem of valuation of intangibles and the specific problem of valuation of goodwill. Also, the absence of marketable value makes the determination of realizable value difficult. McKeown, however, has shown that the realizable values may be either known or can be imputed.[44] On the other hand, there is the problem of valuation of liabilities. Should they be valued at their contractual amounts or at the amounts required to fund the liabilities? Chambers made a

---

[43]John C. McKeown, "Usefulness of Exit Value Accounting Statements in Satisfying Accounting Objectives," in *Objectives of Financial Statements: Selected Papers*, Vol. 2, p. 227.

[44]J. C. McKeown, "An Empirical Test of a Model Proposed by Chambers," *The Accounting Review* (January 1971), pp.12–29.

strong case for valuing liabilities at their contractual amounts. He points out that, "At a given time the issuer owes the bondholders the contractual amount of the bonds, whatever the price at which the bonds are traded."[45]

Fourth, the abandonment of the realization principle at the point of sale and the consequent assumption of liquidation of the firm's resources contradict the established assumption that the firm is a going concern.

Finally, the current exit price system does not take into account changes in the general price level.

Other Notions of Current Values

Other proposals have been made for the implementation of current-value accounting. In this section, we shall examine these proposals, grouping them for convenience in the following categories:

1. Essential versus nonessential assets
2. Value to the firm
3. SEC replacement cost proposal
4. Combination of values
5. Edwards and Bell's concept of business income

Essential Versus Nonessential Assets   In October 1975, the Australian Institute of Chartered Accountants and the Australian Society of Accountants published an exposure draft advocating the disclosure of supplementary current-value–based financial statements by July 1, 1977. Although that deadline was postponed, the Australian Accounting Standards Committee published a preliminary exposure draft on *A Method of Current Value Accounting* in June 1975. The exposure draft introduce a form of current-value accounting that uses different treatments for "essential" and "nonessential" assets. **Essential** assets are determined in reference to "the expected role of particular assets in the entity's operations in the immediately foreseeable future, that is, broadly speaking, continuing use of termination of use."[46] A **nonessential** asset is valued at its current exit price, while an essential asset is valued at its current entry price. The holding gains and losses on "essential" assets are credited or debited to a revaluation account, while the holding gains and losses on nonessential assets are included in income. Liabilities are valued at their contractual amounts. This valuation of liabilities is also the position taken by Chambers, who contends that:

> No amount shall be shown as liability unless it represents an amount owed to and legally recoverable by a creditor. Whether the due date is near or distant is immaterial. Long-dated obligations may become due and payable if any circumstances threaten the security of creditors.[47]

The essential versus nonessential distinction shows a modification of the current entry price system to reflect economic realities. In other words, exit price is a preferred alternative for those assets for which there is no future use.

---

[45] R. J. Chambers, "Continuously Contemporary Accounting," *Abacus* (September 1970), pp. 643–47.

[46] Australian Accounting Standards Committee, *A Method of Current Value Accounting* (Sidney: Australian Institute of Chartered Accountants and the Australian Society of Accountants, June 1975), par. 16.

[47] R. J. Chambers, *Accounting for Inflation*, par. 30.

Value to the Firm   In the United Kingdom, the "Report of the Inflation Accounting Committee," chaired by F. E. P. Sandilands, was issued in September 1975.[48] Known as the "Sandilands Report," it concluded that the following developments are necessary for changes in the law of corporations:

1. The same unit of measure should be used for all users.
2. The operating profit should be disclosed separately from the holding gains and losses.
3. The financial statements should include relevant information for assessing the liquidity of the company.

The most important recommendation of the "Sandilands Report," however, was the use of the "value to the firm" as a valuation base. Under this approach, assets are valued at an amount that represents the opportunity costs to the firm, that is, the maximum loss that might be incurred if the firm is deprived of these assets. Thus, the value to the firm in most cases will be measured by the replacement cost, given that replacement cost represents the amount of cash necessary to obtain an equivalent or identical asset. If the replacement cost is greater than the net realizable value and the discounted cash-flow value, the value to the firm will be: (1) the discounted cash-flow value if it is greater than net realizable value, given that it is preferable to use the asset than to sell it; and (2) the net realizable value if it is greater than the discounted cash flow, given that it is preferable to sell the asset than to use it.

Accounting based on the "value to the firm" was also described as **current cost accounting (CCA).**

The Sandilands Report also recommends that all holding gains and losses be excluded from current cost profit, which leads to:

(i) All unrealized gains arising from the reevaluation of fixed assets (and stock, where applicable) should be shown in reevaluation reserves in the balance sheet.

(ii) Realized holding gains arising on fixed assets should similarly be included in movements in balance sheet reserves.

(iii) The cost of sales adjustment (where applicable) should be taken to a balance sheet "stock adjustment reserve," whether it is positive or negative.

(iv) Extraordinary gains should be classed as "extraordinary items" (which) implies that they may be included in profit for the year, provided they are shown separately and distinguished from current cost profit.

(v) Operating gains should be shown "above the line" in the profit and loss account (earnings statement) as current cost profit for the year.[49]

The report recommends also that a "summary statement of total gains and losses for the year" appear immediately after the income statement. Such a summary statement may be illustrated as follows:

---

[48]F. E. P. Sandilands, *Report of the Inflation Accounting Committee* (London: HMSO, Cmmo, 6225, September 1975).

[49]*Ibid.*, para. 621.

Current costs profit after tax (as shown in profit and loss account)		£XXX
Extraordinary items less tax		XXX
Net profit after tax and extraordinary items		£XXX
Movements in reevaluation reserves net of tax		
Stock adjustment reserve	£XXX	
Reevaluation Reserves: Gain or loss due to changes in the bases of valuation of assets	XXX	
Other gains or losses	XXX	XXX
Total gain (loss) for the year after tax		£XXX

SEC Replacement Cost Proposal   As a first step to correcting some of the limitations of historical cost accounting, the Securities and Exchange Commission mandated replacement cost as the method of disclosure for large corporations. In March 1976, the SEC issued *Accounting Series Release No. 190*, which called for supplementary disclosure of replacement cost information by all SEC registrants with inventories, gross property, plant, and equipment that aggregate more than $100 million and that make up more than 10 percent of total assets.[50] Replacement cost was defined as the lowest amount that would have to be paid in the normal course of business to obtain a new piece of equipment operating at productive capacity. The regulation requires the designated firms, first, to estimate the current replacement cost of inventories and productive capacity and, second, to restate cost of goods sold and services, depreciation, depletion, and amortization for the two most recent full fiscal years on the basis of replacement cost of equivalent productive capacity.

The SEC proposal is a timid attempt to show the impact of inflation on fixed assets and inventory rather than on all monetary and nonmonetary assets. The SEC explicitly stated its objectives in Regulation 210.3.-17 as follows:

> The purpose of this rule is to provide information to investors which will assist them in obtaining an understanding of the current cost of operating the business which cannot be obtained from historical cost financial statements taken alone. . . . A secondary purpose is to provide information which will enable investors to determine the current cost of inventories and productive capacity as a measure of the current economic investment in these assets existing at the balance sheet date.[51]

Combination of Values   The combination of values approach has been suggested as a way of avoiding some of the disadvantages of the current exit price,

---

[50]*Accounting Series Release No. 190*, "Notice of Adoption and Amendments to Regulation S-X Requiring Disclosure of Certain Replacement Cost Data" (Washington, D. C.: Securities and Exchange Commission, 1976).

[51]SEC Regulation 210.3-17, "Current Replacement Cost Information, Statement of Objectives."

current entry price, and capitalization methods. The Canadian Accounting Research Committee's preliminary position favors a combined use of current entry and current exit prices.[52] More specifically, the following values are advocated:

Monetary assets should be shown at discounted cash flow except for short-term items where the time value of money effect is small. . . .

Marketable securities should be valued at current exit price with adjustments for selling costs. . . .

In general, inventory items should be valued at current entry prices. . . .

Normally, long-term intercorporate investments should be valued at current entry prices. . . .

Fixed assets should normally be valued at replacement cost-new (less applicable depreciation calculated on the basis of the estimated useful life of the assets held). . . .

In general, intangible values should be valued at current value. . . .

Liabilities should be shown at the discounted value of future payments except for short-term items when the time value of money effect is small. . . .[53]

A similar combination of values approach was proposed by Sprouse and Moonitz, except that they in fact advocate common dollar current value statements.[54]

Although the combination of values approach may appear to rest on arbitrary rules, advocates of the approach suggested specific decisions rules for the choice of a valuation method based on the market opportunity costs of assets.[55]

The opportunity cost of an action is the value of the benefits foregone as a result of the choice of the proposed action rather than the best option.

The opportunity cost of an asset is indicated by one of the following decision rules:

1. If $C > \bar{R} > S^*$,   use the asset until replacement is required;
2. if $C > S > \bar{R}$,   use the asset until replacement is required;
3. if $R > C > \bar{S}$,   use the asset but do not replace it;
4. if $S > C > \bar{R}$,   sell the asset and replace for resale rather than use;
5. if $S > \bar{R} > C^*$,   sell the asset and replace for resale rather than use; and
6. if $R^* > \bar{S} > C$,   sell the asset and do not replace.

Where

    C = Capitalized value of the asset

    R = Replacement cost of the asset (current entry price)

    S = Net realizable value (current exit price)

---

[52] Accounting Research Committee Discussion Paper, *Current Value Accounting* (Toronto, Ontario: Canadian Institute of Chartered Accountants, August 1976), p. 28.

[53] *Ibid.*, pp. 66–68.

[54] R. T. Sprouse and M. Moonitz, "A Tentative Set of Accounting Principles for Business Enterprises," *Accounting Research Study No. 3* (New York: AICPA, 1962).

[55] Barton, *An Analysis of Business Income Concepts*, pp. 45–46.

* refers to the opportunity cost
  – refers to the nonrelevant value in the comparison.[56]

From the above rules, we can state the following valuation bases:

    1. Use the replacement cost of the assets for all situations in which the assets need to be replaced, as in (1), (2), (4), and (5).

    2. Use the net realizable value of the assets for all situations in which the assets should be used but not replaced, as in (3), and where they should be sold and not replaced, as in (6).

If we add to these two rules a decision rule advocating the valuation of monetary assets and liabilities at their capitalized values, we end up with a combination of values approach that easily may be justified conceptually and practically.

The combination of values approach was deemed relevant by the FASB Study Group on the Objectives of Financial Statements within a particular set of financial statements:

> The Study Group believes that the objectives of financial statements cannot be best served by the exclusive use of a single valuation basis. The objectives that prescribe statements of earnings and financial position are based on user's needs to predict, compare, and evaluate earning power. To satisfy these information requirements, the Study Group concludes that different valuation bases are preferable for different assets and liabilities. That means that financial statements might contain data based on a combination of valuation bases. . . . Current replacement cost may be the best substitute for measuring the benefits of long-term assets held for use rather than sale. Current replacement cost may be particularly appropriate when significant price changes or technological developments have occurred since the assets were acquired. . . . Exit value may be an appropriate substitute for measuring the potential benefit or sacrifice of assets and liabilities expected to be sold or discharged in a relatively short time.[57]

Edwards argues also for a combination of values, as follows:

> A firm that values its assets at exit prices derived from markets in which the firm is normally a buyer reports *unusual* values—those which would obtain in a liquidation situation, at least so far as the assets being so valued are concerned. To employ such values when liquidation is not contemplated is surely misleading. . . .
>
> I am not convinced of the merit of adopting as a normal basis for asset valuations in the going concern, exit prices in buyer markets. These are unusual values suitable for unusual situations. . . .
>
> The point at issue, of course, is not *whether* to value by current entry or exit prices, but *when* to shift from entry to exit values. . . .
>
> The principle . . . that all assets and liabilities of the going concern should be valued at current prices except for those that the firm normally sells . . . would come close to a rule of "replacement cost or net realizable

---

[56]*Ibid.*, p. 46.
[57]*Objectives of Financial Statements*, pp. 41–43.

value, whichever is higher," . . . [except for] a firm which is temporarily selling at a loss.[58]

The Concept of Business Income   Edwards and Bell introduced the concept of **business income**, which others labeled "money income."[59] To explain the components of business, or money, income, we shall highlight the ways in which it differs from accounting income.

We defined accounting income as the difference between the realized revenues arising from the transactions of the period and the corresponding historical costs. In presenting replacement cost income, we also showed that (1) the current operating profit, representing the difference between the realized revenues and the corresponding replacement cost, and (2) the realized holding gains and losses, representing the difference between the replacement costs of the units sold and the historical costs of the same units, constitute the two types of gains that are included in the accounting income. The realized holding gains and losses also may be divided into two elements: First, the holding gains and losses realized and accrued during the period and, second, the holding gains and losses realized during the period but accrued during previous periods. More specifically, accounting income (P_a) may be expressed as:

$$P_a = x + y + z$$

where

> x = current operating profit
>
> y = realized and accrued holding gains of the period
>
> z = realized holding gains of the period accruing in previous periods.

Business income differs from accounting income in two ways: it is based on replacement cost valuation and it recognizes only the gains accruing during the period. More specifically, the business income comprises, first, the current operating profit (x) as defined earlier, second, the realized and accrued holding gains of the period (y), and third, the unrealized holding gains and losses accruing in the period. Business income (P_b) may be expressed as:

$$P_b = x + y + w$$

where

> x and y are as defined above, and
>
> w = unrealized holding gains and losses.

Thus, the difference between business and accounting income is:

$$P_b = P_a - z + w$$

In other words, the business income is equal to the accounting income less the realized holding gains of the period accruing in previous periods and plus the

---

[58]Edgar O. Edwards, "The State of Current Value Accounting," *The Accounting Review* (April 1975), pp. 235–45.

[59]Edwards and Bell, *The Theory and Measurement of Business Income*; R. H. Parker, and G. C. Harcourt, eds., *Readings in the Concept and Measurement of Income* (New York: Cambridge University Press, 1969), pp. 17–18.

EXHIBIT 5-6

Reconciliation of Business or Money Income with Accounting Income

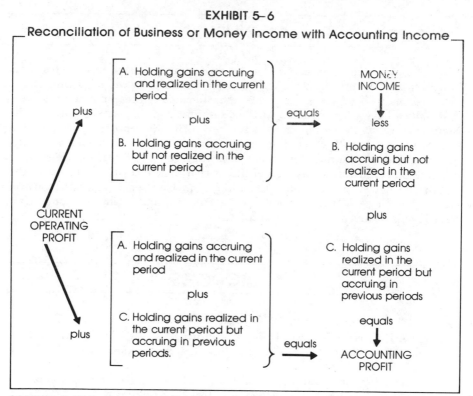

SOURCE: R. H. Parker and G. C. Harcourt, eds., *Readings in the Concept and Measurement of Income* (New York: Cambridge University Press, 1969), p. 6.

unrealized holding gains and losses. A reconciliation of business, or money, income with accounting income is shown in Exhibit 5–6.

This difference may be illustrated by the following example. Assume 1,000 units of a given product were acquired at a price of $1 per unit. At t_1, their replacement cost was $2 per unit. The 1,000 units were sold at t_2 for $3 per unit when replacement cost was $2.50 per unit. Exhibit 5–7 shows the differences between the business income and the accounting income for both periods t_1 and t_2.

EXHIBIT 5-7

Accounting and Business Incomes

Period	x (1)	y (2)	z (3)	w (4)	P_a (1)+(2)+(3)	P_b (1)+(2)+(4)
t_{0-1}	—	—	—	$1,000	—	$1,000
t_{0-2}	$500	$500	$1,000	—	$2,000	1,000
Total	$500	$500	$1,000	$1,000	$2,000	$2,000

Conclusions

The accounting model for current-value accounting discussed in this chapter is based on the interpretation of the "Hicksian" concept of capital maintenance, meaning physical productive capacity maintenance. Different notions of current values have been proposed in the literature and in practice, namely, the capitalized value, the current entry price, the current exit price, and a combination of these values. Each method presents definite advantages compared with historical cost accounting. The major disadvantage of any of the current-value methods and of historical cost accounting is that none recognizes changes in the purchasing power of the dollar. Accordingly, in Chapter 6 we shall focus on general price-level adjusted historical cost accounting and in Chapter 7 on general price-level adjusted current-value accounting.

References

Historical Cost

Ijiri, Y. "A Defense of Historical Cost Accounting." In *Asset Valuation and Income Determination*. Ed. R. R. Sterling. Lawrence, Kansas: Scholars Book Co., 1971, pp. 1–14.

Ijiri, Y. "The Significance of Historical Cost Valuation," *The Foundation of Accounting Measurement*. Englewood Cliffs, N.J.: Prentice-Hall, 1967, pp. 64–67.

Kohler, E. L. "Why Not Retain Historical Cost?" *The Journal of Accountancy* (October 1963), pp. 35–41.

Littleton, A. C. "The Significance of Invested Cost." *The Accounting Review* (April 1952), pp. 167–73.

Mautz, R. K. "A Few Words for Historical Cost." *Financial Executive* (January 1973), pp. 23–27, 93–98.

Capitalization

Alexander, Sidney S. "Income Measurement in a Dynamic Economy." Rev. David Solomons in *Studies in Accounting Theory*, ed. W. T. Baxter and S. Davidson. Homewood, Ill.: R.D. Irwin, 1962, pp. 126–200.

Barton, A. D. "Expectations and Achievements in Income Theory." *The Accounting Review* (October 1974), pp. 664–81.

Bierman, H., Jr., and S. Davidson. "The Income Concept—Value Increment or Earnings Predictor." *The Accounting Review* (April 1969), pp. 239–46.

Bromwich, M. "The Use of Present Valuation Models in Published Accounting Reports." *The Accounting Review* (July 1977), pp. 587–96.

Mattessich, R. "On the Perennial Misunderstanding of Asset Measurement by Means of 'Present Values.'" *Cost and Management* (March–April 1970), pp. 29–31.

Parker, B. H., and G. C. Harcourt, eds. *Readings in the Concept and Measurement of Income*. New York: Cambridge University Press, 1969.

Shwayder, K. "A Critique of Economic Income as an Accounting Concept." *Abacus* (August 1967), pp. 23–35..

Shwayder, K. "The Capital Maintenance Rule and the Net Asset Valuation Rule." *The Accounting Review* (April 1969), pp. 304–16.

Current Entry Price

Drake, D. F., and N. Dopuch. "On the Case of Dichotomizing Income." *Journal of Accounting Research* (Autumn 1965), pp. 192–205.

Prakash, P., and S. Sunder. "The Case Against Separation of Current Operating Profit and Holding Gain." *The Accounting Review* (January 1979), pp. 1–22.

Revsine, L. "Replacement Cost Accounting," *Contemporary Topics in Accounting Series.* Englewood Cliffs, N.J.: Prentice-Hall, 1973.

Rosenfield, P. "Current Replacement Value Accounting—A Dead-End." *The Journal of Accountancy* (September 1975), pp. 63–73.

Rosenfield, P. "Reporting Subjective Gains and Losses." *The Accounting Review* (October 1969), pp. 788–97.

Stamp, E. "The Valuation of Assets." *Chartered Accountant Magazine* (November 1975), pp. 67–69.

Current Exit Price

Bedford, N. M., and J. C. McKeown. "Net Realizable Value and Replacement Cost." *The Accounting Review* (April 1972), pp. 333–38.

Chambers, R. J. *Accounting, Evaluation and Economic Behavior.* Englewood Cliffs, N.J.: Prentice-Hall, 1966 (reprinted 1974 by Scholars Book Co., Houston, Texas)

Chambers, R. *Accounting for Inflation, Exposure Draft.* Sydney, Australia: University of Sydney, August 1975.

Chambers, R. *Accounting for Inflation, Methods and Problems.* Sydney, Australia: University of Sydney, August 1975.

Chambers, R. "NOD, COG and PUPU See How Inflation Teases." *The Journal of Accountancy* (February 1975), pp. 56–62.

Staubus, G. J. "Current Cash Equivalent for Assets: A Dissent." *The Accounting Review* (October 1967), pp. 650–61.

Sterling, R. R. *Theory of the Measurement of Enterprise Income.* Lawrence, Kansas: University of Kansas Press, 1970.

Questions

5–1 Discuss the relevance of the income concept.

5–2 Describe accounting income.

5–3 What are some of the advantages and disadvantages of accounting income?

5–4 Discuss the evolution of the economic concept of income.

5–5 Describe the different concepts of capital maintenance.

5–6 List and describe the different notions of current value.

5–7 Evaluate current entry price accounting.

5–8 Evaluate capitalization accounting.

5–9 Evaluate the current exit price accounting.

5–10   Explain the Edwards and Bell concept of business income.

5–11   The following data are presented for Repaco, Inc.:

Rapaco, Inc.
Balance Sheet
May 31, 19X4

Assets

Cash		$ 50,000
Inventory, FIFO cost (6,000 units at $5.00)		30,000
Land		15,000
Building	$220,000	
Less Accumulated Depreciation	55,000	165,000
Equipment	90,000	
Less Accumulated Depreciation	45,000	45,000
		$305,000

Liabilities and Shareholders' Equity

Income Taxes Payable	$ 30,000
Mortgage Payable	65,000
Capital Stock	150,000
Retained Earnings	60,000
	$305,000

Transaction data during the year ending May 31, 19X5

(1)   Cash sales for the year totaled (50,000 × $12.00) $600,000.

(2)   Purchase for the year totaled (52,000 × $7.00) $364,000.

(3)   Other expenses including depreciation totaled $175,000.

(4)   The building has an estimated useful life of 20 years and the equipment has an estimated useful life of 10 years. Neither asset is expected to have any salvage value at the end of its useful life. Building and equipment were purchased five years ago.

(5)   The income tax rate is 50 percent of reported income including realized holding gains and losses.

(6)   At year-end, the replacement cost of inventory was $8.00 per unit.

(7)   The land had an appraised value of $20,000 at year-end.

(8)   The replacement cost of the building is $250,000 and of the equipment $120,000, which represents gross value at the year-end.

(9)   All transactions are assumed to have been uniformly incurred over the year.

Required:

Prepare a comparative balance sheet and income statement for 1975 using generally accepted accounting principles and replacement cost.

(Society of Management Accountants, adapted 1975)

5–12   The audited quarterly statements of income issued by many corporations to their stockholders are prepared on the same basis as annual statements, the statement for each quarter reflecting the transactions of that quarter.

Required:

a.   Explain why problems arise in using such quarterly statements to predict the income (before extraordinary items) for the year.

b.   Discuss the ways in which quarterly income may be affected by the behavior of the costs recorded in a Repairs and Maintenance of Factory Machinery account.

c. Do such quarterly statements give management opportunities to manipulate the results of operations for a quarter? Explain or give an example.

5–13 The controller of Navar Corporation wants to issue to stockholders a quarterly income statement that will predict annual results. He proposes to allocate all fixed costs for the year among quarters in proportion to the number of units expected to be sold in each quarter, stating that the annual income can then be predicted through use of the following equation:

$$\frac{\text{Annual}}{\text{income}} = \frac{\text{Quarterly}}{\text{income}} \times \frac{100\%}{\text{Percent of unit sales applicable to quarter}}$$

Navar expects the following activity for the year:

	Unit	Average Per Unit	Total (in thousands)
Sales revenue:			
First quarter	500,000	$2.00	$1,000
Second quarter	100,000	1.50	150
Third quarter	200,000	2.00	400
Fourth quarter	200,000	2.00	400
	1,000,000		$1,950
Costs to be incurred:			
Variable:			
Manufacturing		$0.70	$ 700
Selling and Administrative		0.25	250
		$0.95	$ 950
Fixed:			
Manufacturing			$ 380
Selling and Administrative			220
			$ 600
Income before income taxes			$ 400

Required (ignore income taxes):

a. Assuming that Navar's activities do not vary from expectations, will the controller's plan achieve his objective? If not, how can it be modified to do so? Explain and give illustrative computations.

b. How would the effect of variations of actual activity be treated in Navar's quarterly income statements?

c. What assumption has the controller made regarding inventories. Discuss.

(AICPA adapted)

5–14 Section 446 of the 1954 Internal Revenue Code states: "Taxable income shall be computed under the method of accounting on . . . which the taxpayer regularly computes his income in keeping his books"; the method employed shall "clearly reflect income." Among the permissable methods are: (1) "the cash receipts and disbursement method" and (2) "an accrual method."

Required:

Generally accepted accounting principles normally require the use of accrual accounting to "fairly present" income. If the cash receipts and disbursements method of accounting will "clearly reflect" taxable income, why does this method not usually also "fairly present" income?

(AICPA adapted)

5–15 A. D. Barton made the following statement in "Expectations and Achievements in Income Theory" in *The Accounting Review* (October 1974), pp. 664–5:

> The case for dominant position of *ex-ante* present value income rests on the needs of investors for information about the future income prospects of the firm. Investors in business enterprises, i.e., owners, are interested in the prospects of future income from investments, and it is differences in these future prospects which determine the allocation of their investment funds. Ideally, they require information on the expected income to be earned in each form of investment so that they can select those promising the highest returns. The appropriate measures for this are present value income and its corollary, the present value of assets. They do not invest money in firms just because of past financial performances.

Do you agree with this evaluation of present-value accounting? Discuss.

5–16 N. M. Bedford and J. C. McKeown made the following statement in "Comparative Analysis of Net Realizable Value and Replacement Costing" in *The Accounting Review* (April 1972), p. 338:

> On balance, it seems to the authors that advantages accrue to both net realizable value and current replacement cost valuations. It is our conclusion that the complexities of modern economic life require both calculations. We contend that attempts to find simple unequivocal answers to complex problems are bound to fail. Complex problems require complex solutions. Clearly, the accounting profession must start presenting multiple valuations and make multiple disclosures in their annual report. Simple income statements and balance sheets of the past were designed for a much simpler society. This analysis of the non-trivial valuation issue (Net realizable value vs. current replacement cost) indicates that multiple and complex, but precise, annual reports are now required if the accounting profession is to comply with its ethical requirements to provide useful information.

Do you agree with the authors' conclusion? Discuss.

chapter six

General Price-Level Accounting

In Chapter 5, we introduced the radical school of thought associated with the adoption of current-value accounting. We also established that a neoclassical school exists as a middle ground between the classical school of historical cost accounting and the radical school of current-value accounting. This option consists of the restatement of historical cost financial statements prepared in accordance with generally accepted accounting principles in terms of the same unit of general purchasing power. Known as general price-level accounting, or general price-level adjusted historical cost accounting, this school differs from current-value accounting and historical cost accounting by its complete renunciation of the stable monetary unit postulate. Also, we should emphasize at the outset that general price-level accounting and current-value accounting are competing alternatives for dealing with the problems created by inflation. General price-level accounting reflects changes in the general price level, while current-value accounting reflects changes in the specific price level. In general price-level accounting, the change in the unit of measure is measured.

In this chapter, we shall analyze the conceptual and operational features of general price-level accounting information and the means of providing such information.

General Price-Level Restatement of Historical Cost Financial Statements

Historical cost accounting assumes that the monetary unit is either stable or that the changes in its value are not material. It is well recognized, however, that the general purchasing power of the dollar has been continually declining. General purchasing power, which refers to the ability of the monetary unit to purchase goods or services, is inversely related to the price of goods or services for which it may be exchanged. When the price of goods or services increases, the movement is referred to as inflation, which is also a decrease in the general purchasing power of money. When the price of goods or service decreases, the movement is referred to as deflation, which is also an increase in the general purchasing power of money. Because historical cost accounting does not recognize these changes in the general purchasing power of money, the balance sheet contains diverse kinds of assets and liabilities that refer to different dates and that are expressed in dollars having different purchasing power. General price-level accounting is a method for correcting this situation by completely restating the historical cost financial statements in a way that reflects changes in the purchasing power of the dollar.

Changes in the purchasing power of the dollar are measured by means of index numbers. A **price index** is the ratio of the average price of a group of goods or services at a given date and the average price of a similar group of goods or services at another date, known as the base year, when the price index is equal to 100. Price indexes that measure the changes in prices on a general basis reflect the purchasing power of the dollar. Such indexes are used to restate the historical cost basis amounts on the financial statements in terms of units of purchasing power at a base year or at the end of the current period. So that intercompany comparisons will be meaningful, the established common date to which dollars are to be restated in terms of general purchasing power is the end of the current period.

To introduce the steps required in the preparation of general price level statements, we shall use a simplified model drawn from the discussions introduced by Chambers.[1] Assume that a firm's balance sheet may be divided into monetary items and nonmonetary items. At this level, monetary items may be defined as those items for which amounts are fixed by contract or otherwise, in terms of number of dollars, regardless of changes in price levels. For the period t_0, the balance sheet equation, expressed in dollars at time 0, is:

$$M_0 + N_0 = R_0$$

where

$$M_0 = \text{net monetary items}$$

$$N_0 = \text{net nonmonetary items}$$

$$R_0 = \text{residual equity.}$$

Let us also assume that there is a change in the general price level p. By definition, $p = (P_1/P_0) - 1$, where P_0 is the price index at time 0 and P_1 is the price index at time 1. The balance sheet equation at t_2, restated for the changes in the general price level, is:

$$M_0(1 + p) + N_0(1 + p) = R_0(1 + p)$$

which is equivalent to:

$$M_0 + M_{0p} + N_0 + N_{0p} = R_0 + R_{0p}$$

Given that, by definition, net monetary assets are expressed in fixed amounts of dollars, it is appropriate to remove M_{0p} from each side of the equation and replace M_0 with M_1:

$$M_1 + (N_0 + N_{0p}) = (R_0 + R_{0p}) - M_{0p}$$

This last equation may be interpreted as follows:

1. M_1 represents the net monetary assets at t_1.
2. $N_0 + N_{0p}$ represents the general price-level restated monetary assets at t_1.
3. $R_0 + R_{0p}$ represents the general price-level restated residual equity at t_1.
4. M_{0p} represents the gains or losses on monetary items. By definition, M_0 is equal to net monetary assets (C_0) less monetary liabilities (L_0). The balance sheet equation at t_2 may be restated as follows:

---

[1]R. J. Chambers, *Towards a General Theory of Accounting* (Adelaide, Austrailia: University of Adelaide, 1961) and *Accounting, Evaluation and Economic Behavior* (Englewood Cliffs, N.J.: Prentice-Hall, 1965), pp. 223–27.

$$C_1 + (N_0 + N_{0p}) - L_1 = (R_0 + R_{0p}) - (C_{0p} - L_{0p})$$

or

$$C_1 + (N_0 + N_{0p}) - L_1 = (R_0 + R_{0p}) - C_{0p} + L_{0p}$$

Consequently, L_{0p} represents the gain from the outstanding liabilities during the period, and C_{0p} represents the loss from holding monetary assets from t_0 to t_1.

From the above simplified model, we may develop the methodology required for the restatement of historical cost amounts in traditional financial statements to units of general purchasing power. The following steps are necessary:

1. Obtain the complete set of historical cost financial statements.
2. Determine and obtain an acceptable general price-level index with data on the index numbers available to cover the life of the oldest item on the balance sheet.
3. Classify each item on the balance sheet as either a monetary or a nonmonetary item.
4. Adjust the nonmonetary items by a conversion factor to reflect the current general purchasing power.
5. Calculate the general purchasing power (general price-level) gains or losses arising from holding monetary items.

We shall discuss each of these steps, with the exception of Step 1, in the remainder of this chapter.

Adjusting Specific Items for General Price-Level Changes

Treatment of Monetary Items

Calculation of the General Price-Level Gain or Loss   As previously stated, the amounts of monetary items are fixed by contract or otherwise in terms of number of dollars, regardless of changes in the general or specific price level. Although the amounts are fixed, the value of the monetary items in terms of purchasing power changes. Holders of monetary items, therefore, gain or lose purchasing power because the general level of prices changes. Such gains and losses are called general purchasing power gains or losses, or general price-level gains or losses on monetary items. More specifically, during periods of rising prices: (1) monetary assets lose purchasing power, to be recognized by a general price-level loss, and (2) monetary liabilities gain purchasing power, to be recognized by a general price-level gain. During periods of decreasing prices: (1) monetary assets gain purchasing power, to be recognized by a general price-level gain, and (2) monetary liabilities lose purchasing power, to be recognized by a general price-level loss.

To compute the general price-level gain or loss, the following procedures may be used:

1. Compute the net monetary asset position at the beginning of the period.

For example, if cash and payables at the beginning of the period are $30,000 and $20,000, respectively, the net monetary assets will be $10,000.

2. Restate the net monetary asset position at the beginning of the period in terms of the purchasing power of the dollar at the end of the period. For example, assume the general price-level index was 120 at the beginning of the period and 180 at the end of the period. The net monetary asset position at the beginning of the period, which was $10,000, would be restated to $15,000 [$10,000 × (180/120)].

3. Restate all the monetary receipts of the year to the year-end basis and add the result to the restated net monetary position at the beginning of the period (found in Step 2). Assuming that sales of $20,000 occurred evenly during the year and the average general price index was 150, the adjusted monetary receipts would be restated to $24,000 [$20,000 × (180/150)]. This result is added to the $15,000 found in Step 2 to arrive at a total restated net increase in monetary items of $39,000.

4. Restate all the monetary payments of the year to the year-end basis and deduct the result from the total restated net increase in monetary items found in Step 4. Assume that purchases and expenses of $15,000 also occurred evenly during the year. The adjusted monetary payments would be restated to $18,000 [$15,000 × (180/150)]. This result is deducted from the $39,000 found in Step 3 to arrive at the adjusted computed net monetary assets at the end of the period of $21,000.

5. Deduct the actual net monetary assets at the end of the period from the computed net monetary assets at the end of the period found in Step 4 to obtain the purchasing power gains of $6,000.

Using our example, these five steps may be summarized as follows:

	Monetary Items	
	Unadjusted	Adjusted
Steps 1 and 2	$10,000	$15,000
Step 3	20,000	24,000
Total	$30,000	$39,000
Step 4	15,000	18,000
Total	$15,000	$21,000
Step 5		15,000
Purchasing power gain (or loss)		$ 6,000

To summarize, general price-level gains or losses are computed by restating the net monetary position at the beginning of the period and the net monetary transactions during the period to units of general purchasing power at the end of the period. The result is compared with the actual net monetary position, and the difference is the general price-level gain or loss.

Treatment of the General Price-Level Gain or Loss   A lack of agreement exists on the nature of the general price-level gain or loss and the relevant accounting treatment. The following approaches have been suggested.

First, *Accounting Research Study No. 6, APB Statement No. 3*, and the FASB and the CICA exposure drafts on general price-level accounting have taken the position that the general price-level gain or loss should be included in current income.[2]

The second approach is that only the general price-level loss should be included in current income, while the general price-level gain should be treated as capital items.

Third, both the general price-level gain and loss should be treated as capital items.

Fourth, both the general price-level gain and loss should be included in current income, except for those gains and losses relating to long-term debt, which should not appear until realized through the redemption of the bonds.[3]

Fifth, all price-level gains and losses should be included in current income, except for those arising from monetary items included in shareholders' equity, for example, preferred shares having monetary characteristics.

In spite of the controversy generated by each of these different viewpoints, predominant view in pronouncements of the various accounting bodies favors the first treatment. The AICPA first expressed this viewpoint in 1969 in *APB Statement No. 3:*

> 41. General price-level gains and losses on monetary items arise from changes in the general price-level, and are not related to subsequent events such as the receipt or payment of money. Consequently, the Board has concluded that these gains and losses should be recognized as part of the net income of the period in which the general price level changes.

> 42. A different viewpoint than that expressed in paragraph 41, held by a Board member, is that all of a monetary gain should not be recognized in the period of general price-level increase. Under this view, a portion of the gain on net monetary liabilities in a period of general price-level increase should be deferred to future periods as a reduction of the cost of nonmonetary assets, since the liabilities represent a source of funds for the financing of these assets. The proponent of this view believes that the gain from holding net monetary liabilities during inflation is not realized until the assets acquired from the funds borrowed are sold or consumed in operations. The Board does not agree with this view, however, because it believes that the gain accrues during the period of the general price-level increase and is unrelated to the cost of nonmonetary assets.[4]

The APB conclusion was sustained by the FASB in its exposure draft on the subject, which stated:

---

[2] *Accounting Research Study No. 6,* "Reporting the Financial Effects of Price-Level Changes" (New York: AICPA, 1963), p. 13; APB *Statement No. 3,* "Financial Statements Restated for General Price-Level Changes" (New York: AICPA, June 1969), p. 8; Financial Accounting Standards Board, Exposure Draft, "Financial Reporting in Units of General Purchasing Power" (New York: FASB, December 31, 1974), par. 30; Accounting Research Committee, *Accounting for Changes in the General Purchasing Power of Money* (Toronto: Canadian Institute of Chartered Accountants, July 1975), p. 12.

[3] Perry Mason, *Price Level Changes and Financial Statements—Basic Concepts and Methods* (Columbus, Ohio: AAA, 1956), pp. 23–24.

[4] *APB Statement No. 3,* par. 41–42.

48. The net gain or loss of general purchasing power that results from holding monetary assets and liabilities shall be included in determining net income in units of general purchasing power. No portion of the general purchasing power gain or loss shall be deferred to future periods.

77. General purchasing power gains or losses on monetary assets and liabilities arise from changes in the general price-level while the assets are held or the liabilities are owned. They are not related to subsequent events such as the receipt or payment of money. Consequently, the Board concluded (paragraph 48) that those gains and losses should be recognized in determining general purchasing power income in the period in which general price level changes.[5]

The same position was also reached by the Accounting Standards Steering Committee in the United Kingdom, which published a *Provisional Statement of Standard Accounting Practice No. 7* in May 1974. It justified the position as follows:

16. It has been argued that the gain on long term borrowing should not be shown as profit in the supplementary statement because it might not be possible to distribute it without raising additional finance. This argument, however, confuses the measurement of profitability with the measurement of liquidity. Even in the absence of inflation, the whole of a company's profit may not be distributable without raising additional finance, for example because it has been invested in, or earmarked for investment in nonliquid assets.

17. Moreover, it is inconsistent to exclude such gains when profit has been debited with the cost of borrowing (which must be assumed to reflect anticipation of inflation by the lender during the currency of the loan), and with depreciation on the converted cost of fixed assets.[6]

The Accounting Research Committee in Canada took a similar position.[7] Thus, as a general rule, all price-level gains or losses are recognized in the general price-level income statement. The only exception, recommended in both the FASB and the Canadian positions, concerns gains or losses attributable to preferred shares (monetary preference shares) carried at an amount equal to their fixed redemption or liquidation price, which should be credited or charged to common shareholders' equity in the general price-level balance sheet.

Treatment of Nonmonetary Items and Stockholders' Equity

Nonmonetary items are restated in terms of the current general purchasing power by multiplying the cost of the item as reported on the historical cost—based financial statements by the following conversion factor:

---

[5]FASB Exposure Draft, "Financial Reporting in Units of General Purchasing Power," pars. 48 and 77.

[6]Accounting Standards Steering Committee, *Provisional Statement of Standard Accounting Practice No. 7*, "Accounting for Changes in the Purchasing Power of Money" (London: HMSO, May 1974).

[7]"Accounting for Changes in the General Purchasing Power of Money."

$$\frac{\text{Current Year Index}}{\text{Index When the Nonmonetary Item Was Acquired}}$$

For example, assume that a piece of equipment was acquired for $100,000 on December 31, 19X0, when the general price-level index was 120. The estimated useful life of the asset was four years. Assume, further, that the financial statements at the end of 19X2 are restated in terms of units of general purchasing power. If the current-price index on December 31, 19X3 was 180, the adjustment of the equipment account would be as follows:

	Unadjusted	Conversion Factor	Adjusted
Equipment	$100,000	180/120	$150,000
Accumulated depreciation	50,000	180/120	75,000
Net Equipment	$ 50,000		$ 75,000

The restatement of stockholders' equity, with the exception of retained earnings, is similar to the nonmonetary items. The original invested capital is multiplied by the following conversion factor:

$$\frac{\text{Current Year Index}}{\text{Index When the Capital Was Invested}}$$

Retained earnings, which cannot be adjusted by a single conversion factor, represent net income after dividends accumulated since the creation of the going concern. Retained earnings may be restated as follows:

1.   The first time historical cost financial statements are restated in terms of units of current general purchasing power, retained earnings may be determined simply as a residual after all other items in the balance sheet have been restated.
2.   In the following periods, the end-of-period retained earnings in units of current general purchasing power may be determined by:
   a.   net income in units of current general purchasing power as reported in the general price-level statement (including general price-level gains and losses on monetary items), and
   b.   adjustments resulting from general price-level gains or losses on monetary shareholders' equity items.

An important difference is not apparent between general price-level accounting and current-value accounting. Under current-value accounting, an increase in price of a nonmonetary item results in a holding gain. Under general price-level accounting, the adjustment of historical cost is simply a restatement of a nonmonetary item in terms of the current general purchasing power and no gain or loss is recognized.

The Monetary–Nonmonetary Distinction

The distinction between monetary and nonmonetary items is important because different treatments are applied to the two types of items. Nonmonetary items must be translated into dollars of the same purchasing power at the end of the current period. Monetary items, on the other hand, are already stated in end-of-the-current-period dollars and gain or lose purchasing power as a result of changes in the general price level. The distinction between monetary items and nonmonetary items seems apparent. Monetary items gain or lose purchasing power, while nonmonetary items do not. This reasoning was used in *APB Statement No. 3* and reported by different authors.[8] Determining monetary items according to the expected effect, however—that is, gain or loss of purchasing power—and then calculating the gain or loss is circular reasoning. As Hendriksen points out, it

bases the classification on the assumed effect rather than determining the effect from the classification and a change in the price level.[9]

What is necessary is a definition that will allow the identification of monetary assets apart from their expected effects. *Accounting Research Study No. 6* used the idea of fixed claims to define a monetary item as

one the amount of which is fixed by statute or contract, and is therefore not affected by a change in the general price level.[10]

Because it does not specify how the amount is to be fixed, this definition is inadequate. Thus, to correct for this misspecification, the official definition adopted in the various pronouncements of the accounting bodies considers monetary items as "those whose amounts are fixed by contracts or otherwise fixed in terms of dollars (or whatever is the domestic currency) regardless of changes in specific prices or in the general price level." This definition is general and applies to assets, liabilities, and shareholders' equities that have the specified characteristics. Accordingly, monetary and nonmonetary items are identified and segregated as shown in Exhibit 6–1. Some problem areas exist, however, because some assets and liabilities may combine characteristics of both monetary and nonmonetary items. The problem arises from the various possible degrees of "fixity" implied by the word "fixed" in the definition of a monetary item. Must a monetary item be permanently a monetary item? Because conditions may change, the price of a monetary item need not be fixed permanently. What, then, is the degree of fixity that justifies classifying an item as monetary? The decision remains a matter of professional judgment, as the following problem areas indicate:

First, *preferred shares* are classified as nonmonetary in *APB Statement No. 3*. The FASB exposure draft considers that "preferred stock carried at an amount equal to its fixed liquidation or redemption price is monetary because the claim of the preferred stockholders on the assets of the enterprise is in a fixed number of dollars; preferred stock carried at less than its fixed liquidation or redemption price is nonmonetary but becomes monetary when restated to an amount equal to its fixed liquidation or redemption price." The exposure draft also recommends that "gains or losses of general purchasing power that result from monetary stockholders' equity items, for example, preferred stock that is carried ... at ...

---

[8]L. C. Heath, "Distinguishing between Monetary and Non-Monetary Assets and Liabilities in General Price Level Accounting," *The Accounting Review* (July 1972), pp. 458–68; G. L. Johnson, "The Monetary and Non-Monetary Distinction," *The Accounting Review* (October 1965), p. 823; J. M. Boersema, "The Monetary, Non-Monetary Distinction in Accounting for Inflation," *Cost and Management* (May–June 1975), pp. 6–11.

[9]E. S. Hendriksen, *Accounting Theory* (Homewood, Ill.: R. D. Irwin, 1970), p. 207.

[10]*ARS No. 6*, p. 38.

EXHIBIT 6–1
Classification of Items as Monetary or Nonmonetary

Assets	Monetary	Nonmonetary
Cash on hand and demand bank deposits (U.S. dollars)	X	
Time deposits (U.S. dollars)	X	
Foreign currency on hand and claims to foreign currency	X	
Marketable securities		
Stocks		X
Bonds, other than convertibles	X	
Convertible bonds (until converted, these represent an entitlement to receive a fixed number of dollars)	X	
Accounts and notes receivable	X	
Allowance for doubtful accounts and notes receivable	X	
Inventories		
Produced under fixed contracts and accounted for at the contract price	X	
Other inventories		X
Loans to employees	X	
Prepaid insurance, advertising, rent, and other prepayments		X
Long-term receivables	X	
Refundable deposits	X	
Advances to unconsolidated subsidiaries	X	
Equity investment in uncolsoidated subsidiaries or other investees		X
Pension, sinking, and other funds under an enterprise's control	X	X
Property, plant and equipment		X
Accumulated depreciation of property, plant, and equipment		X
Cash surrender value of life insurance	X	
Purchase commitments — portion paid on fixed price contracts		X
Advances to a supplier — not on a contract	X	
Patents, trademarks, licenses, formulas		X
Goodwill		X
Other intangible assets and deferred charges		X

Liabilities	Monetary	Nonmonetary
Accounts and notes payable	X	
Accrued expenses payable (for example, wages)	X	
Accrued vacation pay (if it is to be paid at the wage rates as of the vacation dates and if those rates may vary)		X
Cash dividends payable	X	
Obligations payable in foreign currency	X	
Sales commitments — portion collected on fixed price contracts		X
Advances from customers — not on a contract	X	
Accrued losses on firm purchase commitment	X	
Deferred income		X
Refundable deposits	X	
Bonds payable and other long-term debt	X	

EXHIBIT 6-1
Classification of Items as Monetary or Nonmonetary (cont.)

Liabilities (cont.)	Monetary	Nonmonetary
Unamortized premium or discount and prepaid interest on bonds and notes payable	X	
Convertible bonds	X	
Accrued pensions obligations	X	X
Obligation under warranties		X
Deferred income tax credits	X	
Deferred investment tax credits		X
Preferred stock		
Carried at an amount equal to fixed liquidation or redemption price	X	
Carried at less than fixed liquidation or redemption price		X
Common stockholders' equity		X

fixed liquidation or redemption price, shall be charged or credited directly to common stockholders' equity in the general purchasing power financial statements."

Second, *deferred income taxes* are classified as nonmonetary in *APB Statement No. 3* on the basis that they are a cost saving deferred as a reduction of the expenses of future periods. A similar classification was retained by the FASB in its exposure draft. The argument is that under the accrual method, tax allocation credits are classified as liabilities, whereas under the deferred method, they are merely deferred credits representing the savings to be amortized to income in future periods. It follows that deferred income taxes would be classified as nonmonetary, given the adoption of the deferred method in the United States. On the other hand, the Canadian Institute of Chartered Accountants recommended that deferred income taxes be treated as monetary, although the deferred method is the required method in Canada. The Canadian Institute of Chartered Accountants' *Handbook* indicates that the deferral should be computed at current tax rates without subsequent adjustment of the accumulated tax allocation debit or credit balances to reflect changes in the tax rates.[11] Consequently, deferred income taxes refer to a fixed amount of money and fall under the definition of a monetary unit.

The FASB Exposure Draft, "Constant Dollar Accounting," changed the classification of deferred income tax items to monetary items. The FASB's position is stated as follows:

Again, although the nonmonetary classification may be technically preferable, the monetary classification provides a more practical solution and identifies the effect of inflation with the period the inflation occurs, rather than with the period the deferred income tax item is reversed.[12]

Third, *foreign currencies on hand, claims to foreign currency, and amounts payable in foreign currency* may be interpreted as either monetary of nonmone-

---

[11]*CICA Handbook* (Toronto: CICA, 1980), Section 3470.19.

[12]FASB Exposure Draft, "Constant Dollar Accounting," (Stamford, Conn.: FASB, March 2, 1979), p. 3.

tary items. If they are perceived as commodities, the price of which may fluctuate, they are nonmonetary. If they are perceived as similar to domestic currency items, they are monetary. A more logical viewpoint is to classify foreign currency items as monetary if they are stated at the closing rate of exchange in the historical cost financial statements, and as nonmonetary if they are stated at historical rates of exchange in the historical financial statements. The FASB exposure draft "Constant Dollar Accounting" classified foreign currencies on hand, claims to foreign currency, and foreign currency obligations as monetary items. The position is stated as follows:

> Although the nonmonetary classification may be technically preferable, and result in somewhat different disclosures, as a practical matter the monetary classification produces essentially the same net effect on aggregate disclosure as restating those foreign currency items as nonmonetary and then reducing them to their net realizable value. The monetary classification obviates that two-step procedure and is more understandable.[13]

Fourth, *long-term debt in foreign currency* also may be interpreted as either monetary or nonmonetary. Again, a logical alternative is to classify long-term debt in a foreign currency as monetary if it is stated at the closing rate of exchange and as nonmonetary if it is stated at the historical rate of exchange.

Fifth, *convertible debt* is perceived to have monetary and nonmonetary characteristics. *ARS No. 6* proposes that convertible debt be treated as monetary when the market price of shares is below the conversion price and as nonmonetary when the market price is at or above the conversion price. Another more accepted position is that convertible bonds should be treated as monetary debt until converted. Until conversion, they represent an obligation to pay a fixed number of dollars.

Price-Level Indexes

A price-level index compares changes in price from one period to another. It may be either a general price-level index or a specific price-level index. A general price-level index has been defined as "a series of measurements, expressed as percentages, of the relationship between the average price of a group of goods and services at a succession of dates and the average price of a similar group of goods and services at a common date. The components of the series are price-index numbers. A price index does not, however, measure the movement of the individual component prices, some of which move in one direction and some in the opposite direction. Thus, the general price-level index is based on a large range of goods and services, while the specific price-level index refers to a particular good or industry. Because general price-level accounting is used to reflect the changes in the purchasing power of the dollar, a general price-level index must be used to restate the historical cost statements in terms of dollars of constant purchasing power.

---

[13]*Ibid.*, p. 2.

Index Formulas

The computations of a general price-level index differ according to the method used to assign weights to prices. Four basic formulas are used. We shall use the following symbols to present these four formulas:

$$p = \text{the price of the commodity or service,}$$

$$q = \text{the quantity of the commodity or service,}$$

$$p_0, q_0 = \text{the price, quantity of the commodity in the base period,}$$

$$p_n, q_n = \text{the price, quantity of the commodity in the current period,}$$

$$p_a, q_a = \text{the price, quantity of the commodity in some average period.}$$

The **Laspeyres** formula assumes the price index is a weighted sum of current period prices divided by a weighted sum of base period prices, where the weights are *base* period quantities of commodities. Such an index, called a *Laspeyres* index, is computed as follows:

$$I = \frac{\Sigma p_n q_0}{\Sigma p_0 q_0}$$

The **Paasche** formula assumes the price index is a weighted sum of current period prices divided by a weighted sum of base period prices, where the weights are *current* period quantities of commodities. Such an index, called a *Paasche* index, is computed as follows:

$$I = \frac{\Sigma p_n q_n}{\Sigma p_0 q_n}$$

The **fixed weighted** formula assumes the price index is a weighted sum of current period prices divided by a weighted sum of base period prices, where the weights are *average* period quantities of commodities. The index is computed as follows:

$$I = \frac{\Sigma p_n q_a}{\Sigma p_0 q_a}$$

The **Fisher** formula assumes that the price index is a geometric average of Laspeyres and Paasche formulas. The index is computed as follows:

$$I = \sqrt{\frac{\Sigma p_n q_n}{\Sigma p_0 q_n} = \frac{\Sigma p_n q_a}{\Sigma p_0 q_a}}$$

Choice of a General Price-Level Index

General price-level accounting uses a conversion factor based on changes in the general price-level index to convert dollars at one date to the number of dollars having the same purchasing power in another date. An appropriate concept of purchasing power and an appropriate general price-level index must be chosen.

Hendriksen presented different concepts of purchasing power, namely, general purchasing power of the dollar, purchasing power of the stockholders, investment purchasing power of the firm, and specific replacement purchasing power.[14] The general purchasing power measured by a general price-level index reflects the changes in the value of money and, consequently, has been deemed most relevant for general price-level accounting. For example, *APB Statement No. 3* states that:

> The purpose of the general price-level restatement procedures is to re-state historical-dollar financial statements for changes in the general purchasing power of the dollar, and this purpose can only be accomplished by using a general price-level index.[15]

Thus, the concept of general purchasing power implies the use of a general price-level index. In the United States, the Department of Commerce and the Department of Labor maintain regularly and publish general price indexes. Among the most important are:

1. *The Consumer Price Index*, prepared by the Bureau of Labor Statistics of the U.S. Department of Labor,
2. *The Wholesale Price Index*, prepared by the Bureau of Labor Statistics of the U.S. Department of Labor,
3. *The Composite Construction Cost Index*, prepared by the Construction Industry Division of the Business and Defense Services Administration of the U.S. Department of Commerce, and
4. *The GNP (Gross National Product) Implicit Price Deflator*, prepared by the Office of Business Economics of the U.S. Department of Commerce.

The two price indexes most commonly suggested for general price-level accounting are the Consumer Price Index (CPI) and the implicit gross national product price delfator. The CPI is a base-weighted index that has been designed to measure the change in the price of a *basket* of retail goods and services acquired by middle-income families of specified size living in urban centers. The Gross National Product Implicit Price Deflator (IPI) is a currently weighted index that has been designed to measure price changes in all goods and services produced in a given year. Both the CPI and the IPI have limitations. The CPI, which is base-weighted, fails to take into account the substitution of relatively lower-price goods that takes place when relative prices change. In other words, the CPI has an upward bias. It overstates the effect of changes in prices on the cost of living. On the other hand, the IPI, which is currently weighted, understates the price increase in the cost of living. For example, Rosen says that:

> In summary, when prices are rising, currently-weighted indexes may have a downward bias (i.e., they tend to understate the percentage price increase), and base-weighted indexes have an upward bias (i.e., they tend to overstate a percentage price increase).[16]

In the debate on the choice between the CPI and the IPI, the IPI is considered

---

[14]E. S. Hendriksen, *Accounting Theory*, 3rd ed. (Homewood, Ill: R. D. Irwin, 1977), pp. 231–36.

[15]*APB Statement No. 3*, p. 13.

[16]L. S. Rosen, *Current Value Accounting and Price-Level Restatements* (Toronto: The Canadian Institute of Chartered Accountants, 1972), p. 40.

the best currently compiled general price-level index. It covers all goods and services produced in the economy, whereas the CPI covers only goods and services purchased by a "typical consumer." Thus, in terms of measuring the extent of overall price changes, the IPI is probably more relevant. Annual estimates are available from 1919, and quarterly estimates are available from 1947.

In its exposure draft "Constant Dollar Accounting," however, the FASB designated the Consumer Price Index for all Urban Consumers (known as the CPI-U) as an index of general purchasing power rather then the Gross National Product Implicit Price Deflator for two reasons. First, the CPI-U has two practical advantages: It is calculated more frequently (monthly instead of quarterly), and it is not revised after its initial publication. Second, the rates of change in the CPI-U and the GNP Implicit Price Deflator tend to be similar and, therefore, use of the CPI-U will tend to produce a comparable result.[17]

Simplified Illustration of General Price-Level Indexing

In the following simplified example, we shall illustrate briefly how general price-level historical cost financial statements may be prepared from historical cost financial statements.

The Smith Company began business on December 31, 19X5, when the price level was 100 (base period). The comparative balance sheets for 19X5 and 19X6 are shown in Exhibit 6–2. The 19X6 income statement appears in Exhibit 6–3.

EXHIBIT 6–2
The Smith Company
Comparative Balance Sheets

	Dec. 31, 19X5 Debit	Dec. 31, 19X5 Credit	Dec. 31, 19X6 Debit	Dec. 31, 19X6 Credit
Monetary Assets	$ 30,000		$ 60,000	
Inventories	30,000	(3,000 units)	20,000	(2,000 units)
Land	40,000		40,000	
Plant and Equipment	50,000		50,000	
Accumulated Depreciation				$ 10,000
Liabilities (1%)		$ 50,000		50,000
Capital Stock		100,000		100,000
Retained Earnings				10,000
Total	$150,000	$150,000	$170,000	$170,000

In addition to the balance sheets and income statement, we have the following supplementary information:

1. The price deflator is as follows:

December 31, 19X5	100
December 31, 19X6	180
Average price index for 1976	120

---

[17]FASB Exposure Draft, "Constant Dollar Accounting," p. 2.

EXHIBIT 6-3

The Smith Company
Income Statement
For the Year Ended December 31, 19X6

Sales (5,000 units at $40)		$200,000
− Cost of Goods Sold		
Beginning Inventory (3,000 units at $10)	$ 30,000	
+ Purchases (4,000 units at $12)	48,000	
	$ 78,000	
− Ending Inventory (2,000 units at $10)	20,000	58,000
Gross Margin		$142,000
− Expenses		
Interest Expense	$ 5,000	
Selling and Administrative Expenses	117,000	
Depreciation	10,000	132,000
Net Income		$ 10,000

2. All the revenues and costs were incurred evenly throughout the year, with the exception of the cost of goods sold and the depreciation expense.

3. The inventory purchases were made at a date when the price-level index was at 150.

4. A LIFO flow is assumed.

5. Depreciation for plant and equipment was accumulated by the straight-line method on a five-year life.

The procedure for restating the historical cost financial statements is as follows:

1. Restate the 19X5 balance sheet to 19X6 price levels. The 19X5 balance sheet adjusted to 19X6 price levels is shown in Exhibit 6–4.

EXHIBIT 6-4

The Smith Company
Balance Sheet
December 31, 19X5

Assets	Unadjusted	Conversion Factor	Adjusted
Monetary Assets	$ 30,000	180/100	$ 54,000
Inventories	30,000	180/100	54,000
Land	40,000	180/100	72,000
Plant and Equipment	50,000	180/100	90,000
Accumulated Depreciation	—		
Total	$150,000		$270,000
Equities			
Liabilities (10%)	50,000	180/100	90,000
Capital	100,000	180/100	180,000
Retained Earnings	—		
Total	$150,000		$270,000

EXHIBIT 6–5
The Smith Company
Balance Sheet
December 31, 19X6

Assets	Unadjusted	Conversion Factor	Adjusted
Monetary Assets	$ 60,000	180/180	$ 60,000
Inventories	20,000	180/100	36,000
Land	40,000	180/100	72,000
Plant and Equipment	50,000	180/100	90,000
Accumulated Depreciation	(10,000)		(18,000)
Total	$160,000		$240,000
Equities			
Liabilities (10%)	50,000	180/180	50,000
Capital	100,000	180/100	180,000
Retained Earnings	10,000	—	10,000
Total	$160,000		$240,000

2. Restate the 19X6 balance sheet to current 19X6 price levels. The 19X6 adjusted balance sheet appears in Exhibit 6–5. At this stage, there is no direct conversion factor for retained earnings. It is simply the amount required to achieve a balance between the assets and equities.

3. Restate the 19X6 income statement to 19X6 price levels. The 19X6 adjusted income statement is illustrated in Exhibit 6–6.

EXHIBIT 6–6
The Smith Company
December 31, 19X6
Income Statement Adjusted to 19X6 Price Levels

	Unadjusted	Conversion Factor	Adjusted
Sales (5,000 units at $40)	$200,000	180/120	$300,000
Cost of Goods Sold			
Beginning Inventory (3,000 units)	30,000	180/100	54,000
Purchases (4,000 units)	48,000	180/150	57,600
Goods Available			$111,600
Ending Inventory (2,000 units)	20,000	180/100	36,000
Cost of Goods Sold	$ 58,000		$ 75,600
Gross Margin	$142,000		$224,400
Other Expenses			
Interest Expense	5,000	180/120	7,500
Depreciation Expense	10,000	180/100	18,000
Selling and Administrative Expenses	117,000	180/120	175,500
Net Operating Profit	$ 10,000		$ 23,400

EXHIBIT 6–7

	Unadjusted	Conversion Factor	Adjusted
Net monetary assets on January 1, 19X6	$ (20,000)	180/100	$ (36,000)
Add monetary receipts during 19X6 Sales	200,000	180/120	300,000
Net monetary items	$180,000		$264,000
Less monetary payments			
Purchases	48,000	180/150	57,600
Interest	5,000	180/120	7,500
Selling and administrative expenses	117,000	180/120	175,500
Total			$240,600
Computed net monetary assets, December 31, 19X6			23,400
Actual net monetary assets, December 31, 19X6			(10,000)
Loss on monetary assets			$ 13,400

4. Calculate the monetary gains or losses from changes in the general price level. This computation is shown in Exhibit 6–7.

5. Prepare a reconciliation of retained earnings as follows:

Retained earnings, January 1, 19X6	$ 0
+ Net profit	23,400
− GPL loss	(13,400)
Retained earnings, January 1, 19X6	$10,000

This is a simplified example of price-level adjustments.

Evaluation
of General Price-Level Accounting

An ongoing controversy has been taking place concerning the relevance of general price-level accounting. We shall present here some of the arguments in favor of and against general price-level accounting as a reflection of the positions taken in the literature and in practice. The number and order of our presentations are no reflection on their relative merits.

Arguments in Favor
of General Price-Level Accounting

A number of arguments have been advanced in favor of general price-level accounting. First, financial statements not adjusted for general price-level changes include diverse kinds of assets and claims expressed in dollars of different purchasing power. General price-level accounting is designed to express the level of changes in the price of these assets and the purchasing power of the claims.

General price-level statements present data expressed in a common denominator, which is the purchasing power of the dollar at the end of the period. Such statements facilitate comparisons between firms because a common unit of measure is used. The FASB stated:

> Changes in the purchasing power of the dollar affect individual enterprises differently, depending on the amount of the change and the age and composition of the enterprise's assets and equities. For example, during periods of inflation, those who hold monetary assets (cash and receivables in fixed dollar amounts) suffer a loss in purchasing power represented by those monetary assets. On the other hand, in periods of inflation, debtors gain because their liabilities are able to be repaid in dollars having less purchasing power. In periods of deflation, the reverse is true. Conventional financial statements do not report the effects of inflation or deflation on individual enterprises.[18]

Second, conventional historical cost accounting does not measure income properly as a result of the matching of dollars of different "size" on the income statement. Expenses incurred in previous periods are set off against revenues that are usually expressed in current dollars. General price-level accounting provides a better matching of revenues and expenses because common dollars are used. A more realistic income relationship is therefore possible through the development of more logical dividend policies. The FASB has stated:

> Investors and others often look to the income statement, or to ratios that are based in part on measures of income, for information about the ability of an enterprise to earn a return on its invested capital. In the conventional income statement, revenues are measured in dollars of current, or at least very recent, purchasing power, whereas certain significant expense items are measured in dollars of different purchasing power of earlier periods. Depreciation and cost of goods sold are two of the most commonly cited examples, although the problem arises whenever amounts in the income statement represent expenditure of dollars of different purchasing power. In periods of inflation, depreciation and cost of goods sold tend to be understated in terms of the purchasing power sacrificed to acquire depreciable assets and inventory. Further, information stated in terms of current general purchasing power may indicate that an enterprise's income tax and dividend payout rates are significantly different in terms of units of money and in units of general purchasing power.[19]

The third argument in favor of general price-level accounting is that it is relatively easy to apply. It merely replaces a "rubber dollar" with a "dated dollar."[20] General price-level accounting represents the least departure from generally accepted accounting principles. As a result, it may be relatively objective and verifiable. These characteristics may make it more acceptable to many firms than current-value accounting.

---

[18]*FASB Discussion Memorandum,* "Reporting the Effects of General Price Level Changes in Financial Statements" (Stamford, Conn.: FASB) p. 8.

[19]*Ibid.*

[20]Elwood L. Miller, "What's Wrong with Price Level Accounting," *Harvard Business Review* (November–December 1978), p. 113.

Fourth, general price-level accounting provides relevant information for management evaluation and use. Thus, the general price-level gain and loss resulting from holding monetary items reflect management's response to inflation. The restated nonmonetary items indicate approximately the purchasing power needed to replace the assets. Finally, general price-level accounting presents to users in general the impact of general inflation on profit and provides more realistic return on investment rates.

The staff of the Accounting Research Division of the AICPA argues the case for the preparation of price-level statements as a means for financial analysis as follows:

> If price-level changes can be measured in some satisfactory manner, and if the effects of those changes can be properly disclosed, the inferences that can be drawn from accounting data will be statistically more reliable. Specifically, for example, all the revenues and expenses in the earnings statement for any one year will be expressed in dollars of the same size and not in a mixture of dollars from different years. Similarly, the various balance-sheet items will all be expressed in terms of a common dollar. Since both the results of operations and financial position will be stated in terms of the same "common dollar," a calculation of a rate of return on invested capital can be made in which both numerator and denominator are expressed in the same units.
>
> Some inferences can be drawn in terms of the various groups interested in business activity. Investors and their representatives (e.g., management, including the board of directors) can tell whether the capital invested in the business has been increased or decreased as the result of all the policies followed and all the financial events that have taken place bearing on the business entity. More specifically, management and owners can tell if the dividend policy actually followed in the past has resulted in distributions out of economic or business capital, and, if not, what proportion of the earnings (adjusted for price-level changes) has in fact been distributed. With price-level adjusted data before them, the directors can tell if a proposed dividend will equal, exceed, or fall short of current earnings, or any other norm or standard they wish to use.
>
> Owners, management, and government can tell if taxes levied on income were less than pretax earnings, and if so, to what extent, and, if not, how much they exceeded pretax earnings. Creditors will be better informed as to the buffer or cushion behind their claims. In addition, employees, as well as investors, and management will have a more reliable gauge of the rate of return to date on the capital employed, and will be able to use the information more intelligently to decide if the business entity has been profitable or not.
>
> Financial statements fully adjusted for the effect of price-level changes will also reveal the losses or gains from holding or owing monetary items. All interested groups then have one important measure of the effect of a changing dollar on their position as debtors or creditors.
>
> Financial data adjusted for price-level effects provide a basis for a more

intelligent, better informed allocation of resources, whether those resources are in the hands of individuals, of business entities or of government.[21]

Arguments Against
General Price-Level Accounting

The case against general price-level accounting may be made on the basis of the following arguments. First, most empirical studies have indicated that the relevance of general price-level information is either weak[22] or not accepted.[23] Further research is warranted before any definite conclusions can be reached on the relevance of general price-level information and its ability to be meaningfully interpreted.

Second, general price-level changes account only for changes in the general price level and do not account for changes in the specific price level. Thus, holding gains and losses on nonmonetary assets are not recognized. Besides, users of general price-level adjusted data may believe that the restated values correspond to current values.

Third, the impact of inflation differs among firms. Capital-intensive firms may be affected by inflation more than those that rely heavily on short-term assets. Similarly, highly leveraged firms stand to gain from inflation. As a result, general price-level accounting may distort normal income. High-leveraged companies will "look good" by showing high general price-level gains. Some of the general price-level gains and losses on monetary items, however, are unrealized and should be excluded from the financial statements and deferred to later periods.

Fourth, the costs of implementing general price-level accounting may exceed the benefits. Miller presents the following arguments:

(a) Companies may lose the ability to use LIFO for tax purposes.
(b) GPP [General Purchasing Power] may result in higher property tax assessments.
(c) Companies must roll forward (restate) prior years each time comparative statements are prepared.
(d) Companies must also provide replacement cost information to the Securities and Exchange Commission (SEC).
(e) Investors may not attempt to understand the statements.
(f) There are better ways to disclose the effect of inflation on a specific company, its assets, its operations, and its future.[24]

Finally, some technical problems beset general price-level accounting. The

---

[21]*Accounting Research Study No. 6*, pp. 14–16.

[22]Russel J. Peterson, "A Portfolio Analysis of General Price-Level Restatement," *The Accounting Review* (July 1975), p. 532; T. R. Dyckman, "Investment Analysis and General Price Level Adjustments," *Studies in Accounting Research No. 1* (Evanston, Ill.: AAA, 1969), p. 17; R. C. Morris, "Evidence of the Impact of Inflation Accounting on Share Prices," *Accounting and Business Research* (Spring 1975), p. 90.

[23]C. T. Horngren, "Security Analysts and the Price Level," *The Accounting Review* (October 1955), pp. 575–81; M. Baker, *Financial Reporting for Security and Investment Decisions* (New York: National Association of Accountants, 1970).

[24]Miller, "What's Wrong with Price Level Accounting?" p. 114.

first problem relates to the choice of an appropriate general price-level index. As stated in a previous section, two general indexes have been suggested for use in price-level accounting: the Consumer Price Index and the Gross National Product Implicit Price Deflator. It has been suggested that if price-level restatements are to be made, only the GNP Price Deflator is sufficiently representative of the entire economy. For this reason, this index is more appropriate for measuring the fluctuations in the exchange value of the dollar. There is, however, a problem of timeliness. The GNP Implicit Price Deflator is only available quarterly compared with the Consumer Price Index, which is available monthly. If the GNP Implicit Price Deflator were adopted, it might be necessary to approximate its effects with the Consumer Price Index for periods for which it is not available as needed. The FASB's decision to adopt the CPI-U resolved this problem.

The second problem is that general price-level accounting requires the identification and the classification of assets and liabilities as monetary or nonmonetary. While there is general agreement on how most items should be classified, some items are subject to different interpretations. Examples are deferred income taxes, preferred shares, foreign currency items, and convertible debt.

The third technical problem is that general price-level accounting uses the same accounting principles as conventional accounting. Only the unit of measurement is changed. Therefore, the restated cost of nonmonetary assets should not exceed current value. For example, the lower of cost or market rule is applied just as it is applied in historical cost accounting. Inventories should not be restated at more than net realizable value. Paragraph 37 of *APB Statement No. 3* recommends a write-down of restated cost to replacement cost only for those nonmonetary assets stated at lower of cost or market, such as inventories or other current assets. It does not consider, however, the write-down of noncurrent assets to replacement costs. Accordingly, the *FASB Discussion Memorandum* on general price-level accounting poses the following questions:

> If the cost of nonmonetary asset is to be restated upward for a decrease in the general purchasing power of the dollar, and the restated amount would exceed replacement cost, recoverable cost or some other defined amount, should the restated amount be limited to such a defined amount in general price level financial statements? Further, if such a limit to restatement is required, should it be required for all nonmonetary assets or only for certain assets (for example, only for inventory)?[25]

Conclusions

In this chapter and in Chapter 5, we have established that all the profit concepts are based on different notions of capital maintenance. Conventional accounting, because it relies on historical cost accounting for the valuation of assets and liabilities, conforms to the money maintenance concept. Current-value accounting, in which assets and liabilities are brought into the financial statements at their current value, conforms to the physical productive capacity maintenance concept. Finally, general price-level accounting, because it relies on a general

---

[25]*FASB Discussion Memorandum*, "Reporting the Effects of General Price-Level Changes in Financial Statements," p. 11.

price-level restatement of the historically based assets and liabilities, conforms to the general purchasing power money maintenance concept.

Each of these accounting methods is based on certain principles and rules. Conventional accounting is based on generally accepted accounting principles, in general, and the historical cost principle and stable monetary unit postulate, in particular. It recognizes neither changes in the general price level nor changes in the specific price level. Current-value accounting is characterized by the complete abandonment of the historical cost principle. It recognizes only changes in the specific price level. General price-level accounting is characterized by the abandonment of the stable monetary unit postulate. It recognizes only changes in the general price level. Each of these methods apparently attempts to correct some of the deficiencies of conventional historical-based accounting but not all of them. Consequently, in Chapter 6, we shall introduce another accounting valuation method based on a recognition of changes in both general and specific price levels.

References

Accounting Principles Board, Statement No. 3. "Financial Statements Restated for General Price Level Changes." New York: AICPA, June 1969.

Accounting Research Committee. *Accounting for Changes in the General Purchasing Power of Money.* Toronto: Canadian Institute of Chartered Accountants, July 1975.

American Institute of Certified Public Accountants, Staff of the Accounting Research Division. "Reporting the Financial Effects of Price Level Changes." *Accounting Research Study No. 6.* New York: AICPA, 1969.

Baker, M. *Financial Reporting for Security and Investment Decisions.* New York: National Association of Accountants, 1970.

Boersema, J. M. "The Monetary, Non-Monetary Distinction in Accounting for Inflation." *Cost and Management* (May–June 1975), pp. 6–11.

Davidson, Sidney, Clyde P. Stickney, and Roman L. Weil. *Inflation Accounting: A Guide for the Accountant and the Financial Analyst.* New York: McGraw-Hill, 1976.

Davidson, Sidney, and Roman L. Weil. "Inflation Accounting." *Financial Analysts Journal* (January–February 1975), pp. 27–31, 70–84.

Dyckman, T. R. "Investment Analysis and General Price Level Adjustments." *Studies in Accounting Research No. 1.* Evanston, Ill.: AAA, 1969.

Financial Accounting Standards Board, Exposure Draft, "Financial Reporting in Units of General Purchasing Power" (Stamford, Conn.: FASB, December 31, 1974).

Heath, L. C. "Distinguishing between Monetary and Non-Monetary Assets and Liabilities in General Price Level Accounting." *The Accounting Review* (July 1972), pp. 458–68.

Horngren, C. T. "Security Analysts and the Price Level." *The Accounting Review* (October 1955), pp. 575–81.

Johnson, G. L. "The Monetary and Non-Monetary Distinction." *The Accounting Review* (October 1965), pp. 821–23.

Largay, James A., III, and John Leslie Livingstone. *Accounting for Changing Prices.* New York: John Wiley & Sons, 1976.
Mason, Perry. *Price Level Changes and Financial Statements—Basic Concepts and Methods.* Columbus, Ohio: AAA, 1956.
Miller, Elwood L. "What's Wrong with Price-Level Accounting?" *Harvard Business Review* (November–December 1978), pp. 111–18.
Morris, R. C. "Evidence of the Impact of Inflation Accounting on Share Prices." *Accounting and Business Research* (Spring 1975).
Peterson, Russel J. "A Portfolio Analysis of General Price-Level Restatement," *The Accounting Review* (July 1975), pp. 525–32.
Rosen, L. S. *Current Value Accounting and Price-Level Restatements.* Toronto: The Canadian Institute of Chartered Accountants, 1972.
Short, Daniel G. "The Impact of Price-Level Adjustment in the Context of Risk Assessment." *Journal of Accounting Research (Supplement 1978),* pp. 259–72.
Staff of the Accounting Research Division. "Reporting the Financial Effects of Price-Level Changes." *Accounting Research Study No. 6,* New York: AICPA, 1963.
Stickney, Clyde P. "Adjustments for Changing Prices." In *Handbook of Modern Accounting.* Ed. Sidney Davidson and Roman Weil. 2nd ed. New York: McGraw-Hill, 1977.

Questions

6–1 What do we mean by general price-level accounting?
6–2 Explain the differences among historical cost accounting, current-value accounting, and general price-level accounting.
6–3 Define and present the computation procedures for general price-level gain or loss.
6–4 What accounting treatments are suggested for general price-level gain or loss?
6–5 Distinguish between monetary assets and liabilities and nonmonetary assets and liabilities.
6–6 Give some examples of monetary assets and liabilities.
6–7 Give some examples of nonmonetary assets and liabilities.
6–8 List and discuss the arguments in favor of and against general price-level accounting.
6–9 The president of Carson, Limited, is concerned about the inflation of the last ten years and its influence on his company's financial statements and return on investment. He purchased the company at the end of 1975 and the net profit of the company has increased each year from $34,975 in 1976 to $68,200 in 1984. On this basis, the president has established that return on shareholders' equity has increased from 7.4 percent to 12.4 percent during this period. He gives you the 1976 and 1984 financial statements of Carson, Limited.

Carson, Ltd.
Comparative Balance Sheet
December 31

	1984	1976
Total Assets	$850,000	$600,000
Liabilities	300,000	125,000
Common Stock	350,000	350,000
Retained Earnings	200,000	125,000
	$850,000	$600,000

Carson, Ltd.
Comparative Income Statements
For the Year Ended December 31

	1984	1976
Sales	$1,200,000	$600,000
Cost of Goods Sold		
Beginning Inventory	150,000	110,000
Purchases	985,000	470,000
	$1,135,000	$580,000
Ending Inventory	180,000	100,000
	955,000	480,000
Gross Profit	245,000	120,000
Expenses		
Selling and Administrative	93,000	56,025
Depreciation	15,000	9,000
	108,800	65,025
Profit before Income Taxes	136,200	54,975
Income Taxes	68,000	20,000
Net Profit for the Year	$ 68,200	$ 34,975

Additional Data

(1) All revenue and expenses, except depreciation, are earned or incurred evenly throughout each of the years.

(2) The beginning inventory for 1984 was acquired when the index was 60.

(3) Common stock was issued when the index was 70. Retained earnings amounted to $132,000 in 1976 and $247,000 in 1984 on the basis of constant December 31, 1984, dollars.

(4) Fixed assets of the company were purchased in 1968 when the index was 75. Some additions were made in 1980 when the index was 125. There were no other transactions affecting fixed assets.

(5) The index of general purchasing power of the dollar was:

	1984
Beginning of the year	170
Average for the year	180
End of the year	185

Required:

a. Prepare an income statement for Carson, Limited, for the year ended December 31, 1984, stating all dollar aggregates in terms of dollars of uniform purchasing power.

b. If the 1977 net income in constant 1984 dollars is $11,000, calculate the return on shareholders' equity on the same basis for 1976 and 1984. (Make all calculations to the nearest $1,000.)

(Society of Management Accountants adapted)

6–10 Published financial statements of U.S. companies are currently prepared on a stable-dollar assumption, even though the general purchasing power of the dollar has declined considerably because of inflation in recent years.

To account for this changing value of the dollar, many accountants suggest that financial statements should be adjusted for general price-level changes. Three independent, unrelated statements regarding general price-level adjusted financial statements follow. Each statement contains some fallacious reasoning.

Statement 1: The accounting profession has not seriously considered price-level adjusted financial statements before because the rate of inflation usually has been so small from year-to-year that the adjustments would have been immaterial in amount. Price-level adjusted financial statements represent a departure from the historical-cost basis of accounting. Financial statements should be prepared from facts, not estimates.

Statement 2: If financial statements were adjusted for general price-level changes, depreciation charges in the earnings statement would permit the recovery of dollars of current purchasing power and, thereby, equal the cost of new assets to replace the old ones. General price-level adjusted data would yield statement-of-financial-position amounts closely approximating current values. Furthermore, management can make better decisions if general price-level adjusted financial statements are published.

Statement 3: When adjusting financial data for general price-level changes, a distinction must be made between monetary and nonmonetary assets and liabilities, which, under the historical-cost basis of accounting, have been identified as "current" and "noncurrent." When using the historical-cost basis of accounting, no purchasing-power gain or loss is recognized in the accounting process, but when financial statements are adjusted for general price-level changes, a purchasing-power gain or loss will be recognized on monetary and nonmonetary items.

Required:

Evaluate each independent statement, identify the areas of fallacious reasoning, and explain why the reasoning is incorrect. Complete your discussion of each statement before proceeding to the next statement.

(AICPA adapted)

6–11 Barden Corporation, a manufacturer with large investments in plant and equipment, began operations many years ago. The company's history has been one of expansion in sales, production, and physical facilities. Recently, some concern has been expressed that the conventional financial statements do not provide sufficient information for investors to make sound decisions. After consideration of proposals for various types of supplementary financial statements to be included in the 19X2 annual report, management has decided to present a balance sheet as of December 31, 19X2, and a statement of income and retained earnings for 19X2, both restated for changes in the general price level.

Required:

a. On what basis can it be contended that Barden's conventional statements should be restated for changes in the general price level?

b. What is the difference between financial statements restated for general price-level changes and current-value financial statements?

c. Distinguish between monetary and nonmonetary assets and liabilities, as the terms are used in general price-level accounting, and give examples of each.

d. Outline the procedures Barden should follow to prepare the proposed supplementary statements.

e. What are the major similarities and differences between the proposed supplementary statements and the corresponding conventional statements?

f. Assuming that in the future Barden will want to present comparative supplementary statements, can the 19X2 supplementary statements be presented in 19X3 without adjustment? Explain.

(AICPA adapted)

6–12 Although cash generally is regarded as the simplest of all assets to account for, certain complexities may arise for both domestic and multinational companies.

Required:

a. Unrealized and realized gains or losses may arise in connection with cash. Excluding consideration of price-level changes, indicate the nature of such gains or losses and the context in which they may arise in relation to cash.

b. How might it be maintained that a gain or a loss is incurred by holding a constant balance of cash through a period of price-level change?

c. Identify and justify the typical accounting treatment accorded these gains or losses.

(AICPA adapted)

6–13 Select the best answer in each of the following. Items are independent of one another except where indicated to the contrary. Give the basis, including computations, for your choice.

The following information applies to Items 1 through 4: Equipment purchased for $120,000 on January 1, 19X1, when the price index was 100, was sold on December 31, 19X3, at a price of $85,000. The equipment originally was expected to last six years with no salvage value and was depreciated on a straight-line basis. The price index at the end of 19X1 was 125; at the end of 19X2, 150; 19X3, 175.

(1) Price-level financial statements prepared at the end of 19X1 would include:

a. Equipment, $150,000; accumulated depreciation, $25,000; and a gain, $30,000

b. equipment, $150,000; accumulated depreciation, $25,000; and no gain or loss

    c. equipment, $150,000; accumulated depreciation, $20,000; and a gain, $30,000

    d. none of the above

(2) Price-level comparative statements prepared at the end of 19X2 would show the 19X1 financial statements amount for equipment (net of accumulated depreciation) at:

    a. $150,000   d. $80,000

    b. $125,000   e. none of the above

    c. $100,000

(3) Price-level financial statements prepared at the end of 19X2 should include depreciation expense of:

    a. $35,000   d. $20,000

    b. $30,000   e. none of the above

    c. $25,000

(4) The general price-level income statement prepared at the end of 19X3 should include:

    a. a gain of $35,000   d. a loss of $5,000

    b. a gain of $25,000   e. none of the above

    c. no gain or loss

(5) If land were purchased at a cost of $20,000 in January 19X1, when the general price-level index was 120 and sold in December 19X6, when the index was 150, the selling price that would result in no economic gain or loss would be:

    a. $30,000   d. $16,000

    b. $24,000   e. none of the above

    c. $20,000

(6) If land were purchased in 19X1 for $100,000 when the general price-level index was 100 and sold at the end of 19X7 for $160,000 when the index was 170, the general price-level statement of income for 19X7 would show:

    a. a price-level gain of $70,000 and a loss of sale of land of $10,000

    b. a gain on sale of land of $60,000

    c. a price-level loss of $10,000

    d. a loss on sale of land of $10,000

    e. none of the above

(7) If the base year is 19X1 (when the general price index = 100) and land is purchased for $50,000 in 19X3, when the general price index is 108.5, the cost of the land restated in 19X1 general purchasing power (rounded to the nearest whole dollar) would be:

    a. $54,250   d. $45,750

    b. $50,000   e. none of the above

    c. $46,083

(8) Assume the same facts as in Item 7. The cost of the land restated to December 31, 19X7, general purchasing power when the general price index was 119.2 (rounded to the nearest whole dollar) would be:

    a. $59,600   d. $45,512

    b. $54,931   e. none of the above

    c. $46,083

(AICPA adapted)

6–14   Select the best answer in each of the following and give the basis for your response.

(1)   In preparing price-level financial statements, a nonmonetary item would be:
   a.   accounts payable in cash
   b.   long-term bonds payable
   c.   accounts receivable
   d.   allowance for doubtful accounts
   e.   none of the above

(2)   In preparing price-level financial statements, monetary items consist of
   a.   cash items plus all receivables with a fixed maturity date
   b.   cash, other assets expected to be converted into cash and current liabilities
   c.   Assets and liabilities whose amounts are fixed by contract or otherwise in terms of dollars, regardless of price-level changes
   d.   assets and liabilities classed as current on the balance sheet
   e.   none of the above

(3)   An accountant who recommends the restatement of financial statements for price-level changes should not support this recommendation by stating that
   a.   purchasing power gains and losses should be recognized
   b.   historical dollars are not comparable to present-day dollars
   c.   the conversion of asset costs to a common-dollar basis is a useful extension of the original cost basis of asset valuation
   d.   assets should be valued at their replacement cost

(4)   When price-level balance sheets are prepared, they should be presented in terms of
   a.   the general purchasing power of the dollar at the latest balance sheet date
   b.   the general purchasing power of the dollar in the base period
   c.   the average general purchasing power of the dollar for the latest fiscal period
   d.   the general purchasing power of the dollar at the time the fiscal statements are issued
   e.   none of the above

(5)   During a period of deflation, an entity usually would have the greatest gain in general purchasing power by holding
   a.   cash
   b.   plant and equipment
   c.   accounts payable
   d.   mortgages payable
   e.   none of the above

(6)   The restatement of historical-dollar financial statements to reflect general price-level changes reports assets at
   a.   lower cost or market
   b.   current appraisal values
   c.   costs adjusted for purchasing power changes
   d.   current replacement cost
   e.   none of the above

(7)   An unacceptable practice for reporting general price-level information is
   a.   the inclusion of general price-level gains and losses on monetary items in the price-level income statement

b. the inclusion of extraordinary gains and losses in the general price-level income statement
c. the use of charts, ratios, and narrative information
d. the use of specific price indexes to restate inventories, plant, and equipment
e. none of the above

(AICPA adapted)

6–15 The controller of the Robinson Company, Mr. Fisher, is discussing a comment you made in the course of presenting your audit report.

"Frankly," he continued, "I agree that we, too, are responsible for finding ways to produce more relevant financial statements that are as reliable as the ones we now produce. For example, suppose the company acquired a finished item of inventory for $40 when the general price-level index was 110. And, later, the item was sold for $75 when the general price-level index was 121 and the current replacement cost was $54. We could calculate a 'holding gain.'"

Required:
a. Explain to what extent and how current replacement costs already are used within generally accepted accounting principles to value inventories.
b. Calculate in good form the amount of the holding gain in Fisher's example.
c. Why do some accounting authorities prefer the use of current replacement cost for both inventories and cost of goods sold to the generally accepted use of FIFO or LIFO?

(AICPA adapted)

6–16 Skadden, Inc., a retailer, was organized during 19X1. Skadden's management has decided to supplement its December 31, 19X4, historical-dollar financial statements with general price-level financial statements. The following ledger trial balance (historical dollar) and additional information have been furnished:

Skadden, Inc.
Trial Balance
December 31, 19X4

	Debit	Credit
Cash and receivable (net)	$ 540,000	
Marketable securities (common stock)	400,000	
Inventory	440,000	
Equipment	650,000	
Equipment — Accumulated depreciation		$ 164,000
Accounts payable		300,000
6% first mortgage bonds, due 19X2		500,000
Common stock, $10 par		1,000,000
Retained earnings, December 31, 19X3	46,000	
Sales		1,900,000
Costs of sales	1,508,000	
Depreciation	65,000	
Other operating expenses and interest	215,000	
	$3,864,000	$3,864,000

Additional Data

(1) Monetary assets (cash and receivables) exceeded monetary liabilities (accounts payable and bonds payable) by $445,000 at December 31, 19X3. The amounts of monetary items are fixed in terms of numbers of dollars regardless of changes in specific prices or in the general price level.

(2) Purchases ($1,840,000 in 19X4) and sales are made uniformly throughout the year.

(3) Depreciation is computed on a straight-line basis, with a full year's depreciation being taken in the year of acquisition and none in the year of retirement. The depreciation rate is 10 percent, and no salvage value is anticipated. Acquisitions and retirements have been made fairly evenly over each year, and the retirements in 19X4 consisted of assets purchased during 19X2, which were scrapped. An analysis of the equipment account reveals the following:

Year	Beginning Balance	Additions	Retirements	Ending Balance
19X2	–	$550,000	–	$550,000
19X3	$550,000	10,000	–	560,000
19X4	$560,000	150,000	$60,000	650,000

(4) The bonds were issued in 19X2, and the marketable securities were purchased fairly evenly over 19X4. Other operating expenses and interest are assumed to be incurred evenly throughout the year.

(5) Assume that Gross National Product Implicit Price Deflators (1958 = 100) were as follows:

Annual Averages	Index	Conversion Factors (19X4 4th Qtr. = 1.000)
19X1	113.9	1.128
19X2	116.8	1.100
19X3	121.8	1.055
19X4	126.7	1.014

Quarterly Averages		Index	Conversion Factors
19X3	4th	123.5	1.040
19X4	1st	124.9	1.029
	2nd	126.1	1.019
	3rd	127.3	1.009
	4th	128.5	1.000

Required:

a. Prepare a schedule to convert the Equipment account balance at December 31, 19X4, from historical cost to general price-level adjusted dollars.

b. Prepare a schedule to analyze in historical dollars the Equipment—Accumulated Depreciation account for the year 19X4.

c. Prepare a schedule to analyze in general price-level dollars the Equipment—Accumulated Depreciation account for the year 19X4.

d. Prepare a schedule to compute Skadden, Inc.'s general price-level gain or loss on its net holdings of monetary assets for 19X4 (ignore income tax implications). The schedule should give consideration to appropriate items on or related to the balance sheet and the income statement.

(AICPA adapted)

6–17 The Melgar Company purchased a tract of land as an investment in 19X4 for $100,000; late in that year, the company decided to construct a shopping center on the site. Construction began in 19X5 and was completed in 19X7; one-third of the construction was completed each year. Melgar originally estimated that the costs of the project would be $1,200,000 for materials, $750,000 for labor, $150,000 for variable overhead, and $600,000 for depreciation.

Actual costs (excluding depreciation) incurred for construction were:

	19X5	19X6	19X7
Materials	$418,950	$434,560	$462,000
Labor	236,250	274,400	282,000
Variable overhead	47,250	54,208	61,200

Shortly after construction began, Melgar sold the shopping center for $3,000,000, with payment to be made in full on completion in December 19X7. One hundred and fifty thousand dollars of the sales price was allocated for the land.

The transaction was completed as scheduled, and now a controversy has developed between the two major stockholders of the company. One feels the company should have invested in land because a high rate of return was earned on the land. The other feels the original decision was sound and that unanticipated changes in the price level affected the original cost estimates.

You are engaged to guide these stockholders in resolving their controversy. As an aid, you obtained the following information:

(1) Using 19X4 as the base year, price-level indexes for relevant years are: 19X1 = 90, 19X2 = 93, 19X3 = 96, 19X4 = 100, 19X5 = 105, 19X6 = 112, and 19X7 = 120.

(2) The company allocated $200,000 per year for depreciation of fixed assets allocated to this construction project. Of that amount, $25,000 was for a building purchased in 19X1 and $175,000 was for equipment purchased in 19X3.

Required:

a. Prepare a schedule to restate in base year (19X4) costs the actual costs, including depreciation, incurred each year. Disregard income taxes and assume that each price-level index was valid for the entire year.

b. Prepare a schedule comparing the original estimated costs of the project with the total actual costs for each element of cost (materials, labor, variable overhead, and depreciation) adjusted to the 19X4 price level.

c. Prepare a schedule to restate the amount received on the sale in terms of base year (19X4) purchasing power. The gain or loss should be determined separately for the land and the building in terms of base year purchasing power and should exclude depreciation.

(AICPA adapted)

6–18   Select the best answer for each of the following items relating to price-level accounting.
   (1)   The valuation basis used in conventional financial statements is
      a.   market value
      b.   original cost
      c.   replacement cost
      d.   a mixture of costs and values
      e.   none of the above
   (2)   An unacceptable practice for presenting general price-level information is
      a.   the inclusion of general price-level gains and losses on monetary items in the general price-level statement of income
      b.   the inclusion of extraordinary gains and losses in the general price-level statement of income
      c.   the use of charts, ratios, and narrative information
      d.   the use of specific price indexes to restate inventories, plant, and equipment
      e.   none of the above
   (3)   When general price-level balance sheets are prepared, they should be presented in terms of
      a.   the general purchasing power of the dollar at the latest balance sheet date
      b.   the general purchasing power of the dollar in the base period
      c.   the average general purchasing power of the dollar for the latest fiscal period
      d.   the general purchasing power of the dollar at the time the financial statements are issued
      e.   none of the above
   (4)   The restatement of historical-dollar financial statements to reflect general price-level changes results in presenting assets at
      a.   lower of cost or market values
      b.   current appraisal values
      c.   costs adjusted for purchasing power changes
      d.   current replacement cost
      e.   none of the above
   (5)   During a period of deflation, an entity would have the greatest gain in general pruchasing power by holding
      a.   cash
      b.   plant and equipment
      c.   accounts payable
      d.   mortgages payable
      e.   none of the above
   (6)   When preparing general price-level financial statements, it would not be appropriate to use
      a.   lower of cost or market in the valuation of inventories
      b.   replacement cost in the valuation of plant assets
      c.   the historical cost basis in reporting income tax expense
      d.   the actual amounts payable in reporting liabilities on the balance sheet
      e.   any of the above

(7) For comparison purposes, general price-level financial statements of earlier periods should be restated to the general purchasing power of the dollar at
a. the beginning of the base period
b. an average for the current period
c. the beginning of the current period
d. the end of the current period
e. none of the above

(8) In preparing price-level financial statements, monetary items consist of
a. cash items plus all receivables with a fixed maturity date
b. cash, other assets expected to be converted into cash, and current liabilities
c. assets and liabilities whose amounts are fixed by contract or otherwise in terms of dollars, regardless of price-level changes
d. assets and liabilities that are classified as current on the balance sheet
e. none of the above

(9) In preparing price-level financial statements, a nonmonetary item would be
a. accounts payable in cash
b. long-term bonds payable
c. accounts receivable
d. allowance for uncollectible accounts
e. none of the above

(10) Gains and losses on nonmonetary assets usually are reported in historical-dollar financial statements when the items are sold. Gains and losses on the sale of nonmonetary assets should be reported in general price-level financial statements
a. in the same period, but the amount will probably differ
b. in the same period and the same amount
c. over the life of the nonmonetary asset
d. partly over the life of the nonmonetary asset and the remainder when the asset is sold
e. none of the above

(11) If land were purchased in 1971 for $100,000 when the general price-level index was 100 and sold at the end of 1980 for $160,000 when the index was 170, the general price-level statement of income for 1980 would show
a. a general price-level gain of $70,000 and a loss on sale of land of $10,000
b. a gain on sale of land of $60,000
c. a general price-level loss of $10,000
d. a loss on sale of land of $10,000
e. none of the above

(12) If land were purchased at a cost of $20,000 in January 1974 when the general price-level index was 120 and sold in December 1980 when the index was 150, the selling price that would result in no gain or loss would be

a. $30,000   d. $16,000
b. $24,000   e. none of the above
c. $20,000

(13) If the base year is 1958 (when the price index = 100) and the land is purchased for $50,000 in 1964 when the general price index is 108.5, the cost of the land restated to 1958 general purchasing-power dollars (rounded to the nearest whole dollar) would be
a. $54,250   d. $45,750
b. $50,000   e. none of the above
c. $46,083

(14) Assume the same facts as in Item 13, above. The cost of the land restated to December 31, 1970, general purchasing power dollars when the price index was 119.2 (rounded to the nearest whole dollar) would be
a. $59,600   d. $45,512
b. $54,931   e. none of the above
c. $46,083

The following information applies to Items 15 through 18: Equipment purchased for $120,000 on January 1, Year 1 when the price index was 100, was sold on December 31, Year 3 at a price of $85,000. The equipment originally was expected to last six years with no salvage value and was depreciated on a straight-line basis. The price index at the end of Year 1 was 125, at Year 2 was 150, and at Year 3 was 175.

(15) The general price-level financial statements prepared at the end of Year 1 would include
a. equipment of $150,000, accumulated depreciation of $25,000, and a gain of $30,000
b. equipment of $150,000, accumulated depreciation of $25,000, and no gain or loss
c. equipment of $150,000, accumulated depreciation of $20,000, and a gain of $30,000
d. equipment of $120,000, accumulated depreciation of $20,000, and a gain of 30,000
e. none of the above

(16) In general price-level comparative financial statements prepared at the end of Year 2, the Year 1 financial statements should show equipment (net of accumulated depreciation) at
a. $150,000   d. $80,000
b. $125,000   e. none of the above
c. $100,000

(17) The general price-level financial statements prepared at the end of Year 2 should include depreciation expense of
a. $35,000   d. $20,000
b. $30,000   e. none of the above
c. $25,000

(18) The general price-level income statement prepared at the end of Year 3 should include
a. a gain of $35,000   d. a loss of $5,000
b. a gain of $25,000   e. none of the above
c. no gain or loss

6–19 The directors of Indexo, Ltd., have adopted a firm policy to convert the financial statement items into common dollars starting January 1, 19X4. The treasurer of the company has prepared comparative financial statements for 19X3 and 19X4, but the directors do not understand the meaning and the calculations of some items in these financial statements.

The unadjusted comparative balance sheets are summarized as follows:

Indexo, Ltd.
Comparative Balance Sheet
at December 31

	19X3	19X4
Monetary assets	$110,000	$125,000
Inventories	50,000	60,000
Land	70,000	70,000
Buildings and equipment	100,000	95,000
	$330,000	$350,000
Liabilities	60,000	65,000
Capital stock	200,000	200,000
Retained earnings	70,000	85,000
	$330,000	$350,000

The 19X4 income statement is as follows:

Revenues		$180,000
Cost of sales	$ 98,000	
Wages	25,000	
Depreciation	5,000	
Taxes	35,000	
Other	2,000	165,000
Net income		$ 15,000

On the basis of the price index of the country, the treasurer has made all necessary adjustments and presented the following statements to the directors.

Balance Sheet
December 31, 19X3

	Unadjusted	Adjustment Factor	Adjusted
Monetary assets	$110,000	125/100	$137,500
Inventories	50,000	125/100	62,500
Land	70,000	125/80	109,375
Buildings and equipment	100,000	125/80	156,250
	$330,000		$465,625

Balance Sheet
December 31, 19X4

	Unadjusted	Adjustment Factor	Adjusted
Monetary assets	$125,000	125/125	$125,000
Inventories	60,000	125/116	64,655
Land	70,000	125/80	109,375
Buildings and equipment	95,000	125/80	148,438
	$350,000		$447,468
Liabilities	$ 65,000	125/125	$ 65,000
Capital stock	200,000	125/70	357,143
Retained earnings	85,000		25,325
	$350,000		$447,468

Income Statement
For the Year Ended December 31, 19X4

	Unadjusted	Adjustment Factor	Adjusted
Revenues	$180,000	125/110	$204,545
Cost of goods sold from stock	50,000	125/100	62,500
Cost of goods sold from purchases	48,000	125/114	52,632
Wages	25,000	125/110	28,410
Depreciation	5,000	125/80	7,812
Taxes	35,000	125/110	39,772
Other	2,000	125/110	2,272
	$165,000		$193,398
Net income	$ 15,000		$ 11,147

Required:

a. Distinguish briefly between monetary and nonmonetary assets and liabilities.

b. Prepare a schedule to establish the loss incurred during the year on monetary items.

c. Prepare a schedule to reconcile the adjusted retained earnings at December 31, 1974.

(Society of Management Accountants adapted)

6–20 Select the best answer for each of the following items.

(1) Which of the following observations is valid?

    a. The amount obtained by adjusting an asset's cost for general price-level changes usually approximates its current fair value.

    b. The amounts adjusted for general price-level changes are not departures from historical cost.

    c. When inventory increases and prices are rising, last in, first out (LIFO) inventory accounting has the same effect on financial statements as amounts adjusted for general price-level changes.

d. When inventory remains constant and prices are rising, LIFO inventory accounting has the same effects on financial statements as amounts adjusted for general price-level changes.

(2) In the context of general price-level adjustments, which of the following is a nonmonetary item?
   a. receivables under capitalized leases
   b. obligations under capitalized leases
   c. minority interest
   d. unamortized discount on bonds payable

(3) When does a general purchasing power loss occur, and when is it recognized?
   a. It occurs when holding net monetary assets during inflation, and it is recognized in units-of-general-purchasing-power financial statements.
   b. It occurs when holding net monetary liabilities during inflation, and it is recognized in units-of-general-purchasing-power financial statements.
   c. It occurs when holding net monetary assets during inflation, and it is recognized in units-of-general-purchasing-power and units-of-money financial statements.
   d. It occurs when holding net monetary liabilities during inflation, and it is recognized in units-of-general-purchasing-power and units-of-money financial statements.

(4) Price-level adjusted financial statements (general purchasing power) have been a controversial issue in accounting. Which of the following arguments in favor of such financial statements is *not* valid?
   a. Price-level adjusted financial statements use historical cost.
   b. Price-level adjusted financial statements compare uniform purchasing power among various periods.
   c. Price-level adjusted financial statements measure current value.
   d. Price-level adjusted financial statements measure earnings in terms of a common dollar.

(5) When discussing asset valuation, the following valuation bases are sometimes mentioned: replacement cost, exist value, and discounted cash flow. Which of these bases should be considered a current-value measure?
   a. replacement cost and exit value only
   b. replacement cost and discounted cash flow only
   c. exit value and discounted cash flow only
   d. replacement cost, exit value, and discounted cash flow

(6) When valuing raw materials inventory at lower of cost or market, what is the meaning of the term "market"?
   a. net realizable value
   b. net realizable value less a normal profit margin.
   c. current replacement cost
   d. discounted present value

(7) If a constant unit of measure during a period of inflation is used, the general purchasing power of the dollar in which some expenses are measured (for assets systematically allocated among accounting

periods) may differ significantly from the general purchasing power of the dollar in which revenue is measured. Which of the following accounting procedures maximizes this effect?

a. reserve method of accounting for bad debts
b. income tax allocation
c. accelerated depreciation
d. valuing inventory at the lower of cost or market

(AICPA adapted)

6–21 (1) Price-level adjusted financial statements are prepared in an effort to eliminate the effects of inflation or deflation. An integral part of determining restated amounts and applicable gain or loss from restatement is the segregation of all assets and liabilities into monetary and nonmonetary classifications. One reason for this classification is that price-level gains and losses for monetary items are currently matched against earnings.

Required:

What are the factors that determine whether an asset or liability is classified as monetary or nonmonetary? In your response, include a justification for recognizing gains and losses from monetary items and not for nonmonetary items.

(2) Proponents of price-level restatement of financial statements state that a basic weakness of financial statements not adjusted for price-level changes is that they are made up of "mixed dollars."

Required:

a. What is meant by the term "mixed dollars" and why is this a weakness of unadjusted financial statements?
b. Explain how financial statements restated for price-level changes eliminate this weakness. Use property, plant, and equipment in your example in this discussion.

(AICPA adapted)

chapter seven

Alternative Asset Valuation and Income Determination Models

In Chapters 5 and 6, we established that income may be recognized only after "capital" has been kept intact. Consequently, income measurement depends on the particular concept of capital maintenance chosen. The various concepts of capital maintenance imply different ways of evaluating and measuring the elements of financial statements. Thus, both income determination and capital maintenance are defined in terms of the **asset valuation base** used. A given asset valuation base determines a particular concept of capital maintenance and a particular income concept. What do we mean by asset valuation base? An asset valuation base is a method of measuring the elements of financial statements, based on the selection of both an attribute of the elements to be measured and the unit of measure to be used in measuring that attribute. As discussed in Chapters 5 and 6, four attributes may be measured and two units of measure may be used. The four attributes of all classes of assets and liabilities that may be measured are: (1) historical cost, (2) current entry price (for example, replacement cost), (3) current exit price (for example, net realizable value), and (4) present value of expected cash flows. The two units of measure that may be used are units of money and units of purchasing power. Combining the four attributes and the two units of measure yields the following eight alternative asset valuation and income determination models.

1. *Historical cost accounting* measures historical cost in units of money.

2. *Replacement cost accounting* measures replacement cost (that is, current entry price) in units of money.

3. *Net realizable value accounting* measures net realizable value (that is, current exit price) in units of money.

4. *Present in value accounting* measures present value in units of money.

5. *General price-level accounting* measures historical cost in units of purchasing power.

6. *General price-level replacement cost accounting* measures replacement cost in units of purchasing power.

7. *General price-level net realizable value accounting* measures realizable value in units of purchasing power.

8. *General price-level present-value accounting* measures present value in units of purchasing power.

Each of these alternatives yields a different financial statement, with different meaning and relevance to its users. In this chapter, we shall evaluate these alternatives using a simplified example to enhance conceptual clarity and comparability among the approaches. The nature of the differences and the basis of comparison among the results of the various alternatives will also be highlighted.

The Nature
of the Differences

As stated above, the differences among the alternative asset valuation basis and income determination models arise from the different attributes to be measured and units of measure to be used. We shall examine each characteristic of the elements of the financial statements in the following sections.

Attributes to Be Measured

The attribute of assets and liabilities refers to what is being measured. As we mentioned, the four attributes are: (1) historical cost, (2) replacement cost, (3) net realizable value, and (4) capitalized, or present, value. Let us define each of these.

Historical cost refers to the amount of cash or cash equivalent paid to acquire an asset or the amount of cash or cash equivalent liability.

Replacement cost refers to the amount of cash or cash equivalent that would be paid to acquire an equivalent or same asset currently or that would be received to incur the same liability currently.

Net realizable value refers to the amount of cash or cash equivalent that would be obtained by selling the asset currently or that would be paid to redeem the liability currently.

Present, or **capitalized, value** refers to the present value of net cash flows expected to be received from the use of the asset or the net outflows expected to be disbursed to redeem the liability.

We may classify these attributes in three ways: First, they may be classified with respect to whether they focus on the past, present, or future. Hence, historical cost focuses on the past, replacement cost and net realizable value focus on the present, and present value focuses to the future.

Second, we may classify these measures with respect to the kind of transactions from which they are derived. Hence, historical cost and replacement cost concern the acquisition of assets or the incurrence of liabilities, while net realizable value and present value concern the disposition of assets or the redemption of liabilities.

The third classification is with respect to the nature of the event originating the measure. Hence, historical cost is based on an actual event, present value on an expected event, and replacement cost and net realizable value on a hypothetical event.

One question that we shall examine in this chapter is: What attribute or attributes of the elements of financial statements should be measured in financial accounting or reporting?

Unit of Measure

Financial accounting measurements may be made in one of two units of measure: units of money or units of general purchasing power. Similarly, each of the attributes that we have defined is measurable in either units of money or units of general purchasing power. In the United States and in most other countries, conventional financial statements are expressed in units of money. Given the continuous decline of the purchasing power of the dollar, however, another unit of measure, the unit of purchasing power, is frequently presented as a preferable alternative because it recognizes changes in the general price level.

Do not confuse the general price level with either the specific price level or the relative price level. A change in the general price level refers to changes in the prices of all goods and services throughout the economy. The reciprocal of such changes would be a change in the general purchasing power of the monetary unit. A change in the specific price level refers to a change in the price of a particular product or service. Current-value accounting differs from historical cost accounting in that changes in the specific price level are recognized on the basis of either replacement cost or net realizable value.

Finally, a change in the relative price level of a commodity refers to the part of the specific price change that remains after the effects of the general price-level change have been eliminated. Thus, if all prices increase by 32 percent and the price of a specific good increases by 10 percent, the relative price change is only 20 percent [(132/110) − 1].

All three types of price changes may be incorporated in the asset valuation and income determination models. Note that both historical cost and current value are expressed in units of money, and general price-level restatements may be made for both.

Another question that we shall examine in this chapter is: What unit of measure should be used to measure any particular attribute of the elements of financial statements?

Basis for Comparison and Evaluation

We have established that the alternative accounting models (historical cost accounting, general price-level accounting, replacement cost accounting, general price-level adjusted replacement cost accounting, net realizable value accounting, general price-level adjusted net realizable value accounting, present-value accounting, and general price-level adjusted present value accounting) are based on a choice of one of four available attributes (historical cost, replacement cost, net realizable value, and present value) and one of two available units of measure (units of money and units of general purchasing power). Now, we shall compare the models on the basis of whether they *avoid timing errors* and *avoid measuring unit errors*, and we shall evaluate them in terms of interpretability[1] and relevance.

Although considered theoretically the best accounting models, the present-value models will not be included in our comparison and evaluation because of their recognized practical deficiencies. First the present-value models require the estimation of future net cash receipts and the timing of those receipts, as well as the selection of the appropriate discount rates. Second, when applied to the valuation of individual assets, they require arbitrary allocation of estimated future net cash receipts and the timing of those receipts, as well as the selection of the appropriate discount rates. Third, when applied to the valuation of individual assets, they require arbitrary allocation of estimated future net cash receipts among the individual assets.[2] Because of this lack of objectivity, the present-value models have been largely rejected as impractical. We shall compare and evaluate the remaining accounting models in this chapter. Each of the criteria for comparison and evaluation will be examined next.

Timing Errors

The criteria for determining what attribute or attributes of the element of financial statements should be measured in financial accounting and reporting should favor the attribute that avoids timing errors. Timing errors occur when changes in

---

[1]S. Basu and J. R. Hanna, *Inflation Accounting: Alternatives, Implementation Issues and Some Evidence* (Hamilton, Ont.: The Society of Management Accountants, 1977); R. R. Sterling, "Relevant Financial Reporting in an Age of Price Changes," *The Journal of Accountancy* (February 1975), pp. 42–51.

[2]A. L. Thomas, *The Allocation Problem in Accounting* (Sarasota, Fla.: AAA, 1969).

value occurring in a given period are accounted for and reported in another period. A preferred attribute would be one that recognizes changes in value in the same period that the changes occur. Ideally, "profit is attributable to the whole process of business activity."[3]

Measuring Unit Errors

The criteria for determining what unit of measure should be used for the attributes of the elements of financial statements should favor the unit of measure that avoids measuring unit errors. Measuring unit errors occur when financial statements are not expressed in units of general purchasing power. A preferred measuring unit would be one that recognizes changes in the general price level in the financial statements.

Interpretability

Our first criterion for evaluation is the interpretability of the accounting model. In other words, the resulting financial statements should be understandable in terms of both meaning and use. According to Sterling:

> When an attribute involves an arithmetical calculation, the "empirical interpretation" of that attribute requires that it be placed in an "if . . . then . . ." statement.[4]

Thus, for an accounting model to be interpretable, it must be placed in an "if . . . then . . ." statement to convey to the user an understanding of its meaning as well as demonstrating one of its uses. Given that we have two possible units of measure, the interpretation of the accounting models, by definition, will be also one of the following choices:

1. If the accounting model measures any of the attributes in units of money, its results are expressed in the number of dollars (NOD) or, as Chambers referred to it, the number of odd dollars (NOOD).[5]

2. If the accounting model measures historical cost in units of general purchasing power, its results still are expressed in NOD.

3. If the accounting model measures current values in units of general purchasing power, its results are expressed in the command of goods (COG) or, as Chambers referred to it, command of goods in general (COGG).[6]

In summary, the accounting models may be interpreted as measuring NOD (number of dollars) or COG (command of goods). When expressed in units of money, the models are measures of NOD, and when reflecting changes in both the specific and general price levels, they are measures of COG.

Relevance

The second criterion for evaluation is the relevance of the accounting model. In other words, the resulting financial statements should be useful. Sterling defines relevance as follows:

---

[3]R. T. Sprouse and M. Moonitz, "A Tentative Set of Broad Accounting Principles for Business Enterprises," *Accounting Research Study No. 3* (New York: AICPA, 1962), p. 55.

[4]Sterling, "Relevant Financial Reporting in an Age of Price Changes," p. 44.

[5]R. J. Chambers, "NOD, COG and PuPu: See How Inflation Teases!" *Journal of Accountancy* (September 1975), p. 61.

[6]*Ibid.*, p. 61.

If a decision model specifies an attribute as an input or as a calculation, then that attribute is relevant to that decision model.[7]

Because decision models are either not available or not well-specified, relevance focuses on what ought to be measured. For our purposes, the problem is to decide whether NOD or COG constitutes the relevant measure. From a normative point of view, the answer is straightforward. Because COG expresses changes in both the specific and general price level, it should be considered the most relevant attribute. COG expresses the goods that could be commanded in either the input or the output market. Thus, COG may be defined in terms of the input market as price-level adjusted replacement cost or in terms of the output market as price-level adjusted net realizable value.

Illustration of the
Different Accounting Models

To illustrate the different accounting models, we shall consider the simplified case of the Monti Company, which was formed January 1, 19X6, to distribute a new product called "Gamma." Capital is composed of $3,000 equity and $3,000 liabilities carrying a 10 percent interest. On January 1, the Monti Company began operations by purchasing 600 units of Gamma at $10 per unit. On May 1, the company sold 500 units at $15 per unit. Changes in the general and specific price levels for the year 19X6 are as follows:

	January 1	May 1	December 31
Replacement cost	$10	$12	$13
Net realizable value	—	$15	$17
General price-level index	100	130	156

A brief description of each accounting model follows, accompanied by illustrations using the given data.

Alternative Accounting Models Expressed in Units of Money

To illustrate and isolate only the timing differences, we shall present first the alternative accounting models that do not reflect changes in the general price level. These models are (1) historical cost accounting, (2) replacement cost accounting, and (3) net realizable value accounting. The income statement and the balance sheet for 19X6, under the three accounting models, are shown in Exhibits 7–1 and 7–2, respectively.

Historical Cost Accounting   Historical cost accounting, or conventional accounting, is characterized primarily by (1) the use of historical cost as the attribute of the elements of financial statements, (2) the assumption of a stable monetary unit, (3) the matching principle, and (4) the realization principle.

---

[7]Sterling, "Relevant Financial Reporting," p. 46.

EXHIBIT 7–1

Monti Company
Income Statements, December 31, 19X6

	Historical Cost	Replacement Cost	Net Realizable Value
Revenues	$7,500[a]	$7,500	$9,200[b]
Cost of Goods Sold	5,000[c]	6,000[d]	7,300[e]
Gross Margin	$2,500	$1,500	$1,900
Interest	300	300	300
Operating Profit	$2,200	$1,200	$1,600
Realized Holding Gains and Losses	Included above	1,000[f]	1,000
Unrealized Holding Gains and Losses	Not applicable	300[g]	300
General Price-Level Gains and Losses	Not applicable	Not applicable	Not applicable
Net Profit	$2,200	$2,500	$2,900

[a] $500 \times \$15 = \$7,500$
[b] $7,500 + \$17 (100) = \$9,200$
[c] $500 \times \$10 = \$5,000$
[d] $500 \times \$12 = \$6,000$
[e] $6,000 + \$13 (100) = \$7,300$
[f] $500 (\$12 - \$10) = \$1,000$
[g] $100 (\$13 - \$10) = \$300$

EXHIBIT 7–2

Monti Company
Balance Sheet, December 31, 19X6

	Historical Cost	Replacement Cost	Net Realizable Value
Assets			
Cash	$7,200	$7,200	$7,200
Inventory	1,000	1,300[a]	1,700[b]
Total Assets	$8,200	$8,500	$8,900
Equities			
Bonds (10%)	$3,000	$3,000	$3,000
Capital	3,000	3,000	3,000
Retained Earnings			
Realized	2,200	2,200[c]	2,000[c]
Unrealized	Not applicable	300	700[d]
Total Equities	$8,200	$8,500	$8,900

[a] $100 \times (\$13) = \$1,300$
[b] $100 \times (\$17) = \$1,700$
[c] May be divided into current operating profit ($1,200) and realized holding gains and losses ($1,000)
[d] Unrealized Operating Gain $400 ($1,700 − $1,300) + Unrealized Holding Gain $300

Accordingly, historical cost income, or accounting income, is the difference between the realized revenues and the corresponding historical costs. As shown in Exhibit 7–1, accounting income is equal to $2,200. What does this figure represent for the Monti Company? Generally, it is perceived as a basis for the computation of taxes and dividends and for the evaluation of performance. Its possible use in various decision models results from the unconditional and long-standing acceptance of this version of income by the accounting profession and the business world. This attachment to accounting income may be explained primarily by the fact that it is objective, verifiable, practical, and easy to understand. Accountants and business persons may prefer accounting income over other measures of income for its practical advantages, and they may fear the confusion that could result from the adoption of another accounting model.

In spite of these practical advantages, the Monti Company's $2,200 accounting income contains both timing and measuring unit errors. First, the accounting income contains timing errors because (1) it includes in a single figure operating income and holding gains and losses that are recognized in the current period and that occurred in previous periods, and (2) it omits the operating profit and holding gains and losses that occurred in the current period but that are recognizable in future periods. Second, the accounting income contains measuring unit errors because (1) it does not take into account changes in the general price level that would have resulted in amounts expressed in units of general purchasing power, and (2) by relying on historical cost as the attribute of the elements of financial statements rather than either replacement cost or net realizable value, it does not take into account changes in the specific price level.

How, then, should we evaluate historical cost financial statements? First, they are interpretable. Historical cost financial statements are based on the concept of money maintenance. The attribute being expressed is the number of dollars (NOD). The balance sheet reports the stocks in NOD at December 31, 19X6, and the income statement reports the change in NOD during the year.

Second, historical cost financial statements are not relevant because the command of goods (COG) is not measured. A measure of COG permits reflection of both the changes in the specific price level and general price level, and therefore, such a measure represents the ability to buy the amount of goods necessary for capital maintenance.

In summary, historical cost financial statements (1) contain timing errors, (2) contain measuring unit errors, (3) are interpretable, and (4) are not relevant.

Replacement Cost Accounting   Replacement cost accounting, as a particular case of current entry price accounting, is characterized primarily by (1) the use of replacement cost as the attribute of the elements of financial statements, (2) the assumption of a stable monetary unit, (3) the realization principle, (4) the dichotomization of operating income and holding gains and loses, and (5) the dichotomization of realized and unrealized holding gains and losses.

Accordingly, replacement cost net income is equal to the sum of replacement cost operating income and holding gains and losses. Replacement cost operating income is equal to the difference between the realized revenues and the corresponding replacement costs. From Exhibit 7–1, the Monti Company's replacement cost net income of $2,500 is composed of (1) replacement cost operating income of $1,200, (2) realized holding gains and losses of $1,000, and (3) unrealized holding gains and losses of $300.

What do these figures represent for the Monti Company? The replacement cost operating income of $1,200 represents the "distributable" income, or the maximum amount of dividends the company can pay and maintain its productive capacity intact. The realized holding gains and losses of $1,000 constitute an indicator of the efficiency of holding resources up to the time of sale. The realizable holding gains and losses are an indicator of the efficiency of holding resources after sale and may act as a predictor of future operating and holding performances.

In addition to these practical advantages, replacement cost net income contains timing errors on only operating profit. It does, however, contain measuring unit errors.

First replacement cost net income contains timing errors because (1) it omits the operating profit that occurred in the current period but that is realizable in future periods, (2) it includes the operating profit that is recognized in the current period but that occurred in previous periods, and (3) it includes holding gains and losses in the same period as they occur.

Second, replacement cost net income contains measuring units errors because (1) it does not take into account changes in the general price level that would have resulted in amounts expressed in units of general purchasing power, and (3) it does take into account changes in the specific price level as it relies on replacement cost as the attribute of the elements of financial statements.

We may evaluate replacement cost financial statements as follows. First, they are interpretable. Replacement cost financial statements are based on the concept of productive capacity maintenance. The attribute being expressed is still the number of dollars (NOD) in the income statement. The asset figures, however, are interpretable as measures of command of goods (COG). The asset figures shown in Exhibit 7–2 are expressed in terms of the purchasing power of the dollar at the end of the year. They reflect changes in both the specific and the general price level, and therefore, they represent the COG necessary for capital maintenance. Second, because COG is the relevant attribute, the replacement net income is not relevant, even though the asset figures are relevant.

In summary, replacement cost financial statements present the following characteristics: (1) they contain operating profit timing errors, (2) they contain measuring unit errors, (3) they are interpretable as NOD for the income and COG for the asset figures, and (4) only the asset figures are relevant as measures of COG.

Net Realizable Value Accounting   Net realizable value accounting, as a particular case of current exit price accounting, is characterized primarily by (1) the use of net realizable value as the attribute of the elements of financial statements, (2) the assumption of a stable monetary unit, (3) the abandonment of the realization principle, (4) the dichotomization of operating income and holding gains and losses.

Accordingly, under net realizable value accounting, net income is equal to the sum of the net realizable value operating income and holding gains and losses. Net realizable value operating income is equal to the operating income arising from sale and the net operating income on inventory. Operating income on sale is equal to the difference between the realized revenues and the corresponding replacement cost of the items sold. Operating income on inventory is equal to the difference between the net realizable value of the items in inventory and the corresponding replacement costs. From Exhibit 7–1, the Monti Company's net realizable value net income of $2,900 is composed of (1) net realizable value operating income of $1,600, (2) realized holding gains of $1,000, and (3) unrealized holding gains and losses of $300.

Note that the net realizable value operating income of $1,600 is composed of operating income on sale of $1,200 and operating income on inventory of $400. Thus, in Exhibit 7-2, unrealized retained earnings equal the some of the unrealized holding gains and losses of $300 and the operating income on inventory of $400.

What do these figures represent for the Monti Company? They are similar to the figures obtained with replacement cost accounting, except for the operating income on inventory, which results from the abandonment of the realization principle and the recognition of revenues at the time of production and at the time of sale. Net realizable value net income indicates the ability of the firm to liquidate and to adapt to new economic situations.

To these practical advantages we may add that net realizable net income contains no timing errors, but it does contain measuring unit errors. It does not contain any timing errors because (1) it reports all operating profit and holding gains and losses in the same period in which they occur, and (2) it excludes all operating and holding gains and losses occurring in previous periods.

Net realizable value net income contains measuring unit errors because (1) it does not take into account changes in the general price level (if it had, it would have resulted in amounts expressed in units of purchasing power), and (2) it does take into account changes in the specific price level because it relies on net realizable value as the attribute of the elements of financial statements.

We may evaluate net realizable value financial statements as follows.

First, they are interpretable. Net realizable value financial statements are based on the concept of productive capacity maintenance. The attribute being measured is expressed in NOD in the income statement and COG in the balance sheet. Unlike replacement cost accounting, under net realizable value, accounting, asset figures are expressed as measures of COG in the output market rather than the input market.

Second, because COG is the relevant attribute, the net realizable value income is not relevant, while the asset figures are relevant.

In summary, net realizable value financial statements present the following characteristics: (1) they contain no timing errors, as shown in Exhibit 7-3, (2) they contain measuring unit errors, (3) they are interpretable as NOD for the net income and COG for the asset figures, and (4) only the asset figures are relevant as measures of COG.

EXHIBIT 7-3
Monti Company
Timing Error Analysis — 19X6

Total Operating and Holding Gains	Historical Cost		Replacement Cost		Net Realizable Value	
	Reported Income	Error	Reported Income	Error	Reported Income	Error
$2,900	$2,200	$700	$2,500	$400	$2,900	0

Alternative Accounting Models
Expressed in Units of Purchasing Power

To illustrate both timing and measuring unit errors, we shall present in this section accounting models that reflect changes in the general price level. These models are (1) general price-level adjusted historical cost accounting, (2) general price-level adjusted replacement cost accounting, and (3) general price-level adjusted net realizable value accounting. Continuing with our example of the Monti Company, the income statement and the balance sheet for 19X6, under the three accounting models, are shown in Exhibits 7–4 and 7–5, respectively. The general price-level gain or loss is shown in Exhibit 7–6.

General Price-Level Adjusted Historical Cost Accounting   General price-level adjusted historical cost accounting is characterized primarily by (1) the use of historical cost as the attribute of the elements of financial statements, (2) the use of units of general purchasing power as the unit of measure, (3) the matching principle, and (4) the realization principle.

Accordingly, general price-level adjusted historical cost income is the difference between the realized revenues and the corresponding historical costs, both expressed in units of general purchasing power. From Exhibit 7–4, general price-level adjusted historical cost income is equal to $1,080. Included in the $1,080 historical cost income is a $180 general price-level gain computed as shown in

EXHIBIT 7–4
General Price-Level Income Statement, December 31, 19X6

	Historical Cost	Replacement Cost	Net Realizable Value
Revenues	$9,000^a	$9,000	$10,700^b
Cost of Goods Sold	7,800^c	7,200^d	8,500^e
Gross Margin	$1,200	$1,800	$ 2,200
Interest	300	300	300
Operating Profit	$ 900	$1,500	$ 1,900
Real Realized Holding Gains and Losses	Included above	(600)^f	(600)
Real Unrealized Holding Gains and Losses	Not applicable	(260)^g	(260)
General Price-Level Gain or Loss	180^h	180	180
Net Profit	$1,080	$ 820	$ 1,220

^{a} $7,500 \times \dfrac{156}{130} = \$9,000$

^{b} $9,000 + (\$17 \times 100 \text{ units}) = \$10,700$

^{c} $5,000 \times \dfrac{156}{100} = \$7,800$

^{d} $6,000 \times \dfrac{156}{130} = \$7,200$

^{e} $7,200 + (\$13 \times 100 \text{ units}) = \$8,500$

^{f} $(\$12 \times \dfrac{156}{130} - \$10 \times \dfrac{156}{100}) \times 500 = (\$600)$

^{g} $(\$13 - \$10 \times \dfrac{156}{100}) \times 100 \text{ units} = (\$260)$

^{h} See Exhibit 7–6

EXHIBIT 7-5
General Price-Level Balance Sheet, December 31, 19X6

	Historical Cost	Replacement Cost	Net Realizable Value
Asset			
Cash	$7,200	$7,200	$7,200
Inventory	1,560[a]	1,300	1,700
Total Assets	$8,760	$8,500	$8,900
Equities			
Bonds (10%)	$3,000	$3,000	$3,000
Capital	4,680[b]	4,680	4,680
Retained Earnings			
Realized	900	900	900
Unrealized	Not applicable	(260)	140[c]
General Price-Level Gain or Loss	180	180	180
Total Equities	$8,760	$8,500	$8,900

[a] $1,000 × $\frac{156}{100}$ = $1,560

[b] $3,000 × $\frac{156}{100}$ = $4,680

[c] Unrealized Operating Gain $400 ($1,700 − $1,300) + Unrealized Holding Gain ($260).

Exhibit 7-5. Again, what does the $1,080 figure represent for the Monti Company? It represents accounting income expressed in dollars that have the purchasing power of dollars at the end of 19X6. In addition to the practical advantages listed for accounting income, general price-level adjusted historical cost income is expressed in units of general purchasing power. For these reasons, the use of such an accounting model may constitute a less radical change for those used to historical cost income than any model based on current value.

In spite of these practical advantages, the general price-level adjusted historical cost income of $1,080 contains timing errors but no measuring unit errors. First, general price-level adjusted historical cost income contains the same timing errors as does historical cost income (see page 224). Second, general price-level adjusted historical cost income contains no measuring unit errors because it does take into account changes in the general price level. It does not, however, take into account changes in the specific price level because it relies on historical cost as the attribute of the elements of financial statements rather than on replacement cost or net realizable value.

Again, how should we evaluate the general price-level adjusted historical cost financial statements presented in Exhibit 7-4 and 7-5? First, they are interpretable. General price-level adjusted historical cost financial statements are based on the concept of purchasing power money maintenance. The attribute being measured is NOD in some cases and COG in other cases. Hence, general price-level adjusted historical cost income and all balance sheet figures with the exception of cash (and monetary assets and liabilities) may be interpreted as NOD measures. Only the cash figure (and monetary assets and liabilities) may be interpreted as a

EXHIBIT 7–6
General Price-Level Gain or Loss, December 31, 19X6

	Unadjusted	Conversion Factor	Adjusted
Net Monetary Assets on			
January 1, 19X5	$ 3,000	156/100	$ 4,680
Add Monetary Receipts			
during 19X6 Sales	7,500	156/130	9,000
Net Monetary Items	$10,500		$13,680
Less Monetary Payments			
Purchases	6,000	156/100	9,360
Interest	300	156/156	300
Total	$ 6,300		$ 9,660
Computed Net Monetary			
Assets, December 31, 19X6			4,020
Actual Net Monetary			
Assets, December 31, 19X6			4,200
General Price-Level Gain			$ 180

COG measure. Second, only the cash figures (and monetary assets and liabilities) are relevant because they are expressed as COG measures.

In summary, general price-level adjusted historical cost financial statements present the following characteristics: (1) they contain timing errors, (2) they contain no measuring unit errors, (3) they are interpretable, and (4) only the cash figures (and monetary assets and liabilities) are relevant as COG measures.

General Price-Level Adjusted Replacement Cost Accounting   General price-level adjusted replacement cost accounting is characterized primarily by (1) the use of replacement cost as the attribute of the elements of financial statements, (2) the use of units of general purchasing power as the unit of measure, (3) the realization principle, (4) the dichotomization of operating income and real realized holding gains and losses, and (5) the dichotomization of real realized and real unrealized holding gains and losses.

Accordingly, general price-level adjusted replacement cost income is equal to the sum of general price-level adjusted replacement cost operating income and real holding gains and losses. The general price-level adjusted replacement cost operating income is equal to the difference between realized revenues and the corresponding replacement costs, both expressed in units of general purchasing power. Similarly, general price-level adjusted replacement cost financial statements eliminate the "fictitious holding gains and losses" to arrive at the "real holding gains and losses." Fictitious holding gains and losses represent the general price-level restatement necessary to maintain the general purchasing power of nonmonetary items. We see from Exhibit 7–4 the general price-level replacement cost net income is equal to $820. Included in the $820 income is a $180 general price-level gain, computed as shown in Exhibit 7–5. Again, what does the $820 figure represent for the Monti Company? It represents the replacement cost net income expressed in units of general purchasing power of the end of 19X7. Such a measure of income has the same advantages that we listed for replacement cost accounting income, with the added advantage of being expressed in units of general purchasing power. For these reasons, general price-level restated replacement cost accounting constitutes a net improvement over replacement cost accounting. Not only does this accounting model use replacement cost as an attribute of the elements of financial statements, but it also uses the unit of general purchasing power as the unit of measure. In spite of these improvements, however, general price-level adjusted replacement cost income contains timing errors but no measuring unit errors. First, general price-level adjusted replacement cost income contains the same timing errors found for replacement cost income (see page 225). Second, general price-level adjusted replacement cost income contains no measuring unit errors because it takes into account changes in the general price level. In addition, it takes into account changes in the specific price level because it adopts replacement cost as the attribute of the elements of financial statements.

How should we evaluate the general price-level adjusted replacement cost financial statements presented in Exhibits 7–4 and 7–5? First, they are interpretable. General price-level adjusted replacement cost financial statements are based on the concept of purchasing power productive capacity maintenance. The attribute we are expressing is COG in both the income statement and the balance sheet. Second, general price-level adjusted replacement cost financial statements are relevant because they are expressed as measures of COG. Note, however, that it is COG in the input rather than the output market.

In summary, general price-level adjusted replacement cost financial statements (1) contain timing errors, (2) contain no measuring unit errors, (3) are interpretable, and (4) are relevant as COG measures in the input market.

General Price-Level Adjusted Net Realizable Value Accounting   General price-level adjusted net realizable value accounting is characterized primarily by (1) the use of net realizable value as the attribute of the elements of financial statements, (2) the use of units of general purchasing power as the unit of measure, (3) the abandonment of the realization principle, (4) the dichotomization of operating income and real holding gains and losses, and (5) the dichotomization of real realized and unrealized gains and losses.

Accordingly, general price-level adjusted net realizable value net income is equal to the sun of the net realizable value operating income and holding gains and losses, both expressed in units of general purchasing power. The general price-level adjusted net realizable value operating income is equal to the sum of operating income arising from sale and operating income on inventory, both expressed in units of general purchasing power. From Exhibit 7–4, the general price-level adjusted net realizable value net income of $1,220 is composed of (1) general price-level adjusted net realizable value operating income of $1,900, (2) real realized holding losses of ($600), (3) real unrealized holding losses of ($200), and (4) general price-level gain of $180.

Note again that the general price-level adjusted net realizable value operating income of $1,900 is composed of general price-level adjusted net realizable value operating income on sale of $1,500 and general price-level adjusted net realizable value operating income on inventory of $400.

In addition to the advantages of net realizable value net income, general price-level adjusted net realizable value net income has the advantage of being expressed in units of general purchasing power. For these reasons, general price-level net realizable value accounting represents a net improvement on net realizable value accounting. Not only does it use net realizable value as an attribute of the elements of financial statements, but also the unit of general purchasing power is the unit of measure.

Thus, general price-level restated net realizable value income contains no timing errors and no measuring unit errors. It contains no timing errors as explained in the discussion of net realizable value accounting (page 226). It contains no measuring unit errors because it is expressed in units of general purchasing power.

How should we evaluate the general price-level adjusted net realizable value financial statements presented in Exhibits 7–4 and 7–5? First, they are interpretable. General price-level adjusted net realizable value financial statements are based on the concept of purchasing power productive capacity maintenance. The attribute being measured is COG in both the income statement and the balance sheet statement. Second, they are relevant because they are expressed as measures of COG. Note that the COG is in the output market rather than the input market.

In summary, general price-level restated net realizable value financial statements (1) contain *no* timing errors, (2) contain no measuring unit errors, (3) are interpretable, and (4) are relevant, as measures of COG in the output market.

Such statements, therefore, meet all the criteria established for the comparison and evaluation of the alternative accounting models, as shown in Exhibit 7–7.

Toward a Solution to the Problem of Financial Reporting and Changing Prices

Early Attempts

Long recognized as a problem in the accounting literature, the issue of accounting for changing prices has been extensively studied by the various accounting standard-setting bodies. The Committee on Accounting Procedure in 1947, 1948, and 1953[8] and the Accounting Principles Board in *Opinion No. 6* on "Status of Accounting Research Bulletins" examined the problems relating to changes in the general price level without any success. These attempts were followed by the AICPA's publication of *ARS No. 6*, "Reporting the Financial Effects of Price Level Changes," in 1963, and by the APB's *Statement No. 3*, "Financial Statements Restated for General Price-Level Changes" in June 1969. Both recommended supplemental disclosure of general price-level information, without any success. The FASB approached the price-level subject at a time when inflation was a major concern in the economy. After issuing a *Discussion Memorandum*, "Reporting the Effects of General Price-Level Changes in Financial Statements," on February 15, 1974; an Exposure Draft, "Financial Reporting in Units of General Purchasing

---

[8]Committee on Accounting Procedure, *ARB No. 33*, "Depreciation and High Costs" (New York: AICPA, December 1974); Committee on Accounting Procedure, letter to AICPA members affirming the recommendations of *ARB No. 33*, October 1943; and Committee on Accounting Procedure, *ARB No. 43*, "Restatement and Revision of Accounting Research Bulletins," Ch. 9, Section A, "Depreciation and High Costs" (New York: AICPA, June 1953).

EXHIBIT 7-7

Error Type Analysis

Accounting Model	Timing Error		Measuring Unit Error	Interpretation		
	Operating Profit	Holding Gains		NOD	COG	Relevance
1. Historical Cost Accounting	Yes	Yes	Yes	Yes	No	No
2. Replacement Cost Accounting	Yes	Eliminated	Yes	Yes (Income statement)	Yes (Asset figures)	Yes (Asset figures only)
3. Net Realizable Value Accounting	Eliminated	Eliminated	Yes	Yes (Income statement)	Yes (Monetary assets and liabilities)	Yes (Monetary assets and liabilities)
4. General Price-Level Adjusted Historical Cost Accounting	Yes	Yes	Eliminated	Yes	Yes	Yes
5. General Price-Level Adjusted Replacement Cost Accounting	Yes	Eliminated	Eliminated	Eliminated	Yes	Yes
6. General Price-Level Adjusted Net Realizable Value Accounting	Eliminated	Eliminated	Eliminated	Eliminated	Yes	Yes

Power," on December 31, 1974; a Research Report, "Field Tests of Financial Reporting in Units of General Purchasing Power," in May 1977; another Exposure Draft, "Financial Reporting and Changing Prices," on December 28, 1978; and an Exposure Draft, supplement to the 1974 proposed statement on general purchasing power adjustments, "Constant Dollar Accounting"; the FASB issued in September 1979 *Statement No. 33*, "Financial Reporting and Changing Prices," which calls for information on the effects of both general inflation and specific price changes.

Financial Reporting and Changing Prices: A Step Forward

Statement No. 33 is truly the result of years of attempts by the diverse standard-setting bodies to develop methods of reporting the effects of inflation on earnings and assets. In its deliberations, the FASB considered a variety of accounting systems, which it grouped under the following headings:[9]

1. Measurement of inventory and property, plant, and equipment
   a. Historical cost
   b. Current reproduction cost
   c. Current replacement cost
   d. Net realizable value
   e. Net present value of expected future cash flows (value in use)
   f. Recoverable amount
   g. Current cost
   h. Value to business (current cost or lower recoverable amount)
2. Concepts of capital maintenance
   a. Financial capital maintenance
   b. Physical capital maintenance (the maintenance of operating capacity)
3. Measuring units
   a. Measurements in nominal dollars
   b. Measurements in constant dollars

The above list suggests that the FASB examined all the alternative asset valuation and income determination models that we have presented in this chapter. The board concluded, however, that supplementary information should be presented according to historical cost/constant dollar accounting and current cost accounting. More specifically, the FASB requires major companies to disclose the effects of both general inflation and specific price changes as supplementary information in their published annual reports. Major companies are those having assets of more than $1 billion (after deducting accumulated depreciation) or those whose inventories and property, plant, and equipment (before deducting accumulated depreciation) amount to more than $125 million. Specifically, major firms are required to report:

1. Income from continuing operations adjusted for the effects of general inflation,
2. The purchasing power gain or loss on net monetary items,
3. Income from continuing operations on a current cost basis,
4. The current cost amounts of inventory and property, plant, and equipment at the end of the fiscal year,

---

[9]*Statement of Financial Accounting Standards No. 33*, "Financial Reporting and Changing Prices" (Stamford, Conn.: FASB, September 1979), pp. 47–48.

5. Increases or decreases in current cost amounts of inventory and property, plant, and equipment, net of inflation.

Qualifying firms are also required to present a five-year summary of selected financial data, including information on income, sales, and other operating revenues, net assets, dividends per common share, and market price per share. In the computation of net assets, only inventories and property, plant, and equipment need to be adjusted for the effects of changing prices. To measure current costs, the firms may use either specific price indexes or other, more direct evidence. Exhibits 7–8, 7–9, and 7–10 illustrate these requirements. Thus, *Statement No. 33* requires two supplementary income computations, one dealing with the

EXHIBIT 7–8

Statement of Income from Continuing Operations
Adjusted for Changing Prices
For the Year Ended December 31, 19X6
(in thousands of average 19X5 dollars)

	As Reported in the Primary Statements	Adjusted for General Inflation	Adjusted for Changes in Specific Prices (Current Costs)
Net sales and other operating revenues	$500,000	$500,000	$500,000
Cost of goods sold	400,000	450,000	455,000
Depreciation and amortization expense	20,000	25,000	26,000
Other operating expense	40,000	40,000	40,000
Interest expense	15,000	15,000	15,000
Provision for income taxes	20,000	20,000	20,000
	495,000	550,000	556,000
Income (loss) from continuing operations	$ 5,000	$ (50,000)	$ (56,000)
Gain from decline in purchasing power of net amounts owed			
Increase in specific prices (current cost) of inventories and property, plant, and equipment held during the year[a]			$ 30,000
Effect of increase in general price level			20,000
Excess of increase in specific prices over increase in the general price level			$ 10,000

[a]At December 31, 19X5, current cost of inventory was $55,000 and current cost of property, plant, and equipment, net of accumulated depreciation was $80,000.

EXHIBIT 7-9

**Five-Year Comparison
of Selected Supplementary Financial Data
Adjusted for Effects of Changing Prices
(in thousands of average 19X5 dollars)**

	Years Ended December 31				
	19X1	19X2	19X3	19X4	19X5
Net sales and other operating revenues	$350,000	$400,000	$420,000	$450,000	$500,000
Historical cost information adjusted for general inflation					
Income (loss) from continuing operations				(29,000)	(20,000)
Income (loss) from continuing operations per common share				(2.0)	(2.00)
Net assets at year-end				100,000	120,000
Current cost information					
Income (loss) from continuing operations				(10,000)	(26,000)
Income (loss) from continuing operations per common share				(1.00)	(2.6)
Excess of increase in specific prices over increase in the general price level				5,000	10,000
Net asset at year-end				120,000	130,000
Gain from decline in purchasing power of net amounts owed				4,500	5,000
Cash dividends declared per common share	2.00	2.05	2.10	2.15	2.20
Market price per common share at year-end	40	30	45	40	39
Average consumer price index	170.5	181.5	195.4	205.0	220.9

EXHIBIT 7-10

Statement of Income from Continuing Operations
Adjusted for Changing Prices
For the Year Ended December 31, 19X6
(in thousands of average 19X5 dollars)

Income from continuing operations, as reported in the income statement		$ 5,000
Adjustments to restate costs for the effect of general inflation		
Cost of goods sold	$(50,000)	
Depreciation and amortization expense	(5,000)	(55,000)
Loss from continuing operations adjusted for general inflation		(50,000)
Adjustments to reflect the difference between general inflation and changes in specific prices (current costs)		
Cost of goods sold	(5,000)	
Depreciation and amortization expense	(1,000)	(6,000)
Loss from continuing operations adjusted for changes in specific prices		$(56,000)
Gain from decline in purchasing power of net amounts owed		$ 5,000
Increase in specific prices (current cost) of inventories and property, plant, and equipment held during the year[a]		30,000
Effect of increase in general price level		20,000
Excess of increase in specific prices over increase in the general price level		$ 10,000

[a]At December 31, 19X5, current cost of inventory was $55,000 and current cost of property, plant, and equipment, net of accumulated depreciation was $80,000.

effects of general inflation and the other with specific price changes. Both types of information are intended to help users in their decisions on investment, lending, and other matters in the following specific ways:

a. Assessment of future cash flows. Present financial statements include measurements of expenses and assets at historical prices. When prices are changing, measurements that reflect current prices are likely to provide useful information for the assessment of future cash flows.

b. Assessment of enterprise performance. The worth of an enterprise can be increased as a result of prudent timing of asset purchases when prices are changing. That increase is one aspect of performance even though it may be distinguished from operating performance. Measurements that reflect current prices can provide a basis for assessing the extent to which past decisions on the acquisition of assets have created opportunities for earning cash flows.

c. Assessment of the erosion of operating capability. An enterprise typically must hold minimum quantities of inventory, property, plant, and equipment and other assets to maintain its ability to provide goods and services. When the prices of those assets are increasing, larger amounts of money investment are needed to maintain the previous levels of output. Information on the current prices of resources that are used to generate revenues can help users to assess the extent to which and the manner in which operating capability has been maintained.

   d. Assessment of the erosion of general purchasing power. When general price levels are increasing, larger amounts of money are required to maintain a fixed amount of purchasing power. Investors typically are concerned with assessing whether an enterprise has maintained the purchasing power of its capital. Financial information that reflects changes in general purchasing power can help with that assessment.[10]

Obviously, because it requires the presentation of both general price-level and specific price-level information *Statement No. 33* is a step forward. It falls short, however, of a total solution, which would require the use of general price-level restated current cost accounting, with general price-level restated replacement cost accounting or general price-level restated net realizable value accounting.

Conclusions

Given the existence of four attributes to measure the elements of financial statements and two units of measure to express these attributes, eight alternative asset valuation and income determination models exist, as follows:

1. Historical cost accounting,
2. Replacement cost accounting,
3. Net realizable value accounting,
4. Present value accounting,
5. General price-level adjusted historical cost accounting,
6. General price-level adjusted replacement cost accounting,
7. General price-level adjusted net realizable value accounting,
8. General price-level adjusted present value accounting.

In this chapter, we compared and evaluated these models on the basis of four criteria: (1) the avoidance of timing errors, (2) the avoidance of measuring unit errors, (3) their interpretability, and (4) their relevance as measures of command of goods.

Although conceptually preferable, the present value models were not included in our comparison and evaluation because of the subjectivity and the uncertainty surrounding their use, which make their implementation currently impractical.

Our comparison of the remaining models showed the general price-level adjusted net realizable value accounting model to be the closest to a preferred

---

[10]*Ibid.*, pp. 1–2.

income position concept because it meets each of the criteria set forth in this chapter. *FASB Statement No. 33*, "Financial Reporting and Changing Prices," falls short of adopting this solution and, instead, requires the disclosure of supplemental information on the effects of both general inflation and specific price changes.

References

Basu, S., and J. R. Hanna. *Inflation Accounting: Alternatives, Implementation Issues and Some Empirical Evidence.* Hamilton, Ont.: The Society of Management Accountants, 1977.

Chambers, R. J. *Accounting, Evaluation, and Economic Behavior.* Englewood Cliffs, N.J.: Prentice-Hall, 1966.

Chambers, R. J. "NOD, CPG and PuPu: See How Inflation Teases!" *The Journal Accountancy* (September 1975), pp. 56–62.

Edwards, Edgar O., and Philip W. Bell. *The Theory and Measurement of Business Income.* Berkeley, Calif.: University of California Press, 1961.

Gynther, R. S. "Capital Maintenance, Price Changes, and Profit Determination." *The Accounting Review* (October 1970), pp. 712–30.

Hanna, J. R. *Accounting Income Models: An Application and Evaluation*, Special Study No. 8. Toronto: Society of Management Accountants of Canada, July 1974.

Kerr, Jean St. G. "Three Concepts of Business Income." In *An Income Approach to Accounting Theory.* Ed Sidney Davidson et al. Englewood Cliffs, N.J.: Prentice-Hall, pp. 40–48.

Louderback, J. G. "Projectability as a Criterion for Income Determination Methods." *The Accounting Review* (April 1971), pp. 298–305.

Parker, P. W., and P. M. D. Gibbs. "Accounting for Inflation—Recent Proposals and their Effects." *Journal of the Institute of Actuaries* (December 1974), pp. 1–10.

Revsine, L., and J. J. Weygandt. "Accounting for Inflation: The Controversy." *Journal of Accounting* (October 1974), pp. 72–78.

Rosen, L. S. *Current Value Accounting and Price-level Restatements.* Toronto: Canadian Institute of Chartered Accountants, 1972.

Rosenfield, Paul. "Accounting for Inflation, A Field Test." *Journal of Accountancy* (June 1969), pp. 45–50.

Rosenfield, Paul. "CPP Accounting. Relevance and Interpretability," *Journal of Accountancy* (August 1975), pp. 52–60.

Rosenfield, Paul. "The Confusion Between General Price Level Restatement and Current Value Accounting." *Journal of Accountancy* (October 1972), pp. 63–68.

Sterling, R. R. "Revelant Financial Reporting in an Age of Price Changes." *Journal of Accountancy* (February 1975), pp. 42–51.

Sterling, R. R. *Theory of Measurement of Enterprise Income.* Lawrence, Kansas: University Press of Kansas, 1970.

Wolk, H. I. "An Illustration of Four Price Level Approaches to Income Measurement." *Accounting Education: Problems and Prospects.* Ed. J. Don Edwards. American Accounting Association, 1974, pp. 415–23.

Zeff, S. A. "Replacement Cost: Member of the Family, Welcome Guest, or Intruder." *The Accounting Review* (October 1962), pp. 611–25.

Questions

7–1 List and discuss the differences among the attributes of the elements of financial statements to be measured.

7–2 List and discuss the differences among the units of measure that may be used to measure the attributes.

7–3 Define and explain timing errors.

7–4 Define and explain measuring unit errors.

7–5 List and discuss the bases of evaluation of the alternative asset valuation and income determination models.

7–6 List the principal assumptions and characteristics of the following asset valuation and income determination models:
a. Historical cost accounting
b. Replacement cost accounting
c. Net realizable value accounting

7–7 List the principal assumptions and characteristics of the following asset valuation and income determination models:
a. General price-level adjusted historical cost accounting
b. General price-level adjusted replacement cost accounting
c. General price-level adjusted net realizable value accounting

7–8 What problems are associated with the implementation of the present value accounting models?

7–9 Define each of the following concepts:
a. Realized holding gains and losses
b. Realizable holding gains and losses
c. Fictitious holding gains and losses
d. General price-level gains and losses
e. Specific price level
f. Relative price level
g. Number of dollars, or odd dollars
h. Command of goods
i. Distributable income

7–10 An accountant has prepared four sets of financial statements for Q, Inc. on four different bases: historical cost, current value, historical cost adjusted for general price-level fluctuations, and current value adjusted for general price-level fluctuations. These four sets of statements are presented below in comparative format. The company was incorporated on January 1, 19X4 and began operation on February 1, 19X4.

Additional information:
(1) The general price index at the beginning of the year was 110.
(2) Land and building were acquired on February 15, 19X4. The general price index as of December 31, 19X4, and the average index for 19X4 were 140 and 120 respectively. Assume that the index applicable to the sales made during the year is 125, since more sales were made during the last part of the year. Assume also that the average index (120) applies to merchandise unsold at the end of the year.
(3) The monetary assets as of January 1, 19X4, amounted to $1,100,000. This amount represents the capital invested by the shareholders. There were no monetary liabilities on January 1, 19X4.

Q, Inc.
Balance Sheet
At December 31, 19X4

	Historical Cost	Current Value	Historical Cost Adjusted for General Price-Level Fluctuations	Current Value Adjusted for General Price-Level Fluctuations
Assets				
Cash	$ 778,000	$ 778,000	$ 778,000	$ 778,000
Accounts receivable	40,000	40,000	40,000	40,000
Inventories	20,000	28,000	23,334	28,000
Land	75,000	80,000	91,306	80,000
Building	225,000	300,000	273,912	300,000
Less: Accumulated depreciation	(9,000)	(12,000)	(10,956)	(12,000)
Machinery and equipment	250,000	236,000	280,000	236,000
Less: Accumulated depreciation	(25,000)	(23,600)	(28,000)	(23,600)
	$1,354,000	$1,426,400	$1,447,596	$1,426,400
Liabilities and Shareholders' Equity				
Accounts payable	$ 20,000	$ 20,000	$ 20,000	$ 20,000
Mortgage payable	190,000	190,000	190,000	190,000
Share capital	1,100,000	1,100,000	1,400,000	1,400,000
Unrealized holding gain or (loss)	–	72,000	–	(21,196)
Retained earnings	44,000	44,000	(162,404)	(162,404)
	$1,354,000	$1,426,000	$1,447,596	$1,426,400

Required:

a. What is the major advantage of each of the bases on which the above sets of financial statements are prepared?

b. Analyze the following items and explain how they are determined. (Include the actual computations.)
   (1) General price-level loss
   (2) Unrealized holding gain or loss
   (3) Realized holding gain

c. Compare and comment on the remaining items shown in the four sets of financial statements.

d. List the difficulties that an accountant might have encountered in preparing each set of financial statements with the exception of the historical cost financial statements.

e. Give your recommendations with supporting comments concerning which set or sets of the above financial statements should be presented to shareholders.

(Adapted from Canadian Institute of Chartered Accountants)

Income Statements
For the Year Ended December 31, 1974

	Historical Cost	Current Value	Historical Cost Adjusted for General Price-Level Fluctuations	Current Value Adjusted for General Price-Level Fluctuations
Sales	$ 250,000	$ 250,000	$ 280,000	$ 280,000
Cost of goods sold (see Exhibit A)	100,000	140,000	116,666	140,000
Gross profit on sales	$ 150,000	$ 110,000	$ 163,334	$ 140,000
Out-of-pocket expenses	$ 60,000	$ 70,000	$ 70,000	$ 70,000
Depreciation Building	9,000	12,000	10,956	12,000
Equipment	25,000	23,600	28,000	23,600
Interest expense paid on December 31, 19X4	12,000	12,000	12,000	12,000
	$ 106,000	$ 117,600	$ 120,956	$ 117,600
Operating income or (loss)	$ 44,000	$ (7,600)	$ 42,378	$ 22,400
General price-level loss	–	–	(204,782)	(204,782)
Realized holding gain	–	51,600	–	19,978
Net income or (loss)*	$ 44,000	$ 44,000	$ (162,404)	$ (162,404)

* Income taxes are ignored.

EXHIBIT A

Cost of Goods Sold
For the Year Ended December 31, 19X4

	Historical Cost	Current Value	Historical Cost Adjusted for General Price-Level Fluctuations	Current Value Adjusted for General Price-Level Fluctuations
Inventories January 1, 19X4	–	–	–	–
Purchases 12,000 units	$ 120,000	$ 168,000	$ 140,000	$ 168,000
	$ 120,000	$ 168,000	$ 140,000	$ 168,000
Less: Inventories December 31, 19X4 2,000 units	20,000	28,000	23,334	28,000
Cost of goods sold	$ 100,000	$ 140,000	$ 116,666	$ 140,000

7-11 V Limited was incorporated in 1972 to manufacture a tool for which there has been a rapidly expanding market in Canada. At that time, although production of the tool was relatively simple, it was highly automated, requiring heavy capital investments. The capacity of the manufacturing equipment installed in 1972 had met production demands until unforeseen maintenance cost in 1981 indicated the need for replacement.

The firm's depreciation policy had been to write off fixed assets on a straight-line basis over their expected useful lives. In the case of the manufacturing equipment, it became apparent that the original ten-year life estimate was accurate and that any scrap value would approximately equal the removal costs.

Replacing the manufacturing equipment had been discussed at a recent directors' meeting held to review the 1978 financial statements. The controller had been asked to explain why, despite the fact that the equipment was fully depreciated, there were insufficient funds in the firm to purchase replacement equipment. The controller explained that over the ten-year period there had been a one-third decline in the value of money. It was apparent that the firm would need outside financing to replace the equipment. The discussion then centered on the reporting system in terms of its adequacy for internal management decisions and its adequacy for outside reporting to shareholders and to potential sources of financing.

There had been no significant technological changes in the replacement equipment, and the supplier quoted a price 60 percent in excess of the cost of the existing equipment. The sales manager pointed out that he would have to increase sales by $1,500,000 to produce an after-tax profit of $300,000 to cover the excess replacement cost. He queried whether the annual net profits reported each year were realistic. He had heard about price-level accounting and replacement cost accounting and he now wondered whether these methods might not be beneficial to V Limited.

It soon became apparent that none of the directors understood the implications of price-level and replacement cost accounting. The controller then consulted the company's auditor and requested a report in a week's time on these accounting methods.

Required:
a. Write a short description of price-level accounting and replacement cost accounting, outlining the relationship of each to generally accepted accounting principles.
b. Prepare a general outline of the advantages and disadvantages of each of the two methods and a description of how the two methods may be effectively combined.
c. Explain the benefits to V Limited of the use of a combination of price-level accounting and replacement cost accounting. Call attention to any problems that may arise in implementing of the methods.

(CICA adapted)

7–12 Reg S. Gynther made the following statement in "Capital Maintenance, Price Changes and Profit Determination," in *The Accounting Review* (October 1970), p. 716:

Under the operating capacity concept, profit is not recognized for each firm until its specific operating capacity has been maintained. The concept requires *all* long term capital to be restated (e.g., through a Capital Maintenance Adjustment Account) and this is done in accordance with market buying price changes relating to individual assets held. Total net assets—operating capacity, and the price changes for individual assets have to be accounted for separately because they change in different ways. (To the extent that individual price changes might not be available, specific price indexes are used.)

First, list and explain the different kinds of operating capacity; and second, explain the meaning of the statement.

7–13 R. R. Sterling made the following statement in "Relevant Financial Reporting in an Age of Price Changes," in *The Journal of Accountancy* (February 1975), pp. 50–51:

We should not be arguing that one set of figures is right and another is wrong; instead we should be arguing about which attribute we ought to measure and report. Selection of the attribute that ought to be measured requires precise criteria, rigorously applied.

Discuss the validity of the above statement.

7–14 R. J. Chambers made the following statement in "NOD, COG and PuPu: See How Inflation Teases!" in *The Journal of Accountancy* (September 1975), p. 60:

These two things—changes in specific prices and changes in the general level of prices—occur concurrently in inflation. But they do not arise from the same causes and they are not the same in effect on any person or firm. Their effects on any firm depend on its asset and debt composition and on the sources of its income. If we are to account for what occurs in an inflationary period, therefore, we must take account of both things concurrently, period by period. If we do not account for both, we do not represent the effects of inflation.

Discuss the validity of the above statement.

7–15 R. J. Chambers made the following statement in the same article mentioned in Question 7–14 with reference to what has been conveniently called Pu Pu (purchasing power units), p. 60:

It is easy to see that this is what Pu Pu accounting entails. The financial statements it yields are expressed in dollars—not some other kinds of Pu Pus. The dollars are admitted to be different from time to time; there is not a Pu Pu which is invariant through time, even in Pu Pu accounting. Unquestionably, a Pu Pu is a dated dollar, having the general purchasing power of a dollar at the date which identifies it—in particular, in a balance sheet, the date of the balance sheet.

Discuss the validity of the above statement.

7–16 Mr. Joe May has come to you and asked for an explanation of the effect of inflation on his business. You have taken the following transactions from his records in order to prepare comparative statements and to isolate some variations in price level.

The general price index for 19X4 indicated the following changes in the purchasing power of the dollar:

January 1, 19X4	200
July 1, 19X4	205
December 31, 19X4	210

The following purchases were made:

January 1, 19X4	1,000 items at $3.00 per unit
July 1, 19X4	500 items at $3.30 per unit
December 31, 19X4	500 items at $3.50 per unit
January 15, 19X5	500 items at $3.70 per unit

The year-end inventories are valued according to the first-in, first-out method (FIFO). The company's year end is December 31.

Required:
a. Assuming that no sales were made during 19X4, determine the valuation of the year-end inventories for balance sheet presentation under the following methods:
   (1) Historical cost
   (2) Adjusted cost on the basis of the general price index
   (3) Replacement cost
State the basis of each of your valuations and explain why the amounts differ.
b. Assuming that the company sold 50 percent of its inventory on December 31, 19X4, at a selling price of $4.20 per unit, prepare a comparative income statement using the following methods:
   (1) Historical cost
   (2) Adjusted cost on the basis of the general price index
   (3) Replacement cost
c. Using this comparative income statement, explain the composition of the net income figure under the historical cost method, showing clearly the impact of the general price increase, timing of purchases, and profit from sales.

(Society of Management Accountants adapted)

7–17   Part 1.   Advocates of current value accounting propose several methods for determining the valuation of assets to approximate current values. Two of the methods proposed are replacement cost and present value of future cash flows.

Required:
Describe each of the two methods cited above and discuss the pros and cons of the various procedures used to arrive at the valuation for each method.

Part 2.   The financial statements of a business entity could be prepared by using historical cost or current value as a basis. In addition, the basis could be stated in terms of unadjusted dollars or dollars restated for changes in purchasing power. The various permutations of these two separate and distinct areas are shown in the following matrix:

	Unadjusted Dollars	Dollars Restated for Changes in Purchasing Power
Historical cost	1	2
Current value	3	4

Block number 1 represents the traditional method of accounting for transactions in use today, wherein the absolute (unadjusted) amount of dollars given up or received is recorded for the asset or liability obtained (relationship between resources). Amounts recorded in the method described in block number 1 reflect the original cost of the asset or liability and do not give effect to any change in value of the unit of measure (standard of comparison). This method assumes the validity of the going concern and stable monetary unit concepts. Any gain or loss (including holding and purchasing power gains or losses) resulting from the sale or satisfaction of amounts recorded under this method is deferred in its entirety until sale or satisfaction.

Required:

For each of the remaining matrix blocks (2, 3, and 4) respond to the following questions. Limit your discussion to nonmonetary assets.

a. How will this method of recording assets affect the relationship between resources and the standard of comparison?

b. What is the theoretic justification for using each method?

c. How will each method of asset valuation affect the recognition of gain or loss during the life of the asset and, ultimately, from the sale or abandonment of the asset? Your response should include a discussion of the timing and magnitude of the gain or loss and conceptual reasons for any difference from the gain and loss computed using the traditional method.

(AICPA adapted)

chapter eight

The Future Scope of Accounting

The objective of financial accounting is to communicate information resulting from the transactions of a firm. Such transactions are primarily the exchange of goods and services between two or more economic entities. Several limitations are inherent in this definition. First, the exchanges recognized by conventional accounting are limited to goods and services and do not include changes in human capital. Second, this definition limits the transactions to exchanges between two or more legal and economic entities. Thus, exchanges between a firm and its social environment are ignored for all practical purposes. Third, most transactions are actual or past events so that the future financial position and performance of a firm are not reflected in the financial statements. Fourth, the cost of debt capital is recognized by conventional accounting while the cost of equity capital is not. Finally, a need exists for a worldwide set of generally accepted accounting principles. The future scope of accounting should embrace solutions to these and other problems and controversial issues. In this chapter, we shall discuss some of the ideas presented in the literature and in practice for dealing with these new challenges. Five principal new developments are presented, namely, **socioeconomic accounting, human resource accounting, accounting for the cost of capital, the reporting of financial forecasts,** and **the trend toward multinational accounting.**

Socioeconomic Accounting

The Nature of Socioeconomic Accounting

Conventional financial accounting focuses on the results of transactions between two or more economic entities. Exchanges between a firm and its social environment are practically ignored. Socioeconomic accounting, which is aimed at correcting this omission, is based on the following thesis:

> The technology of an economic system imposes a structure on its society which not only determines its economic activities but also influences its social relationships and well-being. Therefore a measure limited to economic consequences is inadequate as an appraisal of the cause-effect relationships of the total system; it neglects the social effects.[1]

Socioeconomic accounting, therefore, is the process of ordering, measuring, and disclosing the impact of exchanges between a firm and its social environment. Socioeconomic accounting is an expression of a corporation's social responsibilities and a new call for general corporate accountability. Exchanges between a firm and society consist primarily of the use of social resources. If the activities of a firm lead to a depletion of social resources, the result is a **social cost**; if they lead to an increase in social resources, the result is a **social benefit.** The objective of socioeconomic accounting is precisely to measure and disclose the costs and benefits to society created by the production-related activities of a business enterprise. More precisely, the objective is to **internalize** these social costs and social benefits in order to determine a more relevant and exhaustive result, which is the **socioeconomic profit** of a firm. Because this may require the

---

[1]S. C. Mobley, "The Challenges of Socio-Economic Accounting," *The Accounting Review* (October 1970), p. 767.

use of techniques from other relevant disciplines, Linowes has defined socio-economic accounting as "the application of accounting in the field of social sciences. These include sociology, political science and economics."[2] Among the suggested dimensions of socioeconomic accounting are: national income accounting, evaluation of social programs, the role of accounting in economic development, the development of social indicators, and social audit.[3] It is the recognition and measurement of social costs and social benefits, however, that is the basic objective of socioeconomic accounting.

Social Costs and Benefits: Externalities

Most economists agree that perfect competition in all markets leads to a position of maximum social welfare, given the assumptions that underlie this analysis.[4] If markets are highly competitive and consumers and producers rationally attempt to reach a maximum level of satisfaction, then the available resources will be allocated in a way that maximizes social welfare. Thus, prices provide automatic, socially valid guidelines for investment and production. In the case in which an obstruction of the private market prices exists, however, then the marginal social cost will not equal the marginal social benefit, and maximum social welfare will not be achieved. The indirect effects of this situation, considered in economics under various labels, such as "third party effects," "spillover effects," and more clearly, "external economies or diseconomies," are the social costs and social benefits not considered by the private marginal cost pricing rule. Thus, an externality arises whenever a firm's activities have a negative or a positive impact on the environment for which the firm is not held accountable. If the impact is positive, it is called an external economy or social benefit; if the impact is negative, it is an external diseconomy or social cost.

To date, economists' attempts to ascertain the monetary value of externalities and bring them within the scope of economic analysis has not been successful. We shall discuss some of the reasons in the following paragraphs.

Some categories of external diseconomies, manifestly important ones, do not lend themselves easily to measurement. Also, the chain of causality may be quite complex. For example: "Air pollution is not only the result of, and not proportionate of the volume of production and the emissions of residual waste products, it is also governed by the interactions of a whole series of variables which may react upon one another."[5]

It is difficult to attribute to a specific sector of the economy the consequences of some external diseconomies that depend on complementary economic ac-

---

[2]D. F. Linowes, "Socio-Economic Accounting," *The Journal of Accountancy* (November 1970), p. 37.

[3]See D. F. Linowes, "Socio-Economic Accounting," pp. 37–42. See also L. M. Savoie, "Social Accounting—An Opportunity for Service," *The CPA* (November 1967), p. 3; D. F. Linowes, "The Need for Accounting in Developing Social Systems," *The Journal of Accountancy* (March 1970), pp. 62–65; C. W. Churchman, "On the Facility, Felicity, and Morality of Measuring Social Changes," *The Accounting Review* (January 1971), pp. 30–35; R. A. Bauer and D. Fern, Jr., *The Corporate Social Audit* (New York: Russel Sage Foundation, 1972).

[4]W. Baumol, *Economic Theory and Operation Research* (New York: John Wiley and Sons, 1958).

[5]W. Knapp, "Environmental Disruption and Social Cost: A Challenge to Economics," *Kylos* (December 1970), p. 836.

tivities. As Knapp explains, "Environmental and social costs must be looked upon as the outcome of an interaction of several complex systems (economic, physical, meteorological, biological, etc. . . .) in which a plurality of factors interplay through a 'feedback' process."[6]

External diseconomies and social costs depend for their measurement on the magnitude of the perception and awareness of the issue in a particular society. In other words, it is a question of social evaluation. How much importance does organized society attribute to the tangible and intangible values involved?

Moreover, some of the consequences of externalities are intangibles (Ridker speaks of *psychic costs*)[7] and, as such, even if the available monetary estimates of social costs were complete, the measures would have to be considered fragmentary because some of the social losses, which are intangible in character, must be evaluated in other than monetary terms.

Otto A. Davis and A. H. Whinston have made distinction between separable and nonseparable externalities.[8] In the case of separable externalities, only total costs are affected, not marginal (incremental) costs. For example, if Firm A builds installations that so reduce the natural ventilation that the management of a neighboring hotel must install a central air conditioner, the total cost function of the hotel would be increased by a fixed outlay, while its marginal cost would stay constant. In the case of nonseparable externalities, the marginal cost is affected. In other words, "the difference between the separable and nonseparable cases lies in the fact that externality enters the cost function in a multiplicative manner rather than in a strictly additive way." The distinction between separable and nonseparable externalities increases the difficulties of measuring and computing the appropriate charges to be levied.

Davis and Whinston discussed also the complex problem of assessing the value of reciprocal externalities.[9] A reciprocal externality is one that raises the costs for Firm B, when Firm B carries on a production process that creates another externality that raises the costs for Firm A. Nonseparable reciprocal externalities are likely to lead to a merger of firms, because neither one can reach maximum profit without the other.

Such measurement difficulties may explain some of the reluctance of firms to adopt socioeconomic accounting and the urgency to develop a taxonomy for the measurement of social performance that embraces not only social costs but also social contributions, or social benefits. In fact, one author considered the primary social costs of business enterprises to be the following:

1. The social costs resulting from the impairment of *human factor of production*
2. The social costs of air pollution
3. The social costs of water pollution
4. The social costs of depletion and destruction of animal resources
5. The social costs of premature depletion of energy resources
6. The social costs of technological change
7. The social costs of soil erosion, soil depletion, and deforestation

---

[6]*Ibid.*, p. 834.

[7]R. G. Ridker, *Economic Costs of Air Pollution* (New York: Praeger, 1978).

[8]A. Davis and A. H. Whinston, "Externalities, Welfare, and the Theory of Games," *The Journal of Political Economy* (June 1962), p. 120.

[9]*Ibid.*

8. The social costs of unemployment and idle resources[10]

Similarly, the National Association of Accountants' Committee on Accounting for Corporate Social Performance has classified the major domains of corporate concern for social performance as: (1) community involvement, (2) human resources, (3) physical resources and environmental contributions, and (4) product or service contribution.

Community involvement comprises activities that primarily benefit the general public, such as corporate philanthropy, housing construction and financing, health services, volunteer activities of employees, food programs, and community planning and improvement.

Classified under *human resources* are areas that benefit employees, such as training and job enrichment programs, working conditions, promotions policies, and employee benefits.

Under the classification of *physical resources and environmental contributions* are such concerns as air and water quality and control of noise pollution, as well as the conservation of resources and the disposal of solid wastes.

Product or service contribution considers the impact of the company's product or service on society, taking into account such considerations as product quality, packaging, advertising, warranty provisions, and product safety."[11]

Desirability
of Socioeconomic Accounting

The desirability of socioeconomic accounting may be indicated by three factors: (1) corporate response, (2) individual users' responses, and (3) the market response.

While social reporting is still in an early state of development, the corporate response has been encouraging. More and more companies are making some form of social disclosure with varying degrees of information on the social impact of their activities.[12] The most comprehensive social report is that of Abt Associates, Inc., made under the heading "Social Audit." The social audit of Abt Associates is shown in an appendix to this chapter. Note that the social reports include a social income statement and a social balance sheet. The social income statement shows social costs and benefits to the company and shareholders, to the staff, to clients and the general public and to the community. The social balance sheet discloses staff assets, organizational assets, the use of public goods, financial assets, and physical assets.

Two field studies have been conducted to determine the impact of social disclosure on investment decisions.[13] In a survey of institutional investors,

---

[10]W. Knapp, *The Social Costs of Private Enterprises* (Cambridge, Mass.: Harvard University Press, 1950), p. 13.

[11]National Association of Accountants, Committee on Accounting for Social Performance, "Accounting for Social Performance," *Management Accounting* (February 1974), pp. 39–41.

[12]M. Epstein, E. Flamholtz, and J. J. McDonough, "Corporate Social Accounting in the United States of America: State of the Art and Future Prospects," *Accounting Organizations and Society,* 1, No. 1 (1976), 23–42.

[13]B. Longstreth and D. Rosenbloom, *Corporate Social Responsibility and the Institutional Investor* (New York: Praeger, 1973); A. Belkaoui, "The Impact of Socio-Economic Accounting Statements on the Investment Decision: An Empirical Study," Working Paper 78-21, Faculty of Administration, University of Ottawa, 1978.

Longstreth and Rosenbloom found that 57 percent of the respondents indicated that they considered social factors in addition to economic factors when making investment decisions. In a field experiment, Belkaoui presented different forms of social reports, varying in their accounting treatment of pollution costs, to groups of bank officers, practicing accountants, and students. The results of the experiment suggested that pollution cost had an influence on investment decisions.

Similarly, market-based studies have been conducted to assess the relevance to investors of certain social responsibility disclosures of firms by empirically assessing their impact on security returns.[14] Belkaoui reported that the price behavior of firms making social disclosure was different from the price behavior of firms not making the disclosure. Spicer found that pollution control records were useful for assessing a firm's total and systematic risk. Finally, Ingram found that the information content of a firm's social responsibility disclosure depends on the market segment with which the firm is identified. Implicitly, such market studies investigae two views of the possible impact of social disclosure on the market. One view maintains that "ethical investors" form a clientele that responds to demonstrations of social concern.[15] A second view is summed up in the Beams-Fertig thesis, which holds that corporations reporting the least activity in avoiding social cost will appear more successful to investors and will be favored by the market.[16]

Human Resource Accounting

The Usefulness of Human Resources

The objective of financial accounting is to provide information relevant to the decisions of users. Investors should be provided with all the information necessary to make their decisions. Thus, users may need to have adequate information about one "neglected" asset of a firm—the human asset. More specifically, investors may greatly benefit from a knowledge of the extent to which the human assets of an organization have been increased or decreased during a given period. The conventional accounting treatment of human resource outlays consists of *expensing* all human capital formation expenditures, while similar outlays on physical capital are *capitalized*. A more valid treatment would be to capitalize human resource expenditures in order to yield future benefits and reveal when such benefits can be measured.[17] In fact, this last treatment has created a new

---

[14]A. Belkaoui, "The Impact of the Disclosure of the Environmental Effects of Organizational Behavior on the Market," *Financial Management* (Winter 1976), pp. 26–31. B. Spicer, "Investors, Corporate Social Performance and Information Disclosure: An Empirical Study," *The Accounting Review* (January 1978), pp. 94–111. R. W. Ingram, "An Investigation of Information Content of (Certain) Social Responsibility Disclosures," *Journal of Accounting Research* (Autumn 1978), pp. 270–85.

[15]J. G. Simon, C. W. Pavers, and J. P. Gunnemann, *The Ethical Investor* (New Haven: Yale University Press, 1972).

[16]F. A. Beams and P. E. Fertig, "Pollution Control Through Social Cost Conversion," *The Journal of Accountancy* (November 1971), pp. 37–42.

[17]AAA Committee, *A Statement of Basic Accounting Theory* (Evanston, Ill.: American Accounting Association, 1966) p. 35.

concern with the measurement of the cost or value of human resources to an organization and the development of a new field of inquiry in accounting known as **human resource accounting.** A broad definition of human resource accounting is:

> The process of identifying and measuring data about human resources and communicating this information to interested parties.[18]

This definition implies three major objectives of human resource accounting, namely (1) identification of "human resource value," (2) measurement of the cost and value of people to organizations, and (3) investigation of the cognitive and behavioral impact of such information.

Human resource accounting has led to a few applications, such as those of R. G. Barry Corporation, Touche Ross & Company and a midwest branch of a mutual insurance company.[19] In spite of the lack of enthusiasm by many firms to disclosing the value of their human assets, most empirical studies investigating the cognitive and behavioral impact show a favorable predisposition of users to the human resource accounting information.[20] One may wonder, in fact, why R. G. Barry Corporation, a small shoe manufacturing company listed on the American Stock Exchange, would develop a human resource accounting system. As one of its officers rhetorically observed:

> Why in the world is a little company with good—but unspectacular— growth, good—but unromantic—products, good—but unsophisticated—technology, good—but undramatic—profitability interested in the development of a system of accounting for the human resources of the business? This is a fair question and deserves an answer.[21]

To answer this question and any similar questions asked by other corporations, we may cite three facts: First, capitalization of human resource cost is conceptually more valid than the expensing approach. Second, the information on "human assets" is likely to be relevant to a great variety of decisions made by external or internal users or both. And third, accounting for human assets constitutes an explicit recognition of the premise that people are valuable organizational resources and an integral part of a mix of resources.

Human Resource Value Theory

The concept of human value may be derived from the general economic value theory. Like physical assets, individuals or groups may be attributed a value because of their ability to render future economic services. In line with the economic thinking that associates the value of an object with its ability to render benefits, the individual or group value is usually defined as the present worth of

---

[18]"Report of the Committee on Human Resource Accounting," *Committee Reports,* Supplement to vol. 48 of *The Accounting Review,* 1973, p. 169.

[19]R. L. Woodruff, "Human Resource Accounting," *Canadian Chartered Accountant* (September 1970), pp. 2–7; M. O. Alexander, "Investments in People," *Canadian Chartered Accountant* (July 1971), pp. 38–45; E. Flamholtz, "Human Resource Accounting: Measuring Positional Replacement Costs," *Human Resource Management* (Spring 1973), pp. 8–16.

[20]N. S. Elias, "The Effects of Human Asset Statements on the Investment Decision: An Experiment," *Empirical Research in Accounting: Selected Studies, 1972,* Supplement to vol. 10, *Journal of Accounting Research,* pp. 215–33.

[21]Woodruff, "Human Resource Accounting," p. 2.

the services rendered to the organization throughout the individual's or the group's expected service life.

How do we determine the value of a human asset? To measure and disclose "human resource value," we need a theoretical framework, or "human resource value theory," to explicate the nature and determinants of the value of people to an organization. Basically, two models exist of the nature and determinant of human resource value, one advanced by Flamholtz and one by Likert and Bowers.[22] We shall discuss each of these models in the following paragraphs.

Determinants of Individual Value   In Flamholtz's model, the measure of a person's worth is his or her expected realizable value. Flamholtz's model suggests that such a measure of individual value results from the interaction of two variables: (1) the individual's expected conditional value, and (2) the probability that the individual will maintain membership in the organization.

Conditional value is the amount the organization would potentially realize from a person's services. It is a multidimensional variable comprising three factors: *productivity, transferability,* and *promotability.* The elements of conditional value are perceived to be the product of certain attributes of the person and certain dimensions of the organization. Two individual determinants are identified as important, namely the person's skills and "activation level." Similarly, the organizational determinants that interact with the individual values are identified as the organizational role of the individual and the "rewards" that people expect from the different aspects of their membership in a firm.

The probability of maintaining the organizational membership is considered to be related to a person's degree of job satisfaction.

Determinants of Group Value   While Flamholtz's model examined the determinants of an individual's value to an organization, Likert and Bower's model examined the determinants of group value. Intended to represent the "productive capability of the human organization of any enterprise or unit within it,"[23] the model identifies three variables that influence the effectiveness of a firm's "human organization":

1. The *causal* variables are independent variables which can be directly or purposely altered or changed by the organization and its management and which, in turn, determine the course of developments within an organization. These causal variables include only those which are controllable by the organization and its management. General business conditions, for example, although an independent variable, are *not* viewed as causal since they are not controllable by the management of a particular enterprise. Causal variables include the structure of the organization and management's policies, decisions, business and leadership strategies, skills, and behavior.

2. The *intervening* variables reflect the internal state, health and per-

---

[22]E. Falmholtz, "Toward a Theory of Human Resource Value in Formal Organizations," *The Accounting Review* (October 1972), pp. 666–78; R. Likert and D. G. Bowers, "Improving the Accuracy of P/L Reports by Estimating the Change in Dollar Value of the Human Organization," *Michigan Business Review* (March 1973), pp. 15–24.

[23]Likert and Bowers, "Improving the Accuracy of P/L Reports," p. 15.

formance capabilities of the organization; that is, the loyalties, attitudes, motivations, performance goals, and perceptions of all members and their collective capability for effective action.

3. The *end-result* variables are the dependent variables which reflect the results achieved by that organization, such as its productivity, costs, scrap loss, growth, share of the market and earnings.[24]

The model states that certain casual variables induce certain levels of intervening variables, which yield certain levels of end-result variables. The casual variables are managerial behavior, organizational structure, and subordinate peer behavior. The intervening variables are such organization processes as perception, communication, motivation, decision making, control, and coordination. The end-result variables are health and satisfaction and productivity and financial performances.

Measures of Human Assets

Measurement methods based on monetary measures are historical, or acquisition, cost, replacement cost, opportunity cost, the compensation model, and adjusted discounted future wages. The principal nonmonetary measure is the "survey of organizations."

The Historical, or Acquisition, Cost Method   The historical, or acquisition, cost method consists of capitalizing all the costs associated with recruiting, selecting, hiring, and training, and then amortizing these costs over the expected useful life of the asset, recognizing losses in case of liquidation of the asset or increasing the value of the asset for any additional cost expected to increase the benefit potential of the asset. Similar to any of the conventional accounting treatments for other assets, this treatment is practical and objective in the sense that the data are verifiable.[25]

Several limitations exist, however, to the use of these measurements. First, the economic value of a human asset does not necessarily correspond to its historical cost. Second, any appreciation or amortization may be subjective, with no relation to any increase or decrease in the productivity of the human assets. Third, because the costs associated with recruiting, selecting, hiring, training, placing, and developing employees may differ from one individual to another within a firm, historical cost does not result in comparable human resource values.

The Replacement Cost Method   The replacement cost method consists of estimating the costs of replacing a firm's existing human resources. Such costs will include all the costs of recruiting, selecting, hiring, training, placing, and developing new employees to reach the level of competence of existing employees. The principal advantage of the replacement cost method is that it is a good surrogate for the economic value of the asset in the sense that market considerations are essential in reaching a final figure. Such a final figure is also generally intended to be conceptually equivalent to a notion of a person's economic value.[26]

---

[24]*Ibid.*, p. 17.

[25]N. W. E. Glautier and B. Underdown, "Problems and Prospects of Accounting for Human Assets," *Management Accounting* (March 1973), p. 99.

[26]E. Flamholtz, *Human Resource Accounting* (Los Angeles: Dickenson Publishing, 1974), p. 190.

Several limitations exist, however, to the use of the replacement cost method. First a firm may have a particular employee whose value is perceived as greater than the relevant replacement cost. Second, there may be no equivalent replacement for a given human asset.[27] Third, as noted by Likert and Bowers, managers asked to estimate the cost of completely replacing their human organization may have difficulty doing so, and different managers may arrive at quite different estimates.[28]

The Opportunity Cost Method   Hekimian and Jones proposed the opportunity cost method to overcome the limitations of the replacement cost method.[29] They suggested that human resource values be established through a competitive bidding process within the fim, based on the concept of "opportunity" cost. More specifically, using this method, investment center managers will bid for the scarce employees they need to recruit. These "scarce" employees all come from within the firm and include only those who are the subject of a recruitment request by an investment center manager. In other words, employees not considered "scarce" are not included in the human asset base of the organization.

Obviously, several limitations exist to the use of the opportunity cost method. First, the inclusion of only "scarce" employees in the asset base may be interpreted as "discriminatory" by the other employees. Second, the less profitable divisions may be penalized by their inability to outbid for the recruitment of better employees. Third, the method may be perceived as artificial and even immoral.[30]

The Compensation Model   Given the uncertainty and the difficulty associated with determining the value of human capital, Lev and Schwartz suggest the use of a person's future compensation as a surrogate of his or her value.[31] Accordingly, the "value of human capital embodied in a person of age τ is the present value of his remaining future earnings from employment." This valuation model is expressed as:

$$V_\tau = \sum_{t=\tau}^{T} \frac{I(t)}{(1 + r)^{t-\tau}}$$

where

V_τ = the human capital value of a person τ years old,

$I(t)$ = the person's annual earnings up to retirement,

r = a discount rate specific to the person,

T = retirement age.

---

[27]J. S. Hekimian and J. G. Jones, "Put People on Your Balance Sheet," *Harvard Business Review* (January–February 1967), p. 108.

[28]R. Likert and D. G. Bowers, "Organizational Theory and Human Resource Accounting," *American Psychologist*, 24, No. 6 (1969), 588.

[29]Hekimian and Jones, "Put People on Your Balance Sheet," pp. 108–109.

[30]D. Elovitz, "From the Thoughtful Businessman," *Harvard Business Review* (May–June 1967), p. 59.

[31]B. Lev and A. Schwartz, "On the Use of the Economic Concept of Human Capital in Financial Statements," *The Accounting Review* (January 1971), p. 105.

Because V_τ is an ex-post value, given that $I(t)$ is obtained only after retirement and because V_τ ignores the possibility of death before retirement age, Lev and Schwartz refined the valuation model as follows:

$$E(V_T^*) = \sum_{t=\tau}^{T} P_\tau(t + 1) \sum_{i=\tau}^{t} \frac{I_1^*}{(1 + r)^{t-\tau}}$$

where

$$I_1^* = \text{the future annual earnings,}$$
$$E(V_T^*) = \text{the expected value of a person's human capital,}$$
$$P_\tau(t) = \text{the probability of a person dying at age } t.$$

The principal limitation of the compensation model is the subjectivity associated with the determination of the level of future salary, the length of expected employment within the firm, and the discount rate.

The Adjusted Discounted Future Wages Method   Hermanson proposed using an adjusted compensation value as a proxy of the value of an individual to a firm.[32] The discounted future wages are adjusted by an "efficiency factor" intended to measure the relative effectiveness of the human capital of a given firm. This efficiency factor is measured by a ratio of the return on investment of the given firm to all other firms in the economy for a given period. It is computed by the following expression:

$$\text{Efficiency Ratio} = \frac{5\dfrac{RF_0}{RE_0} + 4\dfrac{RF_1}{RE_1} + 3\dfrac{RF_2}{RE_2} + 2\dfrac{RF_3}{RE_3} + \dfrac{RF_4}{RE_4}}{15},$$

where

RF_i = the rate of accounting income on owned assets for the firm for the year i.

RE_i = the rate of accounting income on owned assets for all firms in the economy for the year i.

i = years (0 to 4).

The justification of this ratio rests on the thesis that differences in profitability are primarily due to differences in human asset performance. Thus, it is necessary to adjust the compensation value by the efficiency factor. ·

Nonmonetary Measures   Many nonmonetary measures of human assets may be used, such as a simple inventory of skills and capabilities of people, the assignment of ratings or rankings to individual performance, and measurement of

---

[32]R. H. Hermanson, "Accounting for Human Assets," Occasional Paper No. 14 (East Lansing, Mich.: Bureau of Business and Economic Research, Graduate School of Business Administration, Michigan State University, 1964).

attitudes. The most frequently used nonmonetary measure of human value is derived from Likert and Bowers' model of the variables that determine "the effectiveness of a firm's human organization." A questionnaire based on the theoretical model called "survey of organizations" was designed to measure the "organizational climate."[33] The results of such a questionnaire may serve as a nonmonetary measure of human assets by portraying employees' perceptions of the working atmosphere in the firm.

Accounting for the Cost of Capital

The Nature of Anthony's Proposal

Conventional financial accounting does not take into account and allocate to operations the cost of equity as it does other costs. Consequently, accounting for the cost of capital is a process of allocating the costs of various types of capital to a firm's operations along with other normal production costs. Anthony has suggested such an absorption of the cost of equity as a way of making financial accounting reports more meaningful guides for management.[34] In conventional financial accounting, interest, which refers only to the cost of using debt capital, is accounted for as a period cost, and no charge is recognized for the use of equity capital. Under Anthony's proposal, interest refers to both the cost of debt and the cost of equity and is accounted for as other costs. In other words, similarly to a firm's labor, material, and factory overhead, the interest incurred for the use of capital in the production process should be included in inventory and cost of goods sold. Anthony argues that accounting principles concerning interest should be the same as those of economics and that accounting for the cost of capital would define "accounting profit" in the same way that "economic profit" is defined. Young visualizes four substantial and interrelated changes in current accounting procedures if Anthony's proposal is adopted by the Financial Accounting Standards Board:

1. An interest charge would be applied to common shareholders' equity.
2. Costs of goods sold would include an interest charge for capital tied up in the plant and equipment used for manufacturing.
3. The cost of inventory held for sale or use in future periods would include an interest cost if the holding period were significantly long.
4. The cost of new plant assets would include the interest cost for equity capital used during the construction period.[35]

---

[33]J. C. Taylor and D. G. Bowers, *The Survey of Organizations* (Ann Arbor, Mich.: Institute for Social Research, 1972).

[34]R. N. Anthony, "Accounting for the Cost of Equity," *Harvard Business Review* (November–December 1973), pp. 88–102. *Accounting for the Cost of Interest* (New York: Lexington Books, 1975).

[35]D. W. Young, "Accounting for the Cost of Interest: Implications for the Timber Industry," *The Accounting Review* (October 1976), p. 788.

A Method of Accounting
for the Cost of Capital

Anthony's proposal may be subject to two problems: (1) the problem of measuring the cost of equity capital, and (2) the problem of accounting for the cost of capital per se.

While the measurement of the cost of debt capital, or more precisely of debt interest, does not present an insurmountable problem in most cases, the measurement of the cost of equity capital does present certain difficulties that are well recognized in the field of corporate finance. Despite these difficulties, management may use judgment to compute explicitly or implicitly the cost of equity capital. One expedient method is to deduct the cost of debt from a total cost of capital, debt, and equity combined to estimate the cost of equity.

For the problem of accounting for the cost of capital, Anthony suggests first creating an "interest pool," similar to any overhead cost pool, which is debited by the debt interest and equity interest incurred, with an offsetting credit to retained earnings and cash or debt interest payable. Second, the interest pool is divided by the total capital employed to determine a weighted interest rate for the year. Third, this weighted interest rate is used to determine the amount of interest cost to be applied to cost objectives. More precisely, the interest pool will be credited, and one or several of the following accounts will be debited: cost of goods sold, inventory, plant, and general. This account would have the following entries:

Interest Pool

From Debt	X	To Cost of Goods Sold	T
From Equity	Y	To Inventory	U
		To Plant	V
		To General	W
	Z		Z

Thus, the approach has four effects on a firm's financial statements:

1. The cost of sales is increased by the amount of interest added as a cost of the goods sold.
2. The inventory, plant, and other assets are increased by the amount of interest added as a product cost.
3. Income is decreased by the amount of interest added as a period cost.
4. Retained earnings are increased by the amount of equity interest.

Illustration of the Use
of Anthony's Proposal

To illustrate actual practices using Anthony's proposal, assume that Del Cerro Manufacturing Company has $10,000 of 5 percent bonds and $10,000 in common stock and retained earnings, and the cost of equity capital to the firm is 10 percent. The firm manufactures a particular brand of cognac, which is not sold until the fifth year after production. The income statements and balance sheets reflecting the firm's situation under present practice and applying Anthony's proposal as shown in Exhibits 8–1 and 8–2.

EXHIBIT 8-1

Present Practice
Del Cerro Manufacturing Company
Income Statements

	Each of Years 1-4	Year 5
Sales	$ 0	$10,000
Cost of Goods Sold	0	5,000
Gross Margin	$ 0	$ 5,000
Interest on Debt	$ (500)	500
Net Income (Loss)	$ (500)	$ 4,500

Del Cerro Manufacturing Company
Balance Sheets

	Year					
	0	1	2	3	4	5
Cash	$15,000	$14,500	$14,000	$13,500	$13,000	$22,500
Inventory	5,000	5,000	5,000	5,000	5,000	0
Total	$20,000	$19,500	$19,000	$18,500	$18,000	$22,500
Debt	$10,000	$10,000	$10,000	$10,000	$10,000	$10,000
Capital	10,000	9,500	9,000	8,500	8,000	12,500
Total	$20,000	$19,500	$19,000	$18,500	$18,000	$22,500

Evaluation of Anthony's Proposal

The following arguments may be made in favor of accounting for the cost of capital. First, such an accounting will properly record the increasing investment necessary when holding an asset over time and show a proper economic value for the asset. Second, it will reduce the overestimation of the accounting profit that does include the cost of equity. Third, it will provide a comparable valuation of self-constructed assets and purchased assets. Under conventional accounting, purchased assets include the cost of the supplier's equity and debt capital, while self-constructed assets are assumed to have used no capital. Finally, Anthony suggests that reporting interest as an element of cost would facilitate the work of government agencies that rely on accounting information for public policy.[36] Anthony cited as examples rate setting, price control, defense contracting, and public concepts about profit.

Some limitations also may be associated with Anthony's proposal to account for the cost of capital. First, a determination of the cost of equity is not sufficiently accurate and reliable, although Anthony suggests that the cost of equity figure from firm to firm would be set by the FASB. Second, the proposal to account for the cost of capital may be seen as a violation of the principle of conservatism

---

[36]R. N. Anthony, "Accounting for the Cost of Equity," p. 96.

EXHIBIT 8-2
Anthony's Proposal
Del Cerro Manufacturing Company
Income Statements

	Each of Years 1–4	Year 5
Sales	$ 0	$10,000
Cost of Goods Sold	0	(13,605.1)
Gross Margin and Net Income	$ 0	$ (3,105.1)

Del Cerro Manufacturing Company
Balance Sheets

			Year			
	0	1	2	3	4	5
Cash	$15,000	$14,500	$14,000	$13,500	$13,000	$22,500
Inventory	5,000	6,500	8,100	9,810	11,641	0
Total	$20,000	$21,000	$22,100	$23,310	$24,641	$22,500
Debt	$10,000	$10,000	$10,000	$10,000	$10,000	$10,000
Capital	10,000	11,000	12,000	13,310	14,641	12,500
Total	$20,000	$21,000	$22,000	$23,310	$24,641	$22,500

in the sense that it recognizes revenue before it is realized. Third, there are problems that are related to the cost of equity *per se*. Should the cost of equity be assumed to be constant over time or does it vary with the interest rate? Should the cost of equity and the cost debt be obtained by applying the rate against the book value or the market value of debt?

Toward Capitalizing the Cost of Capital

The issue of accounting for interest cost has been continually debated in the accounting literature, leading to a number of attempts by the standard-setting bodies to resolve the questions. In 1971, a Special Committee on Interest in Relation to Cost set up by the American Institute of Accountants (as it was then known) suggested that interest on investment should not be included in production cost. A committee appointed by the Accounting Principles Board in 1971 to study the question of capitalizing interest cost had its activities terminated before a position could be issued. Because an increasing number of registrants were capitalizing interest, the SEC issued, on June 21, 1974 *ASR No. 163*, "Capitalizing of Interest by Companies Other Than Public Utilities," declaring a moratorium on the trend to capitalize interest by other than public utilities. It explained its action as follows:

> It does not seem desirable to have an alternative practice grow up through selective adoption by individual companies without careful con-

sideration of such a change by the Financial Accounting Standards Board, including the development of systematic criteria as to when, if ever, capitalization of interest is desirable.

In approaching the issue, the FASB considered the following three alternatives:

1. Accounting for interest on debt as an expense of the period in which it is incurred.

2. Capitalizing interest on debt as part of the cost of an asset when prescribed conditions are met.

3. Capitalizing interest on debt and imputed interest on stockholders' equity as part of the cost of an asset when prescribed conditions are met. This corresponds to Anthony's proposal.

In its *Statement No. 34*, the FASB adopted the second method.[37] The assets qualifying for interest capitalization include facilities under construction for a company's own use and assets intended for sale or lease that are constructed as separate or discrete projects, such as ships and real estate developments. Inventories that are routinely manufactured or otherwise produced in large quantities on a repetitive basis do not quality. The capitalization period begins when three conditions are present: The company has made expenditures for the asset, work on the asset is in progress, and interest cost is being incurred.

The FASB position as stated in *Statement No. 34* fails to give comprehensive accounting recognition to an imputed interest cost for equity capital as proposed by Anthony. It recognizes the capitalization of interest on debt only for a narrow range of qualifying assets. For example, inventories that need a long time to age, such as whiskey, wine, and tobacco, do not qualify for interest capitalizaton under the standards set forth in *Statement No. 34*.

Public Reporting
of Corporate Financial Forecasts

Faced with the challenge by diverse users to develop more relevant financial reporting techniques, accountants and nonaccountants alike have recommended that forecasted information be incorporated into financial statements. Proposals have varied from the suggestion that budgetary data be disclosed to the suggestion that public companies provide earnings forecasts in their annual or interim reports and prospectuses. One of the objectives of financial reporting set forth in the Trueblood Report supported this type of disclosure:

> An objective of financial statements is to provide information useful for the predictive process. Financial forecasts should be provided when they will enhance the reliability of users' predictions.[38]

Although the objective does not constitute a strong recommendation for

[37]*Financial Accounting Standards Statement No. 34*, "Capitalization of Interest Cost" (Stamford, Conn.: FASB, October 1979).

[38]Report of the Study Group on the Objectives of Financial Statements, *Objectives of Financial Statements* (New York: AICPA, 1973), p. 13.

corporate financial forecasts, steps have been taken to ensure that forecasts are included in accounting reports. In Great Britain, the revised version of the English *City Code on Take-Overs and Mergers* required that profit forecasts be included in takeover bid circulars and prospectuses.[39] In the English case, the interest of the accounting profession was created by the requirement that not only must "the assumptions, including the commercial assumptions," be stated but the "accounting bases and calculations must be examined and reported on by the auditors or consultant accountants."[40] In the United States, the SEC first announced in February 1973 its intention to require companies disclosing forecasts to conform with certain rules to be laid down by the commission. In April 1976, in reaction to public criticism, the SEC called for voluntary filings of forecasts. This new situation presents some challenges, namely, in terms of the definition of earnings forecasts, of whether the disclosure should be mandatory or optional, and of the possible advantages of such disclosures.

The first problem concerns determining which forecasted items are to be disclosed. The two possibilities are disclosing budgets or disclosing probable results, or forecasts. A distinction may be made because budgets are prepared for internal use and, for motivational reasons, may be stated in a way that differs from expected results. Ijiri makes the distinction as follows:

> Forecasts are estimates of what the corporation considers to be the most likely to occur, whereas budgets may be inflated from what the corporation considers to be most likely to occur in order to take advantage of the motivational function of the budget.[41]

From the point of view of the user, therefore, the disclosure of forecasts rather than budgets may be more relevant to decision needs. In fact, the trend seems to be in favor of the disclosure of forecasts of specific accounts in general and earnings in particular.

The second problem is whether the disclosure of earnings forecasts should be mandatory or optional. Each position may be easily justified. The principal argument in favor of mandatory disclosure is that it creates a similar and uniform situation for all companies. Mandatory disclosure, however, may create an unnecessary burden in terms of competitive advantage, and exceptions would have to be allowed for certain firms, for example private companies, companies in volatile industries, companies in the process of major changes, and companies in a development stage.[42] Another argument against mandatory disclosure is that some firms lack adequate technology, experience, and competence to disclose adequate forecasts, and the outlays to correct the situation may create an unnecessary burden. Such a firm may doubt the benefits of forecasts disclosure that could justify the cost of installing a new reporting system.

The third problem concerns the desirability of publication. Several arguments have been advanced against the reporting of corporate financial forecasts. It has been pointed out, for example, that both companies and analysts have been

---

[39]*The City Code on Take-Overs and Mergers*, revised February 1972.

[40]*Ibid.*, Rule 16.

[41]Yuji Ijiri, "Improving Reliability of Publicly Reported Corporate Financial Forecasts," in *Public Reporting of Corporate Financial Forecasts*, ed. P. Prakash and A. Rappaport, (Chicago: Commerce Clearing House, 1974), p. 169.

[42]R. J. Sycamore, "Public Disclosure of Earnings Forecasts by Companies," *The Chartered Accountant Magazine* (May 1974), pp. 72–75.

unsuccessful in accurately forecasting earnings. Daily pointed out that budgeted "information must be reasonably accurate to be relevant; otherwise, investors would have no confidence in the information and consequently not utilize it."[43] Both his study and McDonald's study[44] support the contention that, on the average, management earnings forecasts are likely to be materially inaccurate. A number of factors may affect the accuracy of forecasts, for example, the length of time covered by the forecast, the nature of the industry in which the company operates, the external environment, and the degree of sophistication and experience of the company making the forecast. Ijiri classified the primary issues involved in corporate financial forecasts as (1) reliability, (2) responsibility, and (3) reticency.[45] **Reliability** is related to the relative accuracy of the forecasts, **responsibility** to the possible legal liabilities of firms making forecasts and accountants auditing the forecasts, and **reticency** to the degree of silence and inaction of the firm put under competitive disadvantage by forecast disclosure. Similarly, Mautz suggested that three kinds of differences must be considered in evaluating the overall usefulness of published forecasts: "1. differences in the forecasting abilities of publicly owned firms; 2. differences in the attitudes with which managements in publicly owned companies might be expected to approach the forecasting task; 3. differences in the capacities of investors to use forecasts."[46] Finally, given the difficulties associated with identifying and estimating forecasts, what is it that an accountant is expected to attest? Mautz suggests the following range of possibilities: (1) arithmetic accuracy, (2) internal integrity of the forecast data, (3) consistency in the application of accounting principles, (4) adequacy of disclosure, (5) reasonableness of assumptions, and (6) reasonableness of projections.[47]

The Trend Toward Multinational Accounting

Although it has not yet reached the level of conceptualization of the other subfields of accounting, multinational (international, transnational, or global) accounting has become a full-fledged subfield within the accounting discipline. Wierich, Avery, and Anderson, who have provided a useful framework for viewing multinational accounting,[48] distinguished three definitional approaches: (1) a universal system (2) a descriptive and informative approach, and (3) accounting

---

[43]R. A. Daily, "The Feasibility of Reporting Forecasted Information," *The Accounting Review* (Ocobter 1971), pp. 686–92.

[44]C. L. McDonald, "An Empirical Examination of the Reliability of Published Predictions of Future Earnings," *The Accounting Review* (July 1973), pp. 565–80.

[45]Y. Ijiri, "Improving Reliability of Publicly Reported Corporate Financial Forecasts," p. 163.

[46]R. K. Mautz, "A View from the Public Accounting Profession," in *Public Reporting of Corporate Financial Forecasts*, ed. P. Prakash and A. Rappaport (Chicago: Commerce Clearing House, 1974), p. 102.

[47]*Ibid.*, p. 110.

[48]Thomas R. Weirich, Clarence G. Avery, and Henry R. Anderson, "International Accounting: Varying Definitions," *International Journal of Accounting* (Fall 1971), pp. 79–87.

practices of foreign subsidiaries and parent companies. They stated these definitional approaches as follows:

World Accounting. In the framework of this concept, international accounting is considered to be a universal system that could be adopted in all countries. A worldwide set of generally accepted accounting principles (GAAP), such as the set maintained in the United States, would be established. Practices and principles would be developed which were applicable to all countries. This concept would be the ultimate goal of an international accounting system.

International Accounting. A second major concept of the term international accounting involves a descriptive and informative approach. Under this concept, international accounting includes *all* varieties of principles, methods and standards of accounting of *all* countries. This concept includes a set of generally accepted accounting principles established for each country, thereby requiring the accountant to be multiple principle conscious when studying international accounting. . . . No universal or perfect set of principles would be expected to be established. A collection of all principles, methods and standards of all countries would be considered as the international accounting system. These variations result because of differing geographic, social, economic, political and legal influences.

Accounting for Foreign Subsidiaries. The third major concept that may be applied to international accounting refers to the accounting practices of a parent company and a foreign subsidiary. A reference to a particular country or domicile is needed under the concept for the effective international financial reporting. The account is concerned mainly with the translation and adjustment of the subsidiary's financial statement. Different accounting problems arise and different accounting principles are to be followed depending upon which country is used as a reference for translation and adjustment purposes.[49]

These three approaches point to the ultimate objective: achieving a world accounting system or a worldwide set of generally accepted accounting principles. The major obstacles are the material differences characterizing generally accepted accounting principles as applied in various countries. The differences in international accounting and in accounting for foreign subsidiaries, which result primarily from differences in the business environment from one country to another, are problems in need of correction. Mueller identified four elements of differentiation.[50]

1. *State of economic development.* National economies vary in terms of their extent of development and in terms of nature, from the developed to the developing countries.

2. *State of business complexity.* National economies vary in terms of their

---

[49]*Ibid.*, pp. 80–81.

[50]G. G. Mueller, "Accounting Principles Generally Accepted in the United States Versus Those Generally Accepted Elsewhere," *International Journal of Accounting Education and Research*, Vol. 3, No. 2 (Spring 1968), pp. 92–93.

technological and industrial know-how, creating differences in their business needs as well as their business output.

3. *Shade of political persuasion.* National economies vary in terms of their political systems, from the centrally controlled economy to the market-oriented economy.

4. *Reliance on some particular system of law.* National economies vary in terms of their supporting legal system. They may rely on either a common law or code law system; they may use protective legislation and unfair trade and anti-trust laws, for example.

These differences in the business environment cause differences in multinational accounting practices and a clustering of financial accounting principles. Mueller, for example, used the four elements of differentiation to identify ten distinct sets of business environments, as follows:

1. United States/Canada/The Netherlands—There is a minimum of commercial or companies legislation in the environment. Industry is highly developed; currencies are relatively stable. A strong orientation to business innovation exists. Many companies with widespread international business interests are headquartered in these countries.

2. British Commonwealth (excluding Canada)—Comparable companies legislation exists in all Commonwealth countries and administration procedures and social order reflect strong ties to the mother country. There exists an intertwining of currencies through the so-called "sterling block" arrangement. Business is highly developed but often quite traditional.

3. Germany/Japan—Rapid economic growth has occurred since World War II. Influences stemming from various United States military and administrative operations have caused considerable imitation of many facets of the United States practices, often by grafting United States procedures to various local traditions. The appearance of a new class of professional business managers is observable. Relative political, social, and currency stability exists.

4. Continental Europe (excluding Germany, The Netherlands and Scandinavia)—Private business lacks significant government support. Private property and the profit motive are not necessarily in the center of economic and business orientation. Some national economic planning exists. Political swings from far right to far left, and vice versa, have a long history in this environment. Limited reservoirs of economic resources are available.

5. Scandinavia—Here we have developed economies, but characteristically slow rates of economic and business growth. Governments tend toward social legislation. Companies acts regulate business. Relative stability of population numbers is the rule. Currencies are quite stable. Several business innovations (especially in consumer goods) originated in Scandinavia. Personal characteristics and outlooks are quite similar in all five Scandinavian countries.

6. Israel/Mexico—These are the only two countries with substantial success in fairly rapid economic development. Trends of a shift to

more reliance on private enterprise are beginning to appear; however, there is still a significant government presence in business. Political and monetary stability seem to be increasing. Some specialization in business and the professions is taking place. The general population apparently has a strong desire for higher standards of living.

7. South America—Many instances are present of significant economic underdevelopment along with social and educational underdevelopment. The business base is narrow. Agricultural and military interests are strong and often dominate governments. There is considerable reliance on export/import trade. Currencies are generally soft. Populations are increasing heavily.

8. The Developing Nations of the Near and Far East*—Modern concepts and ethics of business have predominantly Western origins. These concepts and ethics often clash with the basic oriental cultures. Business in the developing nations of the Orient largely means trade only. There is severe underdevelopment on most measures, coupled with vast population numbers. Political scenes and currencies are most shaky. Major economic advances are probably impossible without substantial assistance from the industrialized countries. OPEC member countries are developing more rapidly since 1973.

9. Africa (excluding South Africa)*—Most of the African continent is still in early stages of independent civilization and thus little native business environment presently exists. There are significant natural and human resources. Business is likely to assume a major role and responsibility in the development of African nations.

10. Communist Nations—The complete control by central governments places these countries in a grouping all its own.[51]

*These areas are obviously treated very generally; exceptions exist for a few given countries.

These groupings are likely to affect the development of accounting and the formulation of accounting principles and explain the diversity of practices used from one country to another. What is needed, however, is a worldwide harmonization of financial accounting principles. A first step toward this goal was the creation in June 1973 of the International Accounting Standards Committee (IASC), with joint representation of professional accounting bodies from Australia, Canada, France, Germany, Japan, Mexico, The Netherlands, the United Kingdom, and Ireland. Since then, the membership has increased. The objectives of the IASC are:

1. To establish and maintain an International Accounting Standards Committee with a membership and powers set out below whose function will be to formulate and publish, in the public interest, standards to be observed in the presentation of audited accounts and financial statements and to promote their worldwide acceptance and observance.
2. To support the standards promulgated by the Committee.

---

[51] Mueller, "Accounting Principles," pp. 93–95. Reprinted by permission.

3. To use their best endeavors in their own countries:
   a. to ensure that published accounts comply with these standards or that there is disclosure of the extent to which they do not and to persuade governments, the authorities controlling securities markets, and the industrial and business community that published accounts should comply with these standards;
   b. to ensure that the auditors satisfy themselves that the accounts comply with these standards. If the accounts do not comply with these standards, the audit report should either refer to the non-compliance in the accounts or should state the extent to which they do not comply;
   c. to ensure that, as soon as practical, appropriate action is taken with respect to auditors whose audit reports do not meet the requirements of (b), above.
4. To seek to secure similar general acceptance and observance of these standards internationally.

In addition to the IASC, other international accounting organizations have emerged with similar objectives, contributing to the harmonization of accounting principles throughout the world. These include the International Congresses of Accountants, the International Federation of Accountants, the International Conference on Accounting Education, the InterAmerican Accounting Association, the Union Européenne des Experts Comptables Economiques et Financiers, the Confederation of Asian and Pacific Accountants, the Accountants International Study Group, and the International Committee on Accounting Cooperation.[52]

The road to internationally uniform accounting standards and principles is not without obstacles. One critic observes:

> The growth of multinational business interests and the expansion of governmental and quasi-governmental assistance make the prospect of compatible worldwide accounting most appealing. Unfortunately, the solution is too simple and the problem too complex. However desirable such a monolithic concept appears, practical impediments to such uniformity must be clearly recognized so that accountants and users of financial information will not rely on the prospect of uniformity as a cure-all for the problems accruing from international accounting diversity.

> Traumatic evidence of the practical obstacles to uniformity are the controversies presently rampant on the American Accounting scene. If one well-organized professional group cannot reach agreement on basic procedures, how much more difficult will it be to establish world standards? . . . As with all social sciences, accounting contains an inherent flexibility which permits it to adapt to diverse financial requirements. This adaptability is at the same time one of the chief values to accounting and one of the chief obstacles to uniformity.[53]

---

[52]For more information on these organizations, see *An Introduction to Multinational Accounting,* by Frederick D. S. Choi and G. G. Mueller (Englewood Cliffs, N.J.: Prentice-Hall, 1978), pp. 156–75.

[53]Irving L. Fantl, "Case Against International Uniformity," *Management Accounting* (May 1971), p. 13.

Other writers have maintained that financial statements can reflect only one point of view, that of the company's country of domicile. As Mueller observes:

> The notion of a single domicile for financial statements means that each set of financial statements necessarily has a nationality, reflects style and customs at a particular point of time and has an individual viewpoint or character. Financial statements are anchored in a single set of underlying account data prepared within a framework of quite specific accounting standards, methods and procedures. Restatement of financial statements to a different set of accounting principles produces different relationships between individual account balances and financial ratios. The meaning and implication of these new relationships may convey an entirely different financial substance to statement readers in other countries.[54]

Conclusions

The new scope of financial accounting requires more extensive disclosure of information, because a greater variety of information is deemed relevant for economic decision making. The new data are a result of attempts to account for the social impact of firms' activities, for changes in human capital, for the cost of equity capital, for financial forecasts, and for international accounting standards. Such extensive disclosure is a new and difficult challenge that will require not only the development of new measurement and reporting techniques but also the possible expanding of the boundaries of the attest function. Accountants and users of tomorrow will need to have a better grasp of the relationship between accounting and other disciplines in the social sciences, of the extent of their responsibilities, and of the need for continuing education.

References

Socioeconomic Accounting

Bauer, R. A., and F. Dan, Jr. *The Corporate Social Audit.* New York: Russel Sage Foundation, 1972.

Beams, F. A., and P. E. Fertig. "Pollution Control Through Social Cost Conversion." *The Journal of Accountancy* (November 1971), pp. 37–42.

Belkaoui, A. "The Accounting Treatment of Pollution Costs." *The Certified General Accountant* (August 1973), pp. 19–21.

Belkaoui, A. "The Impact of Socio-Economic Accounting Statements on the Investment Decision—An Empirical Study." *Accounting, Organizations and Society*, in press.

Belkaoui, A. "The Impact of the Disclosure of the Environmental Effects of Organizational Behavior on the Market." *Financial Management* (Winter 1976), pp. 26–31.

---

[54]G. G. Mueller, "The International Significance of Financial Statements," *Illinois CPA* (Spring 1965), p. 10.

Belkaoui, A. "Whys and Wherefores of Measuring Externalities." *The Certified General Accountant* (January–February 1975), pp. 29–32.

Churchman, C. W. "On the Facility, Felicity, and Morality of Measuring Social Change." *The Accounting Review* (January 1971), pp. 30–35.

Epstein, M., E. Flamholtz, and J. J. McDonough. "Corporate Social Accounting in the United States of America: State of the Art and Future Prospects." *Accounting, Organizations and Society*, 1, No. 1 (1976), 23–42.

Estes, R. W. *Accounting and Society*. New York: Melville, 1973.

Estes, R. W. "Socio Economic Accounting and External Diseconomies." *The Accounting Review* (April 1972), pp. 284–90.

Ingram, R. W. "An Investigation of the Information Content of (Certain) Social Responsibility Disclosures." *Journal of Accounting Research* (Autumn 1976), pp. 270–85.

Knapp, W. *The Social Costs of Private Enterprises*. Cambridge, Mass.: Harvard University Press, 1950.

Linowes, D. F. "An Approach to Socio-Economic Accounting." *The Conference Board Record* (1972), pp. 58–61.

Linowes, D. F. "Socio-Economic Accounting." *The Journal of Accountancy* (November 1968), pp. 37–42.

Longstreth, B., and D. Rosenbloom. *Corporate Social Responsibility and the Institutional Investor*. New York: Praeger, 1973.

Mobley, S. C. "The Challenges of Socio-Economic Accounting." *The Accounting Review* (October 1970), pp. 767–68.

"Report of the Committee on Environmental Effects of Organizational Behavior," *The Accounting Review*, supplement to vol. 48 (1969).

Seidler, L. J., and L. L. Seidler. *Social Accounting: Theory, Insurance Cases*. New York: Melville, 1975.

Simon, J. G., C. W. Pavers, and J. P. Gunnemann. *The Ethical Investor*. New Haven: Yale University Press, 1972.

Human Resource Accounting

Alexander, Michael O. "Investments in People." *Canadian Chartered Accountant* (July 1971), pp. 38–45.

Brummet, R. Lee, Eric G. Flamholtz, and William C. Pyle. "Human Resource Measurement: A Challenge for Accountants." *The Accounting Review* (April 1968), pp. 217–24.

Committee on Human Resource Accounting. "Report of the Committee on Human Resource Accounting." *The Accounting Review*, supplement to vol. 48 (1973), pp. 169–85.

Dittman, D. A., H. A. Juris, and L. Revsine. "On the Existence of Unrecorded Human Assets: An Economic Perspective." *Journal of Accounting Research* (Spring 1976), pp. 49–65.

Elias, N. S. "The Effects of Human Asset Statements on the Investment Decision: An Experiment." *Empirical Research in Accounting: Selected Studies, 1972.* Supplement to vol. 10, *Journal of Accounting Research*, pp. 215–40.

Flamholtz, E. "A Model for Human Resource Valuation: A Stochastic Process with Service Rewards." *The Accounting Review* (April 1971), pp. 253–67.

Flamholtz, E. "Assessing the Validity of a Theory of Human Resource Value: A Field Study." *Empirical Research in Accounting: Selected Studies, 1972.* Supplement to vol. 10, *Journal of Accounting Research*.

Flamholtz, E. *Human Resource Accounting.* Los Angeles: Dickenson Publishing, 1974.

Flamholtz, E. "On the Use of the Economic Concept of Human Capital in Financial Statements: A Comment." *The Accounting Review* (January 1972), pp. 148–52.

Flamholtz, E. "Toward a Theory of Human Resource Value in Formal Organizations." *The Accounting Review* (October 1972), pp. 666–78.

Hekimian, James C., and Curtis H. Jones. "Put People on Your Balance Sheet." *Harvard Business Review*, 45 (January–February 1967), 105–13.

Hendricks, J. A. "The Impact of Human Resource Accounting Information on Stock Investment Decisions: An Empirical Study." *The Accounting Review* (April 1976), pp. 292–305.

Hermanson, R. H. "Accounting for Human Assets." Occasional Paper No. 14. East Lansing, Mich.: Bureau of Business and Economic Research, Graduate School of Business Administration, Michigan State University, 1964.

Lev, Baruch, and Aba Schwartz. "On the Use of the Economic Concept of Human Capital in Financial Statements." *The Accounting Review* (January 1971), pp. 103–12.

Likert, Rensis, and David G. Bowers. "Improving the Accuracy of P/L Reports by Estimating the Change in Dollar Value of the Human Organization." *Michigan Business Review* (March 1973), pp. 15–24.

Likert, Rensis, and David G. Bower. "Organizational Theory and Human Resource Accounting." *American Psychologist*, 24, No. 6 (1969), 585-92.

Likert, Rensis, and William C. Pyle. "A Human Organizational Measurement Approach." *Financial Analysts Journal* (January–February 1971), pp. 75–84.

Taylor, James C., and David G. Bowers. *The Survey of Organizations.* Ann Arbor, Mich.: Institute for Social Research, 1972.

Tomassini, L. A. "Assessing the Impact of Human Resource Accounting: An Experimental Study of Managerial Decision Preferences." *The Accounting Review* (October 1977), pp. 904–14.

Accounting for the Cost of Capital

Anthony, R. N. "Accounting for the Cost of Equity." *Harvard Business Review* (November–December 1973), pp. 88–102.

Anthony, R. N. *Accounting for the Cost of Interest.* New York: Lexington Books, 1975.

Russel, G. "Accounting for the Cost of Capital." *Cost and Management* (July–August 1974), pp 50–52.

Young, D. W. "Accounting for the Cost of Interest: Implications for the Timber Industry." *The Accounting Review* (October 1976), pp. 788–99.

Reporting of Financial Forecasts

Austin, D. R. "The Feasibility of Reporting Forecasted Information." *The Accounting Review* (October 1971), pp. 686–92.

Burton, J. C. "Financial Forecasts." *The Chartered Accountant Magazine* (November 1973), pp. 35–39.

Cooper, W. W., N. Dopuch, and T. Keller. "Budgetary Disclosures and Other Suggestions for Improving Accounting Reports." *The Accounting Review* (October 1968), pp. 640–48.

Copeland, R. M., and R. J. Marioni. "Executive Forecasts of Earnings Per Share Versus Forecasts of Naive Models." *Journal of Business* (October 1972), pp. 134–51.

Elgers, P., and J. Clark. "Forecasted Income Statements: An Investor Perspective." *The Accounting Review* (October 1973), pp. 668–79.

Gillis, J. G. "Corporate Forecasts: Legal Aspects." *Financial Analysts Journal* (January–February 1973), pp. 35–40.

Gonedes, N. J., N. Dopuch, and S. H. Penman. "Disclosure Rules, Information Production, and Capital Market Equilibrium: The Case of the Forecast Disclosure Rules." *Journal of Accounting Research* (Spring 1976), pp. 89–137.

Gray, William S., J. F. Gillis, and S. S. Stewart. "Disclosure of Corporate Forecasts to the Investor." *The Financial Analyst Federation* (March 1973), pp. 15–20.

Kapnick, H. E. "Will Financial Forecasts Really Help Investors." *Financial Executive* (August 1977), pp. 111–90.

McDonald, C. L. "An Empirical Examination of the Reliability of Published Predictions of Future Earnings." *The Accounting Review* (July 1973), pp. 565–80.

Patell, J. M. "Corporate Forecasts of Earnings Per Share and Stock Price Behavior: Empirical Tests." *Journal of Accounting Research* (Autumn 1976), pp. 246–76.

Prakash, Prem, and Alfred Rappaport, eds. *Public Reporting of Corporate Financial Forecasts.* Proceedings of a Conference Sponsored by the Center for Advanced Study in Accounting and Information Systems, Graduate School of Management, Northwestern University. Chicago: Commerce Clearing House, 1974.

Securities and Exchange Commission. "Disclosure of Projections of Future Economic Performance." Release No. 33-5363 and No. 34-9984, February 2, 1973.

Shank, J. K., and J. B. Caffee, Jr. "Case of the Fuqua Forecasts." *Harvard Business Review* (November–December 1973), pp. 34–56.

Shank, J. K., and J. B. Caffee, Jr. "The Pros and Cons of Forecast Publication." *Business Horizons* (October 1973), pp. 43–49.

Sycamore, R. J. "Public Disclosure of Earnings Forecasts by Companies." *The Chartered Accountant Magazine* (May 1974), pp. 77–75.

The Trend Toward Multinational Accounting

Belkaoui, Ahmed, Alfred Kahl, and Josette Peyrard. "Information Needs of Financial Analysts: An International Comparison." *Journal of International Education and Research in Accounting* (Fall 1977), pp. 19–27.

Belkaoui, Ahmed. "The Role of Accounting in Economic Development: Another Point of View." *The Chartered Accountant Magazine* (November 1974), pp. 16–18.

Choi, Frederick D. S., and G. G. Mueller. *An Introduction to Multinational Accounting.* Englewood Cliffs, N.J.: Prentice-Hall, 1978.

Committee on International Accounting Operations and Education, 1976–78. *Accounting Education and the Third World.* Sarasota, Fla.: American Accounting Association, 1978.

Mueller, G. G., and L. M. Walker. "The Coming of Age of Transnational Financial Reporting." *The Journal of Accountancy* (July 1976), pp. 67–74.

Scott, William R. "The Role of Accounting in Economic Development." *The Chartered Accountant Magazine* (July 1974), pp. 8–9.

Tyra, Anita I. "Financial Disclosure Patterns in Four European Countries." *International Journal of Accounting* (Spring 1970), pp. 89–99.

Young, J. M. "Accounting in a Free Economy." *The Accounting Review* (July, 1959), pp. 442–51.

Questions

8–1 What do we mean by socioeconomic accounting?

8–2 What do we mean by human resources accounting?

8–3 What do we mean by accounting for the cost of capital?

8–4 Define *externality, social cost,* and *social benefit.*

8–5 What are the determinants of individual and group value to an organization?

8–6 Discuss each of the monetary measures of human assets.

8–7 Discuss each of the nonmonetary measures of human assets.

8–8 Explain the method of accounting for the cost of capital.

8–9 What are the principal advantages and disadvantages of public reporting of corporate financial forecasts?

8–10 Mr. H. S. Kulshrestha made the following statement in "Accounting as a Social Science," in *The Chartered Accountant* (of India) (October 1964), p. 208:

> Accounting, when born, must not have been more dismal a subject than economics. At least, it has never been condemned as a "Gospel of Mammon." But later on, as all know, when economics aimed at the welfare of man as a member of society, it got popular and now occupies an important position among the social sciences. Accounting, however, continued serving individuals. As a result, the economist acted as a thinker, author and orator on society; whereas the accountant worked at the desk shabbily dressed and "sincere" to his master. The secret of this significant development in and popularity of economics lay in its social approach to the well-being of man, which unfortunately accounting failed to have.

Do you agree with the above statement? Why or why not?

8–11 Do accountants care about the welfare of society?

8–12 What is a social audit?

8–13 Compare Anthony's proposal with *FASB Statement No. 34.*

8–14 "It would seem that a firm's employees, its human resources, can be one of the most significant assets utilized by the firm. Despite this fact, conventional accounting procedures make no provision for entering the value of human resources in the balance sheet. Costs associated with the firm's employees are invariably charged to income as incurred." This fact has led many writers to the conclusion that more attention must be paid to the problems of accounting for human resources.

Required:
a. Many different methods of accounting for the human resources of a company have been studied. List and briefly explain six methods that have been examined by Michael Gilbert in his article, "The Asset Value of Human Organization."
b. In an attempt to develop an accounting system for human resources, R. L. Woodruff, in his article "Human Resource Accounting," describes seven functional accounts. List and briefly explain five of these functional accounts.

(SMA adapted)

8–15 Elmo Company operates several plants at which limestone is processed into quicklime and hydrated lime. The Bland Plant, where most of the equipment was installed many years ago, continually deposits a dusty white substance over the surrounding countryside. Citing the unsanitary condition of the neighboring community of Adeltown, the pollution of the Adel River, and the high incidence of lung disease among workers at Bland, the state's Pollution Control Agency has assessed a substantial penalty, which will be used to clean up Adeltown. After considering the costs involved (which could not have been reasonably estimated before the Agency's action), Elmo decides to comply with the Agency's orders, the alternative being to cease operations at Bland at the end of the current fiscal year. The officers at Elmo agree that the air pollution control equipment should be capitalized and depreciated over its useful life, but they disagree over the period(s) to which the penalty should be charged.
Required:
Discuss the conceptual merits and reporting requirements of accounting for a penalty as a (1) charge to the current period, (2) correction of prior periods, and (3) capitalizable item to be amortized over future periods.

(AICPA adapted)

8–16 Elmo's Davis Plant causes approximately as much pollution as Bland. Davis, however, is located in another state, where there is little likelihood of governmental regulation, and Elmo has no plans for pollution control at this plant. One of Elmo's officers, Mr. Pearce, says that uncontrolled pollution at Davis constitutes a real cost to society, which is not recorded anywhere under current practice. He suggests that this "social cost" of the Davis Plant be included annually in Elmo's income statement. Further, he suggests that measurement of this cost is easily obtainable by reference to the depreciation on Bland's pollution control equipment.
Required:
a. Is Mr. Pearce necessarily correct in stating that costs associated with Davis's pollution are entirely unrecorded? Explain.
b. Evaluate Mr. Pearce's proposed method of measuring the annual "social cost" of Davis's pollution.
c. Discuss the merit of Mr. Pearce's suggestion that a "social cost" be recognized by a business enterprise.

(AICPA adapted)

8–17 "It would seem that a firm's employees, its human resources, can be one of the most significant assets utilized by the firm. Despite this fact, conventional accounting procedures make no provision for entering the value of human resources in the balance sheet. Costs associated with the firm's employees are invariably charged to income as incurred." This fact has led many writers to the conclusion that more attention must be paid to the problems of accounting for human resources.

Many accountants still believe, however, that the problems of accounting for human resources have not been properly settled and that it is preferable to charge these costs to income as incurred.

Required:

a. Give arguments or reasons that may be used by writers to support the accounting treatment of entering the value of human resources in the balance sheet.

b. Give arguments or reasons that may be used by *accountants* to support the accounting treatment of charging all these expenses to income.

(SMA adapted)

8–18 G. G. Mueller and Lauren M. Walker made the following statement in "The Coming of Age of Transnational Financial Reporting," in *The Journal of Accounting* (July 1976), p. 67:

> "Multinational business is the prime generator of transnational financial reporting needs. Thus, with all the current political, legal and moral attacks unleashed upon the multinational corporation, one might simply assume that before long the multinational corporation will meet its fate on one guillotine or another and the problem of transnational financial reporting will go away."

Do you agree with the above statement? Discuss.

Abt Associates, Inc., Annual Report, 1973*

Abt Associates, Inc.
Social and Financial Balance Sheet 1973

Assets		1973	1972
1.	**Staff Assets**		
	Staff Available Within One Year (note 1)	$ 6,384,000	$ 4,166,000
	Staff Available After One Year (note 1)	15,261,000	12,567,000
	Training Investment (note 2)	2,051,000	971,000
		23,696,000	17,704,000
	Less Accumulated Training Obsolescence (note 2)	503,000	248,000
	Total Staff Assets	$23,193,000	$17,456,000
2.	**Organizational Assets**		
	Creation and Development of Organization		
	Research (note 3):	$ 437,000	$ 352,000
	Child Care (note 4)	7,000	7,000
	Social Audit (note 4)	32,000	18,000
	Total Organizational Assets	$ 476,000	$ 377,000
3.	**Use of Public Goods**		
	Public Services Paid For Through Taxes (Net of Consumption) (note 5)	$ 365,000	$ 160,000
4.	**Financial Assets (note 9)**		
	Cash	$ 91,000	$ 365,000
	Accounts Receivable, Less Allowance for Doubtful Accounts	2,083,000	1,285,000
	Unbilled Contract Costs and Fees	1,789,000	1,539,000
	Other Current Financial Assets	42,000	46,000
	Other Long-Term Financial Assets	39,000	89,000
	Total Financial Assets	$ 4,044,000	$ 3,324,000
5.	**Physical Assets (note 9)**		
	Land	$ 310,000	$ 307,000
	Buildings	1,710,000	1,737,000
	Improvements	222,000	152,000
	Equipment, Furniture and Fixtures	242,000	137,000
		2,484,000	2,333,000
	Less Accumulated Depreciation	204,000	111,000
		2,280,000	2,222,000
	Office Building Under Construction	225,000	—
	Total Physical Assets	$ 2,505,000	$ 2,222,000
	Total Assets	$30,583,000	$23,539,000

Social assets and liabilities are identified in lightest type.

* Reprinted by permission of Abt Associates, Inc.

Liabilities and Equity	1973	1972
1. Staff Liabilities		
Staff Wages Payable (note 6)	$23,193,000	$17,456,000
2. Organizational Liabilities		
Organizational Financing Requirements (note 7)	$ 563,000	$ 351,000
3. Public Liabilities (note 8)		
Environmental Resources Used Through Pollution:		
Paper	$ 11,000	$ 5,000
Electricity	76,000	41,000
Commuting	37,000	20,000
Total Public Liabilities	$ 124,000	$ 66,000
4. Financial Liabilities (note 9)		
Notes Payable (Short Term)	$ 514,00	$ 1,112,000
Accounts Payable	1,081,000	539,000
Accrued Expenses	875,000	596,000
Federal Income Taxes	109,000	78,000
Deferred Federal Income Taxes	52,000	35,000
Notes Payable (Long Term)	1,092,000	757,000
Leasehold Interest in Property	128,000	127,000
Total Financial Liabilities	$ 3,851,000	$ 3,244,000
Stockholders' Equity (note 9)		
Common Stock	$ 295,000	$ 295,000
Additional Paid-In Capital	1,491,000	1,491,000
Retained Earnings	912,000	516,000
Total Stockholders' Equity	$ 2,690,000	$ 2,302,000
Society's Equity		
Society's Equity Generated by Increases (Decreases) in Net Social Assets (note 10)	$ 154,000	$ 120,000
Total Liabilities and Equity	$30,583,000	$23,539,000

Note 1
Company staff is considered a social asset. Valuation of the asset is based on year-end payroll, discounted to present value, the discount rate being a function of mean staff tenure (averaged over previous years) and salary profiles over time. Discount rate for 1973 was .9604 for staff available within one year (1972: .9634) and 2.296 for those available after one year (1972: 2.906), based on a mean staff tenure of 3.8 years (1972: 4.6 years).

Note 2
Training investment has been estimated from a staff survey conducted in January 1974. 1973 training expenditures, identified in the Social and Financial Income Statement, have been added to the 1972 balance. Training obsolescence is based on a straightline depreciation of training investment over the mean staff tenure.

Note 3
Creation and development of organization is equated to the replacement cost of paid-in capital, computed by weighing the capital stock account from 1965 (the year of the company's founding) to the present by the deflator for Gross Private Fixed Investment. The replacement cost of total paid-in capital less actual cost constitutes a social asset.

Note 4
Investments in research in child care and the social audit by the company accrue as a social asset.

Note 5
Taxes paid by the company are considered a social contribution or benefit, while public services consumed by the company are considered social costs. When the company does not consume public services equal to taxes paid, a net social asset is produced. The change in this asset from 1972 to 1973 is equal to the difference between the value of public services consumed and total taxes paid, as identified in the Social and Financial Income Statement.

Note 6
This amount does not constitute a liability in the legal sense. It is a liability contingent upon future utilization of staff on contract or administrative tasks.

Note 7
The company's financing requirements are considered to be an opportunity cost to society. This cost is equated to the difference between mean borrowing during the year and year-end borrowing.

Note 8
The use of environmental resources through pollution generated by company operations is considered a cumulative social liability. The change between 1972 and 1973 figures is equal to the social costs identified in the Social and Financial Income Statement.

Note 9
Financial and physical assets, financial liabilities and stockholders' equity are items conventionally accounted for. The individual line items are the same as in the Financial Balance Sheet; they have been rearranged and rounded off for integration into the social balance sheet.

Note 10
Society's investment in the company is created by recognizing the difference between the net increase in the value of social assets and social liabilities.

Note 11
Conventional financial accounting fails to adjust for public services flowing from society to the corporation. These public services constitute a social cost, corresponding to an "invisible subsidy" to the company — which is offset by conventionally accounted tax payments. Federal and state public services consumed by the company are calculated by multiplying the ratio of company revenues to total federal or state corporate revenues times the total of federal or state corporation tax collections. The company's share of local services consumed is computed by multiplying the ratio of the average daily work force of the company to total local population by total local taxes, subtracting the share of the local budget going to education (30.6% in 1973; 29% in 1972) since the staff does not use local public education.

Note 12
In its operations, the company contributes to the degradation of environmental resources through pollution. The cost of pollution abatement is considered analogous to public services provided by society.

Note 13
The company consumed 1,723,593 kWH of electric power in 1973 and 1,542,524 kWH in 1972. The cost of abatement of air pollution created by the production of this power is estimated at $.02 per kWH.

Note 14
The company generated 1,727,440 commuting trip miles in 1973 and 783,750 miles in 1972 (3,622 and 3,438 per staff member, respectively). The cost of abatement of air pollution caused by automobile commuting is estimated at $.01 per mile.

Note 15
A substantial portion of the company's activities are expressed in tangible form through the printed word. The company used 170 tons of paper in 1973 and 102 tons in 1972. The cost of

abatement of water pollution created by the manufacture of this paper is estimated at $35 per ton.

Note 16
The most significant development in the company has been the increase in staff. Total number of employees (in annual average full-time equivalents) increased from 228 in 1972 to 477 in 1973. This increase is reflected in the totals reported in the social and financial income statement. Figures are therefore reported in terms of per employee in the footnotes to clarify qualitative developments.

Note 17
Total annual payroll has been broken down into pay for time worked, vacation and holidays, and sick leave. As a cost to the company, salaries for time worked have been broken down further into compensation for work and training investment (see Note 21).

Abt Associates, Inc.
Social and Financial Income Statement 1973*

Benefits (Income)	1973	1972
1. To Company/Stockholders		
Contract Revenues and Other Income	$15,224,000	$ 6,995,000
Federal Services Consumed (note 11)	195,000	129,000
State Services Consumed (note 11)	80,000	46,000
Local Services Consumed (note 11)	32,000	22,000
Environmental Resources Used Through Pollution (note 12)		
Electricity (note 13)	35,000	31,000
Commuting (note 14)	17,000	10,000
Paper (note 15)	6,000	4,000
Total	$15,589,000	$ 7,237,000
2. To Staff (note 16)		
Salaries for Time Worked (note 17)	$ 5,399,000	$ 2,688,000
Career Advancement (note 18)	602,000	332,000
Vacation and Holidays (note 17)	571,000	298,000
Health and Life Insurance (note 19)	361,000	140,000
Sick Leave (note 17)	127,000	53,000
Parking (note 20)	124,000	59,000
Food Services (note 21)	51,000	24,000
Quality of Work Space (note 22)	16,000	25,000
Child Care (note 23)	11,000	5,000
Credit Union (note 24)	8,000	4,000
Total	$ 7,270,000	$ 3,628,000
3. To Clients/General Public		
Value of Contract Work at Cost (note 35)	$15,224,000	$ 6,995,000
Staff Overtime Worked but not Paid (note 36)	1,056,000	883,000
Federal Taxes Paid by Company	349,000	272,000
State and Federal Tax Worth of Net Jobs Created (note 37)	327,000	174,000
State Taxes Paid by Company	100,000	62,000
Contributions to Knowledge (Publications) (note 38)	54,000	18,000
Total	$17,110,000	$ 8,404,000

*Net social income is identified in lightest type.

Benefits (Income)	1973	1972
4. To Community		
Local Taxes Paid by Company	$ 63,000	$ 71,000
Local Tax Worth of Net Jobs Created (note 39)	52,000	40,000
Environmental Improvements (note 40)	18,000	22,000
Total	$ 133,000	$ 133,000

Costs (Expenditures)	1973	1972
1. To Company/Stockholders		
Salaries Paid (Exclusive of Training Investment and Fringe Benefits (notes 17, 25)	$ 4,319,000	$ 2,150,000
Training Investment in Staff (notes 17, 25)	1,080,000	538,000
Direct Contract Costs (note 26)	5,596,000	1,921,000
Overhead/General and Administrative Expenditures Not Itemized (note 26)	1,649,000	925,000
Vacation and Holidays (note 17)	571,000	298,000
Improvements, Space and Environment (note 27)	384,000	151,000
Federal Taxes Paid (note 26)	349,000	272,000
Health and Life Insurance (note 19)	201,000	96,000
Sick Leave (note 17)	127,000	53,000
State Taxes Paid (note 26)	100,000	62,000
Local Taxes Paid (note 26)	63,000	71,000
Food Services (note 21)	51,000	24,000
Child Care (note 27)	11,000	5,000
Company School and Tuition Reimbursement (note 28)	2,000	1,000
Miscellaneous and Public Offering of Stock (note 26)	154,000	23,000
Interest Payments (note 26)	171,000	107,000
Income Foregone on Paid-In Capital (note 29)	276,000	276,000
Total	$15,104,000	$ 6,973,000
2. To Staff		
Opportunity Costs of Total Time Worked (note 30)	$ 6,455,000	$ 3,571,000
Absence of Retirement Income Plan (note 31)	58,000	43,000
Layoffs and Involuntary Terminations (note 32)	31,000	15,000
Inequality of Opportunity (note 33)	11,000	26,000
Uncompensated Losses Through Theft (note 34)	1,000	1,000
Total	$ 6,556,000	$ 3,656,000
3. To Clients/General Public		
Cost of Contracted Work	$15,224,000	$ 6,995,000
Federal Services Consumed (note 11)	195,000	129,000
State Services Consumed (note 11)	80,000	46,000
Environmental Resources Used Through Pollution (note 12)		
Electricity (note 13)	35,000	31,000
Commuting (note 14)	17,000	10,000
Paper (note 15)	6,000	4,000
Total	$15,557,000	$ 7,215,000
4. To Community		
Local Services Consumed (note 11)	$ 32,000	$ 22,000
Total	$ 32,000	$ 22,000

Net Income		1973	1972
1. To Company/Stockholders: Financial		$ 396,000	$ 298,000
	Social (note 41)	89,000	(34,000)
2. To Staff (note 42)		714,000	(28,000)
3. To Clients/General Public		1,553,000	1,189,000
4. To Community (note 43)		99,000	111,000
Total Net Social Income		$ 2,455,000	$ 1,238,000
Total Net Social and Financial Income Generated by Company Operations		$ 2,851,000	$ 1,536,000

Note 18

Career advancement is expressed as the added earning power from salary increases for merit or promotion. The annualized salary increases in 1973 amounted to $602,000, as compared to $332,000 in 1972; the average increases per employee were $1,262 in 1973 and $1,456 in 1972.

Note 19

The value of health and life insurance provided by the company is assumed to be equal to the cost of purchasing comparable coverage individually by full-time staff. For each dollar spent, the company generates $1.80 of benefits per employee. Benefits per employee amount to $757 in 1973 and $614 in 1972.

Note 20

The company offers free parking to employees at all its locations. This constitutes an "invisible income" to staff, corresponding to the savings in terms of parking costs over alternative locations. Free parking privileges are assumed to be worth $30 per month. Benefits per employee have remained virtually unchanged (1973: $260, 1972: $259).

Note 21

The company subsidizes the operation of food services on its premises, in the interest of work efficiency and staff congeniality, saving the time and public resources otherwise needed to commute to other eating facilities. The average value of subsidies per employee has increased slightly from $105 in 1972 to $107 in 1973.

Note 22

The company provides its employees with floor space exceeding industry standards (average of 90 square feet/employee). The value of actual square footage in excess of industry standards has been estimated at $6.50/square foot. As a result of company employment growth, the average benefit per employee has decreased from $111 in 1972 to $33 in 1973.

Note 23

The company subsidizes the operation of a day care center on its premises, in the interest of working parents of pre-school children. The average value of subsidies per employee has remained stable (approximately $22.50).

Note 24

The Abt Associates Employees Federal Credit Union provides benefits to staff in the form of lower interest rates for loans and higher dividends for deposits than commercially available. The value of these benefits has been estimated at $8,000 for 1973 and $4,000 for 1972. The average benefit per employee has been approximately $18 for both years.

Note 25

The staff survey indicates that company employees spend an average 20% of their time in training, decreasing from a high of 25% during the first year to about 15% by the fourth year.

This percentage has been applied to total salaries for time worked to delineate training investment.

Note 26
Figures have been taken from the financial income statement, adjusted for itemized expenditures.

Note 27
Actual expenditures on building maintenance.

Note 28
The company encourages employees to take courses at local universities related to the work performed by offering a 50% tuition subsidy to qualified staff.

Note 29
"Income Foregone on Paid-In Capital" has been estimated as the opportunity cost to stockholders of having paid-in capital tied up in the company. The opportunity cost is equivalent to the expected return on an investment in a medium-risk venture, estimated at 12%.

Note 30
The opportunity cost of work to staff is equivalent to salaries received for regular working hours plus the value of overtime worked but not paid.

Note 31
Currently, the company does not offer retirement income to its employees. In the staff survey conducted in January 1974, 73% of the respondents indicated a strong interest in a retirement income plan. Its absence therefore constitutes an opportunity cost to staff in terms of benefits routinely available in other employment. The average annual cost of purchasing a standard retirement income plan outside the company has been estimated at $1,935. For 1973, 30 employees were eligible for a standard retirement income plan, compared to 22 in 1972.

Note 32
The cost of layoffs and involuntary terminations to staff is estimated to be one month's salary to each terminee, based on the assumption that the mean time to next employment is one month. The average cost per employee has decreased slightly from $66 in 1972 to $65 in 1973, as has the percentage of employees involuntarily terminated from 6.9 to 6.5 percent.

Note 33
Inequality of opportunity is defined in terms of the costs to individuals of the income loss equal to the difference between what the minority or female individual earns and what a non-minority or male individual doing the same job with the same qualifications earns. The social cost of inequality of opportunity was incurred entirely by women, as a result of a strongly discriminatory labor market that company policy was not completely able to overcome within national wage-price constraints. However, company efforts in 1973 led to an absolute decrease in the total cost of the inequality of opportunity from $26,000 in 1972 to $11,000 in 1973, corresponding to a decrease in the per-employee cost from $114 in 1972 to $23 in 1973.

Note 34
Prior to the establishment of security measures, employees have suffered losses through theft of personal property. In some instances, employees were not reimbursed for such losses. This cost per employee was reduced by half in 1973.

Note 35
A survey of clients indicated that the evaluation of contract value at cost understates the true value to the general public of the work performed by the company. Clients estimated that the actual value of contracts exceeded cost by a factor of up to nine. However, the response rate for this survey was insufficient for reliable statistical estimates of the actual value of

contracts to clients or the general public. The figures reported indicate a slight increase in contact value per employee ($32,000 in 1973 vs. $31,000 in 1972).

Note 36

The 1972 social audit showed an average overtime for professional staff of 33% over regular working hours. Partially in response to that finding, reduction of excessive overtime became company policy. The 1973 staff survey showed a decrease of overtime to 20% of regular working hours. The monetary value of unpaid overtime per employee decreased from $3,873 in 1972 to $2,214 in 1973. The total value of overtime constitutes an "invisible subsidy" of clients an the general public by company staff.

Note 37

The expansion of the company has created 218 additional jobs. The tax value of these additional jobs for the federal and state governments has been computed as 20% of the average starting salary of $12,000, weighted by the proportion of a full year that these (net) new jobs have been effective,

Note 38

Publications by company staff constitute additions to the stock of social knowledge. These contributions are evaluated at the average market rate for similar publications. The average value per employee increased from $79 in 1972 to $113 in 1973, reflecting an increase of publications from one for every fourth employee to one for every third employee.

Note 39

The local tax worth of net jobs created has been computed as the additional revenue to the community in terms of sales taxes, excise taxes on cars, and real estate taxes for private homes.

Note 40

The company contributed to aesthetic improvements of the environment through landscaping ($8,000 in 1973) and the paving over of a dirt lot for a parking lot (rental value of 1973: $10,000). These improvements constitute a benefit to the community.

Note 41

The 1972 net social loss to the company/stockholders results from the relatively high opportunity cost of paid-in capital which was not entirely offset by social contributions to the operations of the company.

Note 42

The change from a net social loss to staff in 1972 ($123 per employee to a social gain in 1973 ($1,497 per employee) is largely a result of the company's success in decreasing the extent of overtime worked but not paid. In addition, this change reflects improvements in the social efforts by the company.

Note 43

The slight decrease in the net social income to the community can be attributed to the fact that physical improvements (new building, landscaping) following the employment expansion of the company have begun late in 1973 and will therefore become effective in 1974 only, while the social costs of increased use of public services from the expanded staff have been immediate.

chapter nine.

Accounting: A Multiple Paradigm Science

Not long ago, a contempt for accounting existed within and without the university. In an address to the American Association of University Instructors in Accounting on December 29, 1923, Henry Rand Hatfield described the situation as follows:

> I am sure that all of us who teach accounting in the universities suffer from the implied contempt of our colleagues, who look upon accounting as an intruder, a Saul among the prophets, a pariah whose very presence detracts somewhat from the sanctity of the academic halls. It is true that we ourselves speak of the science of accounts, or of the art of accounting, even of the philosophy of accounts. But accounting is, alas, only a pseudo-science unrecognized by J. McKeen Cattel: its products are displayed neither in the salon nor in the national academy; one finds it discussed by neither realist, idealist nor phenomenalist. The humanists look down upon us as beings who dabble in the sordid figures of dollars and cents instead of toying with infinities and searching for the elusive soul of things; the scientists and technologists despise us as able only to record rather than to perform deeds.[1]

Fortunately, the situation has changed. The various surveys of research findings are evidence of the academic status of accounting.[2] Accounting research has used different methodologies and different theories to examine all possible issues of interest to the field. Initially, in the early 1970s, such a priori research was criticized as being of doubtful value or theoretically deficient.[3] Gonedes and Dopuch also contended in 1970 that an a priori model that justifies the superiority of a set of accounting procedures is not possible. Fortunately for this research, Wells, in a seminal article in 1976, defended a priori research as a necessary step in a revolution in accounting thought.

Wells proceeded to show that events in accounting seem to follow the pattern of successful revolution described by Kuhn, and thus the discipline of accounting is emerging from a state of crisis. Briefly, as discussed in Chapter 2, Kuhn's thesis is that a science is at any given point dominated by a specific paradigm. Anomalies and a crisis stage may follow, ending in a revolution in which the

---

[1]Henry Rand Hatfield, "A Historical Defense of Bookkeeping," *The Journal of Accountancy* (April 1924), pp. 241–53. Also reprinted in *Studies in Accounting Theory*, ed. W. T. Baxter and S. Davidson (Homewood, Ill.: Richard D. Irwin, 1962).

[2]N. Dopuch and L. Revsine, eds., *Accounting Research 1960–1970: A Critical Evaluation*, Monograph 7 (Urbana, Ill.: Center for Internation Education and Research in Accounting, University of Illinois, 1973); A. R. Abdel-Khalik and T. F. Keller, eds., *The Impact of Accounting Research on Practice and Disclosure* (Durham, N. C.: Duke University Press, 1978); N. Gonedes and N. Dopuch, "Capital Market Equilibrium, Information Production and Selecting Accounting Techniques: Theoretical Framework and Review of Empirical Work," *Studies On Financial Accounting Objectives: 1974*, Supplement to vol. 12 *Journal of Accounting Research*, pp. 48–129.

[3]Carl L. Nelson, "A Priori Research in Accounting," in *Accounting Research 1960–1970: A Critical Evaluation*, Monograph 7, ed. Dopuch and Revsine (Urbana, Ill.: Center for International Education and Research in Accounting, University of Illinois, 1973), pp. 3–18; N. Gonedes and N. Dopuch, "Capital Market Equilibrium, Information Production and Selecting Accounting Techniques: Theoretical Framework and Review of Empirical Work," p. 32; Thomas S. Kuhn, "The Structure of Scientific Revolutions," *International Encyclopedia of Unified Science*, 2nd enlarged Edition (Chicago: University of Chicago Press, 1970), pp. 10–15.

reigning paradigm is replaced by a new dominant paradigm. Central to Kuhn's idea is the definition of a paradigm. Assuming for the time being that such a definition is possible, the next step is to identify the paradigms in accounting. This step was taken by the American Accounting Association with its publication of *Statement on Accounting Theory and Theory Acceptance* (SOTATA).[4] The statement looks at developments in accounting thought from a "philosophy of science" perspective, that is, in terms of Kuhn's ideas of how progress occurs in science. It identifies three dominant theoretical approaches, namely (1) the "classical ('true income' and inductive)" approach, used both by the "normative deductionists" and the "chiefly, positive inductive writers," (2) the "decision–usefulness" approach, used by those who stress decision models and those who focus on decision makers (behavioral accounting and market level research), and (3) the "information economics" approach, with a distinction made between the "single individual case" and the "multi-individual case." One of the arguments made in the statement, which is of great relevance to this study, is that the increasing varieties of accounting theories and approaches suggest the existence of several competing paradigms. The statement even suggests what these competing paradigms might be.

For example, one paradigm, which could be labeled the "anthropological approach" specifies the professional practices of accountants as the empirical domain of accounting. Following this paradigm, accounting theory is formulated as a rationalization of, and by drawing inferences from, extant accounting practices. Another paradigm rests largely upon the behavior of stock markets to provide the empirical domain over which accounting theory is constructed and applied. Still another general view of accounting specifies the decision processes of individuals and/or extant decision theories as the empirical domain of accounting theory. This tripartite categorization can be further expanded to incorporate both the ideal income approach and the information economics approach, each of which suggests a somewhat unique empirical domain of accounting.[5]

What appears is that, first, if Kuhn's ideas as applied to accounting by Wells are accepted, accounting has reached a stage of development that qualifies it as a science, and second, if SOTATA's suggestions are accepted, accounting is multiple paradigm science. Two issues emerge from the acceptance of both Wells's and SOTATA's suggestions. First, an adequate definition of a paradigm is needed that avoids the confusion between theories and paradigms by considering theories as mere components of paradigms and allows differentiation between competing paradigms. The confusion between theories and paradigms and the problem of differentiation between competing paradigms are two of the limitations of Wells's and SOTATA's suggestions.[6] Second, accounting, like most sciences, lacks a

[4]American Accounting Association, Committee on Concepts and Standards for External Financial Reports, *Statement on Accounting Theory and Theory Acceptance* (Sarasota, Fla.: AAA, 1977).

[5]*Ibid.*, p. 47.

[6]K. V. Peasnell, "Statement of Accounting Theory and Theory Acceptance: A Review Article," *Accounting and Business Research* (Summer 1978), pp. 217–25; Nils H. Hakansson, "Where We Are in Accounting: A Review of 'Statement on Accounting Theory and Theory Acceptance,'" *The Accounting Review* (July 1978), pp. 717–25; Paul Danos, "A Revolution in Accounting Thought? A Comment," *The Accounting Review* (July 1977), pp. 746–47.

single comprehensive paradigm, and the competing paradigms in accounting should be properly identified and delineated for a proper conception of the state of accounting.

The Notion of a Paradigm

Central to Kuhn's ideas of how science progresses is the notion of a **paradigm**. Before the publication of Kuhn's "Structure of Scientific Revolutions," "paradigm" was primarily a grammatical term, as Kuhn himself admits, that was used for

> an accepted model or pattern . . . for example, *"amo, amas, amat,"* is a paradigm because it displays the pattern to be used in conjugating a large number of latin verbs, e.g., in producing *"laudo, laudas, laudat."*[7]

Unfortunately, Kuhn uses the term in a different and inconsistent manner.[8] In the first edition of his book, he says that "paradigm" encompasses "the entire constellation of beliefs, values, techniques, and so on shared by members of a given community."[9] In the application to accounting, Wells uses paradigm as a disciplinary matrix. In SOTATA, paradigms were defined as conceptual and instrumental frameworks that "provide models from which spring particular coherent traditions of scientific research." In fact, Masterman identifies twenty-one different senses in which Kuhn uses the term "paradigm."[10] As we mentioned in Chapter Two, Kuhn responded to these criticisms with a narrow definition of paradigm in an epilogue to his second edition, as follows:

> The concrete puzzle solutions which when employed as models of examples, can replace explicit rules as a basis for the solution of the remaining puzzles of normal science.[11]

Although this definition is narrow, it is still vague, and it does not alleviate the major criticisms directed toward Kuhn's change from the view that paradigms rise and fall as a result of political factors to the view that one paradigm wins over another for good reasons, including "accuracy, scope, simplicity, fruitfulness and the like."[12] The first view is eloquently explained by Ritzer as follows:

> One paradigm wins out over another because its supporters have more *power* than those who support competing paradigms and *not* necessarily because their paradigm is "better" than its competitors. For example, the paradigm whose supporters control the most important journals in a field

---

[7]Kuhn, "The Structure of Scientific Revolutions," p. 23.

[8]Dudley Shapere, "The Structure of Scientific Revolutions" (Review), *Philosophical Review*, 73 (1964), 383–94.

[9]Kuhn, "The Structure of Scientific Revolutions," p. 175.

[10]Margaret Masterman, "The Nature of a Paradigm," in *Criticism and the Growth of Knowledge*, ed. Imre Lakatos and Alan Musgrave (Cambridge: Cambridge University Press, 1970).

[11]Kuhn, "The Structure of Scientific Revolutions," p. 105.

[12]Thomas Kuhn, "Reflections on My Critics," in *Criticism and the Growth of Knowledge*, ed. Imre Lakatos and Alan Musgrave (Cambridge: Cambridge University Press, 1970), pp. 231–78.

and thereby determine what will be published is more likely to gain preeminence than paradigms whose adherents lack access to prestigious outlets for their work. Similarly, positions of leadership in a field are likely to be given to supporters of the dominant paradigm and this gives them a platform to enunciate their position with a significant amount of legitimacy. Supporters of paradigms that are seeking to gain hegemony within a field are obviously at a disadvantage since they lack the kinds of power outlined above. Nevertheless they can, by waging a political battle of their own, overthrow a dominant paradigm and gain that position for themselves.[13]

Philipps argued that the reasons advanced in the second view are in fact paradigm dependent.[14] Ritzer agreed with Philipps that the emergence of a paradigm is essentially a political phenomenon and offered the following definition of a paradigm:

A paradigm is a fundamental image of the subject matter witin a science. It serves to define what should be studied, what questions should be asked, how they should be asked, and what rules should be followed in interpreting the answer obtained. The paradigm is the broadest unit of consensus within a science and serves to differentiate one scientific community (or subcommunity) from another. It subsumes, defines and interrelates the exemplars, theories, methods, and instruments that exist within it.[15]

Central to Ritzer's definition is that a paradigm has the following four basic components:

1. An **exemplar,** defined as "a piece of work that stands as a model for those who work within the paradigm";
2. An **image of the subject matter;**
3. **Theories;**
4. **Methods** and instruments.

The paradigm concept, as defined by Ritzer, may be used to analyze scientific communites or subcommunities in accounting. As stated earlier, accounting lacks a single comprehensive paradigm and is instead a multiple paradigm science. Each of accounting's paradigms is striving for acceptance and even domination within the discipline. We shall use the paradigm concept, as defined by Ritzer, to identify and delineate the competing paradigms in accounting. In agreement with SOTATA's suggestions, we shall consider the basic accounting paradigms to be the following:

1. The anthropological–inductive paradigm
2. The true income–deductive paradigm
3. The decision usefulness–decision model paradigm.
4. The decision usefulness–aggregate market behavior paradigm

---

[13]George Ritzer, "Sociology: A Multiple Paradigm Science," *The American Sociologist* (August 1975), pp. 15–17.

[14]D. Philipps, "Paradigms, Falsification and Sociology," *Acta Sociologica,* 16 (1973), 13–31.

[15]Ritzer, "Sociology: A Multiple Paradigm Science," p. 157.

5. The decision usefulness–decision maker–individual user paradigm
6. The information economics paradigm

We shall consider each of these paradigms in the remainder of this chapter.

The Anthropoligical–Inductive Paradigm

Exemplars

Several studies qualify as exemplars of the anthropological–inductive paradigm, namely the works by Hatfield, Gilman, Littleton, Paton and Littleton, and Ijiri.[16] The authors of these studies share a concern for a descriptive–inductive approach to the construction of an accounting theory and a belief in the value of extant accounting practices. Ijiri, for example, views accounting as concerned primarily with the functioning of accountability relationships among interested parties. The objective measurement is viewed as the measurement of the economic performance of the firm. On the basis of discussions of research methodology and the role of logic in theory construction and policy formulation in accounting, Ijiri presents accountability as a descriptive theory of accounting:

> What we are emphasizing here is that current accounting practice can be better interpreted if we view accountability as the underlying goal. We are also suggesting that unless accounting is viewed in this manner, much of the current practice would appear to be inconsistent and irrational.[17]

Ijiri also presents an axiomatic model of existing accounting practice, evaluating the significance of historical cost in terms of accountability and decision making in defense of his paradigm against the criticisms of current-cost and current-value advocates.

Littleton arrived at accounting principles from observations of accounting practices. Such inductively derived principles were supported by the test of experience and incorporated the goals implicit in practice. For example, he states:

> Teachers of bookkeeping and later of accounting and auditing found it necessary to supplement the accumulated rules and descriptions of procedure by explanations and justifications. This was done in order that study should be something more than the memorizing of rules. Hence it

---

[16]H. R. Hatfield, *Accounting* (New York: D. Appleton & Company, 1927); S. Gilman, *Accounting Concepts of Profit* (New York: The Ronald Press, 1939); A. C. Littleton, *Structure of Accounting Theory*, Monograph No. 5 (Sarasota, Fla.: AAA, 1953); W. A. Paton and A. C. Littleton, *An Introduction to Corporate Accounting Standards*, Monograph No. 3 (Sarasota, Fla.: AAA, 1940); and Y. Ijiri, "Theory of Accounting Measurement," *Studies in Accounting Research, No. 10* (Sarasota, Fla.: AAA, 1975).

[17]*Ibid.*, p. 37.

is appropriate to say that both the methods of practice and the explanations of theory were inductively derived out of experience.[18]

Good theory is practice-created and moreover is practice conditioning. Finally, whenever evidence of integration among accounting ideas is found, it will strengthen the conviction that accounting doctrine contains the possibility of being built into a system of coordinated explanations and justifications of what accounting is and what it can become.[19]

Two other studies qualify as exemplars—the articles by Gordon and by Watts and Zimmerman.[20] Both argue that management will select the accounting rule that will tend to smooth income and the rate of growth in income. Gordon theorized on income smoothing as follows:

Proposition 1. The criterion a corporate management uses in selecting among accounting principles is the maximization of its utility or welfare. . . .

Proposition 2. The utility of a management increases with (1) its job security, with (2) the level and rate of growth in the management's income, and with (3) the level and rate of growth in the corporation's size. . . .

Proposition 3. The achievement of the management goals stated in Proposition 2 is dependent in part on the satisfaction of stockholders with the corporation's performance. That is, other things the same, the happier the stockholders the greater the job security, income, etc. of the management. . . .

Proposition 4. Stockholders' satisfaction with a corporation increases with the average rate of growth in the corporation's income (or the average rate of return on its capital) and the stability of its income. This proposition is as readily verified as Proposition 2.

Theorem. Given that the above four propositions are accepted or found to be true, it follows that a management would within the limits of its power, i.e., the latitude allowed by accounting rules, (1) smooth reported income, and (2) smooth the rate of growth in income. By smooth the rate of growth in income we mean the following: If the rate of growth is high, accounting practices which reduce it should be adopted and vice versa.[21]

Several empirical tests in the income smoothing literature left Gordon's model unconfirmed. Also, his assumptions that shareholder satisfaction is solely a positive function of income and that increases in stock prices always follow increases in accounting income have been seriously contested. To avoid the pit-

[18]Littleton, *Structure of Accounting Theory*, p. 185.

[19]*Ibid.*, p. 31.

[20]R. L. Watts and J. L. Zimmerman, "Toward a Positive Theory of the Determination of Accounting Standards," *The Accounting Review* (January 1968), pp. 112–34; M. J. Gordon, "Postulates, Principles and Research in Accounting," *The Accounting Review* (April 1964), pp. 251–63.

[21]Gordon, "Postulates, Principles and Research in Accounting," pp. 261–62.

falls that may exist in Gordon's model, Watts and Zimmerman attempted to provide a positive theory of accounting by exploring the factors influencing management's attitudes on accounting standards. They assumed at the outset that management's utility is a positive function of the expected compensation in future periods and a negative function of the dispersion of future compensation. Their analysis shows that the choice of accounting standards can affect a firm's cash flow through taxes, regulation, political costs, information production costs, and management compensation plans:

> The first four factors increase managerial wealth by increasing the cash flows and, hence share price. The last factor can increase managerial wealth by altering the terms of the incentive compensation.[22]

Image of the Subject Matter

To those who adopt the anthropological–inductive paradigm, the basic subject matter is existing accounting practices and managements' attitudes toward those practices. Proponents of this view argue in general that either techniques may be derived and justified on the basis of their tested use or that management plays a central role in determining the techniques. Consequently, the objective of accounting research associated with the anthropological–inductive paradigm is to understand, explain, and predict existing accounting practices. For example, Ijiri viewed the mission of the approach as follows:

> This type of inductive reasoning to derive goals implicit in the behavior of an existing system is not intended to be pro-establishment to promote the maintenance of the status quo. The purpose of such exercise is to highlight where changes are most needed and where they are feasible. Changes suggested as a result of such a study have a much better chance of being actually implemented.[23]

Theories

Two kinds of theories may be considered to be part of the anthropological–inductive paradigm. The first kind deals with all the attempts made to explain and justify existing accounting practices: namely, the historical cost approach to asset valuation, conventional cost allocation techniques, bookkeeping techniques, and so on. The second kind of theory deals with attempts to explain management's role in the determination of techniques and includes the income smoothing hypothesis and the beginnings of a positive theory of accounting.

Methods

Those who accept the anthropological–inductive paradigm tend to use two kinds of techniques. Those interested in explaining and justifying existing accounting practices rely either on analytical techniques or survey research and observational methods. Those primarily interested in explaining management's role in the determination of techniques rely basically on empirical techniques.

---

[22]Watts and Zimmerman, "Toward a Positive Theory of the Determination of Accounting Standards," p. 14.

[23]Ijiri, *Theory of Accounting Measurement*, p. 28.

The True Income–Deductive Paradigm

Exemplars

Studies that qualify as exemplars of the true income–deductive paradigm are the works by Paton, Canning, Sweeney, MacNeal, Alexander, Edwards and Bell, Moonitz, and Sprouse and Moonitz.[24] These authors share a concern for a normative–deductive approach to the construction of an accounting theory and, with the exception of Alexander, a belief that, ideally, income measured using a single valuation base would meet the needs of all users. They are also in complete agreement that current price information is most useful to users making economic decisions. Paton, for example, presented a restatement of the theory of accounting consistent with the conditions and needs of the business enterprise as a distinct entity or personality in refutation of the propietary theory of accounts view. In his view, accounting plays a significant and relevant role in the firm and in society:

> If the tendencies of the economic process as evidenced in market prices are to be reflected rationally in the decisions of business managers, efficient machinery for the recording and interpreting of such statistics must be available; and a sound accounting scheme represents an essential part of such a mechanism. . . .

> To put the matter in very general terms, accounting, in so far as it contributes to render effective the control of the price system in its direction of economic activity, contributes to general productive efficiency, and has a clear-cut social significance, a value to the industrial community as a whole.[25]

Paton's theory of the accounting system consisted of a logical discussion and justification of the accounting structure in terms of the fundamental classes of accounts, the proprietorship and liabilities, the property and equity accounts, the types of transactions, the expense and revenue and supplementary accounts, the account classification, the periodic analysis, and the concepts of debit and credit. He states:

---

[24]W. A. Paton, *Accounting Theory* (New York: The Ronald Press, 1922); J. B. Canning, *The Economics of Accountancy* (New York: The Ronald Press, 1929); H. W. Sweeney, *Stabilized Accounting* (New York: Harper & Brothers, 1936); K. MacNeal, *Truth in Accounting* (Philadelphia: University of Pennsylvania Press, 1939); S. S. Alexander, "Income Measurement in a Dynamic Economy," *Five Monographs on Business Income* (New York: The Study Group on Business Income, The American Institute of (Certified Public) Accountants, 1950). See also: S. S. Alexander, "Income Measurement in a Dynamic Economy," revised by D. Solomons, *Studies in Accounting Theory*, ed. W. T. Baxter and S. Davidson (Homewood, Ill.: Richard D. Irwin, 1962); E. O Edwards and P. W. Bell, *The Theory and Measurement of Business Income* (Berkeley: University of California Press, 1961); M. Moonitz, "The Basic Postulates of Accounting," *Accounting Research Study No. 1* (New York: AICPA, 1961); R. T. Sprouse and M. Moonitz, "A Tentative Set of Broad Accounting Principles for Business Enterprises," *Accounting Research Study No. 3* (New York: AICPA, 1962).

[25]Paton, *Accounting Theory*, p. 8.

The liberal view that, ideally, all bona fide value changes in either direction, from whatever cause, should be reflected in the accounts has been adopted without argument. To show that all possible types of situations and transactions can be handled in a rational manner in accordance with the principles enunciated is a chief reason for this attitude.[26]

Image of the Subject Matter

To those who adopt the true income–deductive paradigm, the basic subject matter is first, the construction of an accounting theory on the basis of a logical and normative reasoning and conceptual rigor, and second, an ideal income concept based on other than historical cost. MacNeal states the argument for an ideal income concept as follows:

> There is one correct definition of profits in an accounting sense. A profit is an increase in net wealth. A loss is a decrease in net welath. This is an economist's definition. It is terse, obvious, and mathematically demonstrable.[27]

Alexander, who argues also for an ideal income concept, states:

> We must find out whether economic income is an ideal from which accounting income differs only to the degree that the ideal is practically unattainable, or whether economic income is inappropriate even if it could conveniently be measured.[28]

Theories

The theories that emerged from the true income–deductive paradigm presented alternatives to the historical accounting system. In general, the following five theories or schools of thought may be identified:[29]

1. Price-level adjusted (or current purchasing power) accounting.[30]
2. Replacement cost accounting.[31]
3. Deprival value accounting.[32]

---

[26]*Ibid.*, pp. 8–9.

[27]MacNeal, *Truth in Accounting*, p. 295.

[28]Alexander, "Income Measurement in a Dynamic Economy," p. 159.

[29]M. C. Wells, "A Revolution in Accounting Thought," *The Accounting Review* (July 1976), pp. 471–82.

[30]Ralph Coughenour Jones, *The Effects of Price Level Changes* (Sarasota, Fla.: AAA, 1956); Perry Mason, *Price Level Changes and Financial Statements* (Sarasota, Fla.: AAA 1971).

[31]Edgar O. Edwards and Philipe W. Bell, *The Theory and Measurement of Business Income* (Berkeley: University of California Press, 1961); R. L. Mathews, "Price-Level Accounting and Useless Information," *Journal of Accounting Research* (Spring 1965), pp. 133–55; R. S. Gynther, *Accounting for Price-Level Changes: Theory and Procedures* (New York: Pergamon, 1966); Lawrence Revsine, *Replacement Cost Accounting* (Englewood Cliffs, N.J.: Prentice-Hall, 1973).

[32]W. T. Baxter, "Accounting Values: Sale Price Versus Replacement Cost," *Journal of Accounting Research* (Autumn 1967), pp. 208–14; F. K. Wright, "A Theory of Financial Accounting," *Journal of Business Finance* (Autumn 1970), pp. 51–69; Edward Stamp, "Income and Value Determination and Changing Price Levels: An Essay Towards a Theory," *The Accountants' Magazine* (June 1971), pp. 277–92; Geoffrey Whittington, "Asset Valuation, Income Measurement and Accounting Income," *Accounting and Business Research* (Spring 1974), pp. 96–101.

4. Continuously contemporary (net realizable value) accounting.[33]
5. Present value accounting.[34]

Each of these theories presents alternative methods of asset valuation and income determination alleged to overcome the defects of the historical cost system.

Methods

Those who accept the true income–deductive paradigm generally use analytical reasoning to justify the construction of an accounting theory or to argue the advantages of a particular asset valuation/income determination model other than historical cost accounting. These authors generally proceed from objectives and postulates about the environment to specific methods.

The Decision Usefulness–
Decision Model Paradigm

Exemplars

Chambers's "Blueprint" article was among the first to point to the decision usefulness–decision model paradigm:

> It is therefore a corollary of the assumption of rational management that there shall be an information-providing system; such a system is required both as a basis for decisions and as a basis for reviewing the consequences of decisions. . . . A formal information-providing system would conform with two general propositions.
>
> The first is a condition of all logical discourse. The system should be logically consistent; no rule or process can be permitted which is contrary to any other rule or process. . . . The second proposition arises from the use of accounting statements as a basis for making decisions of practical consequence. The information yielded by any such system should be relevant to the kinds of decision the making of which it is expected to facilitate.[35]

Chambers did not pursue this view of the decision usefulness–decision model. He preferred to base an accounting theory on the usefulness of "current cash equivalents," rather than on the decision models of specific user groups. Similarly, May[36] offered a list of uses of financial accounts without explicitly using the decision model approach to formulate an accounting theory. According to May, financial accounts are used as:

---

[33]R. J. Chambers, *Accounting, Evaluation and Economic Behavior* (Englewood Cliffs, N.J.: Prentice-Hall, 1966); Robert R. Sterling, "On Theory Construction and Verification," *The Accounting Review* (January 1971), pp. 12–29.

[34]David Solomons, "Economic and Accounting Concepts of Income," *The Accounting Review* (July 1961), pp. 374–83; Kenneth W. Lemke, "Asset Valuation and Income Theory," *The Accounting Review* (January 1966), pp. 33–41.

[35]R. J. Chambers, "Blueprint for a Theory of Accounting," *Accounting Research* (January, 1955), pp. 21–22.

[36]G. O. May, *Financial Accounting* (New York: Macmillan, 1943), p. 19.

1. A report of stewardship
2. A basis for fiscal policy
3. A criterion of the legality of dividends
4. A guide to wise dividend action
5. A basis for the granting of credit
6. Information for prospective investors
7. A guide to the value of investments already made
8. An aid to government supervision
9. A basis for price or rate regulation
10. A basis for taxation

In fact, the article by Sterling and the one by Beaver, Kennelly, and Voss[37] may be considered the true exemplars of the decision usefulness–decision model paradigm. First, Beaver et al. examined the origin, relationship to the facilitation of decision making, and the potential difficulties associated with the implementation of the predictive ability criterion. According to this criterion, alternative methods of accounting measurement are evaluated in terms of their ability to predict economic events. According to Beaver et al.:

> The measure with the greatest predictive power with respect to a given event is considered to be the "best" method for that particular purpose.[38]

The predictive ability criterion is presented as a purposive criterion in the sense that accounting data ought to be evaluated in terms of their purposes or use, which are generally accepted in accounting to be the facilitation of decision making. The predictive ability criterion is assumed to be relevant even with a low specification of the decision model. According to Beaver et al.:

> Because prediction is an inherent part of the decision process, knowledge of the predictive ability of alternative measures is a prerequisite to the use of the decision-making criterion. At the same time, it permits tentative conclusions regarding alternative measurements, subject to subsequent confirmation when the decision models eventually become specified. The use of predictive ability as a purposive criterion is more than merely consistent with accounting's decision-making orientation. It can provide a body of research that will bring accounting closer to its goal of evaluation in terms of a decision-making criterion.[39]

Second, Sterling examined the development of criteria by which the various measures of wealth and income are to be judged. Given the conflicting viewpoints about the objective of accounting reports, usefulness was chosen as the overriding criterion. Sterling emphasizes the importance of usefulness over such requirements of a measurement method as objectivity and verifiability.[40]

Because of the diversity of the decision makers and the inherent economic and physical impossibility of providing all the information that users want, Ster-

---

[37]R. R. Sterling, "Decision Oriented Financial Accounting," *Accounting and Business Research* (Summer 1972), pp. 198–208; W. H. Beaver, J. W. Kennelly, and W. M. Voss, "Predictive Ability as a Criterion for the Evaluation of Accounting Data," *The Accounting Review* (October 1968), pp. 675–83.

[38]Beaver et al., "Predictive Ability," p. 675.

[39]*Ibid.*, p. 680.

[40]Sterling, "Decision Oriented Financial Accounting," p. 198.

ling opted for usefulness as relevant to decision models. He states:

> The basis for selection that I prefer is to supply information for rational decision models. The modifier "rational" is defined to mean those decision models that are most likely to allow decision makers to achieve their goals.[41]

In summary, an accounting system should be designed to provide relevant information to rational decision models. The accounting system cannot supply all the information desired by all decision makers and therefore, we must decide to exclude some kinds of information and to include other kinds. Restricting the decision models to rational ones permits the exclusion of a raft of data based upon the whims of decision makers. It permits us to concentrate on those models that have been demonstrated to be effective in achieving the decision makers' goals.[42]

Image of the Subject Matter

To those who adopt the decision usefulness–decision model paradigm, the basic subject matter is the usefulness of accounting information to decision models. Information relevant to a decision model or criterion is determined and then implemented by choosing the best accounting alternative. Usefulness to a decision model is equated with relevance to a decision model. For example, Sterling states:

> If a property is specified by a decision model, then a measure of that property is relevant (to that decision model). If a property is not specified by a decision model, then a measure of that property is irrelevant (to that decision model).[43]

Theories

Two kinds of theories may be included within the decision usefulness–decision model paradigm. The first kind deals with the different kinds of decision models associated with business decision making, for example, EOQ, PERT, linear programming, capital budgeting, buy versus lease, make or buy, and so on. The information requirements for most of these decision models are fairly well specified. The second kind deals with the different economic events that may affect a going concern, such as bankruptcy, takeover, merger, and bond ratings. Theories linking accounting information to these events are still lacking. Developing such theories is the primary objective of those working within the decision usefulness–decision model paradigm.

Methods

Those who accept the decision usefulness–decision model paradigm tend to rely on empirical techniques to determine the predictive ability of selected items of information. The general approach has been to use discriminant analysis to classify firms in one of several a priori groupings, dependent upon the firms' individual financial characteristics.

---

[41]*Ibid.*, p. 199.

[42]*Ibid.*, p. 201.

[43]*Ibid.*, p. 199.

The Decision Usefulness–
Decision Maker–Aggregate
Market Behavior Paradigm

Exemplars

The exemplars for the aggregate market paradigm are the papers by Gonedes[44] and by Gonedes and Dopuch.[45] In his pioneering paper, Gonedes extended the interest in decision usefulness from the individual user response to the aggregate market response. Arguing that the market reactions (for example, anticipatory price reactions) to accounting numbers should govern the evaluation of these numbers' informational content and of the procedures used to produce these numbers, Gonedes developed the aggregate market paradigm. It is implied that accounting produces numbers that have informational content as indicated by market reactions. To the counterarguments that, first, the procedures used to produce the numbers may have induced market inefficiencies and, second, that recipients may have been conditioned to react to accounting numbers, in a particular manner, Gonedes argued that if both cases were true, the opportunity to earn an abnormal profit by those possessing this knowledge will provide a basis for its demise within the context of an efficient capital market. In their award-winning paper, Gonedes and Dopuch provide a theoretical framework for the approach of assessing the desirability or effects or both of alternative accounting procedures. Their approach relies on the use of prices of (rates of returns on) firms' ownership shares. Gonedes and Dopuch concluded that the price domain analysis is sufficient for assessing the effects of alternative accounting procedures or regulations but not sufficient for assessing the desirability of alternative accounting procedures or regulations. This conclusion was based primarily on one market failure case in which information of a public good nature cannot be excluded from nonpurchasers (the free rider problem). In such a case, the prices of firms' ownership shares cannot be used to assess the desirability of alternative accounting procedures or regulations.

Other market failure possibilities that could have been used are the issues of adverse selection[46] and the effect of information on the completeness of markets and efficient risk-sharing arrangements.[47] Gonedes and Dopuch also note that some criticisms of work based upon capital market efficiency, such as by May and

---

[44]Nicholas J. Gonedes, "Efficient Capital Markets and External Accounting," *The Accounting Review* (January 1972), pp. 11–21.

[45]Nicholas J. Gonedes and N. Dopuch, "Capital Market Equilibrium, Information Production, and Selecting Accounting Techniques: Theoretical Framework and Review of Empirical Work," *Studies on Financial Accounting Objectives: 1974*, Supplement to vol. 12 *Journal of Accounting Research*, pp. 48–125.

[46]M. Spence, "Job Market Signalling," *Quarterly Journal of Economics* (August 1973), pp. 356–74.

[47]George A. Akerloff, "The Market for 'Lemons': Quality Uncertainty and the Market Mechanism," *Quarterly Journal of Economics* (August 1970), pp. 488–500; Richard Kihlstrom and M. Pauly, "The Role of Insurance in the Allocation of Risk," *American Economic Review* (May 1971), pp. 100–130; Roy Radner, "Competitive Equilibrium Under Uncertainty," *Econometrica* (January 1968), pp. 60–85; and "Existence of Equilibrium of Plans, Prices and Price Expectations in a Sequence of Markets," *Econometrica* (March 1972), pp. 71–82.

Sundem[48] and Abdel-Khalik,[49] treat remarks on assessing effects as if they were remarks on assessing desirability.

Another contemporary piece of work that may be seen as an exemplar for the aggregate market behavior paradigm is William Beaver's "The Behavior of Security Prices and Its Implications for Accounting Research (Methods)."[50] Beaver raises the importance of the relationship between accounting data and security behavior. He argues that it is inconceivable that optimal information systems for investors could be selected without a knowledge of how accounting data are impounded in prices because these prices determine wealth, and wealth affects the multiperiod investment decisions of individuals.

Image of the Subject Matter

To those who adopt the aggregate market behavior paradigm, the basic subject matter is the aggregate market response to accounting variables. These authors agree that in general the decision usefulness of accounting variables could be derived from the aggregate market behavior, or as presented by Gonedes and Dopuch, only the effects of alternative accounting procedures or speculations could be assessed from aggregate market behavior. The view of Gonedes and Dopuch is that the selection of the accounting information system is determined by aggregate market behavior.

Theories

The relationship between aggregate market behavior and accounting variables has been based on the theory of capital market efficiency. According to this theory, the market for securities is deemed efficient in the sense that (1) market prices "fully reflect" all publicly available information and, by implication, (2) market prices react instantaneously and unbiasedly to new information. The theory implies that, on average, the abnormal return (return in excess of the equilibrium-expected return) to be earned from using a set of extant information in any trading scheme is zero.[51] Thus, any change in the information set will automatically result in a new equilibrium.

Methods

Those who accept the aggregate market behavior paradigm tend to use a variant of either the two-parameter asset pricing model or the dividend (earnings) capitalization model when they do empirical research.

The capital asset pricing model asserts that there is a linear relationship between the systematic risk of an individual security and its expected return, such that the greater the ride the higher the expected return.[52] This model also

---

[48]Robert G. May and Gary L. Sundem, "Cost of Information and Security Prices: Market Association Tests for Accounting Policy Decisions," *The Accounting Review* (January 1973), pp. 80–90.

[49]A. Rashad Abdel-Khalik, "The Efficient Market Hypotheses and Accounting Data: A Point of View," *The Accounting Review* (October 1972), pp. 791–93.

[50]William H. Beaver, "The Behavior of Security Prices and Its Implications for Accounting Research (Methods)," in American Accounting Association, *Report of the Committee on Research Methodology in Accounting*, Supplement to vol. 47, *The Accounting Review* (1972), pp. 407–37.

[51]Eugene Fama, "The Behavior of Stock Market Prices," *Journal of Business* (January 1965), pp. 34–105.

states that the only variable that determines differential expected returns among securities is the systematic risk (that is, either its covariance with the market portfolio or its β, which is a measure of its responsiveness to the market factor). The capital asset pricing model is then an equilibrium pricing model. In general, accounting research has relied instead on the "market model," which specifies the stochastic process generating the individual security returns. Simply, the market model assumes that the return on each security is linearly related to the market return:

$$R_{it} = \alpha_i + \beta_i R'_{mt} + u_{it}$$

where

$$E(u_{it}) = 0$$
$$G(R'_{mt}, u_{it}) = 0$$
$$G(u_{it}, u_{jt}) = 0$$

R_{it} = return on security i in period t

R'_{mt} = aggregate rate of return on all securities in the market

u_{it} = stochastic portion of the individualistic factor expressing that portion of security i's return that varies independently of R'_{mt}

α_i, β_i = intercept and slope associated with the linear relationship.

The parameters $(u_{it}, \alpha_i,$ and $\beta_i)$ are estimated from a time series ordinary least square regression of the individual security returns against the market returns. The differences between the actual returns and the estimated returns are the abnormal returns. These abnormal returns are then aggregated and used to assess the effect(s) of information on capital market agents' behavior. One variant of this approach is to construct an Abnormal Performance Index (API). Used initially in the seminal Ball and Brown study,[53] API is computed in the following manner:

$$API_T = \frac{1}{N} \sum_{i=1}^{N} \prod_{t=1}^{T} (1 + u_{it})$$

where

T = number of time periods,

N = number of securities, and

u_{it} = same as above.

---

[52] William F. Sharpe, "A Simplified Model for Portfolio Analysis," *Management Science* (January 1963), pp. 377–92; John Lintner, "The Valuation of Risk Assets and the Selection of Risky Investments in Stock Portfolios and Capital Budgets," *Review of Economics and Statistics* (February 1965), pp. 13–37; and "Security Prices, Risk and Maximal Gains from Diversification," *Journal of Finance* (December 1965), pp. 587–616; Jan Mossin, "Equilibrium in a Capital Asset Market," *Econometrica* (October 1966), pp. 768–82.

[53] Ray Ball and Philip Brown, "An Empirical Evaluation of Accounting Income Numbers," *Journal of Accounting Research* (Autumn 1968), pp. 159–78.

The *API* reflects the abnormal return that would have been caused from holding a portfolio and knowing the earnings figure in advance of the market. It is a measure of information in a foreknowledge sense. More specifically, a positive (negative) *API* associated with positive (negative) earning forecast error is assumed to indicate the positive association between unexpected earnings and prices. Evidently, this method depends on the earnings expectation model used.

Under the dividend (earnings) capitalization model, the equilibrium price of an ownership share equals the discounted value of all future dividends to be received, discounted at the cost of equity capital. To account for uncertainty, various ad hoc adjustments are introduced, rather than being implied by some explicit theory of valuation under uncertainty.

The Decision Usefulness–Decision Maker–Individual User Paradigm

Exemplars

The articles by Bruns, Hofstedt and Kinard, and Birnberg and Nath[54] may be considered exemplars of the individual user paradigm. Bruns proposed hypotheses that relate the user of accounting information, the relevance of accounting information for decisions, the decision maker's conception of accounting, and other available information to the effect of accounting information on decisions. These hypotheses are also developed in a model that identifies and relates some factors that may determine when decisions are affected by accounting systems and information. Hofstedt and Kinard argue for a behavioral accounting research, stemming from the realization that accounting information is both a cause and an effect of human behavior and that an accounting system could be designed to influence behavior. They defined behavioral accounting research as the study of the behavior of accountants and nonaccountants as it is influenced by accounting functions and reports. These authors show that such an endeavor is a proper area of inquiry and worthy of research, and they propose a research strategy.

Birnberg and Nath investigated the implications of behavioral science for managerial accounting. They presented examples of how behavioral science theories may be used to perceive the accounting process and develop testable hypotheses about it. The principal rationale for this endeavor is that the implementation of accounting techniques depends on the human element responses and the interaction of the individual or group with the accounting system.

Image of the Subject Matter

To those who adopt the individual user paradigm, the basic subject matter is the individual user response to accounting variables. These authors argue that, in general, the decision usefulness of accounting variables may be derived from

[54]William J. Bruns, Jr., "Accounting Information and Decision Making: Some Behavioral Hypotheses," *The Accounting Review* (July 1968), pp. 469–80; Thomas R. Hofstedt and James C. Kinard, "A Strategy for Behavioral Accounting Research," *The Accounting Review* (January 1970), pp. 38–54. Jacob G. Birnberg and Raghu Nath, "Implications of Behavioral Science for Managerial Accounting," *The Accounting Review* (July 1967), pp. 468–79.

human behavior. In other words, accounting is viewed as a behavioral process. The AAA Committee on Behavioral Science Content of the Accounting Curriculum hypothesized that "the very process of accumulating information, as well as the behavior of those who do the accumulating, will affect the behavior of others."[55] Consequently, the objective of behavioral accounting research is to understand, explain, and predict human behavior in an accounting context. The individuals of interest to this paradigm are internal and external users of accounting, producers and attesters of information, and the general public or their surrogates. Behavioral accounting research related to the external reporting environment has addressed four overall issues: (1) the adequacy of financial statement disclosure, (2) the usefulness of financial statement data, (3) attitudes about corporate reporting issues, and (4) materiality judgments.[56] Behavioral accounting research related to the internal reporting environment has addressed two overall issues: behavioral budgeting and behavioral control.

Theories

Much of the research associated with the individual user paradigm has been conducted without the explicit formulation of a theory. In general, the alternative to developing theories proper to behavioral accounting has been to borrow theories from other fields and disciplines. Such borrowed theories generally have been found to be adequate in explaining and predicting human behavior in an accounting context. Some examples are the use of linguistic relativism to explain the impact of accounting information on the user's behavior,[57] the use of sociolinguistics to explain the differences in the linguistic behavior of users and producers,[58] the use of the entropy concept to study aggregation in accounting,[59] the use of Weber's Law from psychophysics to study judgments of numerical data,[60] the use of models from the psychology of information processing to study the decision-making process,[61] the use of dissonance theory to explain compliance with APB opinions,[62] the use of functional fixity to study the impact of data on

---

[55] American Accounting Association, "Report of the Committee on Behavioral Science Content of the Accounting Curriculum," *The Accounting Review*, supplement to vol. 46 (1971), p. 247.

[56] Thomas R. Dyckman, Richard Gibbins, and Robert J. Swieringa, "Experimental and Survey Research in Financial Accounting: A Review and Evaluation," in *The Impact of Accounting Research in Financial Accounting and Disclosure on Accounting Practice*, ed. A. Rashad Abdel-Khalik and Thomas F. Keller (Durham, N.C.: Duke University Press, 1978), pp. 48–105.

[57] Ahmed Belkaoui, "Linguistic Relativity in Accounting," *Accounting, Organizations and Society* (October 1978), pp. 97–104.

[58] Ahmed Belkaoui, "The Interprofessional Linguistic Communication of Accounting Concepts: An Experiment in Sociolinguistics," *The Journal of Accounting Research* (Autumn 1980), in press.

[59] A. Rashad Abdel-Khalik, "The Entropy Lax, Accounting Data and Relevance to Decision Making," *The Accounting Review* (April 1974), pp. 271–83.

[60] Jerry Rose et al., "Toward an Empirical Measure of Materiality," *Journal of Accounting Research*, supplement to vol. 8 (1970), pp. 138–56.

[61] R. Libby and B. L. Lewis, "Human Information Processing Research in Accounting: The State of the Art," *Accounting, Organizations and Society* (September 1977), pp. 245–68.

[62] Blaine A. Ritts, "A Study of the Impact of APB Opinions on Practicing CPAs," *Journal of Accounting Research* (Spring 1974), pp. 93–111.

users,[63] and the use of information inductance, whereby the behavior of an individual is affected by the information he is required to communicate.[64]

Methods

Those who accept the individual user paradigm tend to use all the methods favored by behaviorists, namely, observation techniques, interviews, questionnaires, and experimentation. Because a laboratory provides a controlled setting, experimentation is the preferred method. Laboratory experiments may be popular because the individual user paradigm is quite recent. Such experiments may be only starting points for further validation. For example, Hofstedt and Kinard contend that the success of laboratory experiments "leads to more general hypotheses and to theories whose validity and applicability can be tested by subsequent field studies, both quasi-experimental and purely observational."[65]

The Information Economics Paradigm

Exemplars

The exemplars for the information economics paradigm are articles by Feltham,[66] Crandall,[67] and Feltham and Demski.[68] In his pioneering paper, Feltham provided a framework for determining the value of a change in the information system from the point of view of the person making an information decision, known as the decision maker. The framework relies on the individual components required to compute the expected payoff for a particular information system. The components are a set of possible actions at each period within a time horizon, a payoff function over the events that occur in the periods, probabilistic relationships between past and future events, events and signals from the information system as well as past and future signals, and a set of decision rules as a function of the signals. The framework states that the value of changing from one information system to another is equal to the difference between the expected payoffs of the two alternatives.

Crandall examined the usefulness of information economics to the future development of accounting theory and offered the "Applied Information Economics" approach as a new mainstream for accounting theory.[69] Simply, this

---

[63] Yuji Ijiri, Robert K. Jaedicke, and Kenneth E. Knight, "The Effects of Accounting Alternatives on Management Decisions," ed. Robert K. Jaedicke, Yuji Ijiri, and Oswald Neilsen, *Research in Accounting Measurement* (Sarasota, Fla.: AAA, 1966), pp. 186–99.

[64] Prem Prakush and Alfred Rappaport, "Information Inductance and Its Significance for Accounting," *Accounting, Organizations and Society*, 2, No. 1, (1977), 29–38.

[65] Hofstedt and Kinard, "A Strategy for Behavioral Accounting Research," p. 54.

[66] Gerald A. Feltham, "The Value of Information," *The Accounting Review* (October 1968), pp. 684–96.

[67] Robert H. Crandall, "Information Economics and Its Implications for the Further Development of Accounting Theory," *The Accounting Review* (July 1969), pp. 457–66.

[68] Gerald A. Feltham and Joel S. Demski, "The Use of Models in Information Evaluation," *The Accounting Review* (July 1969), pp. 475–66.

[69] In fact, Crandall proposed a partitioning of the field of accounting theory to include the Traditional approach, the Postulational approach, the Traditional Economic Theory approach, and the Applied Information Economics approach.

approach consists of recognizing explicitly each of the components of the information economics model and broadening the scope of accounting design to include all these components. The components are defined as the Filter, the Model, the Channel, Decoding, and the Decision Rule. The implications for the future development of accounting theory are stated as follows:

> The ideal for the development of accounting theory would be the development of a constructive theory of information economics where, in some significant areas of the model, one could develop algorithms that pointed out the theoretically "best" design of the system, given a set of assumptions. . . .[70]

> [The purpose is] to permit the construction and evaluation of information systems for the purpose of maximizing the utility to each user, subject to constraints as to the cost of the system, the decision rules available, the state of the technology, and the feasibility of obtaining information from the real world.[71]

The third exemplar is Feltham and Demski's "The Use of Models in Information Evaluation," which presents and discusses a model of the information choice situation. It views information evaluation in cost-benefit terms and as a sequential process. The entire process is summarized as follows:

> specification of a particular information system, η, results in a set of signals, y, being supplied to the decision maker; the decision maker may then use the resulting information in selecting his action, a; and this action may determine, in parts, the events, x, of the subsequent period. The information evaluation must predict the relationship between each of the above elements: the signal generation process, $\phi(y/\eta)$; the decision maker's prediction and action choice process, $\alpha(y/\eta)$; and the relationship between the actions selected and the events which will occur, $\phi(x/y, \eta, \alpha)$. In addition, he must predict the gross payoff, $w(x)$, he will derive from the events of the subsequent period as well as the cost of operating the particular information system, $w'(y, \eta)$.[72]

Image of the Subject Matter

To those who adopt the information economics paradigm, the basic subject matter is that information is an economic commodity, the acquisition of which amounts to a problem of economic choice. The value of information is viewed in terms of a cost-benefit criterion and within the formal structure of decision theory and economic theory. Accounting information is evaluated in terms of its ability to improve the quality of the optimal choice in a basic choice problem that an individual or a number of heterogenous individuals must resolve. A single individual must select among different actions with different possible outcomes. Assuming a consistent, rational choice behavior governed by the expected utility hypotheses, the action with the higher expected payoff (or utility) is preferred by the individual. Information is desired in this context to revise the probabilities of

---

[70]Crandall, "Information Economics," p. 464.

[71]Ibid., p. 458.

[72]Feltham and Demski, "The Use of Models," p. 626.

the original outcomes. Thus, the individual may face a two-stage process: a first stage during which the information system produces different signals, and a second stage during which the observance of a signal results in a revision of probabilities and a choice of the conditional best action. The information system with the highest expected utility is preferred. Information, therefore, is strictly needed for a systematic probability revision (Bayesian revision), which in turn is used for information analysis on the basis of the subjective expected utility maximization rule.

Theories

The information economics paradigm draws on insights gained from the Theory of Teams developed by Marschak and Radner,[73] statistical decision theory, and the economic theory of choice. What has resulted is a normative theory of information evaluation for the systematic analysis of information alternatives.[74] Central to the information economics paradigm is the traditional economic assumption of consistent, rational choice behavior.

Methods

Those who accept the information economics paradigm generally use analytical reasoning based on statistical decision theory and the economic theory of choice. The approach consists of isolating general relationships and effects of alternative scenarios and applying Bayesian revision analysis and a cost-benefit criterion to analyze questions of accounting policy. The approach relies also on rationality as the major assumption.

Conclusions and Implications: Revolution and Falsification

Accounting may be approached from the point of view of the philosophy of science. Research output in accounting is not considered to be of doubtful value or theoretically deficient but rather as an indication that accounting events follow the pattern of successful revolutions theorized by Kuhn. In this chapter, we have adopted a definition of a paradigm relevant to accounting. The essential components of such a paradigm are exemplars, image of the subject matter, theories, and methods. This definition helps identify and delineate the competing paradigms in the accounting field, which we have identified as (1) the anthropological–inductive paradigm, (2) the true income–deductive paradigm, (3) the decision usefulness–decision model paradigm, (4) the decision usefulness–decision maker–aggregate market behavior paradigm, (5) the decision usefulness–decision maker–individual user paradigm, and (6) the information economics paradigm. Each of these paradigms is the object of investigation and research by established

[73]Jacob Marschak and Roy Rasher, *Economic Theory of Teams* (New Haven: Yale University Press, 1972).

[74]Gerald A. Feltham, "Information Evaluation," *Studies in Accounting Research, No. 5* (Sarasota, Fla.: AAA, 1972); Joel S. Demski, *Information Analysis* (Reading, Mass.: Addison-Wesley, 1972).

communities. A paradigm creates in each of these communities a coherent, unified viewpoint—a kind of *Weltanschauung*—that determines the way a member views accounting research, practice, and even education. In the interests of continuity and progress within the accounting discipline, these paradigms should never be considered absolute and final truthful knowledge. Instead, they should be subjected to constant verification and testing in a search for possible anomalies.

Most scientists and philosophers hold the view that scientific knowledge can never be "proved" knowledge. Karl Popper argues that although no theory can ever be proved "true" with finality, it can be proved "false" with finality.[75] Generally known as the notion of falsification or theory of refutability, the theory holds that to be accredited as scientific, a theory has to be refutable in the sense that if its results turn out to be wrong, then the theory is falsified. Among various types of falsification, the one that comes closest to Kuhn's views is the one termed "sophisticated falsification," which Lakatos summarizes as *"no experiment, experimental report, observational statement or well corroborated low-level falsifying hypothesis alone can lead to falsification. There is no falsification before the emergence of a better theory."*[76] A "better theory" is one that "offers any novel, excess information compared with its predecessor and whether some of the excess information is corroborated."[77] *The difference between Popper's naive falsification and the sophisticated falsification is that the latter requires existence of a better theory. How should the sophisticated falsificationist proceed? Lakatos tells us that the sophisticated falsificationist*

makes unfalsifiable by fiat some (spatio-temporally) singular statements which are distinguishable by the fact that there exists at the time a "relevant technique" such that "anyone who has learned it" will be able to decide that the statement is "acceptable."

. . .This decision is then followed by a second kind of decision concerning the separation of the set of accepted basic statements from the rest. . . . The methodologoical falsificationist realizes that in the "experimental techniques" of the scientist, fallible theories are involved, "in the light of which" he interprets the facts. In spite of this he "applies" these theories, he regards them in the given context not as theories under test but as *unproblematic background knowledge* "which we accept (tentatively) as unproblematic while we are testing the theory."

. . . Furthermore, probabilistic theories may qualify now as "scientific": although they are not falsifiable they can be made "falsifiable" by an *additional (third type) decision* which the scientist can make by specifying certain rejection rules which may make statistically interpreted evidence "inconsistent" with the probabilistic theory.[78]

This may be the attitude to adopt in dealing with the competing paradigms in accounting.

---

[75]Karl Popper, *Conjecture and Refutations* (London: Basic, 1963).

[76]Imre Lakatos, "Falsification and the Methodology of Scientific Research," in *Criticism and the Growth of Knowledge,* ed. Imre Lakatos and Alan Musgrave (Cambridge: Cambridge University Press, 1970), p. 119.

[77]*Ibid.,* p. 120.

[78]*Ibid.,* pp. 106–09.

References

American Accounting Association, Committee on Concepts and Standards for External Financial Reports. *Statement on Accounting Theory and Theory Acceptance.* Sarasota, Fla.: AAA, 1977.

Damos, Paul. "A Revolution in Accounting Thought? A Comment." *The Accounting Review* (July 1977), pp. 746–47.

Hakansson, Nils H. "Where We Are in Accounting: A Review of 'Statement on Accounting Theory and Theory Acceptance.'" *The Accounting Review* (July 1978), pp. 717–25.

Peasnell, K. V. "Statement of Accounting Theory and Theory Acceptance: A Review Article." *Accounting and Business Research* (Summer 1978), pp. 217–25.

Ritzer, George. "Sociology: A Multiple Paradigm Science." *The American Sociologist* (August 1975), pp. 156–57; also *Sociology: A Multiple Paradigm Science.* Boston: Allyn and Bacon, 1975.

Kuhn, Thomas S. "The Structure of Scientific Revolutions." *International Encyclopedia of Unified Science*, 2nd enlarged Edition. Chicago: University of Chicago Press, 1970.

Wells, M. C. "A Revolution in Accounting Thought." *The Accounting Review* (July 1976), pp. 471–82.

Questions

9–1 Show how the pattern of events in accounting follows the pattern of successful revolution as described by Kuhn.

9–2 Define and discuss *paradigm* as it applies to accounting.

9–3 Is accounting a multiple paradigm science? Discuss.

9–4 Explain the following accounting paradigms:
   a. The anthropological–inductive paradigm
   b. The true income—deductive paradigm
   c. The decision usefulness–decision model paradigm
   d. The decision usefulness–decision maker–aggregate market behavior paradigm
   e. The decision usefulness–decision maker–individual user paradigm
   f. The information economics paradigm

9–5 What is the role of falsification in accounting? What is the difference between naive falsification and sophisticated falsification?

9–6 What are the primary contributions of Kuhn, Popper, and Lakatos to the philosophy of science?

Author Index

Coughlan, J. W., 106
Cousineau, A., 40, 105
Cowan, T. K., 27
Cramer, J. J., Jr., 69, 96, 160
Crandall, R. H., 302, 303
Cyert, R. M., 65, 96

Daily, R. A., 264
Danos, P., 287, 306
Davidson, S., 150, 199, 286, 292
Davis, A., 250
Deaken, E., 46
Deinzer, H. T., 123
Delphin, R., Jr.,
Demski, J. S., 27, 56, 302, 303
Dermer, J., 42
Desai, H. B., 38
Devine, C. T., 28, 37, 64, 124, 176
Dickhaut, J. W., 40, 42, 43, 44, 56
Dittman, D. A., 270
Dolphin, R., Jr., 39
Dopuch, N., 27, 40, 53, 57, 96, 160, 173,
     271, 272, 286, 297
Downs, D., 56
Drake, D. F., 160, 172
Driver, M., 43
Dukes, R. E., 49, 53
Dunette, M. D., 43
Dyckman, T. R., 38, 40, 56, 157, 199, 301
Dyer, J., 40

Ecton, W. W., 38
Edminster, R. O., 46
Edwards, E. O., 6, 9, 100, 148, 152, 159,
     170, 238, 252, 293
Eggleton, I. R. C., 40, 42, 43
Einhorn, H. J., 57
Elgers, P., 272
Elias, N. S., 40, 253, 270
Elovitz, D., 256
Enthoven, A. J. H., 29
Epstein, M., 251, 260
Estes, R. W., 28, 260
Estrin, T., 42

Falk, M., 39, 43
Fama, E., 50, 57, 298
Fantl, I. L., 268
Fekrat, A. M., 114, 125
Feltham, G. A., 302, 303, 304
Fern, D., Jr., 249
Fertig, P.E., 13, 252, 269
Financial Accounting Standards Board, 29,
     64, 77, 78, 79, 80, 81, 84, 85, 86, 87,
     88, 89, 90, 91, 96, 121, 125, 149, 183,
     187, 191, 195, 198, 199, 233, 262

Findlay, M. C., 141
Fisher, I., 144
Fisher, L., 47
Flamholtz, E., 251, 253, 254, 255, 270, 271
Fleissner, D., 41
Foster, G., 53
Frank, W., 45, 140
Fremgen, J. M., 7, 8, 27, 104, 114, 124, 125
Frishkoff, P., 121, 125, 126

Gambling, T., 28
Gans, M. S., 96
Geijsbeek, J. B., 8, 27
Gibbins, M., 38, 56, 301
Gibbs, P. M. D., 238
Gillis, J. G., 272
Gilman, S., 100, 289
Glautier, N. W. E., 255
Godurn, L. B., 40
Goetz, B. E., 96
Gonedes, N. J., 27, 48, 52, 53, 57, 272, 286,
     297
Gordon, M. J., 290
Grady, P., 6, 123
Gray, J., 45
Gray, W. S., 272
Green, D., Jr., 45, 46, 115, 125
Greenball, M. N., 57
Griffin, C. H., 27
Gunneman, J. P., 252
Gynther, R. S., 238, 293

Hakansson, N. H., 28, 58, 237, 306
Haley, B., 141
Hanna, J. R., 220, 238
Harcourt, G. C., 172
Harried, A. A., 39
Harrison, R. B., 96
Haslem, J. A., 39
Hatfield, H. R., 10, 100, 286, 289
Hawkins, D. F., 41, 56
Hayes, S. L., III, 48
Heath, L. C., 185, 199
Hekimian, J. S., 256, 271
Hendriks, J. R., 145, 271
Hendriksen, E. S., 5, 7, 110, 126, 185, 190
Hermanson, R. H., 257, 271
Hicks, E. L., 123, 125
Higgins, T. S., 123
Hofstedt, T. R., 38, 40, 41, 43, 56, 104, 300,
     302
Holmes, W., 125
Horngren, C. T., 20, 24, 29, 38, 40, 115,
     124, 125, 197, 199
Horrigan, J. O., 47
Horton, J. J., 47
Hughes, G., 41
Husband, G. R., 67, 124

Weil, R. L., 159, 199
Weirich, T. R., 264
Wells, M. C., 54, 58, 293, 306
Welsh, G. A., 115
Werner, F., 140
Whinston, A., 35
Whinston, A. H., 250
White, J. A., 115
Whitmore, G. A., 141
Whittington, G., 293
Williams, R. J., 96
Williams, T. H., 27, 125
Windal, F. W., 112
Winters, A. A., 96
Wolk, H. I., 238

Woodruff, R. L., 253
Woolsey, S. M., 40, 125
Wright, F. K., 293
Wright, W., 42

Young, D. W., 260, 271
Young, J. M., 273
Yu, S. C., 11, 124

Zeff, A. S., 14, 29, 79, 124, 238
Zimmerman, J. L., 29, 64, 290, 291
Zimmerman, V. K., 13
Zlatkovitch, C. T., 115

Subject Index

315

Money maintenance, 145

n

Neutrality, 93
Nonarticulated view, 82–88
Nonessential asset, 165
Nonmonetary item, 181, 184
Number of dollars, 221
Number of odd dollars, 221

p

Paradigm
    aggregate market behavior, 55
    antropological–inductive, 55, 289–91
    decision usefulness–decision
        maker–individual user, 55, 297–99
    decision usefulness–decision
        maker–aggregate market behavior,
        55, 300–302
    decision usefulness–decision model,
        55, 294–96
    defined, 55, 288–89
    individual user, 55
    information economics, 55, 302–304
    true income–deductive, 55, 292–94
Postulate
    accounting period, 104–105, 142
    entity, 102–103
    going concern, 103–104
    stable monetary, 104–105
    unit of measure, 104–105
Predictive ability, 44–46
Principle
    comparability, 122–23
    conservatism, 119–20
    consistency, 118
    cost, 109–10, 142
    full disclosure, 118–19
    matching, 114–15, 142
    materiality, 120–21
    objectivity, 116–17
    realization, 111–12
    revenue, 110–11, 142
    uniformity, 122–23
Principles
    accounting, 109
    generally accepted, 2
Probabilistic judgment, 41

q

Qualitative characteristic, 78, 92–93

r

Random walk, 50
Relevance, 44, 93, 221
Reliability, 117

Representational faithfulness, 93
Residual equity, 107
Revenue/expense view, 82–88
Revolution, 54, 304

s

Sandilands report, 146
School
    classical, 138
    neoclassical, 138
    radical, 138
Social benefit, 13, 248–49
Social cost, 13, 248–49
Social welfare, 13
Statement of corporate objectives, 76
Statement of future prospects, 76
Statement of money exchange, 75
Statement of transactions, 76
Statement of valued added, 75
Stockholders' welfare maximization
    model, 141
Subjective goodwill, 150
Systematic risk, 52

t

Takeover, 47
Tax determination, 2
Tax planning, 2
Theory
    for accounting, 6
    of accounting, 6
    confirmation, 3
    construction of, 3
    descriptive, 5–6
    entity, 107
    events, 36
    fund, 108
    human resource value, 253–55
    middle range, 4
    normative, 5–6
    positive, 284
    proprietary, 106–107
    validation of, 304
    verification of, 3
Timeliness, 93
Timing error, 220
Trueblood Report, 68–74

u

Understandability, 93
Unit of measure
    purchasing power, 219
    money, 219

v

Validity
    construct, 43